Study and Revise
GCSE
Biology

David Applin

KEY TO SYMBOLS

As you read through this book you will notice the following symbols. They will help you find your way around the book more quickly.

- **Hints & Tips** — shows a handy hint to help you remember something 
- **Facts** — shows you some key facts
- means remember!!! 
- says 'Did you know this?' – interesting points to note 
- points you to other parts of the book where related topics are explained 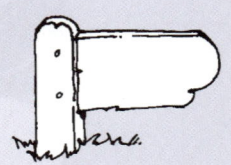
- shows a sequence of linked processes  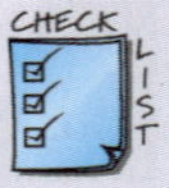
- **Checklist** — refers you from a diagram to a checklist of related points

Acknowledgements

Copyright photographs have been used, with permission, from the following sources:
p. 22 Planet Earth Pictures; **pp. 44, 135** Science Photo Library

Copyright © David Applin 1997, 2004

First published in this edition 2004
exclusively for WHSmith by
Hodder & Stoughton Educational
338 Euston Road
London NW1 3BH

All rights reserved. Apart from any use permitted under UK copyright law, no part of this publication may be reproduced or transmitted in any form or by any means, electronic or mechanical, including photocopying, recording or any information storage and retrieval system, without permission in writing from the Publisher.

Impression number   10 9 8 7 6 5 4 3 2 1
Year   2010 2009 2008 2007 2006 2005 2004

Illustrations: Peter Bull, Simon Cooke, Chris Etheridge, Ian Law, Joe Little, Andrea Norton, Mike Parsons, John Plumb, Dave Poole, Chris Rothero, Anthony Warne

Prepared by Starfish, London

Printed and bound in the UK by Scotprint

A CIP record for this book is available from the British Library

ISBN 0 340 85860 5

Contents

GCSE Biology and this Study and Revise book — 3

1 Introducing biology — 4
- 1.1 Living on Earth — 4
- 1.2 Characteristics of life — 5
- 1.3 Grouping living things — 5
- 1.4 Identifying living things — 9

2 Organisms in the environment — 11
- 2.1 Introducing ecology — 11
- 2.2 Food chains and webs — 15
- 2.3 Ecological pyramids — 18
- 2.4 Distribution of organisms — 20
- 2.5 Population size — 22
- 2.6 Food production — 32

3 Cell activity — 38
- 3.1 Cells at work — 38
- 3.2 Into and out of cells — 39
- 3.3 Cell division — 43
- 3.4 Cells, tissues and organs — 46
- 3.5 Chemicals in living things — 49

4 Green plants as organisms — 57
- 4.1 Photosynthesis — 57
- 4.2 Transport in plants — 61
- 4.3 Plant responses — 64

5 Humans (and other animals) as organisms — 68
- 5.1 Food and diet — 69
- 5.2 The digestive system — 70
- 5.3 Obtaining food — 76
- 5.4 Breathing, gaseous exchange and respiration — 80
- 5.5 Blood and the circulatory system — 84
- 5.6 Senses and the nervous system — 90
- 5.7 Sense organs — 96
- 5.8 Hormones — 97
- 5.9 Maintaining the internal environment — 102
- 5.10 Support and movement — 106

6 Health and disease — 113
- 6.1 Introducing health and disease — 113
- 6.2 More about immunology — 117
- 6.3 Controlling the spread of disease — 119
- 6.4 Fighting infectious diseases — 123

7 Inheritance and evolution — 128
- 7.1 Reproduction — 128
- 7.2 Asexual reproduction in plants — 130
- 7.3 Monohybrid inheritance — 132
- 7.4 Variation — 137
- 7.5 Evolution — 139

8 Biotechnology — 144
- 8.1 Introducing biotechnology — 144
- 8.2 Making use of biotechnology — 147
- 8.3 Eating microorganisms — 152

Answers — 155

Index — 164

GCSE Biology and this Study and Revise book

How to use this book

This *Study and Revise GCSE Biology* book is not intended to replace your school textbooks. As tests and examinations approach, however, many students feel the need to revise from something a good deal shorter than their usual textbook. This book is intended to fill that need. It covers the GCSE Biology specifications for the different Examining Groups.

Make a timetable for revision, using the contents list on page 1 to ensure that you cover all of the topics of your specification. Planned use of time and concentrated study will give you time for other activities and interests as well as work.

Each revision chapter begins with a set of Test yourself questions to give you an idea of how well you have already grasped the topic. There is a set of Round up questions at the end of each chapter. Work out your improvement index from your score on the Round up questions compared with your score on the Test yourself questions.

When the exam arrives

When the exam arrives, you should have confidence if you have revised thoroughly. In the examination room, attempt all the questions you are supposed to answer and make sure that you turn over every page. Many marks have been lost in exams as a result of turning over two pages at once. If you suffer a panic attack, breathe deeply and slowly to get lots of oxygen into your system and clear your thoughts. Your examination is important, but above all, keep it in perspective.

A note on content

Part of the content of *Study and Revise GCSE Biology* is specified by the National Curriculum. This part of the content is required by all the Examining Groups. The rest of the content is extension material chosen by the Examining Groups and there are differences between their specifications. Each Examining Group requires some topics but not others. However, a number of topics (e.g. aspects of health and disease) are part of the specifications of the majority of Examining Groups. Carefully check the specifications of the Examining Group you are following to find out which extension material you need to revise in this book.

I wish you success.

David Applin

Chapter 1 — Introducing biology

How much do you already know? Work out your score on page 155.

Test yourself

1. What would happen to ground temperature if Earth were a) nearer to the Sun b) further from the Sun? [2]

2. a) List the processes which tell you that something is living. [7 × ½]
   b) Put a tick (✓) next to the processes which you think apply to animals. [7 × ½]
   c) Put a cross (✗) next to the processes which you think apply to plants. [6 × ½]
   d) Do plants and animals have the same characteristics? If not, how are they different? [1]

3. Using the forget-me-not and oak tree as examples, explain the meaning of the words 'annual' and 'perennial'. [3]

4. a) What is a biological key used for? [1]
   b) Why are features like exact colour, size and mass not suitable for including in a biological key? [3]

5. List the physical features of soil which make it a suitable place for earthworms to live. [4]

1.1 Living on Earth

PREVIEW

At the end of this section you will:
- understand why Earth is a suitable place for living things (organisms)
- know that soil, air and water are the physical environments in which organisms live.

Why the Earth can support life

Earth is a planet in orbit round a star we call the Sun. It is the only planet we know of that supports life.

★ Earth is close enough to the Sun for its surface temperature to be in the range in which life can exist. The temperature at the Earth's surface varies between −70 °C and 55 °C.

★ Earth is massive enough to have sufficient gravity to hold down an atmosphere of different gases essential for living organisms.

★ The layer of ozone which surrounds Earth reduces the amount of ultraviolet light from the Sun reaching the planet's surface. Too much ultraviolet light destroys living things.

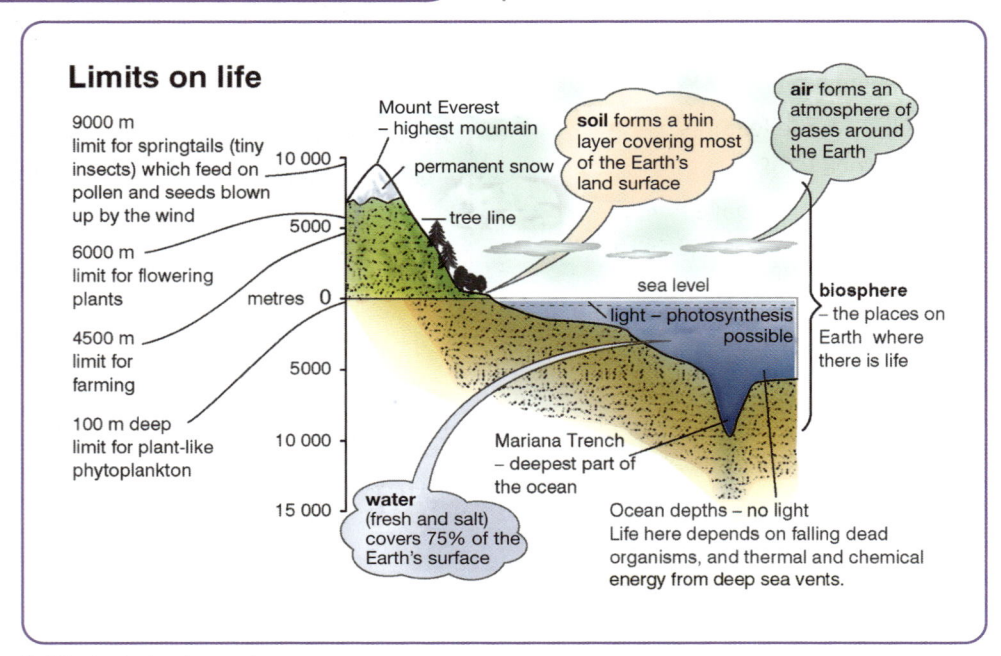

Limits on life

- 9000 m limit for springtails (tiny insects) which feed on pollen and seeds blown up by the wind
- 6000 m limit for flowering plants
- 4500 m limit for farming
- 100 m deep limit for plant-like phytoplankton
- Mount Everest – highest mountain
- permanent snow
- tree line
- sea level
- light – photosynthesis possible
- Mariana Trench – deepest part of the ocean
- Ocean depths – no light. Life here depends on falling dead organisms, and thermal and chemical energy from deep sea vents.
- soil forms a thin layer covering most of the Earth's land surface
- air forms an atmosphere of gases around the Earth
- water (fresh and salt) covers 75% of the Earth's surface
- biosphere – the places on Earth where there is life

Earth's physical environment

Introducing biology

The diagram on the opposite page shows that soil, air and water form Earth's environment.

★ **Soil** is formed when the small particles of rock broken down by the weather, the roots of plants and the different activities of animals mix with **humus** (the decomposed remains of dead plants, animals and other organisms).

★ **Air** consists of: 78% nitrogen; 21% oxygen; 0.035% carbon dioxide; and less than 1% water vapour, argon, xenon and other gases.

★ **Water** fills the seas, oceans, rivers and lakes. About 2% of the Earth's water is locked up as ice, in the soil, in the bodies of living things or as vapour in the atmosphere.

1.2 Characteristics of life

PREVIEW

At the end of this section you will know the characteristics of life:

- Movement
- Respiration
- Sensitivity
- Growth
- Reproduction
- Excretion
- Nutrition

Handy hint

The memory aid **Mrs Gren** will help you remember the characteristics of living things.

More about MRS GREN

The characteristics of life are the features that are common to all living things.

★ **Movement**: animals are able to move from place to place because of the action of **muscles** which pull on the **skeleton**. Plants do not usually move from place to place; they move mainly by **growing**.

★ **Respiration** occurs in cells, and releases energy from food for life's activities. **Aerobic** respiration uses oxygen to release energy from food. **Anaerobic** respiration releases energy from food without using oxygen.

★ **Sensitivity** allows living things to detect changes in their surroundings and respond to them.

★ **Growth** leads to an increase in size. **Development** occurs as the young change and become adult in appearance.

★ **Reproduction** produces new individuals.

★ **Excretion** removes the waste substances produced by the chemical reactions (called **metabolism**) taking place in cells.

★ **Nutrition** either makes food (usually by the process of photosynthesis) or takes in food for use in the body.

Fact file

Respiration is sometimes compared to combustion, but there is a vital difference. When fuel is burnt, energy is quickly released. If cells were to release energy from food as suddenly, the sharp rise in temperature would kill them. Respiration releases energy from food gradually.

Remember

- **Respiration** releases energy from food.
- **Gaseous exchange** takes in oxygen for respiration and removes carbon dioxide produced by respiration.
- **Excretion** removes wastes produced by metabolism.
- **Defecation** (or egestion) removes the undigested remains of food.

1.3 Grouping living things

PREVIEW

At the end of this section you will:

- understand that groups of living things are named according to Linnaeus' system of classification
- know the major groups of plants and animals
- understand binomial names.

Classification

Living things which have features in common are grouped together. Organising living things into groups is called **classification**. Some characteristics are unique to the group; other characteristics are shared with other groups. Groups therefore

Introducing biology

Arachnids
- The body is made up of two parts.
- There are **eight legs**.
- Scorpions, mites and harvestmen are close relatives of spiders.

Cnidarians
- The body has no front or rear. Its parts are arranged evenly in the round.
- Tentacles surround an opening which is both mouth and anus.
- Stinging cells are used to capture prey.

Crustaceans
- The body is made up of two parts.
- There are 14 legs.
- Woodlice are the only **crustaceans** that live on land.
- Crabs, lobsters and prawns are close relatives of woodlice.

Reptiles
- Skin is dry and covered with scales that restrict water loss from the body.
- As a result, reptiles can live in dry environments.
- Lay eggs, each protected by a hard shell.
- As a result, water is not necessary for breeding.

Insects
- The body is made up of three parts: head, thorax and abdomen.
- There are six legs.
- There are usually two pairs of wings, but flies have one pair.

ANIMAL KINGDOM

Phylum Arthropoda
- Class Crustacea — woodlouse
- Class Arachnida — spider
- Class Insecta — fly

Phylum Cnidaria — sea anemone

Phylum Annelida — earthworm

Phylum Chordata
- Class Pisces (fish) — stickleback
- Class Reptillia — lizard
- Class Aves (birds) — thrush
- Class Amphibia — frog
- Class Mammalia — human

Worms
- The body is long and thin.
- The body is made up of many segments.

Fish
- The body is covered with scales.
- Fins control the position of the body in water.
- Gills are surfaces for gaseous exchange. They are exposed to the environment. The gases exchanged are in solution.
- As a result gills lose water easily in dry air.
- As a result fish are restricted to living in water.

Birds
- The body is covered with feathers which:
  > make flying possible
  > keep in heat
  > keep out water.
- The beak is specialised (adapted) differently in different species to deal with different foods.
- Birds lay eggs, protected by a hard shell.

Amphibians
- Live on land but breed in water.
- Development of the young into adults is called a metamorphosis.
- Soft skin is a surface for gaseous exchange. The gases are in solution.
- As a result the skin loses water easily in dry air.
- As a result amphibians are restricted to living in damp places when on land.

Mammals
- Hair helps conserve body heat.
- Young feed on milk produced by the female's breasts (mammary glands).
- Have a small tail bone called the coccyx.

Groups within groups – the major groups of the Animal kingdom and the Plant kingdom are listed, with an example of each. Each major group of plants is called a Division rather than a Phylum.

Introducing biology

Mosses
- Mosses quickly lose water in dry air.
- As a result, mosses live in damp places.
- Roots are absent.
- As a result, water is soaked up by capillary movement over the leaves.
- Stalks grow from moss plants, each carrying a spore capsule filled with spores.
- Each spore is able to develop into a new plant.

REPRODUCE BY MEANS OF SPORES

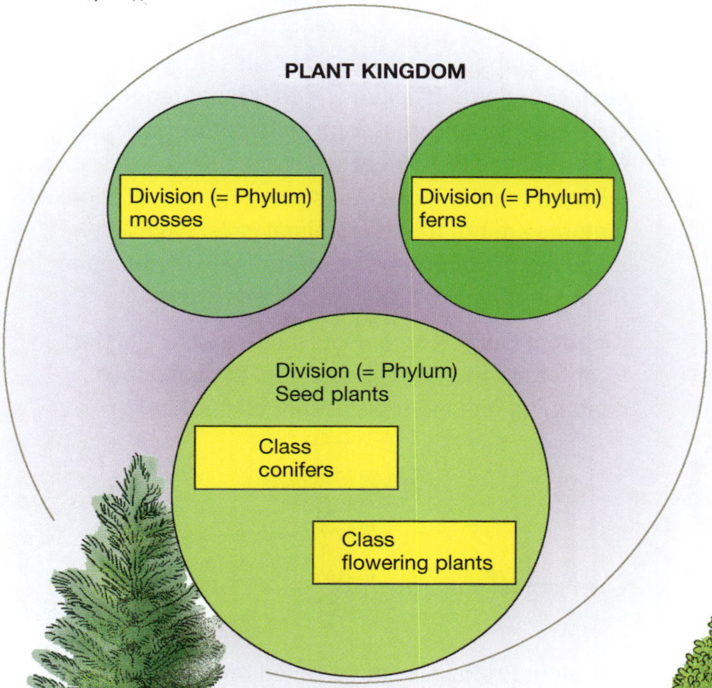

PLANT KINGDOM

Division (= Phylum) mosses

Division (= Phylum) ferns

Division (= Phylum) Seed plants
- Class conifers
- Class flowering plants

Ferns
- A waxy layer waterproofs the plant's surfaces, reducing water loss in a dry atmosphere.
- Roots draw water from the soil.
- Spore capsules containing spores grow in patches on the undersides of leaves.
- Each spore is able to grow into a new fern plant.

REPRODUCE BY MEANS OF SEEDS

Forget-me-not: **annual** – flowers and produces **seeds** in one growing season. The plant then dies.

Oak tree: **perennial** – produces seeds year after year. The plant survives for many years.

Conifers
- Seeds are contained in cones.
- Covered with leaves all year round ('evergreens').
- Roots draw water from the soil.
- Waxy layer waterproofs plant surfaces.

Flowering plants
- Seeds are contained in fruits.
- Leaves of trees/shrubs fall once a year ('deciduous').
- Roots draw water from the soil.
- Waxy layer waterproofs plant surfaces.

7

Introducing biology

combine to form larger groups. The largest group of all is the **kingdom**. Each:
- kingdom contains a number of **phyla**
- phyl**um** (singular) contains a number of **classes**
- class contains a number of **orders**
- order contains a number of **families**
- family contains a number of **genera**
- gen**us** (singular) contains one or more **species**.

Fact file

Classifications that group living things according to the features they have in common with one another are called **natural classifications**. Most natural classifications attempt to show evolutionary relationships between species (see below).

Classifications that group living things according to the way they affect people are **artificial classifications**. For example, plants may be classified as poisonous or edible; animals may be classified as wild or domesticated.

Individuals of the same species are able to sexually reproduce offspring, which are themselves able to reproduce. In other words, the offspring are fertile.

EVOLUTION Page 139.

The genus and the species identify the individual living thing, rather like your first name and family name identify you. For example, humans belong to the genus *Homo* and have the species name *sapiens*; barn owls are called *Tyto alba*.

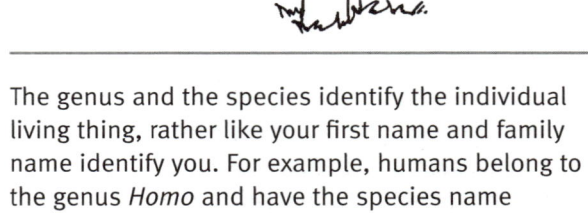

Since the name of each living thing is in two parts, the method of naming is called the **binomial system**. Notice that the genus name begins with a capital letter, the species name begins with a small letter, and the whole name is printed in italics.

The English naturalist John Ray (1627–1705) was the first to organise (classify) plants according to the characteristics that the members of the group have in common. His work paved the way for the Swedish naturalist Carolus Linnaeus (the Latin version of his name Carl von Linné) who published *Systema Naturae* in 1735. The book established the system of naming organisms that we use today.

The five kingdoms

There are five kingdoms. Living things in each kingdom obtain food in different ways. Their structure and body chemistry are different. Each kingdom, therefore, represents a way of life which all its members share. Animal cells and plant cells each contain a distinct nucleus (except red blood cells and the cells that form sieve tubes and xylem). Most plant cells also each contain chloroplasts and a large vacuole. A cell wall surrounds the cell. These features are not found in animal cells. Pages 6–7 show the major groups in the Animal kingdom and Plant kingdom. The other kingdoms are:

Kingdom Fungi – organisms made up of cells that form thread-like structures called **hyphae**, each containing a number of distinct nuclei.

(not to scale)

Kingdom Protista – single-celled organisms. The cell body contains a distinct nucleus within which is the genetic material (DNA).

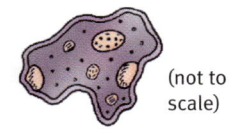

(not to scale)

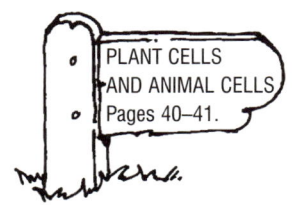

PLANT CELLS AND ANIMAL CELLS Pages 40–41.

Introducing biology

Kingdom Bacteria – single-celled organisms. The cell body is simple in structure compared with the cell body of protists. The cell body does *not* contain a distinct nucleus. The genetic material (DNA) lies in the cytoplasm.

(not to scale)

CELL NUCLEUS Page 41.

Fact file

Viruses are smaller than bacteria. They consist of a coat of protein that surrounds a strand of genetic material (DNA or RNA). Viruses can only reproduce inside living cells (the **host cells**). They:

- insert their genetic material into the host cell. As a result, some of the proteins made by the host cell are viral proteins necessary for the production of new virus particles
- destroy the host cell, which bursts, releasing the new virus particles to infect new host cells.

DNA AND RNA Page 52.

1.4 Identifying living things

PREVIEW

At the end of this section you will:
- know that a key is a set of clues that help identify a particular organism or group of organisms
- understand how to use a dichotomous key
- know that a dichotomous key can be written in different ways.

What is a key?

A **key** is a means of identifying an unfamiliar organism from a selection of specimens. A key consists of a set of descriptions. Each description is a clue that helps in the identification. A set of clues makes the key.

The easiest type of key to use is called a **dichotomous** key. 'Dichotomous' means branching into two. Each time the key branches, you have to choose between alternative statements. The alternative statements may be presented diagrammatically as a chart, or written in pairs or **couplets**. For example, a key to amphibians would begin:

	yes	no
1a The animal has a tail.	**newts**	go to **2**
1b The animal has no tail.	**frogs and toads**	go to **3**

and so on ...

By comparing the pairs of statements with the organism in front of you, you will eventually find one that fits. This identifies the organism. A key is therefore the route to a name. Different keys are used to name different living things.

When making a key, it is important to choose features that are characteristic of the type of organism rather than of the individual itself. For example, shape or proportions and patterns of colour are fairly constant in a type of organism and are therefore useful clues in a key. Size and shades of colour vary from individual to individual and are of limited use.

Introducing biology

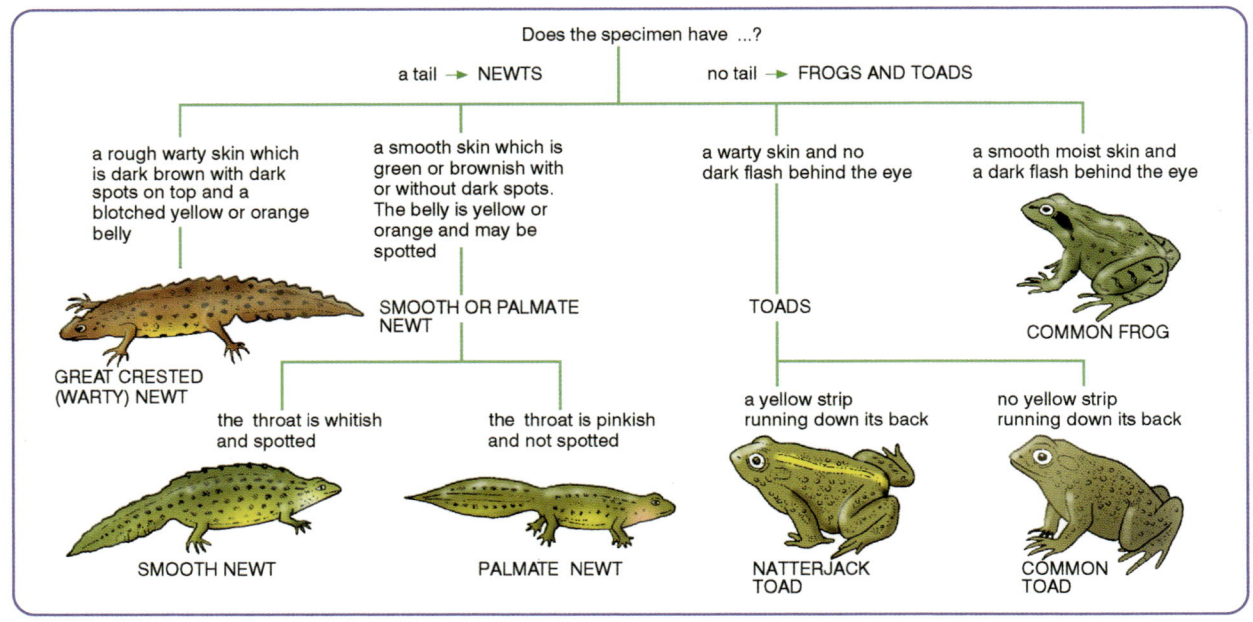

Does the specimen have ...?

- a tail → NEWTS
  - a rough warty skin which is dark brown with dark spots on top and a blotched yellow or orange belly
    - **GREAT CRESTED (WARTY) NEWT**
  - a smooth skin which is green or brownish with or without dark spots. The belly is yellow or orange and may be spotted
    - **SMOOTH OR PALMATE NEWT**
      - the throat is whitish and spotted
        - **SMOOTH NEWT**
      - the throat is pinkish and not spotted
        - **PALMATE NEWT**
- no tail → FROGS AND TOADS
  - a warty skin and no dark flash behind the eye
    - **TOADS**
      - a yellow strip running down its back
        - **NATTERJACK TOAD**
      - no yellow strip running down its back
        - **COMMON TOAD**
  - a smooth moist skin and a dark flash behind the eye
    - **COMMON FROG**

Different ways of writing a key to amphibians

ROUND UP

How much have you improved? Work out your improvement index on page 155.

1. What would happen to Earth's water if Earth were **a)** nearer to **b)** further from the Sun? [2]

2. **a)** Which gas is used during aerobic respiration to release energy from food? [1]
   b) Which gas is produced during aerobic respiration? [1]

3. **a)** Distinguish between respiration and gaseous exchange. [3]
   b) Distinguish between excretion and defecation. [2]

4. In the 1890s, when people saw cars for the first time, many thought that the cars were alive. Imagine that you are a reporter writing a short article for the local newspaper reassuring people that although cars seem to move under their own steam, they are not alive. [8]

5. Match each characteristic of life in column **A** with its description in column **B**.

A characteristics	B descriptions
movement	making or obtaining food
respiration	responding to stimuli
sensitivity	removing waste substances produced by cells
growth	producing new individuals
reproduction	releasing energy from food
excretion	changing position
nutrition	increasing in size

   [7]

6. Different types of animal are listed in column **A**. Match each type with the correct description in column **B**.

A animals	B descriptions
insect	no legs
worm	eight legs
spider	two legs
bird	six legs

   [4]

7. Briefly describe how a biological key is used. [4]

8. Briefly explain how the binomial system of biological names works. [4]

9. A key can be written in couplets. What are 'couplets'? [1]

Organisms in the environment — Chapter 2

How much do you already know?
Work out your score on pages 155–156.

Test yourself

1. Match each term in column **A** with the correct description in column **B**.

A terms	B descriptions
biosphere	the place where a group of organisms lives
community	all the ecosystems of the world
habitat	a group of individuals of the same species
population	all the organisms that live in a particular ecosystem

   [4]

2. a) Why is a food web a more accurate description of feeding in a community than a food chain? [2]
   b) Why do food chains and food webs nearly always begin with plants? [4]

3. a) Why is the pyramid of biomass usually a better description of a community than the pyramid of numbers? [2]
   b) Why is the pyramid of energy the best description of the feeding relationships within a community? [3]

4. Give reasons for the rapid increase in the human population. [4]

5. Weigh up the benefits in food production of intensive farming against the costs to the environment. [5]

2.1 Introducing ecology

PREVIEW

At the end of this section you will understand that:

- an ecosystem is a self-contained part of the biosphere, such as a pond or an oak wood
- the community consists of the organisms that live in a particular ecosystem
- the habitat is the place where a group of organisms live
- a niche is the role each species has in its habitat
- a population is a group of organisms of the same species living in the same place at the same time.

Some ecological terms

Ecology involves studying the relationships between organisms and between organisms and the environment.

The diagram at the top of page 13 shows that all the places on Earth where there is life form the **biosphere**. Each organism is suited (**adapted**) to the place where it lives. This place consists of:
- an **environment** of air, soil or water
- a living **community** of plants, animals, fungi and microorganisms.

Environment and community together form an **ecosystem**, which is a more or less self-contained part of the biosphere. 'Self-contained' means that each ecosystem has its own characteristic organisms not usually found in other ecosystems. These organisms are the living (**biotic**) community of the ecosystem. The physical environment is the non-living (**abiotic**) part, consisting of air, soil or water. The diagram on page 12 shows the different components of an oak wood ecosystem.

The flow chart on page 13 shows the hierarchy of ecological terms.

Fact file

Polar bears are adapted to survive Arctic cold. Their thick fur coat is easily shaken dry and its hairs stay erect, trapping a layer of air, which helps to insulate the body from heat loss because air is a poor conductor of heat. A thick layer of fat (also a poor conductor of heat) under the skin insulates the body from heat loss as well. A polar bear's fur is white, camouflaging it in the landscape of snow and ice. The camouflage makes it difficult for seals, the bear's main food source, to see when danger (the bear) threatens.

Camels are adapted to survive in hot deserts. Fat insulates the body's surfaces exposed to the Sun, in this case restricting heat flow into the body.

Organisms in the environment

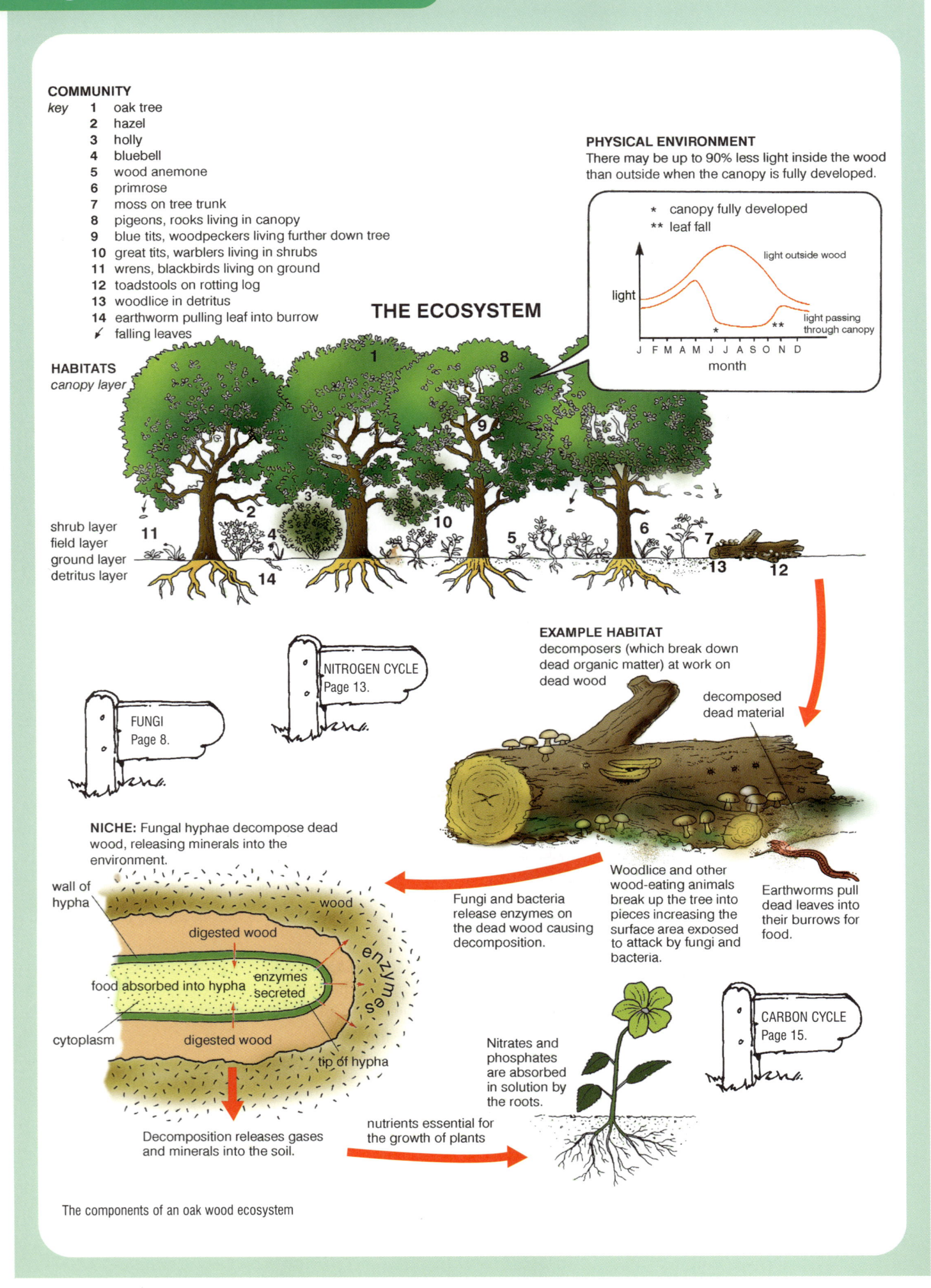

COMMUNITY

key
1. oak tree
2. hazel
3. holly
4. bluebell
5. wood anemone
6. primrose
7. moss on tree trunk
8. pigeons, rooks living in canopy
9. blue tits, woodpeckers living further down tree
10. great tits, warblers living in shrubs
11. wrens, blackbirds living on ground
12. toadstools on rotting log
13. woodlice in detritus
14. earthworm pulling leaf into burrow
↙ falling leaves

PHYSICAL ENVIRONMENT

There may be up to 90% less light inside the wood than outside when the canopy is fully developed.

* canopy fully developed
** leaf fall

light outside wood
light passing through canopy

month: J F M A M J J A S O N D

THE ECOSYSTEM

HABITATS
canopy layer
shrub layer
field layer
ground layer
detritus layer

NITROGEN CYCLE Page 13.

FUNGI Page 8.

EXAMPLE HABITAT
decomposers (which break down dead organic matter) at work on dead wood

decomposed dead material

Fungi and bacteria release enzymes on the dead wood causing decomposition.

Woodlice and other wood-eating animals break up the tree into pieces increasing the surface area exposed to attack by fungi and bacteria.

Earthworms pull dead leaves into their burrows for food.

NICHE: Fungal hyphae decompose dead wood, releasing minerals into the environment.

- wall of hypha
- wood
- digested wood
- enzymes secreted
- food absorbed into hypha
- cytoplasm
- digested wood
- tip of hypha
- enzymes

Decomposition releases gases and minerals into the soil.

nutrients essential for the growth of plants

Nitrates and phosphates are absorbed in solution by the roots.

CARBON CYCLE Page 15.

The components of an oak wood ecosystem

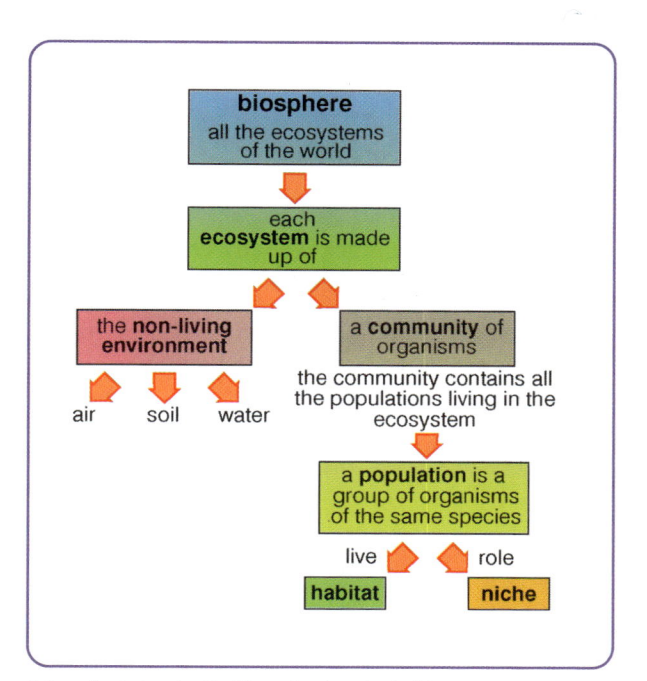

Organisms in the environment

A flow chart showing the hierarchy of ecological terms:

- **biosphere** — all the ecosystems of the world
- each **ecosystem** is made up of:
  - the **non-living environment**: air, soil, water
  - a **community** of organisms — the community contains all the populations living in the ecosystem
    - a **population** is a group of organisms of the same species
      - live → **habitat**
      - role → **niche**

Fact file

The **species diversity index** is a measure of the number of different types (species) of organism in an ecosystem. **Biodiversity** is the term used to refer to the number of different species in an ecosystem.

Decomposition

Notice in the diagram of an oak wood ecosystem that bacteria and fungi release enzymes on to dead organic material, digesting it. The products of digestion are absorbed by the bacteria and fungi and are a source of energy for their growth. Their activities are also the cause of **decomposition**, which releases mineral nutrients into the soil from the **detritus layer**. The mineral nutrients are **absorbed** in solution by the roots of plants. In this way plants obtain the mineral nutrients essential for growth. Animals obtain nutrients by eating plants and/or other animals.

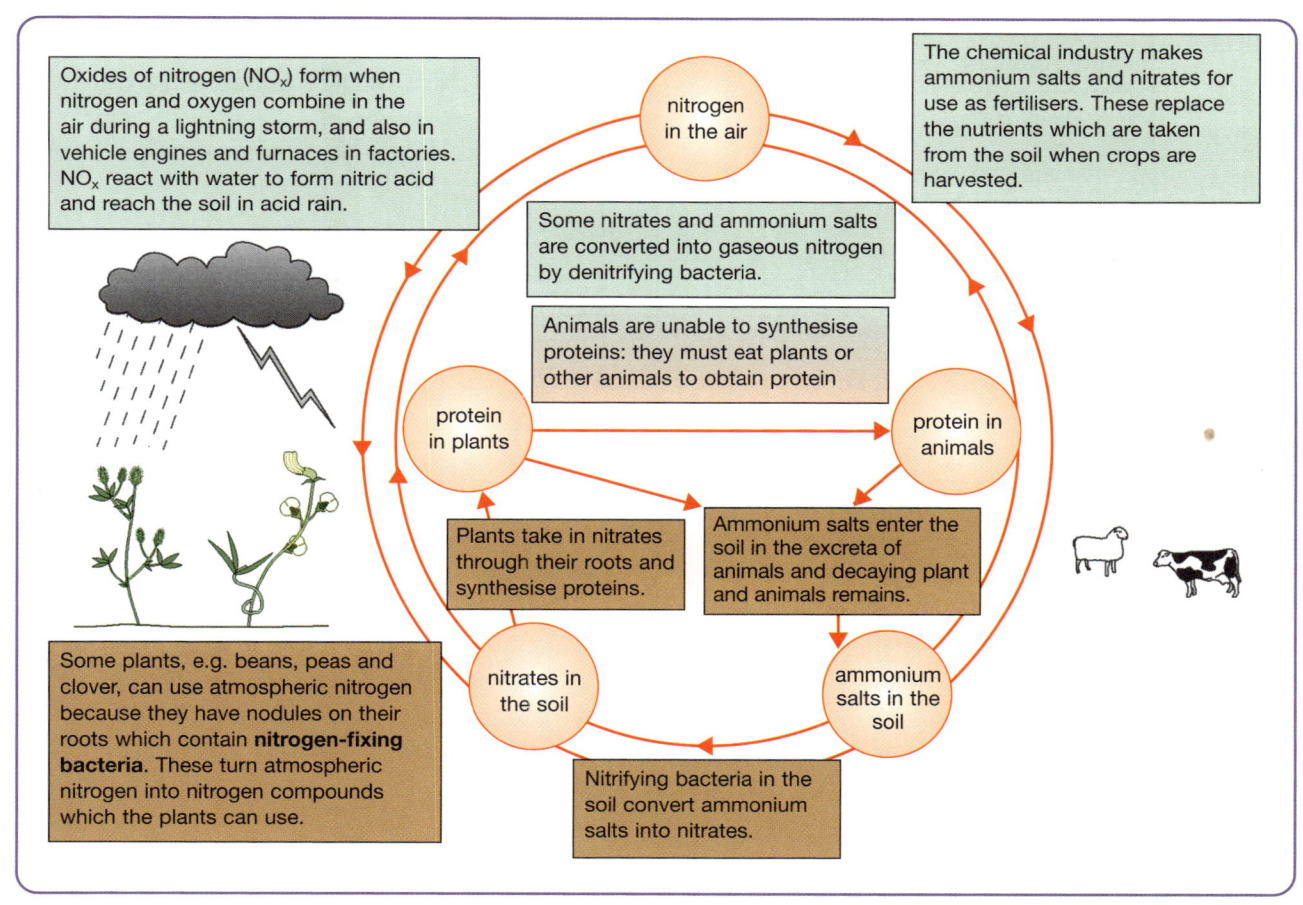

Nitrogen cycle diagram:

- Oxides of nitrogen (NO_x) form when nitrogen and oxygen combine in the air during a lightning storm, and also in vehicle engines and furnaces in factories. NO_x react with water to form nitric acid and reach the soil in acid rain.

- The chemical industry makes ammonium salts and nitrates for use as fertilisers. These replace the nutrients which are taken from the soil when crops are harvested.

- Some nitrates and ammonium salts are converted into gaseous nitrogen by denitrifying bacteria.

- Animals are unable to synthesise proteins: they must eat plants or other animals to obtain protein.

- Plants take in nitrates through their roots and synthesise proteins.

- Ammonium salts enter the soil in the excreta of animals and decaying plant and animals remains.

- Some plants, e.g. beans, peas and clover, can use atmospheric nitrogen because they have nodules on their roots which contain **nitrogen-fixing bacteria**. These turn atmospheric nitrogen into nitrogen compounds which the plants can use.

- Nitrifying bacteria in the soil convert ammonium salts into nitrates.

Cycle nodes: nitrogen in the air → protein in plants → protein in animals → ammonium salts in the soil → nitrates in the soil.

Nitrogen circulates from air to soil to living things and back again in the nitrogen cycle. Most living things cannot make use of nitrogen in the air. Nitrogen-fixing bacteria make nitrogen available in the form of nitrogen compounds, which plants absorb in solution through their roots.

Organisms in the environment

Nitrates are nutrients used by living things to make **protein**. The element **nitrogen** is present in nitrates (e.g. calcium nitrate). Decomposition recycles it from living things to the air, soil and water and back again. The process shown at the bottom of page 13 is called the **nitrogen cycle.**

CARBON CYCLE Page 15.

Remember, in equations we use the following state symbols:

(s)	=	solid
(l)	=	liquid
(g)	=	gas
(aq)	=	aqueous solution

Ammonia and fertilisers

The nitrogen in the air is used to make nitrogenous fertilisers. Under the conditions of the **Haber process** (named after the chemist Fritz Haber) nitrogen combines with hydrogen to form ammonia.

$$\text{nitrogen} + \text{hydrogen} \rightleftharpoons \text{ammonia}$$
$$N_2(g) + 3H_2(g) \rightleftharpoons 2NH_3(g)$$

Ammonia solution can be used as a fertiliser. However, it is more common to use the solid fertilisers ammonium nitrate, ammonium sulphate and ammonium phosphate.

Mixtures of ammonium nitrate, ammonium phosphate and potassium chloride contain the elements nitrogen, phosphorus and potassium, which are nutrients essential for plant growth. They are sold as **NPK fertilisers** (sometimes called **artificial fertiliser**).

Artificial fertiliser (and untreated sewage) entering streams, rivers and the sea causes the water to become richer and richer in nutrients. The process is called **eutrophication**.

★ Water plants increase and grow.

★ Algae increase in number, clouding the water in a greenish scum – an **algal bloom**.

★ When the plant material and algae die, bacteria decompose the organic matter and multiply.

As a result, the bacteria use up the oxygen in the water.

As a result, wildlife dies through lack of oxygen.

PHOTOSYNTHESIS Page 57.

The carbon cycle

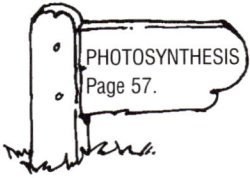

Plants and algae are able to make sugars by the process of **photosynthesis**:

$$\text{carbon dioxide} + \text{water} + \text{sunlight} \xrightarrow{\text{catalysed by chlorophyll}} \text{glucose} + \text{oxygen}$$

All living things obtain energy as a result of **cellular respiration**:

$$\text{glucose} + \text{oxygen} \rightarrow \text{carbon dioxide} + \text{water} + \text{energy}$$

The balance between the processes which take carbon dioxide from the air and those which put carbon dioxide into the air is called the **carbon cycle**. The cycle is shown opposite.

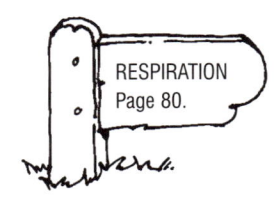

RESPIRATION Page 80.

Organisms in the environment

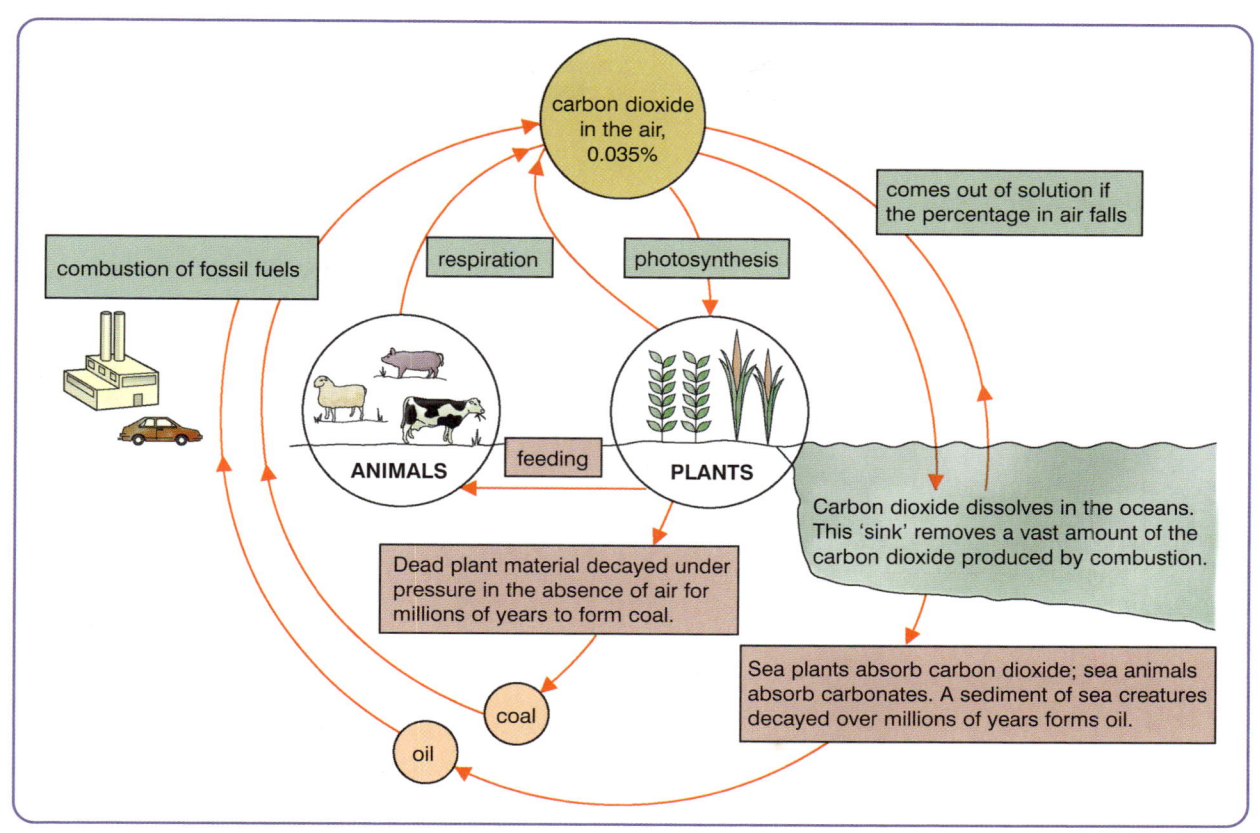

The carbon cycle

2.2 Food chains and webs

> **PREVIEW**
>
> At the end of this section you will:
> - know the meaning of the terms producer, herbivore, carnivore and omnivore
> - understand that energy is transferred along food chains
> - be able to interpret diagrams of food chains and food webs.

Who eats whom?

Finding out 'who eats whom' is one way of describing how a community works. Looking at:
- animals' teeth or mouthparts
- what is in the intestine
- animals feeding
- what food an animal likes best (a **food preference test**)

helps find out what animals feed on.

The working community

Animals fall into three categories according to what they eat.

★ **Herbivores** eat plants.

★ **Carnivores** eat meat.

★ **Omnivores** eat both plants and meat. (Most human beings are omnivorous.)

Most carnivores are **predators** – they catch and eat other animals. The animals caught are their **prey**, and are often herbivores.

Scavengers are carnivores that feed on the remains of prey left by predators, or on the bodies of animals that have died for other reasons such as disease or old age.

A **food chain** shows the links between plants, prey, predators and scavengers. Some examples of food chains are shown on page 16.

Organisms in the environment

Notice in each example that:
- the arrows represent the transfer of food (and therefore food energy) between different organisms
- the arrows point from the organism eaten to the organism which eats it
- the number of links in a food chain is usually four or less.

A **food web** is usually a more accurate description of feeding relationships in a community because most animals eat more than one type of plant or other animal. Some examples of food webs are shown opposite.

Notice in each example that:
- several food chains link up to form a food web
- plants and algae produce food by photosynthesis
- different types of animal eat the same type of food.

Producers

Plants, algae and some bacteria are called **producers** because they use sunlight to produce food by photosynthesis. This is why food chains and food webs always begin with plants (or algae or photosynthetic bacteria). Animals use this food when they eat plants. Even when they eat other animals, predators depend on plant food indirectly since somewhere along the line the prey has been a plant eater. Because they eat food, animals are called **consumers**.

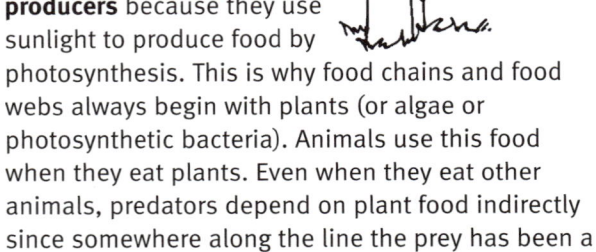

PHOTOSYNTHESIS Page 57.

No light means no photosynthesis, but communities of organisms flourish in the dark of the ocean depths around openings in the sea floor called **vents**. Larva and gases escaping from the vents provide substances for chemical reactions, which produce hydrogen sulphide (H_2S). Different types of bacteria oxidise the sulphide releasing the energy needed for them to make sugars from carbon dioxide (in solution) and water. The bacteria are the producers upon which the food web of the vent community depends.

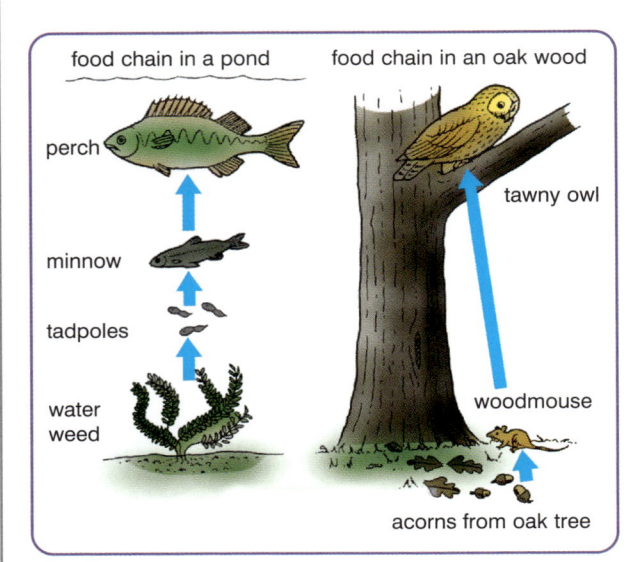

Food chains

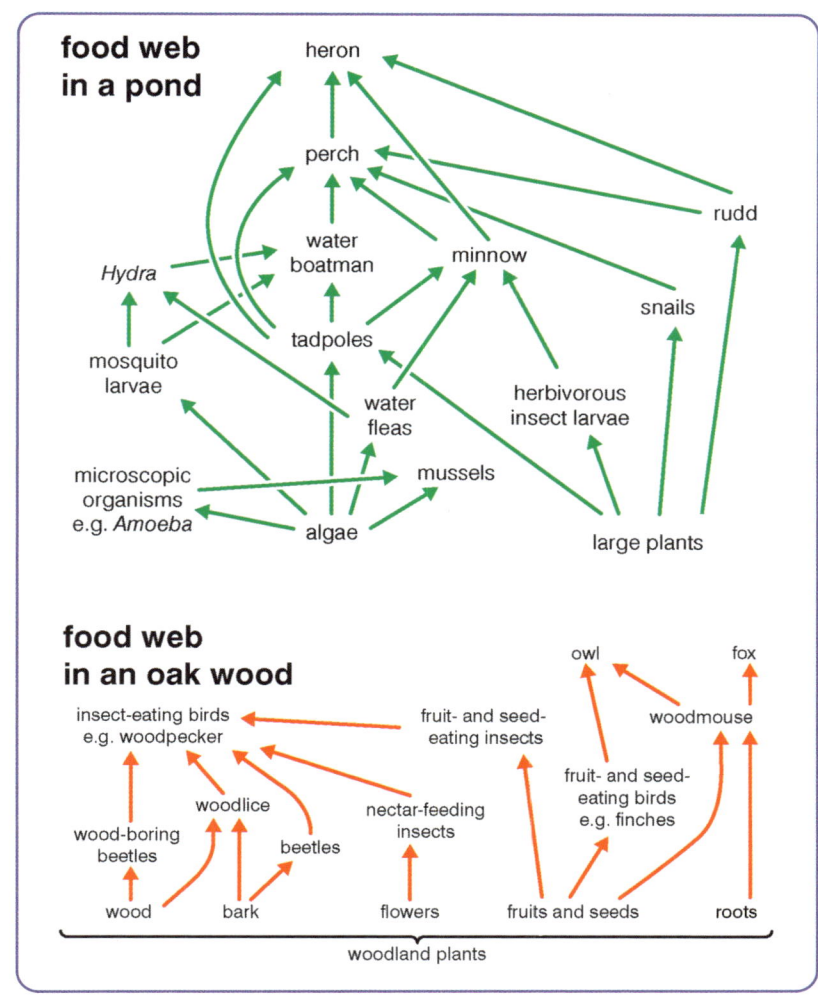

Organisms in the environment

Energy flow

Sunlight underpins life on Earth. Without sunlight, and the photosynthesis which depends on it, most communities would cease to exist.

Through photosynthesis plants convert light energy into the chemical energy of food. A food chain represents one pathway of food energy through the community of an ecosystem. A food web represents many pathways. The diagram below shows the idea.

At each link in the food chain, energy is lost in the waste products produced by organisms and as a result of the metabolism (chemical reactions taking place in the cells) of each living thing. Much of the energy lost is in the form of heat.

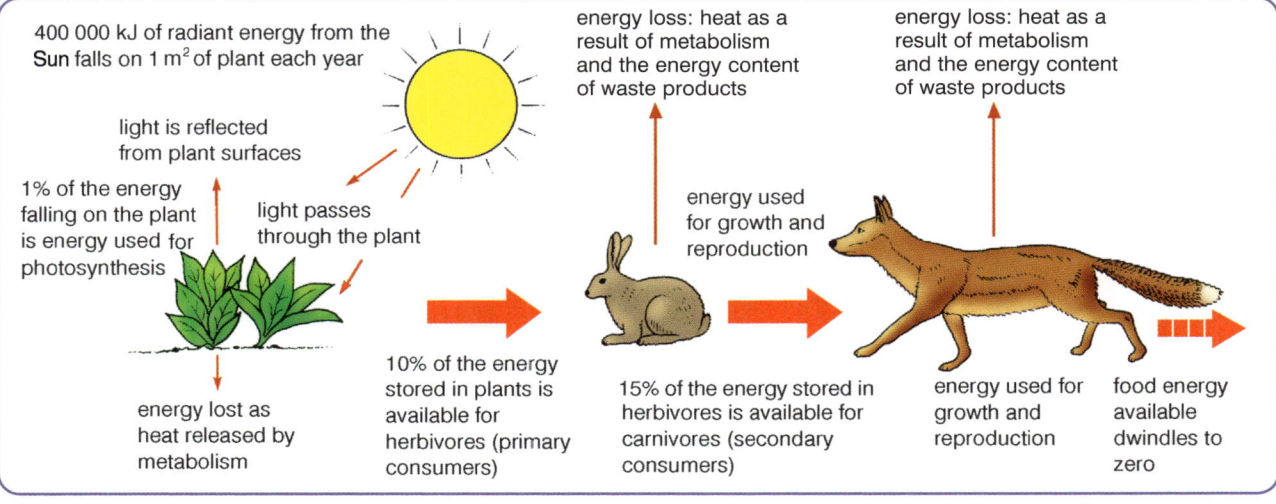

food web in a pond

heron, perch, rudd, water boatman, minnow, snails, Hydra, tadpoles, herbivorous insect larvae, mosquito larvae, water fleas, mussels, microscopic organisms e.g. Amoeba, algae, large plants

food web in an oak wood

owl, fox, insect-eating birds e.g. woodpecker, fruit- and seed-eating insects, woodmouse, woodlice, nectar-feeding insects, fruit- and seed-eating birds e.g. finches, wood-boring beetles, beetles, wood, bark, flowers, fruits and seeds, roots — woodland plants

Food webs

400 000 kJ of radiant energy from the Sun falls on 1 m² of plant each year

energy loss: heat as a result of metabolism and the energy content of waste products

energy loss: heat as a result of metabolism and the energy content of waste products

light is reflected from plant surfaces

1% of the energy falling on the plant is energy used for photosynthesis

light passes through the plant

energy used for growth and reproduction

energy lost as heat released by metabolism

10% of the energy stored in plants is available for herbivores (primary consumers)

15% of the energy stored in herbivores is available for carnivores (secondary consumers)

energy used for growth and reproduction

food energy available dwindles to zero

The flow of energy through a food chain. Notice that only a small proportion of the Sun's radiant (light) energy is used in photosynthesis.

Organisms in the environment

2.3 Ecological pyramids

> **PREVIEW**
>
> At the end of this section you will:
> - understand the term trophic level
> - know how to build a pyramid of numbers
> - be able to interpret pyramids of numbers and pyramids of biomass
> - understand that the pyramid of energy gives the best picture of the relationships between producers and consumers.

Food chains and **food webs** describe the feeding relationships within a community. However, they do not tell us about the numbers of individuals involved. Many plants support a limited number of herbivores which in turn support fewer carnivores.

Trophic levels

Below is a diagram of an ecological pyramid.

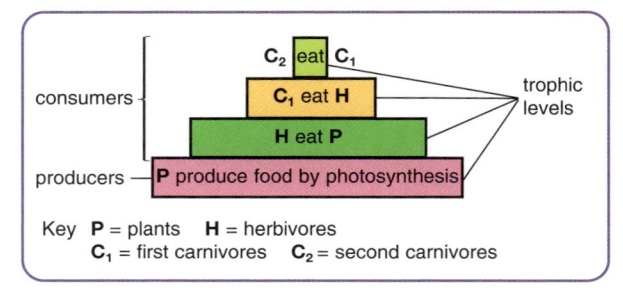

Ecological pyramid

★ The pyramid has several feeding levels called **trophic levels**.

★ Producers (plants/algae/some bacteria) occupy the base of the pyramid.

★ Other trophic levels are made up of consumers:
- **primary** consumers are herbivores (H) that feed on plants
- **secondary** consumers or first/primary carnivores (C_1) are carnivores that feed on herbivores
- **tertiary** consumers or second/secondary carnivores (C_2) are carnivores which feed on first/primary carnivores.

Each trophic level groups together organisms that have similar types of food. For example, a snail and a sheep are herbivores. Both belong to the second (H) trophic level.

The group of organisms in each trophic level is smaller than the one below it. This gives the shape of a pyramid.

Pyramids of numbers

Pyramids of numbers show the *number of organisms* in each trophic level. The table shows the numbers of insects and spiders collected from grass with a sweep net.

sample	number of insects	number of spiders
1	135	5
2	150	10
3	110	10
4	115	5
5	120	15
	630	45
	average = $\frac{630}{5}$ = 126 insects in each sample	average = $\frac{45}{5}$ = 9 spiders in each sample

Samples of insects and spiders collected with a sweep net. Each sample was collected with 10 sweeps while walking around an area of 10 m².

Data like those in the table can be used to plot a pyramid of numbers, as shown below. Half the number of organisms in each trophic level is plotted on one side of the vertical line, the other half is plotted on the other side of the vertical line.

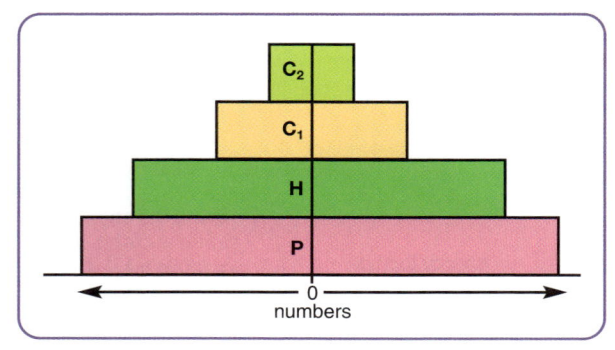

How to plot a pyramid of numbers

18

Organisms in the environment

In grassland, the producers (grasses) and consumers (mainly insects and spiders) are small and numerous. A lot of plants support many herbivores (mostly insects) which in turn support fewer carnivores (mostly spiders). Plotting the number of organisms in each trophic level of the grassland community gives the shape of a pyramid.

Problems with numbers ...

Example 1: the pyramid of numbers for a woodland community below has a point at the bottom as well as the top. This is because relatively few producers (trees) support a large number of herbivores and carnivores. You might think that woodland consumers are in danger of starvation! However, each tree is large and can meet the food needs of many different organisms.

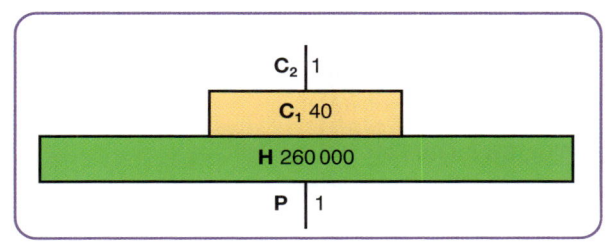

C_2 1
C_1 40
H 260 000
P 1

Pyramid of numbers for a woodland community

Example 2: pyramids of numbers including parasites appear top-heavy, as shown below. Many parasites feed on fewer secondary consumers.

In both these examples, number pyramids are not an accurate description of the feeding relationships in the different communities. Why? Because each number pyramid does not take into account differences in size of the different producers and consumers.

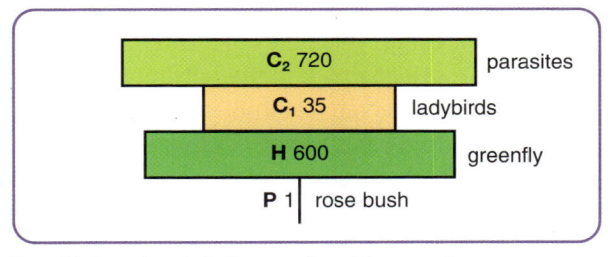

C_2 720 — parasites
C_1 35 — ladybirds
H 600 — greenfly
P 1 — rose bush

Pyramid of numbers including parasites of the secondary consumers (ladybirds)

... and the solution

A **pyramid of biomass** allows for differences in the size of organisms, because the pyramid shows the *amount of organic material* in each trophic level.

- A representative sample of the organisms at each trophic level is weighed.
- The mass is then multiplied by the estimated number of organisms in the community.

In practice, dry mass is used because fresh mass varies greatly as organisms contain different amounts of water. The sample is dried out in a warm oven until there is no further change in mass. The dry mass data are plotted as kilograms of dry mass per unit area (m^2) of the community.

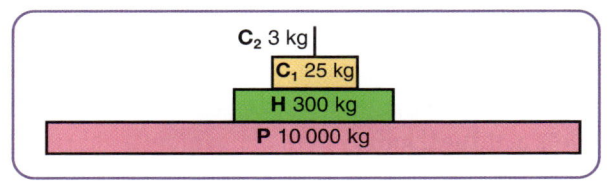

C_2 3 kg
C_1 25 kg
H 300 kg
P 10 000 kg

Pyramid of biomass for a woodland community

Problems with biomass ...

Example 1: the biomass of an organism can vary during the year. For example, an oak tree in full leaf during the summer will have a much greater biomass than in winter without its leaves.

Example 2: some organisms reproduce so quickly that sampling misses the rapid fluctuations in population. For example, below is an upside-down pyramid of biomass for the English Channel. Microscopic algae (producers) only live for a few days but reproduce millions of offspring very quickly. Collecting them over a short period misses this rapid turnover of living material and results in a pyramid which suggests that the biomass of herbivores (H) is greater than that of the producers (P) they feed on.

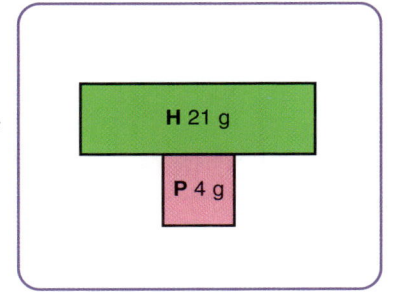

H 21 g
P 4 g

Pyramid of biomass for the English Channel, grams per unit volume (m^3) of water

Organisms in the environment

... and the solution

A **pyramid of energy** gives information about the *amount of energy* at each trophic level over a certain period of time. In other words, the energy pyramid shows the amount of food being produced and consumed in a given time. Its shape therefore is not affected by differences in size, or changes in numbers of individuals.

The food energy in each trophic level is measured by incinerating samples of organisms in a **bomb calorimeter**. The heat given off is a measure of the energy value of the samples and is therefore representative of the food energy in the trophic level to which the sample of organisms belongs. The diagram below shows you the idea.

Notice that:
- feeding transfers food energy from one trophic level to the next (energy flows)
- energy is lost from each trophic level through life's activities, mostly in the form of heat released by the metabolism of cells.

As a result, the amount of food energy in a trophic level is less than the one below it.

As a result, the amount of living material (biomass) in a trophic level is less than the one below it.

Key
- energy lost from each trophic level through life's activities
- flow of food energy through the community from one trophic level to the next (feeding)

sun — light energy captured
C_2 90 kJ
C_1 1600 kJ
H 14 200 kJ
P 87 400 kJ

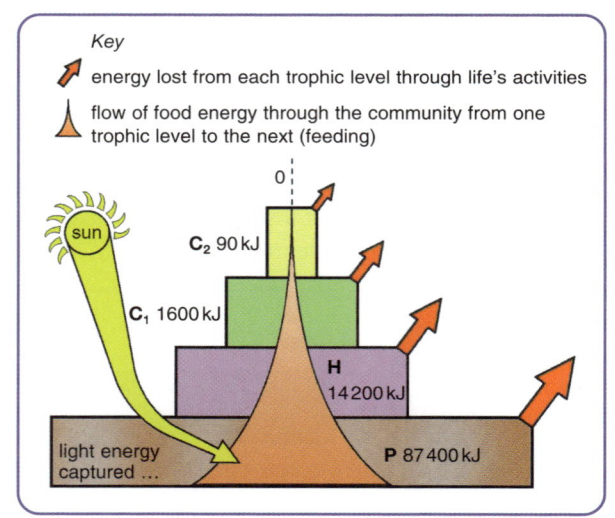

Pyramid of energy for a stream in kJ/m²/year

2.4 Distribution of organisms

PREVIEW

At the end of this section you will:
- understand the effect of environmental factors on the distribution of plants
- know that competition affects the distribution of organisms
- understand that different adaptations enable plants and animals to survive.

Competition between organisms

The distribution of organisms (where living things are found in the environment) is affected by different factors.

★ Physical factors include:
  - the amount of light
  - the abundance of water.

★ Biological factors include:
  - **intraspecific competition** – competition between individuals of the same species
  - **interspecific competition** – competition between individuals of different species
  - **interactions** between predators and prey
  - **adaptations** of organisms for survival in different environments.

Fact file

★ **Competition:** in nature organisms that are rivals for something that is in limited supply are competitors. The 'something' is a resource like water, light, space, food or mates.

★ **Adaptation:** organisms are adapted (suited) to the environment in which they live and to their role (niche – see page 13) in that environment. For example, the larvae (caterpillars) of different species of butterfly eat leaves or other parts of a plant. The adults suck the nectar of flowers.

As a result, competition for food between adults and their offspring is reduced.

Organisms in the environment

★ **Symbiosis:** a general term for close associations between individuals of different species where either one of the partners benefits to the detriment of the other (**parasitism**) or both benefit (**mutualism**). Where one member of the partnership is found, so too is the other, each affecting the distribution of the partner.

Examples of factors affecting the distribution of organisms follow below.

Example 1: intraspecific competition for light

In a wood, the branches of full-grown trees spread in all directions. They touch the branches of neighbouring trees, forming a continuous layer. This is the **canopy** which shades out plants beneath. When a tree is blown over, light floods through the gap in the canopy, stimulating vigorous plant growth on the woodland floor. This sunlit clearing becomes an arena for intense competition between tree seedlings which sprout from seeds that may have lain dormant for years, and then grow into saplings (young trees). Many competitors start out but there is limited space for spreading branches, which also overshadow slower-growing rivals. Many young trees perish along the way. Only the one that grows the fastest will fill the gap in the canopy, finally cutting off the sunlight that signalled the start of the race many years previously.

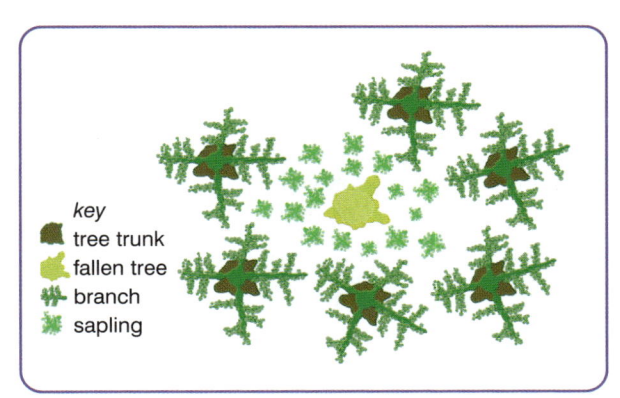

key
- tree trunk
- fallen tree
- branch
- sapling

Which sapling will survive to fill the gap? The length of the branches sets the distance between neighbouring trees, producing a continuous canopy and a regular pattern of tree trunks. The sunlit clearing caused by the fallen tree breaks the pattern and provides opportunities for new plant growth and competition between saplings to complete the canopy once more.

Example 2: intraspecific competition for water

The cacti in the photograph over the page are widely spaced apart, and look as if they have been planted out in a regular arrangement. The pattern appears because the roots of the cacti spread out underground, setting the distance between neighbouring plants. Although many tiny cactus seedlings sprout in a particular area, there is only enough water for some of them to grow into mature plants. Growing cacti are the competitors and water is the resource in short supply.

Fact file

The word '**arid**' is used to describe places where water is in short supply.

Cacti are adapted to grow in hot arid environments. For example, their thick stems store water. Also, the loss of water from the cactus is reduced by:
- spiny leaves reducing the surface area from which water is lost
- shiny surfaces, which reflect light and heat, reducing the evaporation of water from the plant
- shallow roots, which are widespread, providing a large surface area for the absorption of the little water that may be available
- pits in the plant's surface surrounding the stomata. The pits are fringed with hairs and as a result the microenvironment around the stomatal pore is humid, reducing the concentration gradient of water between the inside of the plant and outside. As a result the rate of transpiration is reduced
- a thick waxy cuticle, covering the plant's surfaces.

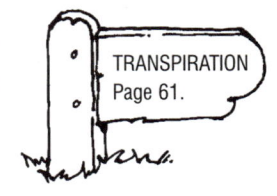

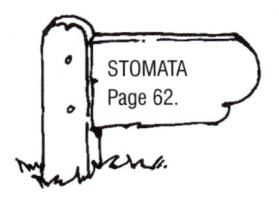

TRANSPIRATION Page 61.

STOMATA Page 62.

Organisms in the environment

Cacti in the Arizona Desert, south-western United States, where rainfall is erratic and infrequent

Example 3: interspecific competition

Competition between different species is usually greatest among individuals that occupy the same trophic level. This competition for the same resource often leads to one species replacing another (called **competitive exclusion**). For example, when two species of clover (both producers) were grown separately, they grew well. However, when grown together one species eventually replaced the other. The reason was that the successful species grew slightly taller than its competitor and overshadowed it. The unsuccessful species received less light. Its rate of photosynthesis and therefore its rate of growth was less than its successful competitor.

Example 4: predator and prey

Predators are adapted to catch prey, and prey are adapted to escape predators. The table summarises their different strategies.

predator	prey
eats a variety of prey species, reducing the risk of starvation should one prey species decline in numbers	large groups (e.g. herds of antelope, shoals of fish) distract predators from concentrating on a particular individual
catches young, old and sick prey	stings and bitter taste deter predators
catches large prey which provides more food per kill	warning coloration tells predators to avoid particular prey
moves to areas where prey is plentiful	camouflage conceals prey
predator tries to run/swim/fly faster than prey	prey tries to run/swim/fly faster than pursuing predator
	shock tactics startle predators

Strategies for predator success and prey survival

2.5 Population size

PREVIEW

At the end of this section you will:
- know how populations increase in size
- understand that the impact of human activity on the environment is related to population size
- be able to identify specific effects of human activity on the environment.

The size of a population

★ A **population** is a group of individuals of the same species living in the same place at the same time.

★ **Births** and **immigration** increase the size of a population.

★ **Deaths** and **emigration** decrease the size of a population.

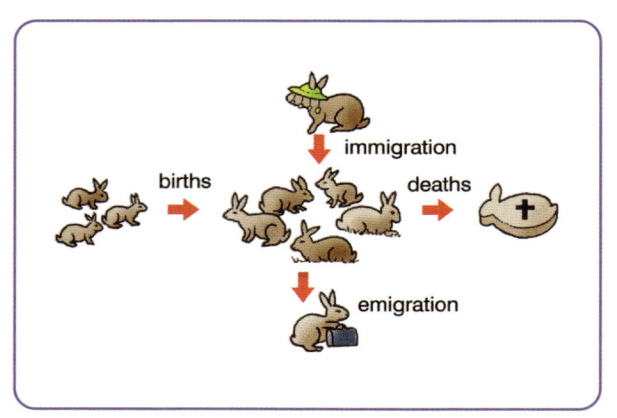

Factors affecting the size of a population

Population growth

The following graph shows that populations grow in a particular way. **Limiting factors** stop populations from growing indefinitely. They include:

shortages of
- food
- water
- oxygen
- light
- shelter

build-up of
- poisonous wastes
- predators
- disease
- social factors.

Organisms in the environment

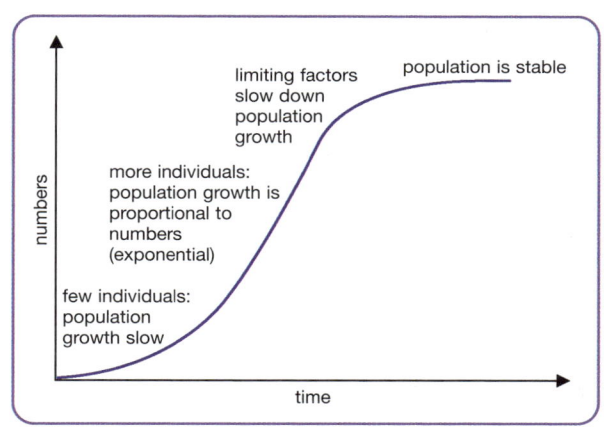

Population growth curve

Predator and prey populations

Predation affects the number of the prey population: if predators are numerous then more prey is caught. The number of prey affects the predator population: if prey is scarce, then some of the predators will starve. The graph below shows the relationships between the numbers of predators and prey.

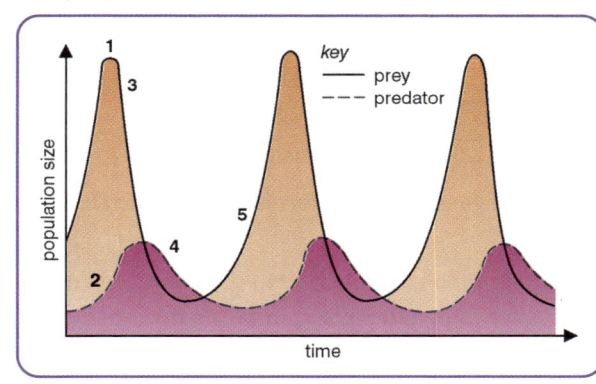

Predator–prey relationships

1 Prey breed and increase in numbers if conditions are favourable (e.g. food is abundant).

2 Predators breed and increase in numbers in response to the abundance of prey.

3 Predation pressure increases and the number of prey declines.

4 Predator numbers decline in response to the shortage of food.

5 Predation pressure decreases and so prey numbers increase ... and so on.

Notice that:
- fluctuations in predator numbers are *smaller* than fluctuations in prey numbers
- fluctuations in predator numbers *lag* behind fluctuations in prey numbers.

Why is this? There are fewer predators than prey, and predators tend to reproduce more slowly than prey.

The human population

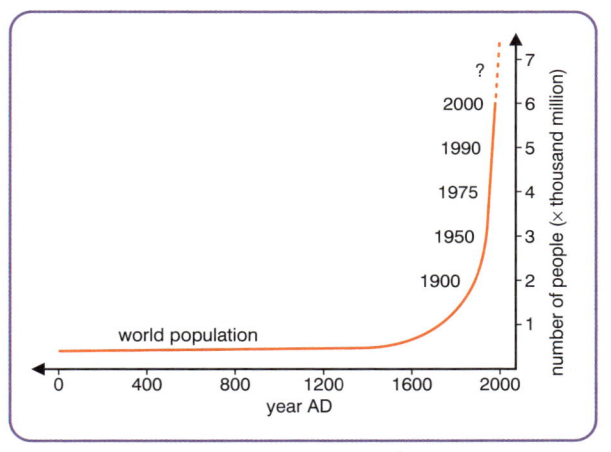

World population growth over the past 2000 years showing predicted future increase based on present trends

This graph shows that the human population has grown dramatically since the beginning of the nineteenth century. Although the populations of Europe, North America and Japan (countries with developed economies) are levelling off, the populations of some other countries with developing economies are still growing rapidly as a result of:
- improvements in food production
- more drugs for the treatment of disease
- improved medical care
- improved public health.

The rate of population growth is affected by the number of young people in the population, particularly women of child-bearing age. The table on page 24 summarises the problem.

A large proportion of the world's population is young so the problems listed in the table are global. The problems are particularly acute in developing countries.

23

Organisms in the environment

problem	result
present birth rate high	adding to the rate of population increase
future birth rate high	as children in the population 'bulge' grow older and have their own children, adding further to the rate of population increase
social services inadequate	large numbers of children put strain on the educational system, medical services and housing

Problems of a young population

In Britain (and other countries with developed economies) the problems are more to do with a population that has an increasing proportion of old people. The diseases of old age (cancer, arthritis, dementia) take up an increasing proportion of the resources available for medical care.

Human impact on the environment

1.5 million years ago: early humans probably moved from place to place in search of food. They hunted animals and gathered plants. Their impact on the environment was no more than that of other medium-sized animals.

10 000 years ago: about 12 million people lived in the world. In the Middle East they harvested wild wheat and other grains. When the grain was ripe, a family could probably gather over a year's supply in just a few weeks. People had little impact on the environment beyond their village.

2000 years ago: people had started to farm. Skills in crafts and tool-making developed. Villages became larger and some grew into towns. People had a much greater impact on the environment – farming the land, using raw materials.

Today: about 6.2 billion (thousand million) people live in the world. In countries with developed economies, food is produced by relatively few people. Industry and technology use raw materials, often obtained from countries with developing economies where environments may be stripped of resources.

The impact of people on the environment is **agricultural, industrial** and **domestic**. Everyone needs food and a home. Many people also want a wide range of manufactured goods. In developed countries large quantities of food are produced and plenty of goods are manufactured. However, pollution is the result of plenty.

★ **Air** is polluted by gases, dust and smoke from cars, factories and houses.

★ **Fresh water** (rivers and lakes) and **seawater** are polluted by:
  - waste from factories
  - 'run off' of agrochemicals (pesticides and fertilisers) from farmland
  - discharge from sewage treatment works
  - 'cooling water' discharged from power stations.

★ **Land** is polluted by waste in the form of:
  - household (domestic) rubbish and waste from factories
  - pulverised ash from coke and coal-fired power stations
  - slag from quarrying and mining operations.

Controlling pollution

What can be done about reducing pollution?

Clean up the gases and liquids discharged into the environment

★ *Power stations* – 'scrubbers' in the chimneys of power stations remove sulphur from the waste gases produced by burning coal, before the gases escape into the atmosphere.

★ *Cars* – catalytic converters fitted to the exhausts of cars remove harmful gases (e.g. carbon monoxide) produced by engines burning fuel.

★ *Drinking water* – stripping nitrates and phosphates from drinking water reduces the risks to human health. The nitrates and phosphates are components of fertiliser which 'runs off' in solution from farmland into rivers and lakes.

Recycle materials

Recycling materials saves raw materials obtained from the environment and the energy needed to manufacture goods.

Organisms in the environment

★ *Costs* of disposing of waste material in landfill sites are reduced.

★ *Space* which would be used for landfill sites is saved.

Reduce the use of harmful materials

★ *Chlorofluorohydrocarbons* (CFCs) are compounds used as propellants in aerosols. They react with ozone in the upper atmosphere. Oxygen is produced and the ozone layer which protects life on Earth from the harmful effects of ultra-violet radiation is gradually destroyed. 'Ozone-friendly' compounds are replacing CFCs in a range of products.

Fossil fuels and nuclear power

Fossil fuels – coal, oil (including petrol) and gas – are a source of energy. Their combustion (burning) releases gases that pollute the environment. The table summarises the problem.

pollutant	source	harmful effect
sulphur dioxide	power stations and factories	causes acid rain which damages trees and other plants. Acid rain also kills wildlife in lakes and ponds
carbon monoxide	engines and factories	combines with haemoglobin (see page 86) better than oxygen. A shortage of oxygen causes headaches and dizziness in affected people. A concentration of 0.1% of carbon monoxide in the air kills
oxides of nitrogen	engines, power stations, factories, mining	cause acid rain (see above). Increase the concentration of ozone in the atmosphere, damaging crops
lead compounds	engines	poison the nervous system, causing damage to the brain. Replacing the lead in petrol with alternative substances and increasing use of *unleaded* petrol is reducing the amount of lead released into the environment

The main pollutants in air

Nuclear reactors are also a source of energy. The safe disposal of the radioactive waste produced by nuclear reactions is a major environmental problem because it:
- *persists* in the environment for thousands of years
- *accumulates* in food chains.

  As a result, human health is affected.
  - The risk of the development of different types of cancer (e.g. leukaemia) increases.
  - Women give birth to deformed babies.

Water pollution

★ Living standards depend on industry, and industry needs water to dispose of wastes. [FARMING Pages 32–36.]

★ Agrochemicals (pesticides and fertilisers) 'run off' from the land into rivers, lakes and the sea.

★ People produce sewage which (treated and untreated) enters rivers and the sea.

  As a result, water is polluted making it:
  - unsafe to drink (unless treated)
  - unsuitable for organisms that depend on clean water to survive.

Organic waste consists of **compounds** containing carbon and originates from animals (including humans) and plants. It is a source of food (**nutrients**) for microorganisms. Sewage and fertilisers are examples. As the water becomes richer and richer in nutrients the microorganisms multiply and rapidly increase in numbers. [FERTILISERS Page 14.]

★ The activities of microorganisms (including **aerobic** bacteria) decompose the organic waste.

Organisms in the environment

As a result, the concentration of dissolved oxygen is reduced and poisonous substances (e.g. ammonia) are released into solution.

As a result, organisms die through lack of oxygen and/or poisoning.

★ Anaerobic bacteria continue the decomposition of the organic waste.

As a result, the water becomes black and unable to support wildlife.

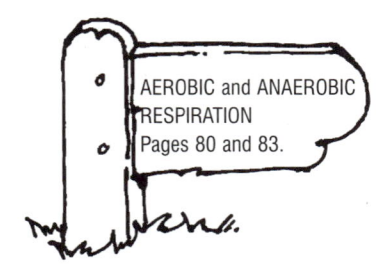

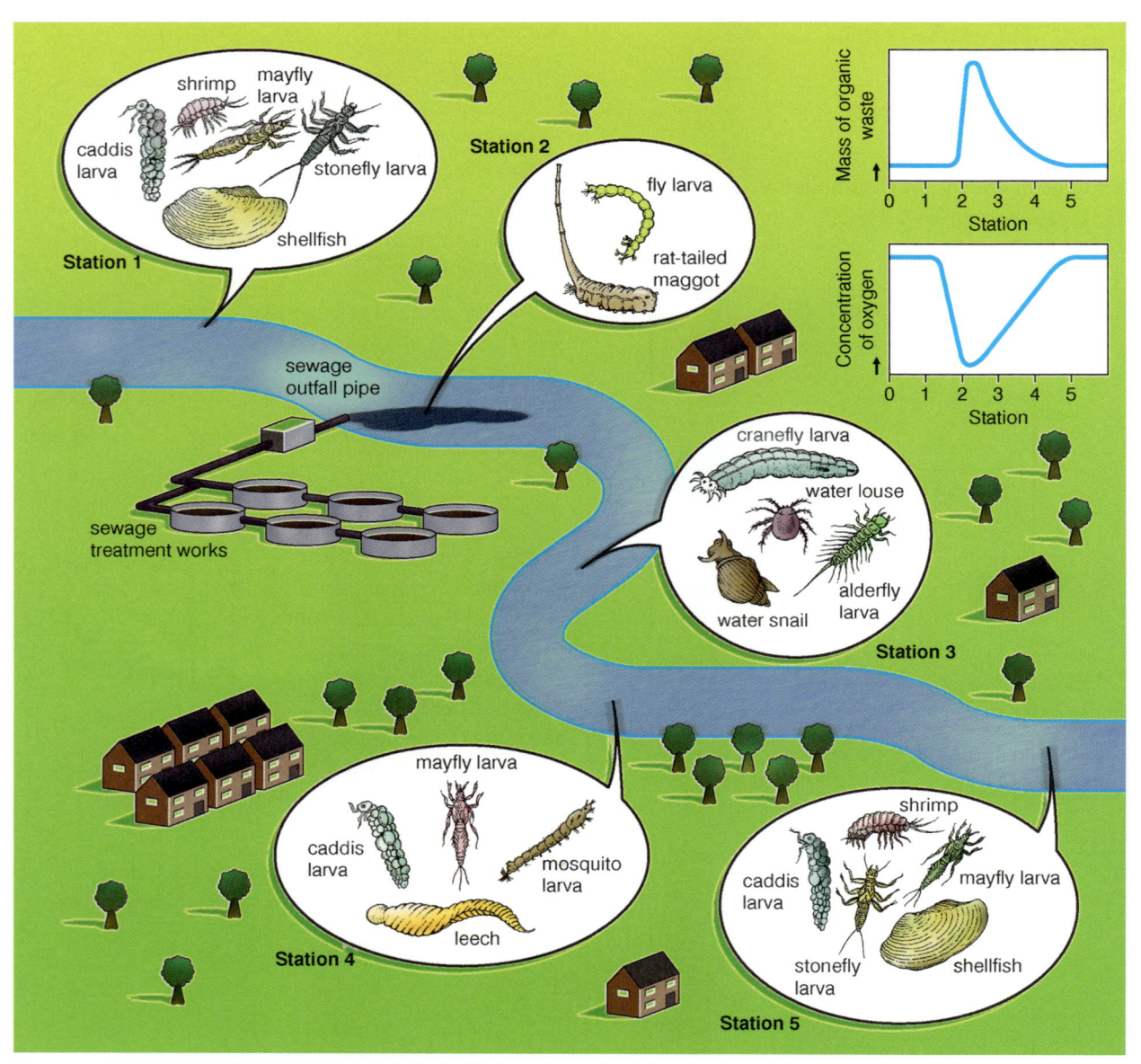

AEROBIC and ANAEROBIC RESPIRATION Pages 80 and 83.

The presence or absence of different species (types) of animal indicates how polluted the water is with organic wastes. Notice that the number of species and types of species at Stations 2, 3 and 4 are less than at Stations 1 and 5. At Station 5, the dilution of sewage is so great that water quality is no longer affected. The species found at Station 5 are the same as those found in the unpolluted waters at Station 1.

Organisms in the environment

The sequence runs:

```
waste enters the water
        ↓
the number of microorganisms
     rapidly increases
```

AEROBIC CONDITIONS

```
the activities of the microorganisms
(decomposition) use up dissolved oxygen
       ↙                    ↘
most types of          a few types of
organism die           organism can survive
because of the         the lack of oxygen
lack of oxygen                ↓
                     their numbers increase
```

ANAEROBIC CONDITIONS

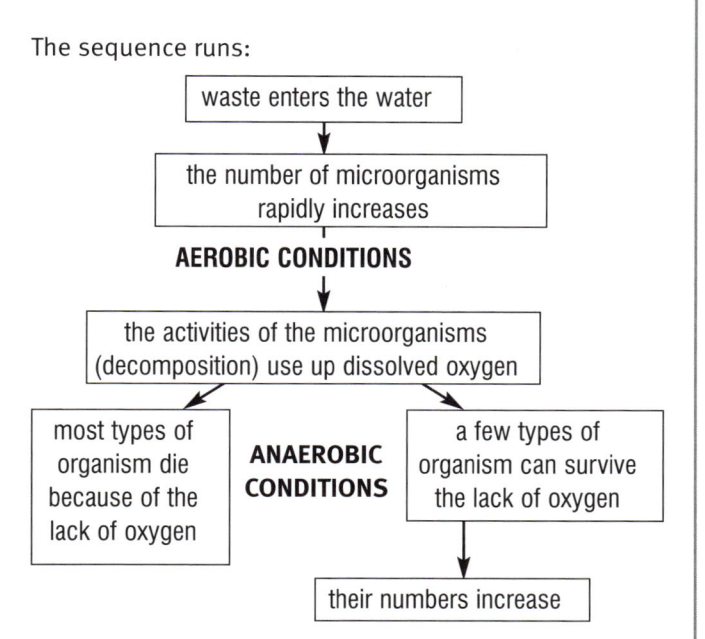

The diagram opposite shows you what happens to the animals of a river that is polluted with sewage and fertiliser.

Notice that the more waste there is in the water, the less oxygen there is in solution (abiotic effect).

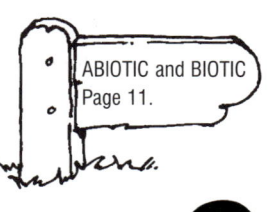

ABIOTIC and BIOTIC Page 11.

As a result, there are fewer types of animal able to survive in the polluted parts of the river (biotic effect).

The greenhouse effect

The Earth receives radiation from the Sun, and also radiates heat into space. Carbon dioxide and water vapour reduce the escape of heat energy from the Earth by means of the **greenhouse effect** (see diagram below). Without these 'blankets' of water vapour and carbon dioxide, the temperature of the Earth's surface would be at −40°C, and life on Earth would be impossible.

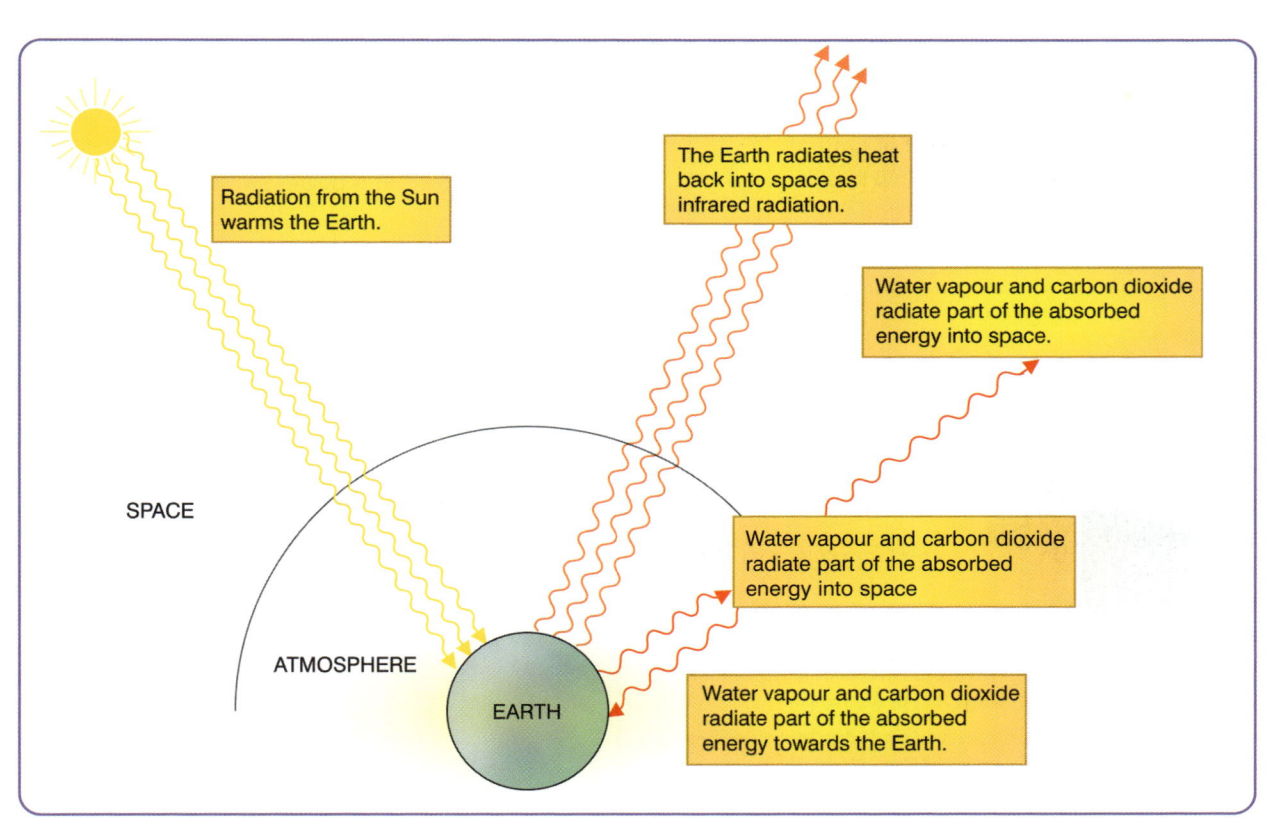

Radiation from the Sun warms the Earth.

The Earth radiates heat back into space as infrared radiation.

Water vapour and carbon dioxide radiate part of the absorbed energy into space.

Water vapour and carbon dioxide radiate part of the absorbed energy into space

Water vapour and carbon dioxide radiate part of the absorbed energy towards the Earth.

SPACE

ATMOSPHERE

EARTH

The greenhouse effect

27

Organisms in the environment

The combustion of fossil fuels is causing an increase in the level of carbon dioxide at a rate which could raise the average temperature of the Earth. One result would be that the massive icecaps of the Arctic and Antarctic regions would slowly begin to melt. The levels of oceans would rise, and coastal areas would be flooded. A rise in temperature could decrease food production over vast areas, e.g. the mid-west USA and Russia. Secondary effects would make matters worse. The increase in temperature would make more water vaporise from the oceans and drive out some of the carbon dioxide dissolved in the oceans to add to a still thicker greenhouse blanket. Other 'greenhouse gases' are methane, chlorofluorocarbons (CFCs), nitrogen oxides and ozone.

CFCs Page 25.

Acid rain

Rain is naturally weakly acidic because it dissolves carbon dioxide from the air. The pH of natural rainwater is 5.2. Rain with a pH below this is described as **acid rain**. Sulphur dioxide released into the atmosphere is the cause. The diagram below shows the major sources of sulphur dioxide in the air and the effects of acid rain:
- damage to lakes and the fish and plants in them
- washing of nutrients out of topsoil, resulting in poor crops and damage to trees
- costly damage to building materials, e.g. limestone, concrete, cement and metal.

What can be done?

Sweden has tackled the problem by spraying tonnes of calcium hydroxide into acid lakes.

Members of the European Union (EU) agreed to make a 60–70% cut in their emissions of sulphur dioxide by 2003. Power stations must make a big contribution to solving the problem. Some lines of attack are listed below.

★ Coal can be crushed and washed with a solvent to remove much of the sulphur content.

★ Fuel oil can be purified at the refinery – at a cost.

★ Sulphur dioxide can be removed from the exhaust gases of power stations. In **flue gas desulphurisation** (**FGD**), jets of wet powdered limestone neutralise acidic gases as they pass up the chimney of the power station.

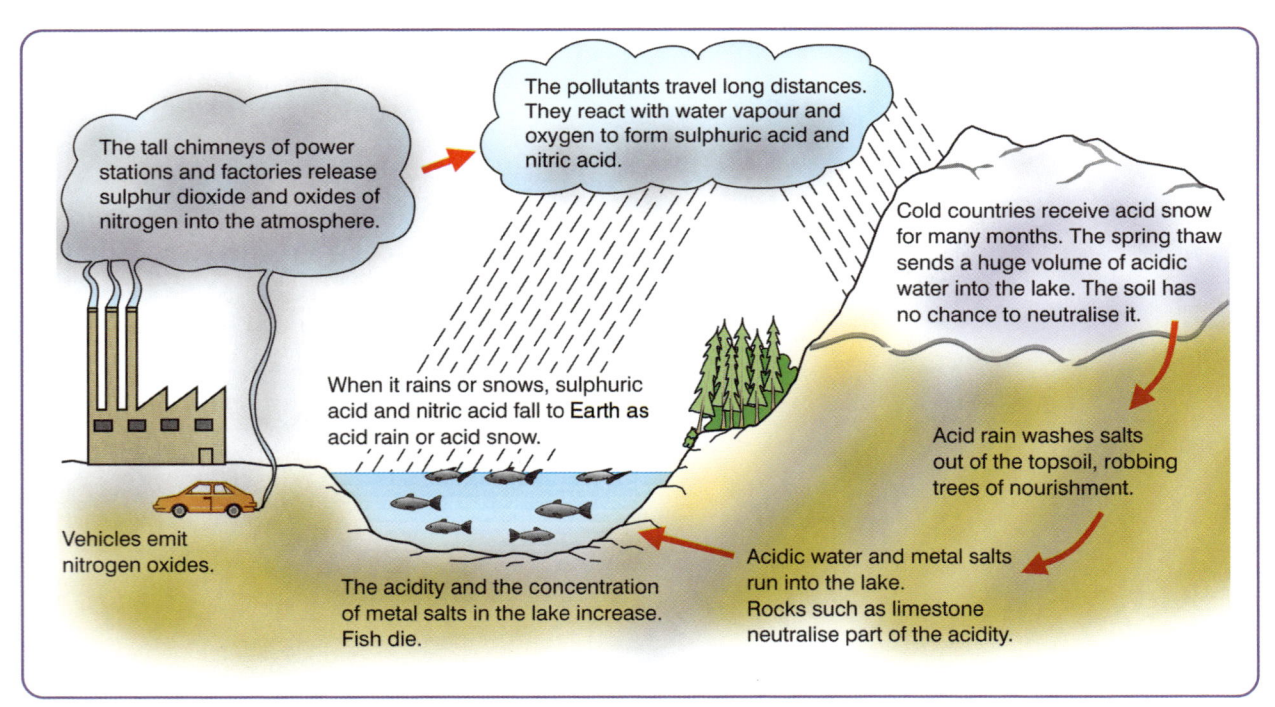

Acid rain; its source and its effect on lake water

Organisms in the environment

★ In a **pulverised fluidised bed combustion** (**PFBC**) furnace, the coal is pulverised (broken into small pieces) and burnt on a bed of powdered limestone, which is 'fluidised' (kept in motion by an upward flow of air). As the coal burns, sulphur dioxide reacts with the limestone.

★ Nuclear power stations do not send pollutants into the air. However, they create the problem of storing radioactive waste.

Managing the environment

Different pressures increase the use of land.
- economic development
- increasing human populations
- the increasing need for food for the increasing population

Case study: tropical rainforest

The diagram below shows you some of the ways people exploit tropical rainforest.

Improvements

Managing tropical rainforests for human benefit and conserving the environment is possible.

★ Stop clearing rainforest.

★ Use resources in a **sustainable** way. For example:
- do not fell valuable hardwoods like teak and mahogany faster than they can be replaced by the reproduction and growth of new trees
- subsidise poor countries so they will not need to make money from forest clearance
- do not use rainforest products faster than they can naturally be replaced, e.g.:
  – rubber latex
  – nuts and fruits
  – plants as sources of new drugs and medicines.

Rainforests girdle the equator covering 14.5 million km^2 of land. The vegetation recycles carbon dioxide and oxygen through photosynthesis. Moisture absorbed by the forest evaporates back into the atmosphere, to fall as rain thousands of miles away. Rainforest is being cleared at a rate of 100 000 km^2 each year for:

cheap beef is exposed to be made into hamburgers

Beef: about 20 000 km^2 of Brazilian forest are cleared each year for cattle ranches.

Opencast mining for metals causes much damage to rainforest.

After clearing, nutrients are used up and the soil is soon exhausted. Semi-desert develops: the ranchers move on to clear a new area.

Logging: only 4% of trees are felled for timber, but another 40% are damaged or destroyed in the process.

How human activities exploit resources and land and produce pollution

Organisms in the environment

Case study: fishing

The diagram below shows you the human threat to stocks of commercially important fish.

Improvements

Managing fish stocks highlights the conflict between *short-term* human needs (food, economical use of expensive equipment) and the health of a particular environment. Using living things for food and as a source of different products only as fast as they can be naturally replaced helps the environment to provide resources in the *long term*.

★ Reducing the intensity of fishing helps balance the numbers of fish being born with the number of fish caught.

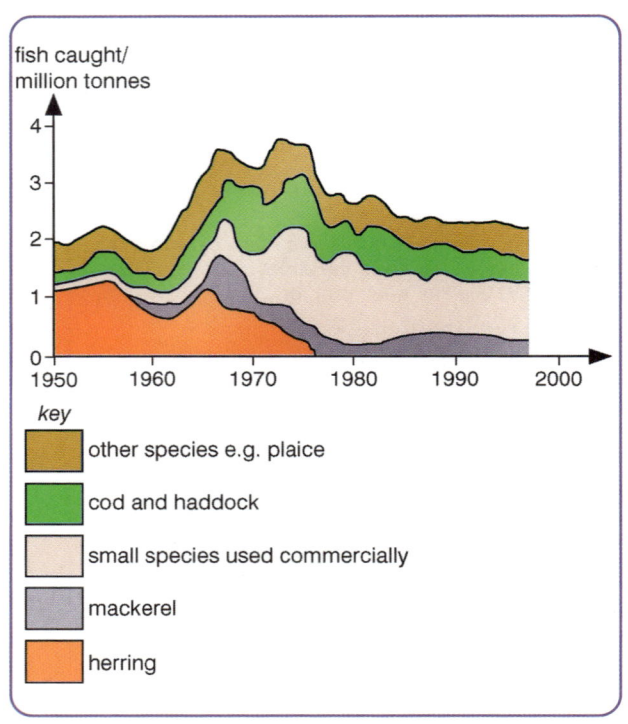

Fishing in the North Sea

★ Increasing the mesh size of nets allows young fish to escape capture.

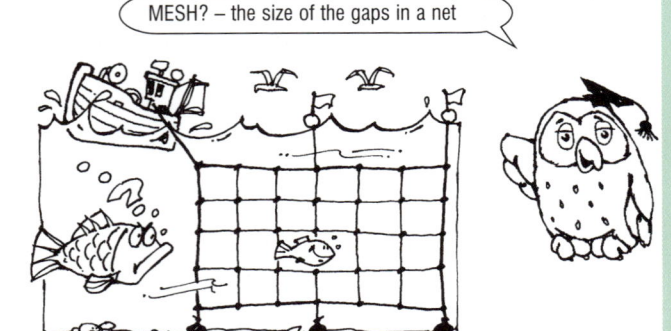

MESH? – the size of the gaps in a net

As a result, more fish mature and reproduce to replace the fish caught.

★ Encourage the catching of little-used species.

Catches of fish are reduced because of:
★ **overfishing:** increased efficiency of fishing methods catches more fish than are replaced by reproduction

★ **pollution:**
- nutrients (e.g. nitrates and phosphates) from sewage works and surplus artificial fertilisers enter rivers which discharge into the North Sea
- pesticides used to protect crops enter rivers which discharge into the North Sea
- metals (e.g. mercury, cadmium, copper) from different industrial processes.

Case study: farming

Soil erosion

Erosion removes the top few centimetres of soil needed to grow crops. The soil may be washed away by rain or blown away by wind. Different human activities increase the risk of soil erosion.

★ **Clearing** land of trees and hedges

As a result, the soil is no longer held in place by the roots of plants.

As a result, there are no leaves to add **humus** which improves the structure and water-holding properties of soil.

Organisms in the environment

★ Poor **farming** methods, for example:
- *overgrazing* of grassland by livestock (e.g. cattle and sheep)
- *cultivating* hillsides without taking account of the slope of the land.

Improvements

Growing crops and raising livestock is possible without damaging the soil.

Erosion by wind is prevented through:
- **reforestation**, which replaces trees and hedgerows

   As a result, roots prevent soil from blowing away.

   As a result, humus is added to the soil.

   As a result, the soil remains fertile, maintaining crop yields.

- **reducing** the numbers of livestock grazing grassland.

   As a result, the yield of grass needed to support livestock is maintained.

Erosion by running water is prevented through:
- **contour ploughing**: furrows lie across the natural slope of the land
- **terracing**: broad shallow ditches lie across the natural slope of the land.

   As a result, water is held back from flowing downhill.

   As a result, soil is *not* washed away.

Agrochemicals

Pesticides (chemicals that kill pests) are very poisonous. Farmers apply pesticides to the land. **Fertilisers** supply **nutrients** which improve the growth of crops.
Compounds of nitrogen (N), phosphorus (P) and potassium (K) – NPK fertilisers – are used in huge quantities.

POLLUTION Page 24.

Remember to read Section 2.6 *Food production* for more details about the impact of pesticides and fertilisers on the environment.

Improvements

★ Alternative methods of pest control (**biological control**) reduce dependence on pesticides.

★ Controlling application of pesticides helps to reduce the damage to wildlife and the environment.

★ Careful use of fertilisers reduces run-off from the land.

Fact file

Before the introduction of pesticides, the management of food production depended on **crop rotation**: a different crop was grown in a particular field each year.

★ Each crop absorbed different nutrients from the soil.

   As a result, the crops' demands for nutrients are spread over a number of years.

★ **Leguminous** plants (e.g. clover) are part of the cycle of crop rotation.

NITROGEN CYCLE Page 13.

   As a result, soil nitrates are replaced by the nitrogen-fixing bacteria, which live in swellings (nodules) on the roots of leguminous plants.

Crop rotation prevents the build up of:
- weeds
- disease-causing organisms which affect crops and maintain the fertility of the soil.

Today farmers use crop rotation and agrochemicals to maintain productivity.

Fact file

The fungus *Phytophthora infestans* causes **late blight** of potatoes. In the 1840s, it wiped out the European potato harvest. Crop rotation and good hygiene help to break the chain of infection. Other control measures include planting seed potatoes selectively bred for resistance to the fungus and spraying plants with fungicide.

Organisms in the environment

Conservation

Our well-being depends on keeping a balance between using and protecting environments. Conservation aims to:

- use renewable resources in a **sustainable** way and reduce the exploitation of non-renewable resources through **recycling** and the discovery of **alternative** materials for the production of goods
- use land so that **conflicting interests** between human needs and the impact of these needs on the survival of wildlife and their environments are reduced
- reduce **pollution** by the development of more efficient industrial processes, which produce less waste and use less energy, and the introduction of more environmentally friendly methods of farming.

Different initiatives attempt to protect wildlife in danger of extinction (**endangered species**) because of human activities.

- ★ **Convention on International Trade in Endangered Species (CITES)** aims to control the trade in, and products from, endangered species.
- ★ **Sites of Special Scientific Interest (SSSIs)** have been established as protected habitats for rare and endangered species.
- ★ **Captive breeding programmes** have saved species from extinction. Rare species are captured and individuals held in zoos where they breed. When numbers have been built up, some individuals are released back into the wild under close supervision.
- ★ **National Parks** have been established to conserve areas of outstanding beauty and scientific interest.
- ★ **Seed banks** are cold stores of seeds. Species of plant threatened with extinction are conserved as seeds in store with a view to building up numbers and conserving genetic material for future breeding programmes.

2.6 Food production

PREVIEW

At the end of this section you will:

- understand why a short food chain makes more food energy available to the consumer than a long food chain
- know that intensive farming produces food in great quantities.

Fact file

- ★ **Intensive farming** means that farmers use different methods to produce as much food as possible from the land available for raising crops (**arable** farming) and the land available for raising animals (**livestock** farming). The methods impose a duty on farmers to limit the damage on natural ecosystems and to treat intensively farmed animals humanely. New laws are being introduced to improve the welfare of farm animals.
- ★ **Productivity** means the amount of food produced (crops or livestock) per unit area of land (e.g. per hectare (ha)).
- ★ **Selective breeding** greatly reduces variation in populations of crops and animals raised for food, because the number of different alleles is reduced.

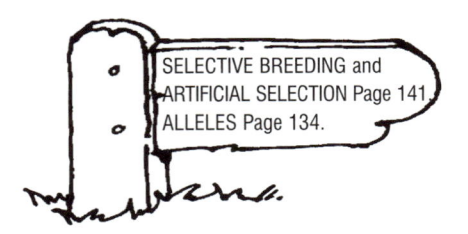

SELECTIVE BREEDING and ARTIFICIAL SELECTION Page 141. ALLELES Page 134.

- ★ Selectively bred plants may need special growing conditions.

Soil

Soil is the lifeblood of farming. Producing food in sufficient quantities at economic prices depends on the quality of the soil in which crops grow and the pasture on which livestock feed. Most soils are a mixture of particles of different sizes. Sand particles are relatively large, clay particles are relatively small. A mixture of both in the right proportions produces a **loam**, the texture of which is ideal for growing plants.

Organisms in the environment

A soil may be acidic, alkaline or neutral. For each type of crop, there is a range of pH over which the plants can be grown successfully. When soils are too acidic, farmers add lime (calcium oxide) which neutralises the excess acid. Adding **peat** (the partly decayed remains of dead organisms) to soil improves the **texture** of the soil. 'Texture' determines the amount of air in the soil and the rate at which water drains from the soil: factors that affect the growth of plants.

Energy and farming

Farms are ecosystems with people as consumers in a food chain of crops and livestock. The amount of food a farm produces depends on:
- the amount of energy entering the farm ecosystem
- the efficiency with which energy is converted into plant and animal tissue.

The energy that enters the system is the **input**. The energy content of the food produced is the **output**.

Shortening the food chain

The inefficiency of energy transfer between trophic levels affects the amount of food available for human consumption. The *fewer* the trophic levels (links in a food chain), the *less* food energy is lost and so the *more* food is available to consumers. Being a **vegetarian** shortens the food chain and reduces the loss of food energy between trophic levels. Output therefore increases.

Energy transfer between producers and consumers is inefficient because:
- some of the plant material is not digested and passes out of the herbivore's body as faeces
- the herbivore uses energy to stay alive
- when the herbivore dies, its body represents 'locked up' energy, some of which transfers to decomposers.

Eating meat is therefore wasteful in terms of food energy. The diagram at the top of the next column illustrates this point. What percentage (%) of the food energy eaten by the cow in a year is available to the consumer as milk and meat?

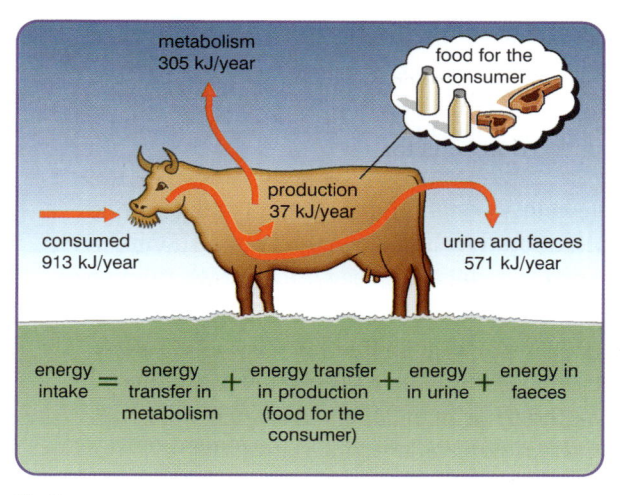

Wasting energy

Farming

The concept map for the intensive farm at work on page 36 shows different technologies at work on the modern intensive farm. The checklist points on page 35 summarise the benefits for food production but also highlight the impact on the environment and the possible risks to human health.

Artificial insemination

Artificial insemination (AI) is widely used to introduce **semen** (and the sperm it contains) from prize bulls (males with desirable characteristics) into cows (which also have desirable characteristics). The advantages of AI are that the technique allows:
- rapid improvement in the characteristics (more meat, more milk) of the cattle herd
- selection of top-quality bulls in order to reduce inbreeding within the herd. The bulls have undergone tests to establish that the characteristics they pass on to their offspring are desirable
- farmers *not* to have the problems and expense of keeping bulls.

A disadvantage of AI is the requirement to detect when the cow is **ovulating** (producing eggs). Mistiming reduces the success rate of AI.

REPRODUCTION Page 128.

Organisms in the environment

Semen is usually **collected** using an **artificial vagina**. The bull inserts his penis into the artificial vagina. The sperm is ejaculated (released from the penis) and collected in a glass tube attached to the artificial vagina.

Following ejaculation, the semen is **diluted** (one ejaculation from a bull contains more sperm than is needed to fertilise one egg from a cow). Dilution of semen is in a solution which:
- provides nutrients that keep the sperm alive
- contains antibiotics preventing infections
- contains salts maintaining a desirable pH and an environment where the movement of water (osmosis) into and out of the sperm cells is appropriate for their survival.

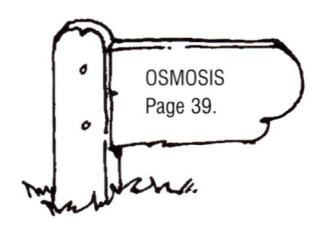

OSMOSIS Page 39.

Diluted semen is frozen in liquid nitrogen at −196°C, **stored** in disposable straws and packed in cylinders ready for transport to the farms where AI is to be carried out.

In vitro fertilisation

Other techniques also allow genetically suitable cows to pass on desirable characteristics to their offspring. For example:
- cows are injected with hormones that stimulate the development and release of eggs
- the eggs are fertilised in the laboratory (*in vitro* fertilisation) with sperm donated by a suitable bull
- the fertilised eggs are transplanted into different regions of the uterus of a substitute (**surrogate**) mother.

The fertilised eggs divide and the embryo develops normally. Eventually the surrogate mother gives birth to offspring, which have inherited the favourable characteristics of the mother (cow) and father (bull).

Organisms in the environment

Checklist for intensive farming

checklist	benefits	impact
1 pesticides	kill pests which damage crops	spray is carried in the wind (**drift**) which can harm wildlife
	food production increases	pesticide **run-off** seeps into groundwater, eventually draining into ponds and river systems, possibly contaminating drinking water and harming wildlife
2 irrigation	brings water to land	**salination**: the Sun's heat evaporates water, increasing the concentration of mineral salts in soil. Eventually land is too 'salty' for crops to grow, reducing crop yields
	food production increases	overwatering: land becomes **waterlogged**, reducing crop yields. In warm countries the threat to human health increases because habitats are created for the spread of water-borne diseases such as malaria and schistosomiasis
3 mechanisation	powerful machinery needs few people to work it, cutting wage costs	land is **cleared** of woods and hedges to make fields larger – large machinery is most efficient in big fields
	more land can be used for farming	habitats are **destroyed** with loss of wildlife
	harvests crop more quickly	soil is **packed**, causing waterlogging
4 manure	spreading manure on land adds humus which improves soil structure	water is needed to **wash manure** into lagoon
		slurry **leaks** from lagoon, seeping into streams and rivers, killing fish and other wildlife
5 monoculture	efficient use of expensive machinery	crop provides **unlimited** food for insects, which feed on plants. Their populations may increase to pest proportions
	reduces labour costs	costs are **high** because crops must be sprayed with pesticides
	high yields mean farmer can take advantage of selling in bulk to obtain best prices for produce	soil **loses** its nutrients, which are replaced with expensive artificial fertilisers
		soil is left **bare** between crops, risking erosion
6 artificial fertilisers	land can be used continuously for growing crops	manufacture of fertilisers **uses** a lot of fuel
	farmers do not need to keep animals for manure	soil structure **deteriorates** and soil erosion increases
	efficiency is increased by specialising in growing one or two crops each year	surplus fertiliser runs off into streams and rivers: this encourages population explosion of algae (called **blooms**) which use up oxygen in the water, killing fish and other wildlife. Surplus fertiliser may also put excess nitrates, a health hazard, into drinking water
	food production is increased, helping feed the world's growing population	

Organisms in the environment

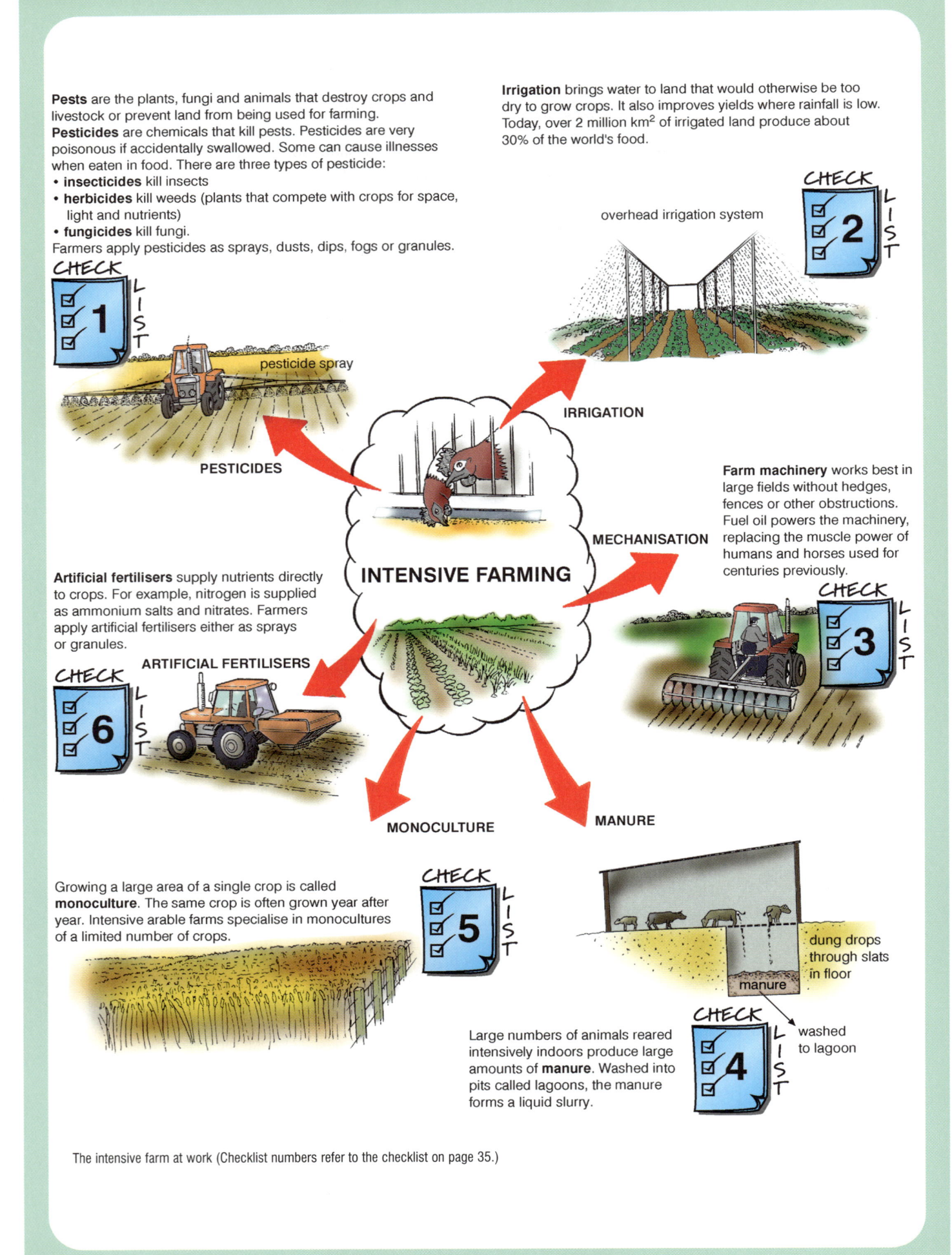

Pests are the plants, fungi and animals that destroy crops and livestock or prevent land from being used for farming.
Pesticides are chemicals that kill pests. Pesticides are very poisonous if accidentally swallowed. Some can cause illnesses when eaten in food. There are three types of pesticide:
- **insecticides** kill insects
- **herbicides** kill weeds (plants that compete with crops for space, light and nutrients)
- **fungicides** kill fungi.

Farmers apply pesticides as sprays, dusts, dips, fogs or granules.

CHECKLIST 1

pesticide spray

PESTICIDES

Irrigation brings water to land that would otherwise be too dry to grow crops. It also improves yields where rainfall is low. Today, over 2 million km^2 of irrigated land produce about 30% of the world's food.

overhead irrigation system

CHECKLIST 2

IRRIGATION

INTENSIVE FARMING

Farm machinery works best in large fields without hedges, fences or other obstructions. Fuel oil powers the machinery, replacing the muscle power of humans and horses used for centuries previously.

CHECKLIST 3

MECHANISATION

Artificial fertilisers supply nutrients directly to crops. For example, nitrogen is supplied as ammonium salts and nitrates. Farmers apply artificial fertilisers either as sprays or granules.

CHECKLIST 6

ARTIFICIAL FERTILISERS

MONOCULTURE

Growing a large area of a single crop is called **monoculture**. The same crop is often grown year after year. Intensive arable farms specialise in monocultures of a limited number of crops.

CHECKLIST 5

MANURE

dung drops through slats in floor

manure

washed to lagoon

Large numbers of animals reared intensively indoors produce large amounts of **manure**. Washed into pits called lagoons, the manure forms a liquid slurry.

CHECKLIST 4

The intensive farm at work (Checklist numbers refer to the checklist on page 35.)

36

Organisms in the environment

ROUND UP

How much have you improved? Work out your improvement index on page 156.

1. Look at pages 12–13. List the different components of an ecosystem. [6]

2. a) Explain the meaning of the word 'abiotic'. [1]
   b) Why is the amount of light an important abiotic influence on life inside a wood? [4]

3. Look at the pond food chain on page 16.
   a) How many links are there in the food chain? [1]
   b) Name the producers. [1]
   c) Briefly explain why they are called producers. [1]
   d) Name the herbivores. [1]
   e) Briefly explain why they are called herbivores. [1]
   f) Name the carnivores. [2]
   g) Briefly explain why they are called carnivores. [1]

4. Why is the efficiency of energy conversion in photosynthesis less than 8%? [3]

5. In what circumstances is the pyramid of numbers an accurate description of the feeding relationships in a community? [1]

6. The diagram shows a pyramid of biomass for a rocky seashore.
   a) Name the producers. [1]
   b) Name the secondary consumers. [1]
   c) Severe weather conditions virtually wipe out the periwinkles. What will be the effect on the biomass of dog whelks and saw wrack? [2]

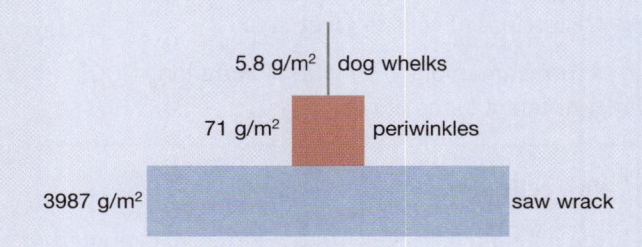

   5.8 g/m² — dog whelks
   71 g/m² — periwinkles
   3987 g/m² — saw wrack

7. Explain the differences between
   a) intraspecific competition and interspecific competition
   b) adaptation and survival
   c) camouflage and warning colouration. [6]

8. The graph shows long-term changes in the numbers of snowshoe hare and its predator the Canadian lynx.

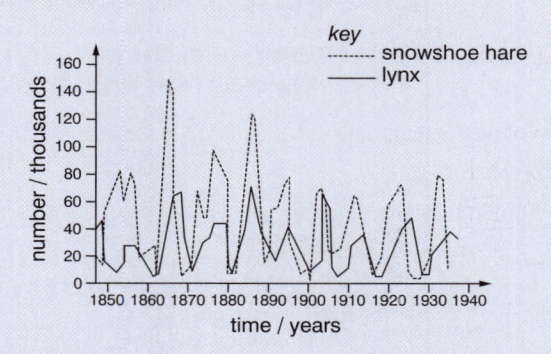

   key
   -------- snowshoe hare
   ——— lynx

   a) Why do the highs and lows in the numbers of lynx lag behind the highs and lows in the numbers of snowshoe hare? [3]
   b) Although the numbers of snowshoe hare and lynx fluctuated between 1850 and 1940, what do you think is the *overall* trend in the population growth of each species between these years? [1]
   c) In 1890, if disease had virtually wiped out the lynx population, what do you think would have happened to the numbers of snowshoe hare? [1]
   d) If the lynx population had recovered from the effects of disease by 1910, what then do you think would have happened to the numbers of snowshoe hare? [2]
   e) If the lynx population had never recovered from the effects of disease, what then do you think would have happened to the numbers of snowshoe hare? Briefly explain your answer. [2]

9. The terms in column **A** refer to different aspects of intensive farming. Match each term with its correct description in column **B**.

A terms	B descriptions
fertiliser	kills plants
herbicide	an unwanted plant
irrigation	supplies plants with nutrients
monoculture	supplies plants with water
weed	a crop plant grown over a large area

   [5]

Chapter 3 — Cell activity

Work out your score on pages 156–7.

Test yourself

1 Match each of the structures in column **A** with its function in column **B**.

A structures	B functions
mitochondrion	partially permeable to substances in solution
plasma membrane	where energy is released from the oxidation of glucose
chloroplast	fully permeable to substances in solution
cell wall	contains the chromosomes
nucleus	where light energy is captured [5]

2 Why do you think the process of active transport requires more energy than diffusion? [1]

3 Explain the difference between
   a) a plasmolysed cell and a turgid cell [4]
   b) a fully permeable membrane and a partially permeable membrane. [3]

4 What is a clone? [1]

5 What is formed by the replication of DNA? [2]

6 a) Why do the cells of a tissue undergo mitosis? [3]
   b) In mitosis, what is the relationship between the number and type of chromosomes in the parent cell and in the daughter cells? [2]

7 Briefly explain the meaning of 'haploid' and 'diploid'. [4]

8 Complete the following paragraph using the words below. Each word may be used once, more than once or not at all.

   types   organism   tissues   organs   cells   an organ

   Living things are made of _____. Groups of similar _____ with similar functions form _____ that can work together as _____. A group of _____ working together form _____ system. [6]

9 Cellulose and chitin are important building materials in living things. Give an example of a structure where each may be found. [2]

10 Briefly explain the difference between saturated and unsaturated fats. [2]

11 What is a nucleotide? [4]

3.1 Cells at work

PREVIEW

At the end of this section you will know that:
- all living things are made of cells
- plant cells and animal cells have structures in common but are also different from one another
- mitochondria and chloroplasts are structures in cells which convert energy from one form to another
- different types of cells are each specialised to perform a particular biological task.

Cell functions

The structures that make up a cell are organised in a way that depends on the **functions** of the cell (the way it works).

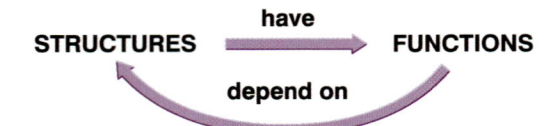

STRUCTURES ⇌ FUNCTIONS
(have / depend on)

Fact file

★ Most cells are too small to be seen with the naked eye.

★ The light microscope helps us to see the structure of cells.

★ The transmission electron microscope reveals cell structures too small to be seen under the light microscope. It enables us to see the structure of cells in great detail.

★ The human body is made of more than 200 different types of cell.

How cells work

The diagram on pages 40–41 is the concept map for **cells at work**. The numbers on the diagram refer to the checklist of points on page 40.

Cell activity

3.2 Into and out of cells

PREVIEW

At the end of this section you will:
- understand that there is constant movement of solutions inside and into and out of cells
- know about diffusion, osmosis and active transport
- know that solutions move along a concentration gradient.

Moving molecules

Cells need a non-stop supply of water and the substances dissolved in it to stay alive. Substances therefore move inside and into and out of cells.

★ **diffusion** – the movement of a substance through a solution or gas *down* its concentration gradient (that is, from a region of high concentration to a region of low concentration of the substance)

★ **osmosis** – the movement of **water** *down* its concentration gradient through a **partially permeable** membrane

★ **active transport** – the movement of a substance through a solution *up* (against) its concentration gradient (that is, from a region of low concentration to a region of high concentration of the substance).

Fact file

Why does sugar sprinkled onto strawberries turn pink? Because it makes the juice come out of the strawberries.

In and out of cells

On page 42 is the concept map for **movement into and out of cells**. The numbers on the concept map refer to the checklist of points below.

Checklist for movement in and out of cells

1. ★ The molecules of a substance move at random, but there is a better than even chance that some molecules will spread (diffuse) from where they are highly concentrated to where they are fewer in number.

   As a result, there is a net movement of molecules from where the substance is in high concentration to where it is in low concentration.

   ★ Diffusion continues until the concentration of the substance is the same throughout the gas or solution.

   ★ The greater the difference in concentration between the regions, the steeper the concentration gradient and the faster the substance diffuses.

2. ★ During active transport, the molecules of a substance pass from where they are in low concentration to where they are in higher concentration.

   As a result, cells may build up stores of a substance which would otherwise be spread out by diffusion.

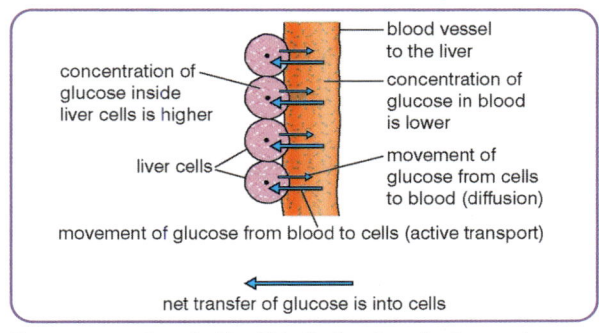

   Glucose passes from the blood into the liver by active transport

   ★ Active transport requires more energy than normal diffusion.

3. ★ The flow of water from a more dilute solution to a more concentrated solution is called **osmosis**.

   ★ A partially permeable membrane is a membrane that allows some substances to pass through but stops others. The passage of substances across such a membrane depends on the: 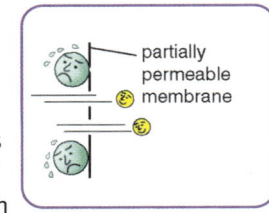
   - size of the molecules
   - size of the membrane pores
   - surface area of the cell membrane
   - steepness of the concentration gradient
   - temperature.

   ★ The changes happening inside plant cells due to osmosis bring about visible changes in the plant.
   - **Plasmolysis** causes a plant to **wilt** through lack of water.
   - The plant recovers following watering, which restores turgor to its cells. Remember that a cell filled with water is said to be **turgid**.

   ★ Osmosis through a partially permeable membrane continues until the concentrations of water on either side of the membrane are equal.

Cell activity

Checklist for cells at work

1. ★ During photosynthesis, oxygen is released into the environment.
   ★ During aerobic respiration, oxygen is used to release energy from food.

   As a result, photosynthesis and aerobic respiration are stages in a cycle, the by-products of one forming the starting point of the other.

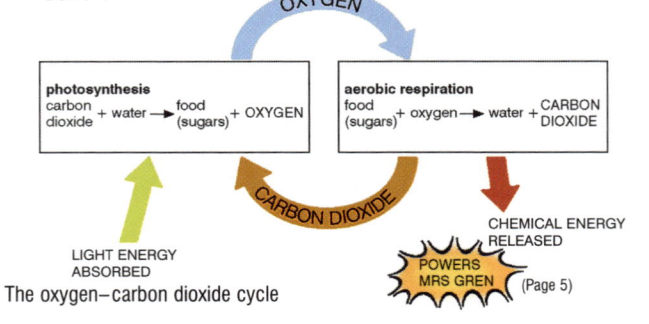

   photosynthesis: carbon dioxide + water → food (sugars) + OXYGEN

   aerobic respiration: food (sugars) + oxygen → water + CARBON DIOXIDE

   LIGHT ENERGY ABSORBED
   CHEMICAL ENERGY RELEASED
   POWERS MRS GREN (Page 5)

   The oxygen–carbon dioxide cycle

   The energy released during aerobic respiration enables:
   - cells to make (synthesise) larger molecules from the combination of smaller ones
   - muscle cells to contract
   - mammals (including humans) and birds to maintain a steady body temperature even though the temperature of the surroundings changes.

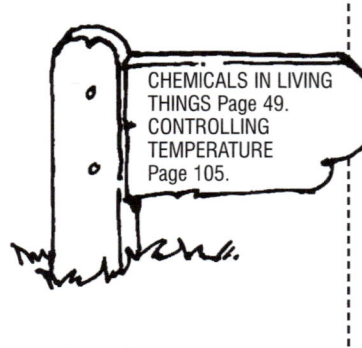

   CHEMICALS IN LIVING THINGS Page 49.
   CONTROLLING TEMPERATURE Page 105.

2. ★ There are different types of cell for different functions.
   ★ Each type of cell is suited (**adapted**) to carry out its function in the animal body or plant body.
   ★ A sheet of cells which covers a body surface is called an **epithelium**.
   ★ Red blood cells do not have nuclei.

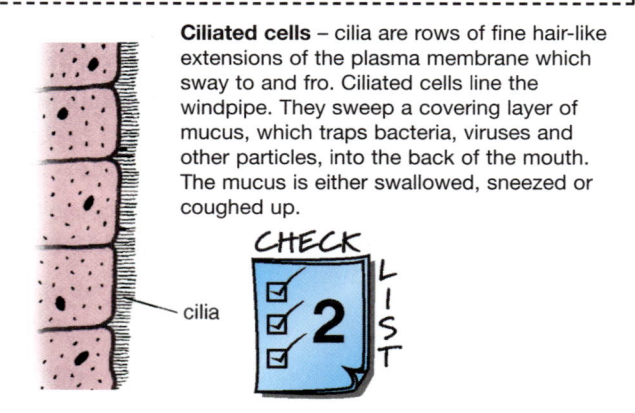

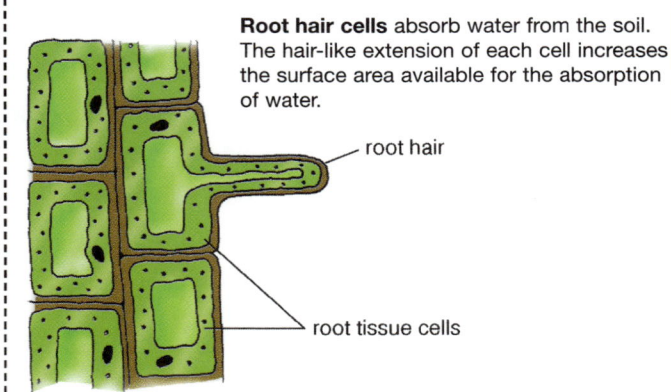

Root hair cells absorb water from the soil. The hair-like extension of each cell increases the surface area available for the absorption of water.
- root hair
- root tissue cells

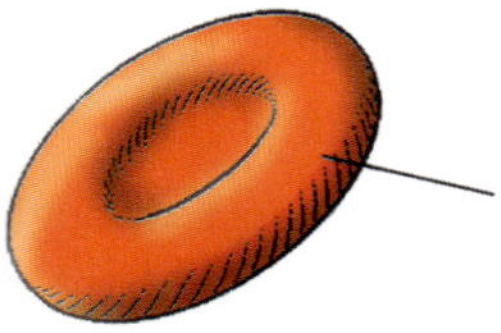

Red blood cells transport oxygen around the body. They contain the pigment haemoglobin which combines with oxygen.
- flattened disc shape increases surface area for the absorption of oxygen

VARIETY OF CELLS

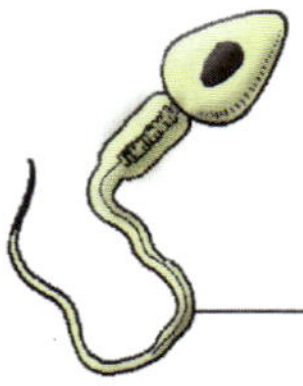

sperm – the male sex cells which swim to the egg
- tail-like flagellum lashes from side to side

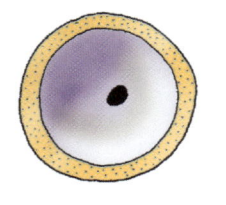

Ovum (egg) – the female sex cell which is fertilised when a sperm fuses with it

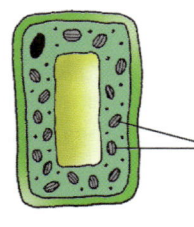

Leaf palisade cells each contain numerous chloroplasts where photosynthesis takes place.
- chloroplasts

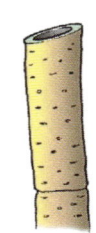

Ciliated cells – cilia are rows of fine hair-like extensions of the plasma membrane which sway to and fro. Ciliated cells line the windpipe. They sweep a covering layer of mucus, which traps bacteria, viruses and other particles, into the back of the mouth. The mucus is either swallowed, sneezed or coughed up.
- cilia

Xylem cells form tubes in the stem, roots and leaves, transporting water to all parts of the plant.

Cells at work

Cell activity

SUNLIGHT ENERGY

captured by chlorophyll, the green pigment which fills each chloroplast

chloroplast

PHOTO-SYNTHESIS Page 57.

PLANT CELLS TRANSFORM ENERGY

LIGHT ENERGY IS CONVERTED TO CHEMICAL ENERGY
$6CO_2 + 6H_2O \rightarrow C_6H_{12}O_6 + 6O_2$
carbon   water   sugar   oxygen
dioxide   (glucose)

CELL STRUCTURE

mitochondria where energy is released from the oxidation of glucose

nucleus contains the chromosomes which carry genes that control the activities of the cell

chloroplasts contain chlorophyll which captures light energy

cell wall made of cellulose, which strengthens it. It is fully permeable to substances in solution

cytoplasm is jelly-like material which fills the cell, giving it shape. It is where most of the chemical reactions (**metabolism**) of the cell take place

vacuole contains cell sap – a solution of sugars and salts

ANIMAL CELL

plasma membrane is partially permeable to substances in solution. It controls the passage of substances into and out of the cell

PLANT CELL

STRUCTURES FOUND IN ANIMAL *AND* PLANT CELLS

STRUCTURES FOUND *ONLY* IN PLANT CELLS

SUGAR

CHECK LIST 1

ANIMAL AND PLANT CELLS TRANSFORM ENERGY

MRS GREN Page 5.

OXYGEN

mitochondrion

oxidation of sugar (glucose)

MOVEMENT
RESPIRATION
SENSITIVITY   POWERS → ENERGY
GROWTH
REPRODUCTION
EXCRETION
NUTRITION

CHEMICAL ENERGY IS RELEASED
$C_6H_{12}O_6 + 6O_2 \rightarrow 6CO_2 + 6H_2O$
sugar   oxygen   carbon   water
(glucose)   dioxide

AEROBIC RESPIRATION Page 80.

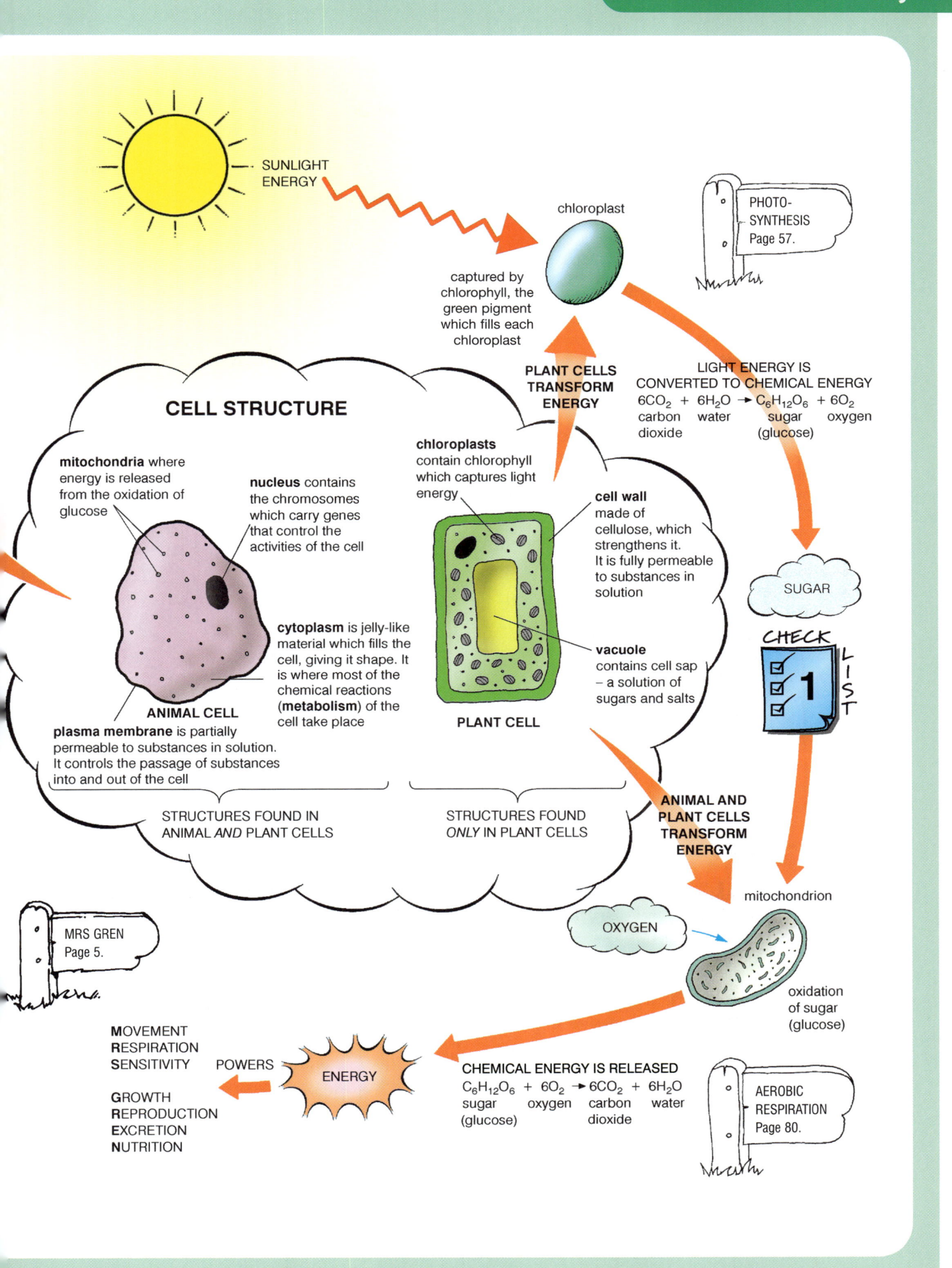

41

Cell activity

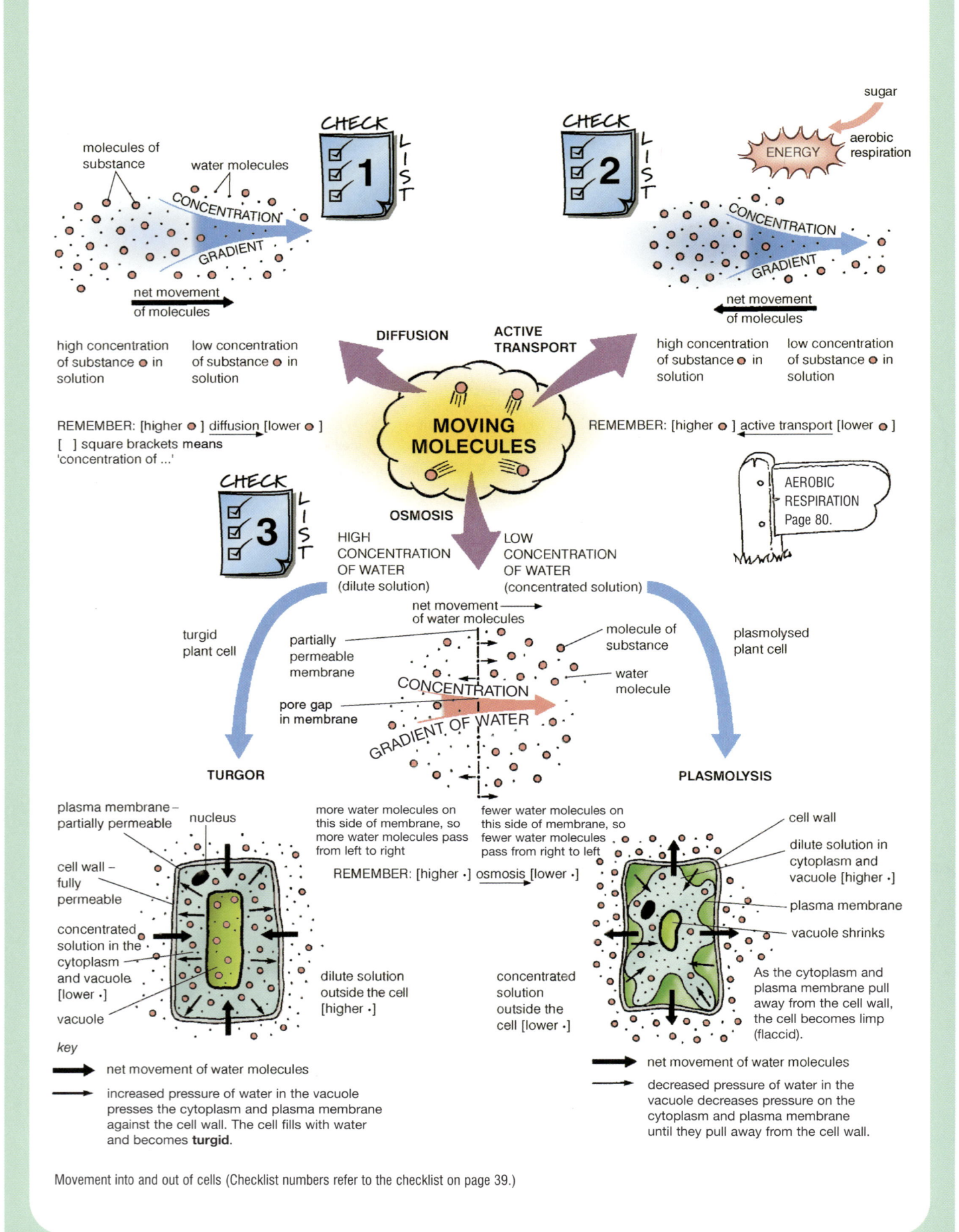

CHECK LIST 1

molecules of substance • water molecules

CONCENTRATION GRADIENT

net movement of molecules →

high concentration of substance • in solution — low concentration of substance • in solution

REMEMBER: [higher •] diffusion [lower •]
[ ] square brackets means 'concentration of ...'

CHECK LIST 2

sugar → ENERGY ← aerobic respiration

CONCENTRATION GRADIENT

← net movement of molecules

high concentration of substance • in solution — low concentration of substance • in solution

REMEMBER: [higher •] ← active transport [lower •]

AEROBIC RESPIRATION Page 80.

MOVING MOLECULES

DIFFUSION — ACTIVE TRANSPORT

OSMOSIS

CHECK LIST 3

HIGH CONCENTRATION OF WATER (dilute solution) — LOW CONCENTRATION OF WATER (concentrated solution)

net movement of water molecules →

partially permeable membrane

pore gap in membrane

CONCENTRATION GRADIENT OF WATER

molecule of substance • water molecule

TURGOR

turgid plant cell

- plasma membrane – partially permeable
- nucleus
- cell wall – fully permeable
- concentrated solution in the cytoplasm and vacuole [lower •]
- vacuole

dilute solution outside the cell [higher •]

more water molecules on this side of membrane, so more water molecules pass from left to right

fewer water molecules on this side of membrane, so fewer water molecules pass from right to left

REMEMBER: [higher •] osmosis [lower •]

PLASMOLYSIS

plasmolysed plant cell

- cell wall
- dilute solution in cytoplasm and vacuole [higher •]
- plasma membrane
- vacuole shrinks

concentrated solution outside the cell [lower •]

As the cytoplasm and plasma membrane pull away from the cell wall, the cell becomes limp (flaccid).

key

→ net movement of water molecules

→ increased pressure of water in the vacuole presses the cytoplasm and plasma membrane against the cell wall. The cell fills with water and becomes **turgid**.

→ decreased pressure of water in the vacuole decreases pressure on the cytoplasm and plasma membrane until they pull away from the cell wall.

Movement into and out of cells (Checklist numbers refer to the checklist on page 39.)

Cell activity

3.3 Cell division

PREVIEW

At the end of this section you will:
- know that new cells (daughter cells) are formed when old cells (parent cells) divide into two
- understand that the cytoplasm and nucleus divide during cell division
- know that the nucleus may divide either by mitosis or meiosis.

How cells divide

On pages 44–45 is the concept map for **cell division**. Study it carefully.

Remember

★ The nucleus of each **cell of the body** (except some of the cells of sex organs) divides by **mitosis**.

★ The nucleus of each of the **cells of the sex organs** that give rise to the sex cells (**gametes**) divides by **meiosis**. Sex cells are produced in the sex organs:
- the **testes** of the male and the **ovaries** of the female in mammals
- the **anthers** (male) and the **carpels** (female) in flowering plants.

SEXUAL REPRODUCTION Pages 128–129.

Mitosis and meiosis

The nucleus contains **chromosomes**, each consisting of a double strand of **deoxyribonucleic acid (DNA)** wound round a core of protein. In cell division, the chromosomes are passed from the **parent** cell to the new **daughter** cells. 'Daughter' does not mean that the cells are female. It means that they are the new cells formed as a result of cell division.

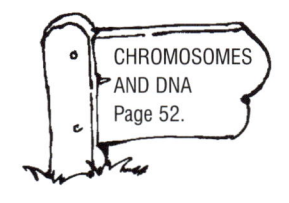

CHROMOSOMES AND DNA Page 52.

Mitosis produces daughter cells with the same number of chromosomes as the parent cell. The daughter cells are described as **diploid** (or **2n**).

Meiosis produces daughter cells with only half the number of chromosomes as the parent cell. The daughter cells are described as **haploid** (or **n**).

The importance of mitosis

The daughter cells each receive an identical full (diploid) set of chromosomes from the parent cell.

ASEXUAL REPRODUCTION Page 130.

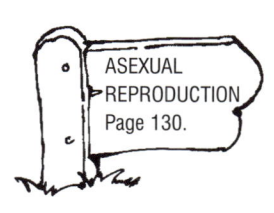

As a result, the parent cell and its daughter cells are genetically identical. They form a **clone**.

As a result, mitosis is the way in which living things:

- **repair damage:** for example, mitosis replaces damaged skin cells with identical new skin cells
- **grow:** for example, the root of a plant grows because root tip cells divide by mitosis to form new root tissue
- **reproduce asexually:** for example, parts of stems can sprout roots and grow into new plants. The new individuals are genetically identical to the parents and are therefore clones.

The importance of meiosis

The daughter cells each receive a half (haploid) set of chromosomes from the parent cell.

As a result, during fertilisation (when sperm and egg join together), the chromosomes from each cell combine.

As a result, the fertilised egg (**zygote**) is diploid but inherits a new combination of genes contributed (50:50) from the parents.

As a result, the new individual inherits characteristics from both parents, not just from one parent as in asexual reproduction.

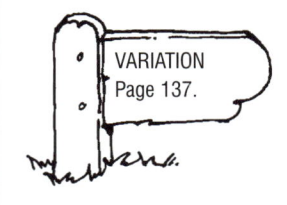

VARIATION Page 137.

Cell activity

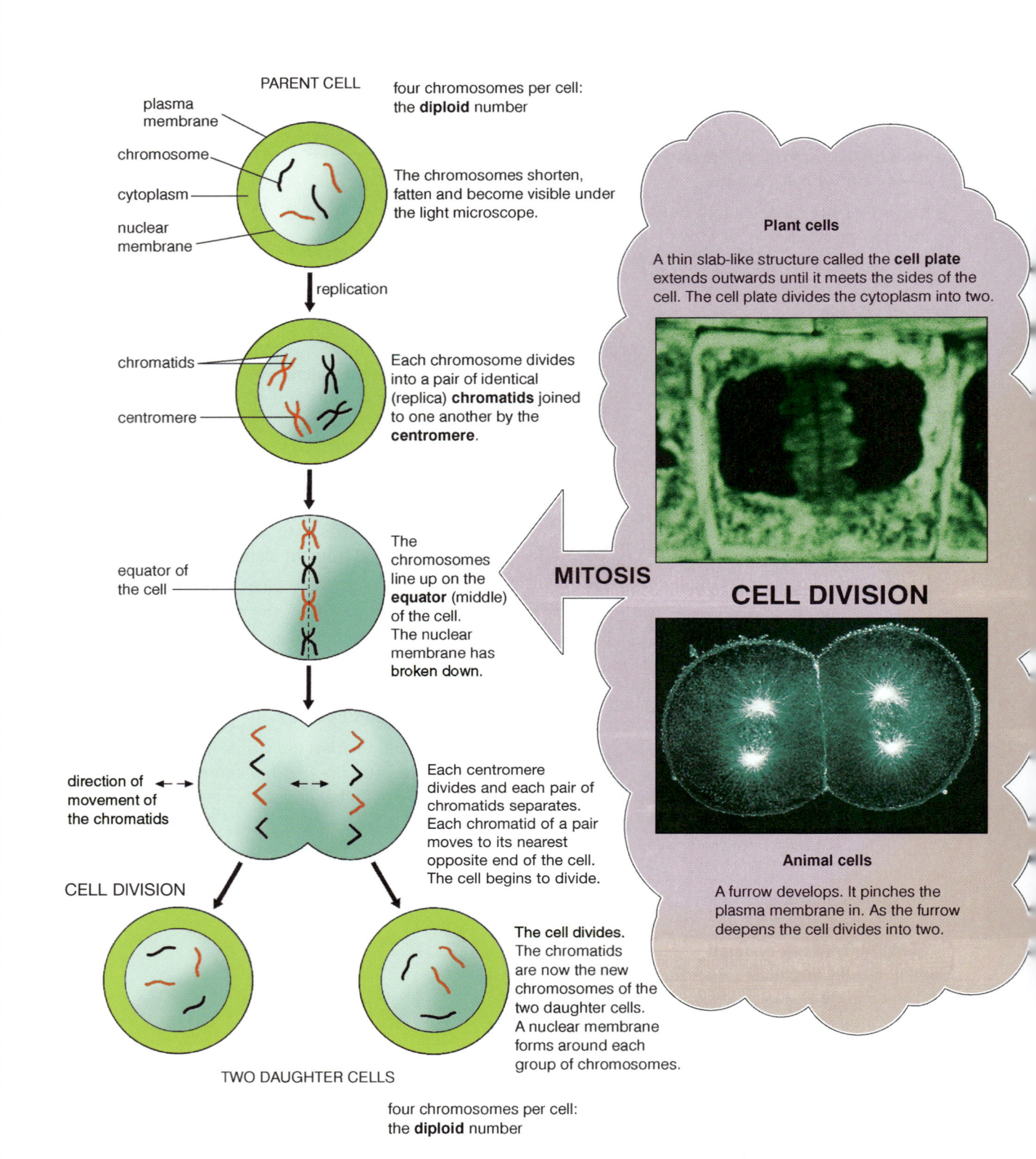

Cell division

PARENT CELL — four chromosomes per cell: the **diploid** number

- plasma membrane
- chromosome
- cytoplasm
- nuclear membrane

The chromosomes shorten, fatten and become visible under the light microscope.

↓ replication

- chromatids
- centromere

Each chromosome divides into a pair of identical (replica) **chromatids** joined to one another by the **centromere**.

- equator of the cell

The chromosomes line up on the **equator** (middle) of the cell. The nuclear membrane has **broken down**.

- direction of movement of the chromatids

Each centromere divides and each pair of chromatids separates. Each chromatid of a pair moves to its nearest opposite end of the cell. The cell begins to divide.

CELL DIVISION

TWO DAUGHTER CELLS

The cell divides. The chromatids are now the new chromosomes of the two daughter cells. A nuclear membrane forms around each group of chromosomes.

four chromosomes per cell: the **diploid** number

MITOSIS — CELL DIVISION

Plant cells

A thin slab-like structure called the **cell plate** extends outwards until it meets the sides of the cell. The cell plate divides the cytoplasm into two.

Animal cells

A furrow develops. It pinches the plasma membrane in. As the furrow deepens the cell divides into two.

Cell activity

PARENT CELL

four chromosomes per cell: the **diploid** number

- plasma membrane
- chromosome
- cytoplasm
- nuclear membrane

The chromosomes shorten, fatten and become visible under the light microscope.

↓ replication

Each chromosome divides into a pair of identical (replica) **chromatids** joined to one another by the **centromere**.

- chromatids
- centromere

Matching chromosomes pair up, forming **homologous pairs**. The nuclear membrane breaks down and homologous pairs of chromosomes line up on the **equator** (middle) of the cell.

- equator of the cell
- homologous pair of chromosomes

Homologous pairs of chromosomes separate, each pair moving to its nearest opposite end of the cell. The cell begins to divide.

← → direction of movement of chromosomes

MEIOSIS

CELL DIVISION

A new nuclear membrane forms around each group of chromosomes and the cell divides.

The nuclear membrane breaks down. The chromosomes (still as pairs of chromatids) arrange themselves on the **equator** (middle) of the cell.

— equator of the cell

Each centromere divides and each pair of chromatids separates. Each chromatid of a pair moves to its nearest opposite end of each cell. The chromatids are now the new chromosomes. Each cell begins to divide.

direction of movement ↕ of chromatids

CELL DIVISION

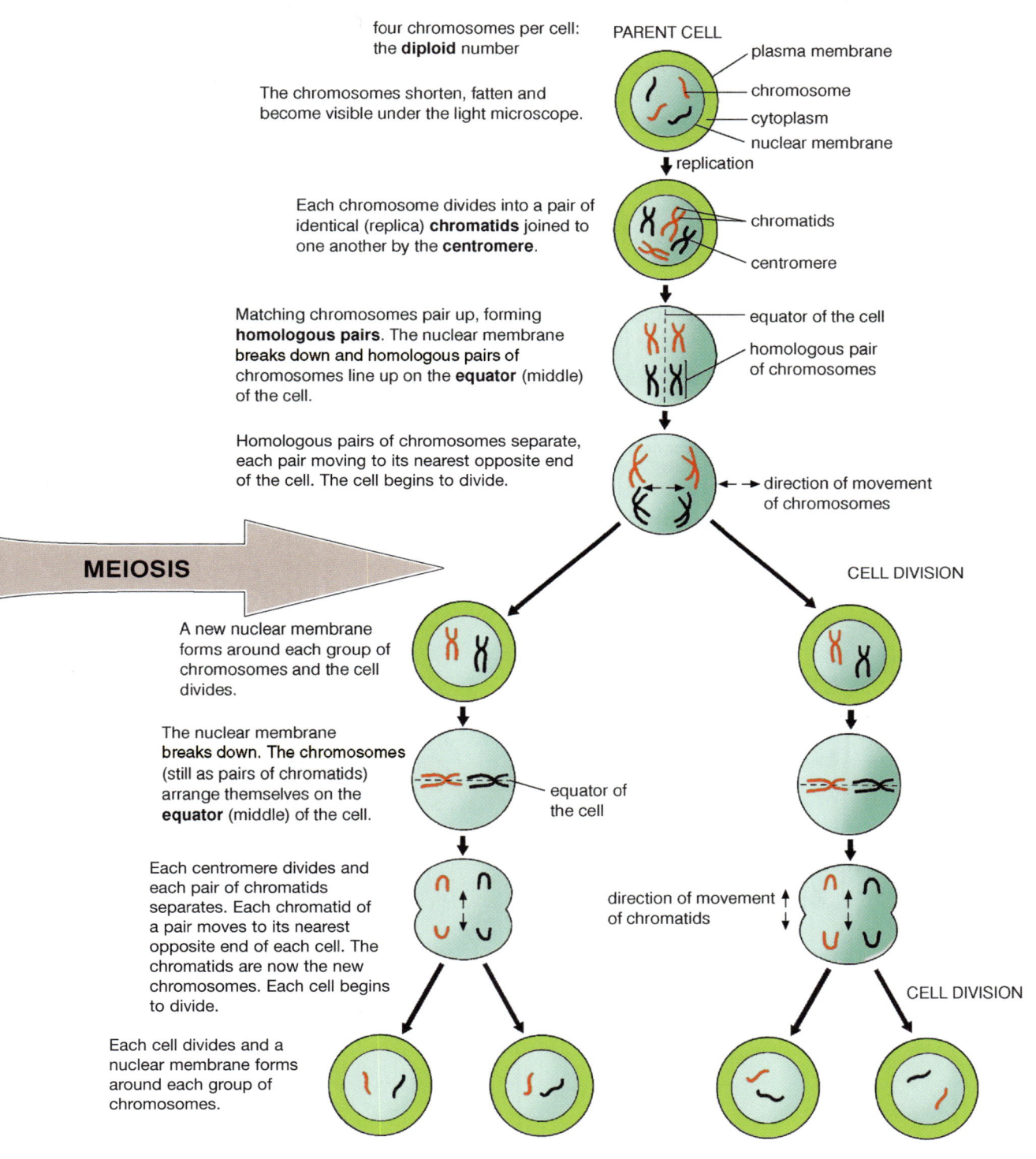

Each cell divides and a nuclear membrane forms around each group of chromosomes.

FOUR DAUGHTER CELLS

two chromosomes per cell: the **haploid** number

45

Cell activity

3.4 Cells, tissues and organs

> **PREVIEW**
>
> At the end of this section you will:
> - understand that cells are organised into tissues, tissues into organs, and organs into organ systems
> - know about the importance of the surface area to volume ratio for living processes
> - understand that organ systems are specialised for exchanging materials.

Building an organ system

Here is the concept map which revises **cells**, **tissues** and **organs**.

Plants and animals are **multicellular**: they are made of many types of cells. Each type of cell is specialised to perform a particular biological task.

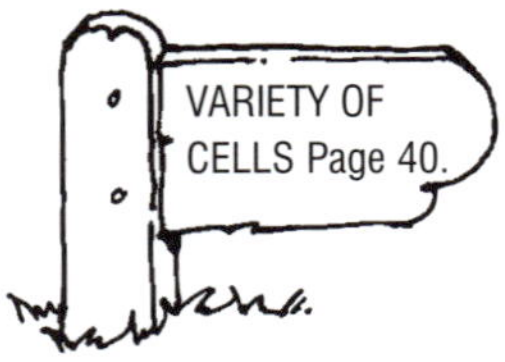

VARIETY OF CELLS Page 40.

★ A group of similar cells makes a **tissue**.

★ Different tissues together make up an **organ**.

★ Different organs combine to make an **organ system**.

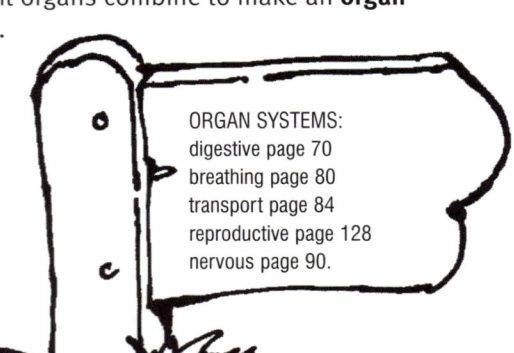

ORGAN SYSTEMS:
digestive page 70
breathing page 80
transport page 84
reproductive page 128
nervous page 90.

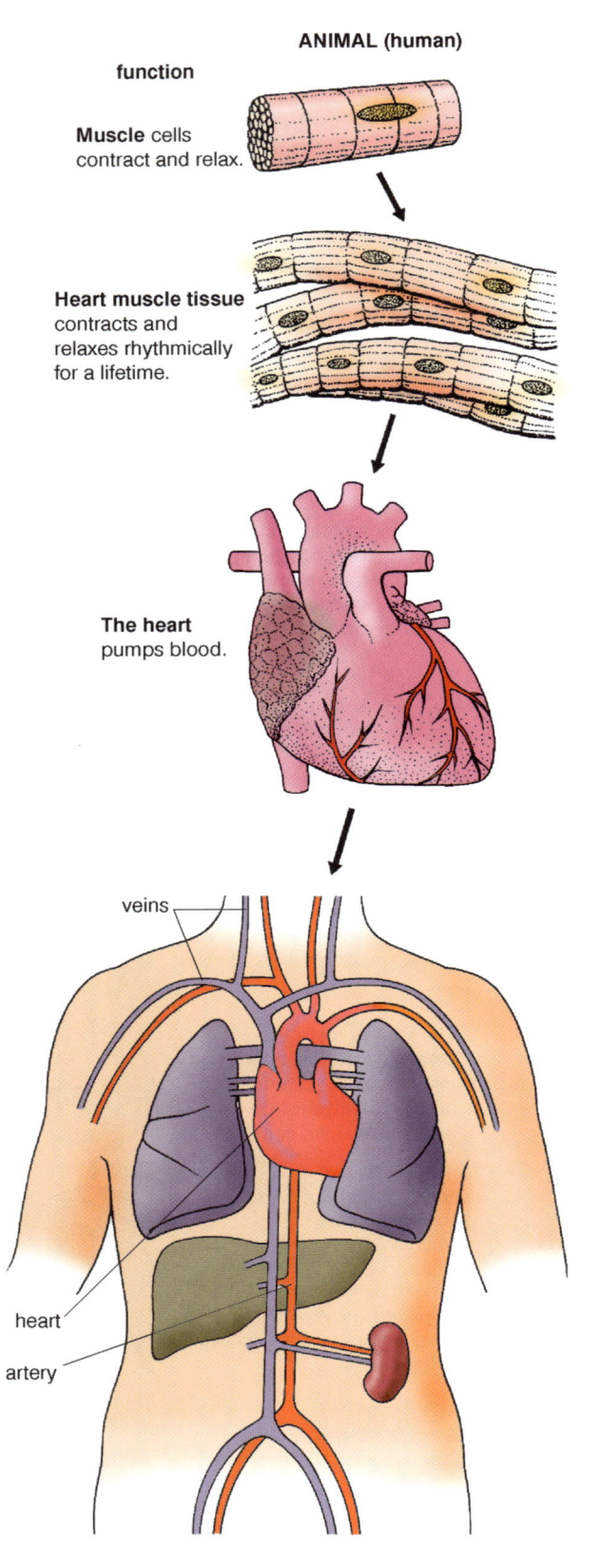

The **heart and blood vessels** transport blood to all parts of the body.

ANIMAL (human)
function

Muscle cells contract and relax.

Heart muscle tissue contracts and relaxes rhythmically for a lifetime.

The heart pumps blood.

veins
heart
artery

Cells to organ systems

Cell activity

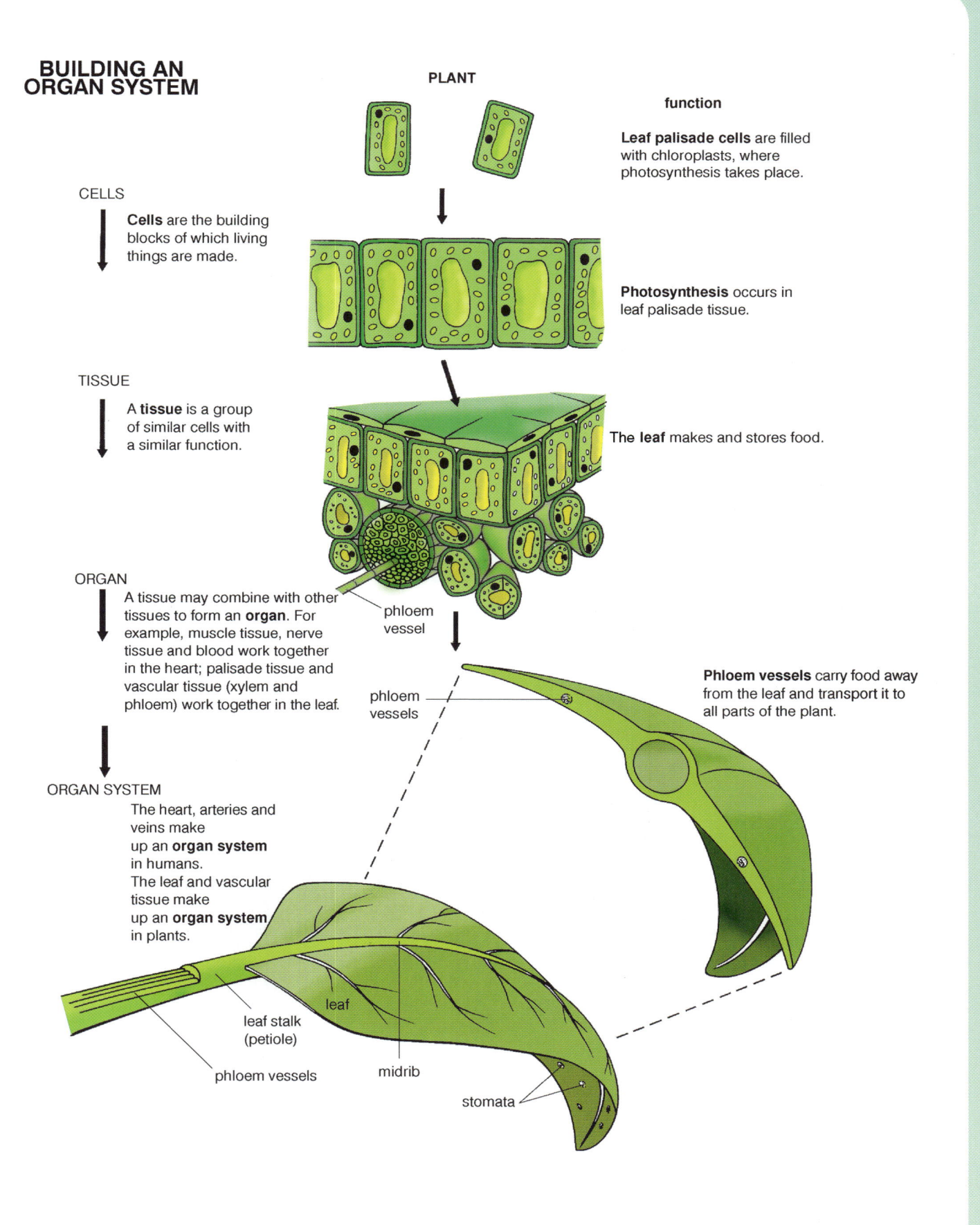

BUILDING AN ORGAN SYSTEM

PLANT

function

CELLS

Cells are the building blocks of which living things are made.

Leaf palisade cells are filled with chloroplasts, where photosynthesis takes place.

TISSUE

A **tissue** is a group of similar cells with a similar function.

Photosynthesis occurs in leaf palisade tissue.

ORGAN

A tissue may combine with other tissues to form an **organ**. For example, muscle tissue, nerve tissue and blood work together in the heart; palisade tissue and vascular tissue (xylem and phloem) work together in the leaf.

The **leaf** makes and stores food.

phloem vessel

ORGAN SYSTEM

The heart, arteries and veins make up an **organ system** in humans. The leaf and vascular tissue make up an **organ system** in plants.

Phloem vessels carry food away from the leaf and transport it to all parts of the plant.

phloem vessels

leaf

leaf stalk (petiole)

phloem vessels

midrib

stomata

47

Cell activity

Surface area to volume ratio

All cells (tissues, organs, organisms) exchange gases, food and other materials with their environment. The exchanges occur mostly by diffusion across surfaces. Look at the calculations for surface area (SA), volume (V) and surface area to volume ratio (SA/V) here.

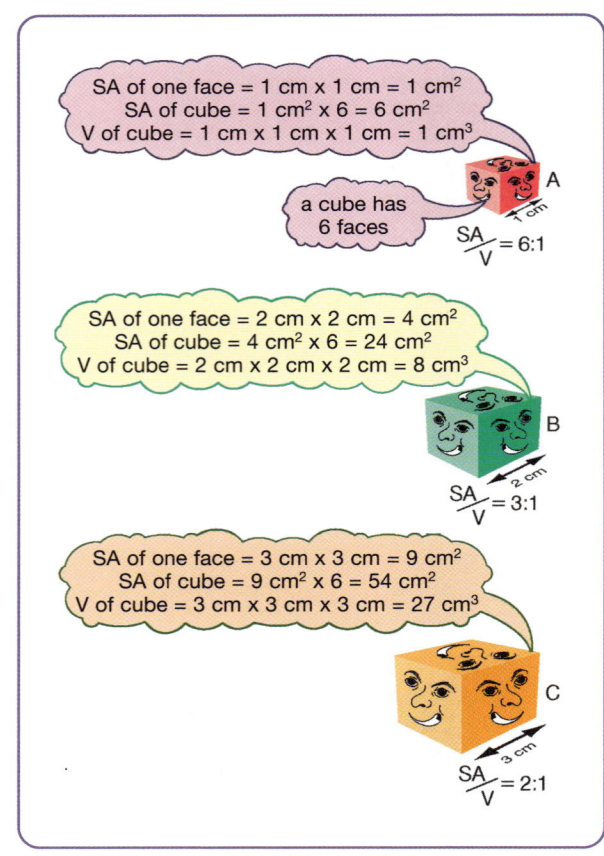

SA of one face = 1 cm × 1 cm = 1 cm^2
SA of cube = 1 cm^2 × 6 = 6 cm^2
V of cube = 1 cm × 1 cm × 1 cm = 1 cm^3

a cube has 6 faces

A
SA/V = 6:1

SA of one face = 2 cm × 2 cm = 4 cm^2
SA of cube = 4 cm^2 × 6 = 24 cm^2
V of cube = 2 cm × 2 cm × 2 cm = 8 cm^3

B
SA/V = 3:1

SA of one face = 3 cm × 3 cm = 9 cm^2
SA of cube = 9 cm^2 × 6 = 54 cm^2
V of cube = 3 cm × 3 cm × 3 cm = 27 cm^3

C
SA/V = 2:1

Cubic arithmetic

- The SA/V of cube B is half that of cube A.
- The SA/V of cube C is two-thirds that of cube B and one-third that of cube A.

Remember

The LARGER the cube becomes, the SMALLER its SA/V.

★ Surface area increases with the **square** (power^2) of the side.

★ Volume increases with the **cube** (power^3) of the side.

Cells (tissues, organs, organisms) are not cube shaped, but the calculations apply to any shape. For example, as a cell grows it:
- takes in more food and gases
- produces more waste substances.

After the cell reaches a certain size, its surface area becomes proportionally too small to meet the needs of the larger volume of living matter inside.

At this point, the cell divides into two smaller daughter cells. This restores the ratio of surface area to volume because the surface area to volume ratio of each daughter cell is greater than that of the parent cell.

As a result, sufficient food and gases can pass across the cell surface into the cell.

As a result, wastes can pass across the cell surface out of the cell.

Fact file

The SA/V of large animals is less than the SA/V of small animals. Large animals, therefore, lose proportionally less body heat than small animals. However, it takes them longer to warm up.

Organ systems specialised for exchanging materials

We all exchange gases, food and other materials between our body and the environment. The exchange happens by diffusion across body surfaces. Special features of organs and organ systems increase the available surface area for the exchange of materials with their surroundings. These features increase the ratio of surface area to volume of the organs and organ systems in question.

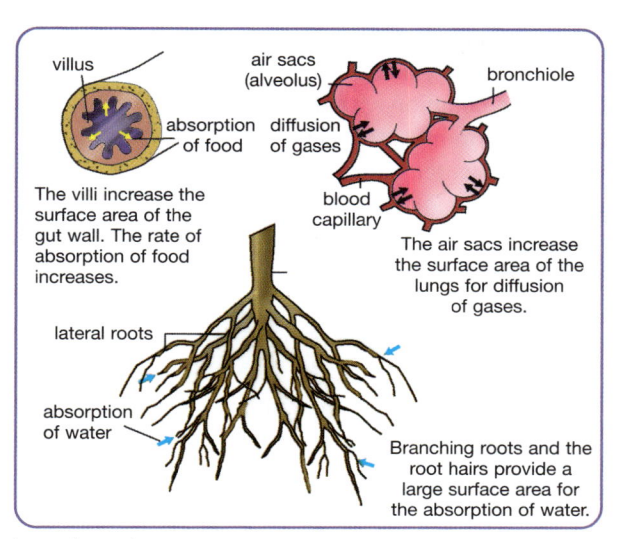

Cell activity

Increasing surface area

- villus — absorption of food
- The villi increase the surface area of the gut wall. The rate of absorption of food increases.
- air sacs (alveolus), bronchiole, diffusion of gases, blood capillary
- The air sacs increase the surface area of the lungs for diffusion of gases.
- lateral roots, absorption of water
- Branching roots and the root hairs provide a large surface area for the absorption of water.

3.5 Chemicals in living things

PREVIEW

At the end of this section you will:
- understand that living things are made from the same elements as other types of matter
- know that carbohydrates, lipids, proteins and nucleic acids are important chemicals in living things
- understand that atoms of carbon are able to combine to form long chains.

Elements for life

All matter is made of chemical elements. Of these elements, six make up more than 95% by mass of living matter. They are:
- carbon (C)
- hydrogen (H)
- nitrogen (N)
- oxygen (O)
- phosphorus (P)
- sulphur (S).

Handy hint

The symbols of the elements arranged in order of abundance in living matter make the memory aid **CHNOPS**.

Compounds for life

Important categories of compounds in living things are:
- **carbohydrates**: major sources of energy and structural materials
- **lipids**: stores of energy
- **proteins**: for building and repairing bodies
- **nucleic acids**: carry a code which enables cells to make proteins.

Fact file

Carbon is the most common element in the substances that make up living things. Carbon atoms can combine to form long chains. Many of the carbon compounds in living things have large molecules (**macromolecules**) formed by small molecules combining.

Carbohydrates

Carbohydrates are compounds containing the elements carbon, hydrogen and oxygen. There are three categories:

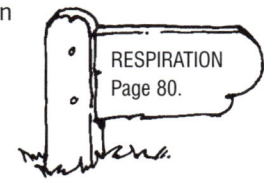

RESPIRATION Page 80.

Monosaccharides are simple sugars. Sweet-tasting **fructose** and **glucose** are examples. Both have the molecular formula $C_6H_{12}O_6$. The six carbon atoms form a ring. Sugars (especially glucose) are an important source of energy in all living things.

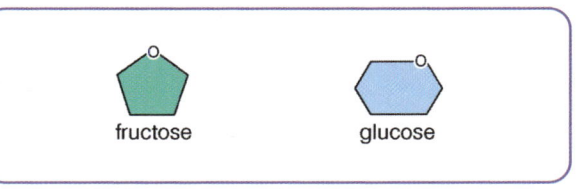

fructose   *glucose*

The structural formulae of fructose and glucose in shorthand form. Although the molecular formula of each sugar is the same, the structural formulae are different.

Disaccharides are more complex sugars. They are formed when two monosaccharides combine. For example, two molecules of glucose combine to form one molecule of **maltose**:

2 glucose → maltose + water

$2C_6H_{12}O_6(aq) \rightarrow C_{12}H_{22}O_{11}(aq) + H_2O(l)$

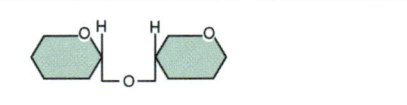

The formula for maltose in shorthand form

49

Cell activity

A molecule of fructose and a molecule of glucose combine to form one molecule of **sucrose**:

glucose + fructose → sucrose + water

Polysaccharides are carbohydrates whose molecules contain hundreds of sugar rings. For example, **starch**, **cellulose** and **glycogen** are polysaccharides. Their molecules consist of long chains of glucose rings.

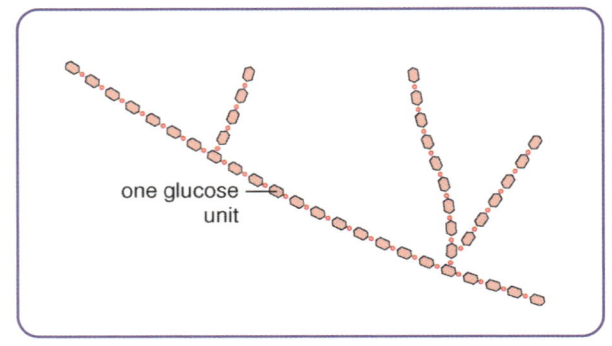

Part of a starch molecule

Polysaccharides differ in the length and structure of their chains. They are important storage and structural materials in living things.

★ **Starch** is a food substance stored in plants. Starch can be converted into glucose, which is oxidised (respired) in cells. Energy is released.

★ **Glycogen** is a food substance stored in animals. Liver cells convert glycogen into glucose, which is oxidised (respired). Energy is released.

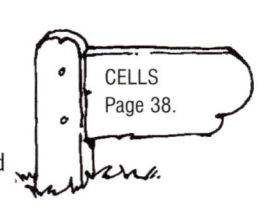

CELLS Page 38.

★ **Cellulose** is an important component of the cell walls of plants.

★ **Chitin** is an important component of the exoskeleton of insects.

Lipids

Lipids are compounds containing the elements carbon, hydrogen and oxygen. There are two types of lipids: **fats**, which are solid at room temperature; and **oils**, which are liquid at room temperature.

Fats and oils are compounds formed between two constituents: **fatty acids** and **glycerol**. A molecule of glycerol can combine with three fatty acid molecules to form a **triglyceride** molecule and three molecules of water. Fats and oils are mixtures of triglycerides.

glycerol + fatty acid ⟶ triglyceride + water

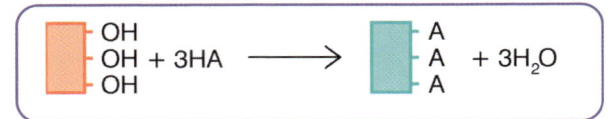

Making a triglyceride

Saturated and unsaturated fats and oils

Fatty acids (and therefore the fats and oils of which they are a part) may be:
- **saturated** – the carbon atoms are joined by single bonds, *or*
- **unsaturated** – the carbon atoms have double bonds between them. If there is one double bond in the molecule, the compound is **monounsaturated**. If there is more than one double bond in the molecule, the compound is **polyunsaturated**.

HEART DISEASE Page 89.

Fats and oils are important as:
- components of cell membranes
- sources of energy
- sources of the fat-soluble vitamins A, D and E
- insulation which helps to keep the body warm
- protection for delicate organs.

Proteins

Proteins are compounds containing the elements carbon, hydrogen, oxygen, nitrogen and sometimes sulphur.

Amino acids are the building blocks which combine to make proteins. Two or more amino acids can combine to form a **peptide**, which can combine with more amino acids to form a **protein**.

Cell activity

Fact file

★ **Peptides** have molecules with up to 15 amino acids.

★ **Polypeptides** have molecules with 15–50 amino acids.

★ **Proteins** have still larger molecules.

There are 20 different amino acids that combine to form proteins. The protein made depends on the type and number of amino acids joining together.

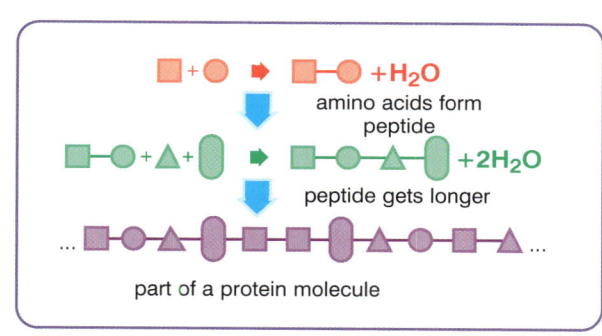

How amino acids combine to form peptides and proteins. Each shape represents a particular type of amino acid.

Proteins are important because:
- they are the materials from which new tissues are made during growth and repair
- most **enzymes** are proteins. Enzymes control the rates of chemical reactions in cells
- some **hormones** are proteins. Hormones control the activities of organisms.

HORMONES Pages 97–102.

Enzymes in action

Enzymes are made by living cells. They are **catalysts** which control the rates of chemical reactions in cells. There are thousands of different enzymes in a cell. Enzymes also speed up the rate of digestion of food in the gut.

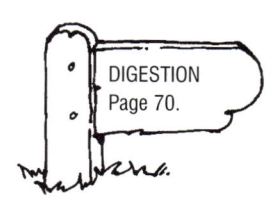

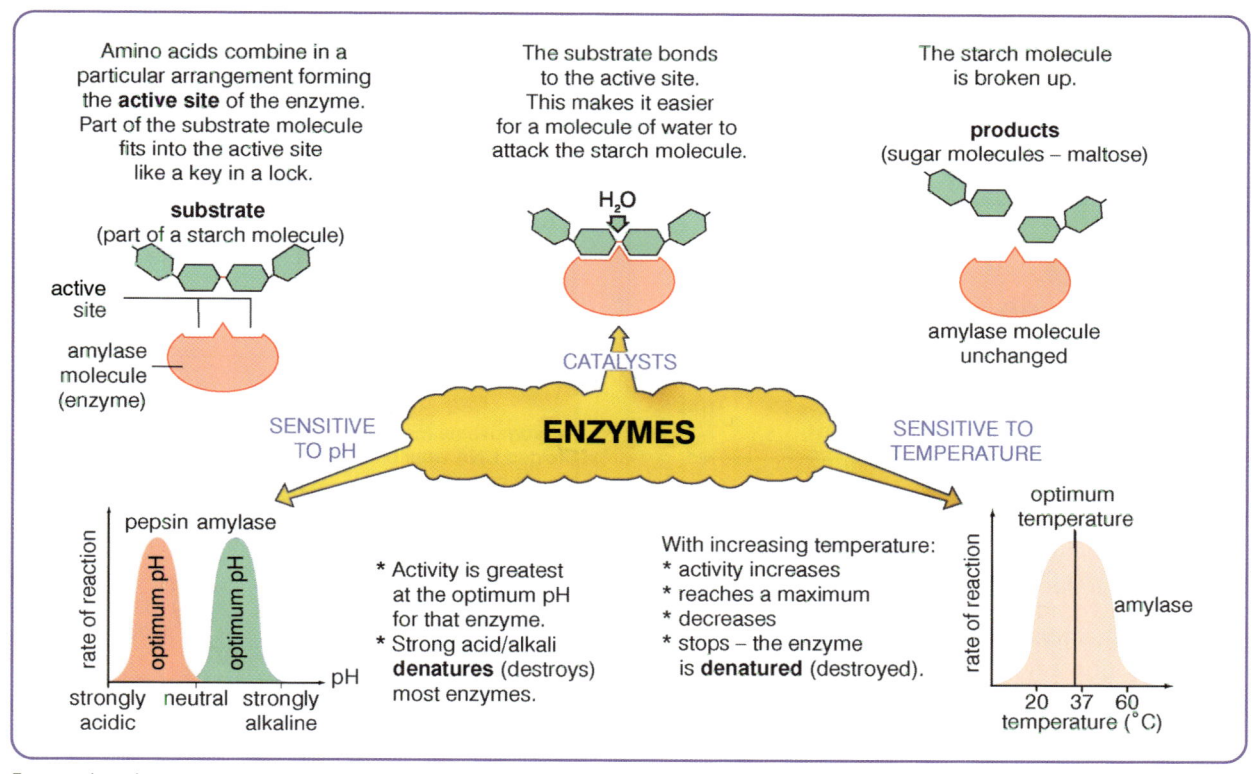

DIGESTION Page 70.

Amino acids combine in a particular arrangement forming the **active site** of the enzyme. Part of the substrate molecule fits into the active site like a key in a lock.

substrate (part of a starch molecule)

active site

amylase molecule (enzyme)

The substrate bonds to the active site. This makes it easier for a molecule of water to attack the starch molecule.

The starch molecule is broken up.

products (sugar molecules – maltose)

amylase molecule unchanged

CATALYSTS

ENZYMES

SENSITIVE TO pH

SENSITIVE TO TEMPERATURE

pepsin   amylase
optimum pH   optimum pH
strongly acidic   neutral   strongly alkaline

* Activity is greatest at the optimum pH for that enzyme.
* Strong acid/alkali **denatures** (destroys) most enzymes.

With increasing temperature:
* activity increases
* reaches a maximum
* decreases
* stops – the enzyme is **denatured** (destroyed).

optimum temperature
amylase
20 37 60
temperature (°C)

Enzymes in action

Cell activity

Enzymes are:
- **specific** in their action – each enzyme catalyses a certain chemical reaction or type of chemical reaction
- sensitive to changes in **pH**
- sensitive to changes in **temperature**.

The substance that the enzyme helps to react is called the **substrate**. The substances formed in the reaction are called **products**.

Nucleic acids

Deoxyribonucleic acid (**DNA**) and **ribonucleic acid** (**RNA**) are nucleic acids.

★ DNA makes up the chromosomes in the nucleus of the cell. The **genes** that carry information from parents to offspring are lengths of DNA. They carry the **genetic code** which enables cells to assemble amino acids in the correct order to make proteins.

★ RNA occurs in the nucleus and cytoplasm of the cell. It transfers the information in the genes to the structures in the cell where proteins are made. The structures are called **ribosomes**.

The structure of DNA

DNA and RNA are large complex molecules made from lots of smaller molecules called **nucleotides**.

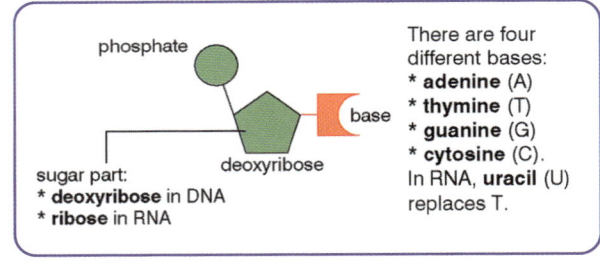

There are four different bases:
* **adenine** (A)
* **thymine** (T)
* **guanine** (G)
* **cytosine** (C).
In RNA, **uracil** (U) replaces T.

sugar part:
* **deoxyribose** in DNA
* **ribose** in RNA

A nucleotide molecule

★ Many nucleotides join together, sugar to phosphate, to form a long strand.

★ Two of these strands link together by **base pairing** to form a molecule of DNA:
- adenine (A) bonds to thymine (T) or *vice versa*
- guanine (G) bonds to cytosine (C) or *vice versa*.

★ The double strand twists into a spiral called a **double helix** – two intertwined spiral strands.

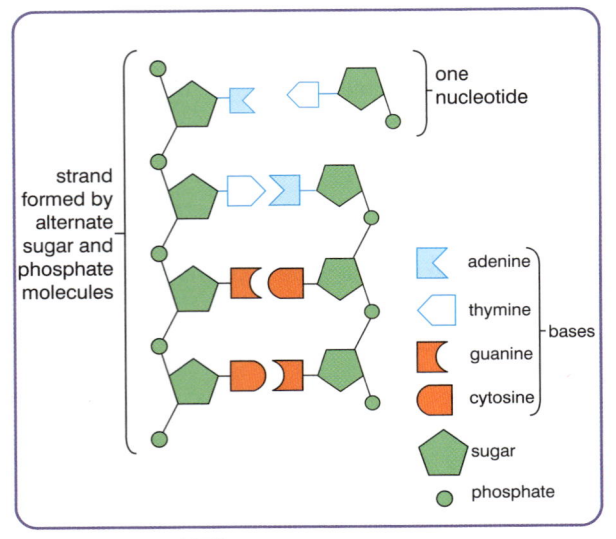

Part of a molecule of DNA

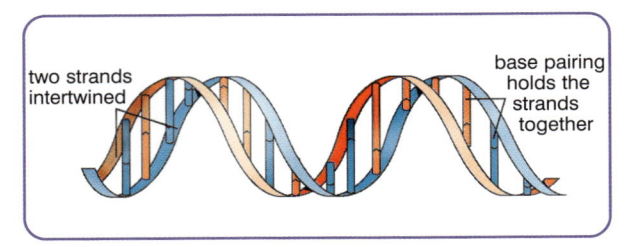

The double helix: two spiral strands connected by their bases

★ A **chromosome** consists of a folded double strand of DNA coiled round a protein core. The DNA part of the structure controls the inheritance of characteristics.

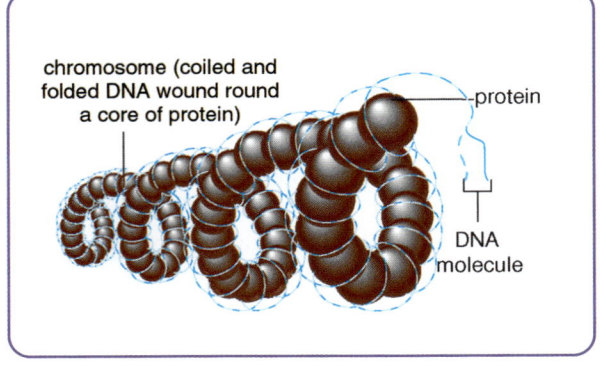

The structure of a chromosome

Cell activity

DNA replication

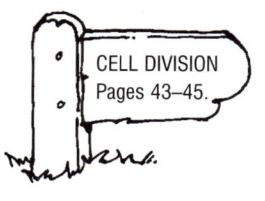

During cell division, the chromosomes **replicate** – they form an identical copy of themselves. This means the DNA molecule must make a copy of itself. The diagram below shows how this happens.

> CELL DIVISION Pages 43–45.

Now you can see why the daughter cells formed by mitosis are genetically identical to each other and to their parent cell. The two new molecules of DNA are each a replica of the original because of the base pairing. A always pairs with T (or *vice versa*), and G always pairs with C (or *vice versa*). All the cells in the body that die are replaced by mitosis, so the new cells are identical to the old ones that gave rise to them.

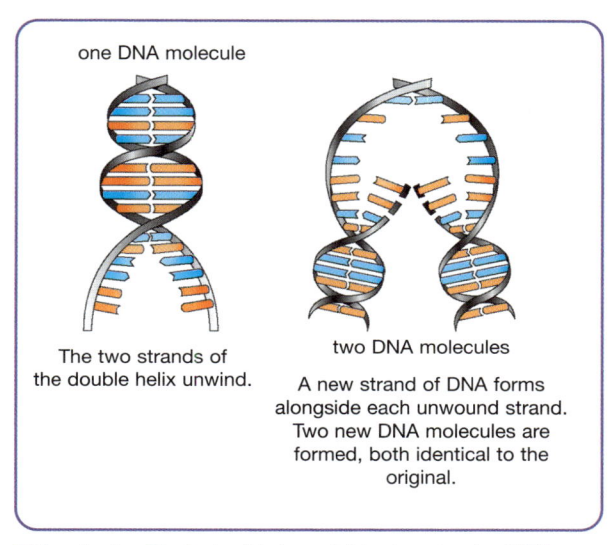

one DNA molecule

The two strands of the double helix unwind.

two DNA molecules

A new strand of DNA forms alongside each unwound strand. Two new DNA molecules are formed, both identical to the original.

DNA replication. The horizontal shapes joining two strands of DNA represent the bases A, T, G and C shown opposite.

Mutation

Hundreds of thousands of nucleotides a second can be added to the replicating DNA. Occasionally the wrong nucleotide adds by mistake. Then the new DNA formed is slightly different from the original. The change in structure of DNA is called a **mutation**.

A mutation may also involve a change in the amount of DNA. In either case, there is a change in the genetic code of the organism.

★ **Gene mutations** occur when the sequence of bases is incorrectly copied during DNA replication (see above). A nucleotide (and its base) may be:
- *inserted:* a base is added
- *deleted:* a base is lost
- *duplicated:* a base is repeated
- *inverted:* a base is turned round
- *substituted:* a base is copied wrongly.

The mutation may result in a new order in which amino acids are assembled resulting in an error in the synthesis of protein (see page 54).

★ **Chromosome mutations** occur when chromosomes break in the early stages of meiosis. Normally, breakage is followed by **crossing-over**. As a result, new combinations of genes are produced, increasing **variation**. However, breakage of chromosomes may have other consequences:
- *deletion:* a chromosome or part of a chromosome is lost
- *translocation:* the broken part of a chromosome joins to another chromosome
- *inversion:* the broken part of a chromosome rejoins the chromosome but after turning through 180°.

The offspring that inherit chromosome mutations from their parents may show a range of abnormalities.

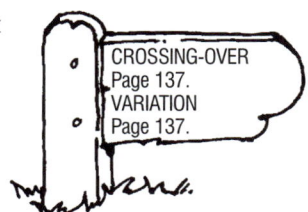

> CROSSING-OVER Page 137. VARIATION Page 137.

The genetic code

★ A **codon** is the length of a DNA molecule that codes for one amino acid. It is three nucleotides long.

★ A **gene** is the length of a DNA molecule that codes for one complete protein.

★ A gene, therefore, is a long line of codons in a particular order. The order of the codons controls the order in which amino acids are assembled to produce a particular protein.

Cell activity

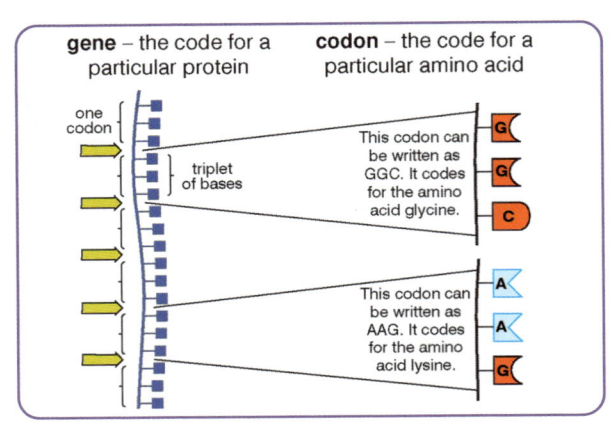

The genetic code

(diagram showing: **gene** – the code for a particular protein; **codon** – the code for a particular amino acid; one codon; triplet of bases; This codon can be written as GGC. It codes for the amino acid glycine. This codon can be written as AAG. It codes for the amino acid lysine.)

Remember that:
- one of the five bases – adenine (A), thymine (T), guanine (G), cytosine (C) or uracil (U) – is a component of a nucleotide
- nucleotides whose base is uracil are not components of DNA but are components of RNA
- a length of DNA consists of a sequence of nucleotides (and therefore bases)
- the sequence of bases of a gene is a set of instructions (one part of the genetic code) which enables a cell to make a particular protein.

Follow the sequence of events. Remember the rules of base pairing and that in RNA uracil (U) replaces thymine (T).

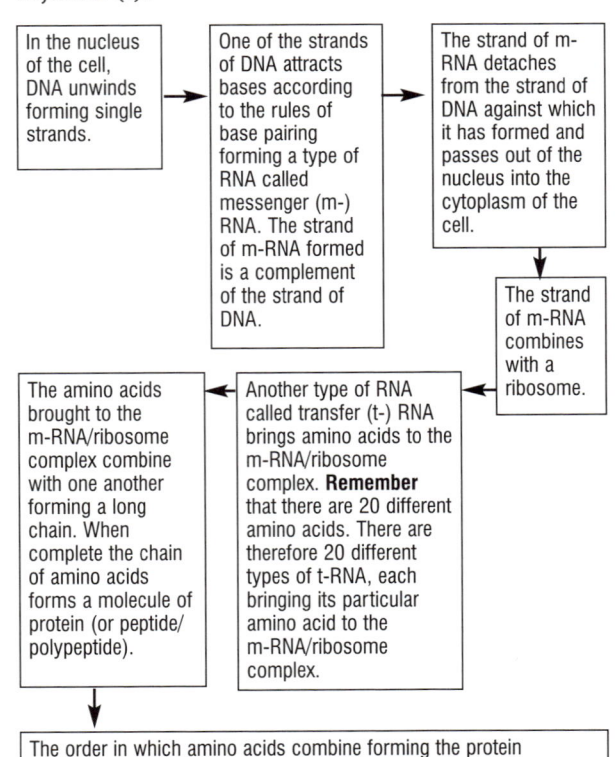

| In the nucleus of the cell, DNA unwinds forming single strands. | → | One of the strands of DNA attracts bases according to the rules of base pairing forming a type of RNA called messenger (m-) RNA. The strand of m-RNA formed is a complement of the strand of DNA. | → | The strand of m-RNA detaches from the strand of DNA against which it has formed and passes out of the nucleus into the cytoplasm of the cell. |

The strand of m-RNA combines with a ribosome.

The amino acids brought to the m-RNA/ribosome complex combine with one another forming a long chain. When complete the chain of amino acids forms a molecule of protein (or peptide/polypeptide). ← Another type of RNA called transfer (t-) RNA brings amino acids to the m-RNA/ribosome complex. **Remember** that there are 20 different amino acids. There are therefore 20 different types of t-RNA, each bringing its particular amino acid to the m-RNA/ribosome complex.

The order in which amino acids combine forming the protein (peptide/polypeptide) molecule is a result of the sequence of codons of the m-RNA which is itself a complement of the sequence of the codons of the strand of DNA against which the m-RNA formed.

The human genome

The word **genome** refers to all of the DNA in all of an organism. Scientists working on the human genome:
- have worked out the sequence order of bases of the lengths of DNA that form our genes
- aim to identify where individual genes are located on chromosomes
- aim to identify the proteins for which the genes are the code.

Nearly all human cells each have about 30–40 thousand genes. These genes determine vulnerability to disease, patterns of behaviour, appearance and all of the other characteristics we inherit from our parents. Samples of cells (white blood cells and sperm) are taken from anonymous volunteers. The DNA extracted from the cells is analysed and its sequence of bases worked out.

The discovery of the sequence of the bases of the human genome is the key that unlocks the possibilities of new drugs and treatments as a result of our knowing the genetic causes of disease.

Fact file

★ The **Human Genome Organisation** was established in the late 1980s to co-ordinate the research of scientists in the USA, UK and other countries working to discover the sequence of the human genome. The organisation receives money from public funds.

★ The **Institute of Genomic Research** was privately funded and set up soon after its founder Craig Venter had applied in 1991 for **patents** on more than 300 human genes. A patent is a legal document that registers a person's (or organisation's) claim for an invention. In the case of genomic research, the invention refers to the base sequence of the DNA that makes up the human genome.

Cell activity

Issues

The publication of the publicly funded and privately funded working draft of the human genome sequence on February 15th 2001 highlights difficult issues that arise from knowing our genetic make up. Here are a number of points for you to think about.

★ Patents stop other people and organisations from making use of genomic information. Exploiting the genome to improve health care may well depend on paying the owners of the patents large sums of money.

★ If our individual genome is part of our medical records, will organisations that provide life insurance require people to be tested for their risk of developing genetically related disease? An unfavourable genetic profile may also make it difficult for people to obtain a mortgage to buy a house.

★ It is likely that genetic testing for intelligence, eye and hair colour and other characteristics will soon be possible. Should parents be able to choose a 'designer' baby?

These are just a few of the issues that you need to think about. The more accurate finished human genome was announced on 14 April 2003.

Cell activity

ROUND UP

How much have you improved? Work out your improvement index on page 157.

1. Which of the structures listed below are found in **a)** animal cells and plant cells **b)** plant cells only?

    **nucleus plasma membrane cell wall
    large vacuole mitochondria chloroplasts
    cytoplasm** [7]

2. Describe what happens in the cells of a plant deprived of water which is then watered. How will the appearance of the plant change? [5]

3. Complete the following paragraph using the words below. Each word may be used once, more than once or not at all.

    **osmosis faster gains down slower partially
    energy against**

    The movement of a substance _____ a concentration gradient is called diffusion. The steeper the concentration gradient, the _____ is the rate of diffusion. Active transport occurs _____ a concentration gradient. The process requires more _____ than diffusion. The diffusion of water through a _____ permeable membrane is called _____. [6]

4. Why is mitosis important for maintaining the health of the tissues of the body? [1]

5. Compare and contrast the processes of mitosis and meiosis by listing the similarities and the differences in different columns. [8]

6. Below is a series of words that describe the organisation of living matter. Arrange the words in the correct sequence, beginning with the simplest level of organisation and ending with the most complex.

    **organs cells organisms organ systems
    tissues** [5]

7. Match each substance in column **A** with its function in column **B**.

A substances	B functions
fat	carries the genetic code
cellulose	insulates the body
DNA	a component of the plant cell wall
polypeptide	a food substance stored in the liver
glycogen	most enzymes are made of this substance
protein	made of about 40 amino acids

    [6]

8. **a)** The following is a sequence of bases for a length of DNA. How many codons are there in the sequence, assuming the first codon begins at the left-hand side and there is no overlap?

    T T A G G A C T G A T C

    b) If each codon codes for one amino acid, how many amino acids are coded for in this length of DNA? [2]

Green plants as organisms — Chapter 4

How much do you already know? Work out your score on page 157.

Test yourself

1. **a)** Name the inorganic substances that are the raw materials for photosynthesis. [2]
   b) Name the gas given off during photosynthesis. [1]

2. Minerals are needed for healthy growth. Match each substance in column **A** with its function in column **B**.

A substances	B functions
nitrogen	used to make cell membranes
phosphorus	used to make chlorophyll
magnesium	used to make protein

   [3]

3. Complete the following paragraph using the words below. Each word may be used once, more than once or not at all.

   active transport   evaporates   increase translocation   osmotic   stomata   xylem osmosis

   Root hairs _____ the surface area available for the uptake of water. Water passes across the root into the _____ by _____. The uptake of minerals in solution is by _____. Water moves through the _____ tissue in unbroken columns connecting the root with the leaves of the plant. Water is lost from the leaves as it _____ through the _____. [8]

4. Different types of tropisms are listed in column **A**. Match each type with the correct description in column **B**.

A tropisms	B descriptions
phototropism	growth movement in response to gravity
geotropism	growth movement in response to touch
hydrotropism	growth movement in response to light
thigmotropism	growth movement in response to water

   [4]

4.1 Photosynthesis

PREVIEW

At the end of this section you will:
- understand the structure of leaves
- know that limiting factors affect the rate of photosynthesis
- be able to identify the minerals that plants need for healthy growth.

Photosynthesis

Photosynthesis is a chemical process that traps the energy of sunlight. Plant cells use the energy to convert carbon dioxide and water into sugars. A summary of the process is:

$$\text{carbon dioxide} + \text{water} \xrightarrow{\text{catalysed by chlorophyll}} \text{glucose} + \text{oxygen}$$

$$6CO_2(g) + 6H_2O(l) \longrightarrow C_6H_{12}O_6(aq) + 6O_2(g)$$

There are lots of different chemical reactions that make up the process of photosynthesis. The reactions happen inside chloroplasts, in the cells of leaves and other green parts of plants.

Leaves

A leaf is a food-making factory. Carbon dioxide and water circulate within the leaf. Light is captured by the pigment chlorophyll, which is packaged in the chloroplasts that pack the cells of the leaf. On pages 60–61 is the concept map for **photosynthesis**, and its checklist of points is on page 59. The diagram below shows you how the plant uses sugars.

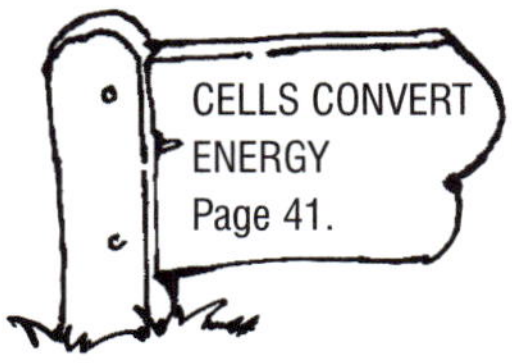

CELLS CONVERT ENERGY — Page 41.

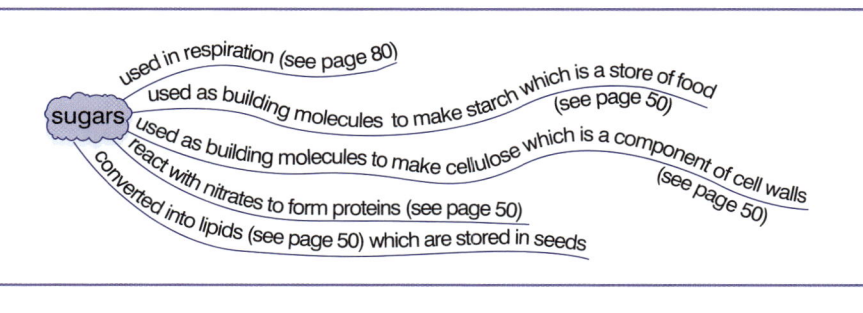

---

sugars
- used in respiration (see page 80)
- used as building molecules to make starch which is a store of food (see page 50)
- used as building molecules to make cellulose which is a component of cell walls (see page 50)
- react with nitrates to form proteins (see page 50)
- converted into lipids (see page 50) which are stored in seeds

Green plants as organisms

Limiting factors

The rate at which plants make sugar by photosynthesis is affected by supplies of **carbon dioxide** and **water**, **temperature** and the **intensity of light**. These factors are called **limiting factors** because if any one of them falls to a low level, photosynthesis slows down or stops. The diagram below illustrates the point. At low concentrations of carbon dioxide, the carbon dioxide limits the rate of photosynthesis, whatever the light level is. Carbon dioxide is the limiting factor. At higher concentrations of carbon dioxide, the rate of photosynthesis increases if the light is bright enough. Light is now the limiting factor.

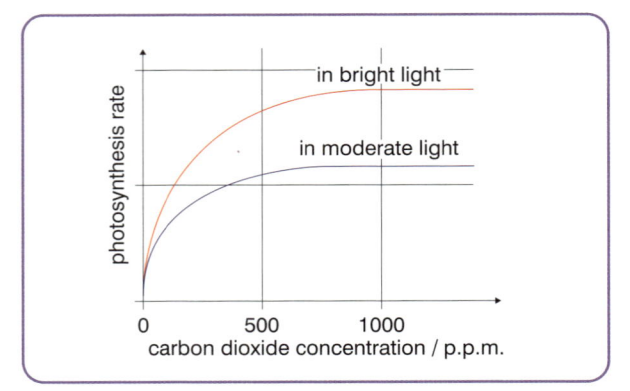

Effect of carbon dioxide concentration on the rate of photosynthesis (carbon dioxide concentration is given in p.p.m., parts per million)

The higher the temperature, the faster the chemical reactions of photosynthesis, within limits. Extreme cold slows the activity of the enzymes which control the chemical reactions of photosynthesis; extreme heat destroys them.

Water is a raw material for photosynthesis. However, water is also the solvent in which most of the reactions of metabolism occur within cells. Singling out the direct effect of the availability of water on photosynthesis is therefore very difficult.

In a greenhouse, conditions are controlled so that limiting factors are eliminated. The diagram in the next column shows this idea.

Greenhouse plants can be grown without soil. The plants are supplied with a solution of all of the substances they need for a healthy existence (nutrient solution). The method is called **hydroponics** (or nutrient culture). Using hydroponics means that:
- plants grow faster
- weeds are eliminated
- pests that live in soil are eliminated
- the quality and taste of crops is improved.

Hydroponic culture requires significant financial investment, and is therefore restricted to crops with high cash value in the market place.

Fact file

Bottles of 'plant food' sold at garden centres contain solutions of some of the important minerals needed for healthy plant growth.

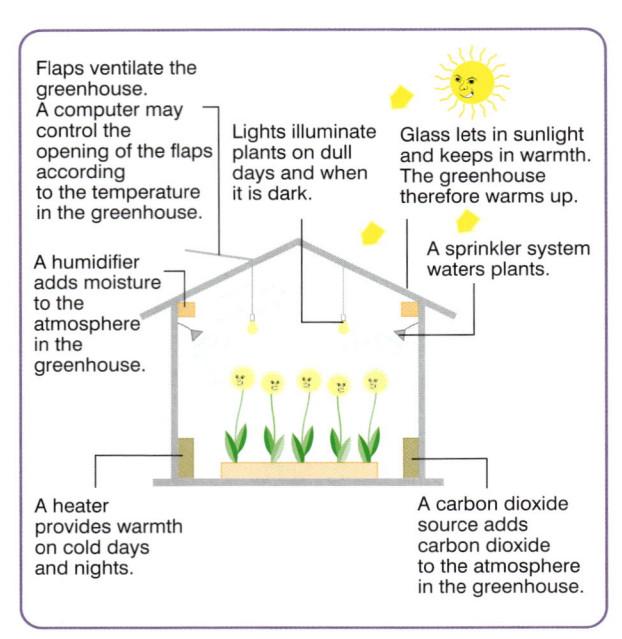

The maximum-efficiency greenhouse

Mineral nutrients

Plants grow using the food (sugars) they make by photosynthesis. Healthy plant growth also depends on **minerals** which are absorbed from the soil through the roots as solutions of salts.

Major elements are needed in quite large amounts.

★ **Nitrogen (N)** is used by plants to make protein.

★ **Phosphorus (P)** is used by plants to make cell membranes. It is also a component of DNA and has an important role in the chemical reactions of photosynthesis and respiration.

★ **Potassium (K)** promotes the activity of enzymes, which control the chemical reactions of photosynthesis and respiration.

Plants deprived of any of the major elements grow less well. Most artificial fertilisers are NPK fertilisers.

Green plants as organisms

Shortage of:
- nitrogen in the form of nitrate ions leads to stunted growth and yellow older leaves
- phosphorus in the form of phosphate ions leads to poor root growth and purple younger leaves
- potassium in the form of potassium ions leads to yellow leaves with dead spots.

Trace elements (micronutrients) are needed in much smaller amounts than major elements.

★ **Magnesium** (Mg) is a component of the chlorophyll molecule.

★ **Iron** (Fe) is also a component of the chlorophyll molecule.

If magnesium and iron are in short supply then leaves become mottled and pale. **Copper** (Cu), **sodium** (Na) and **manganese** (Mn) are also trace elements. Absence of any one of them from the soil leads to poor plant growth.

Checklist for photosynthesis

1 ★ Leaves are arranged so that the lower ones are not overshadowed by those above. The arrangement is called the **leaf mosaic**.

   As a result, more leaves are exposed to direct sunlight.

   ★ The leaf blade is flat.

   As a result, a large surface area is exposed for the absorption of light.

   ★ The leaf blade is thin.

   As a result, light reaches the lower layers of cells in the leaf.

2 ★ Water moves up to leaves in the **transpiration stream**.

   ★ Carbon dioxide enters leaves through the **stomata**.

3 ★ The cells of the upper leaf surface do not contain chloroplasts and are transparent.

   TRANSPIRATION Page 61.

   ★ **Palisade cells** beneath the upper epidermis are column shaped, tightly packed and filled with chloroplasts.

   As a result, many chloroplasts are exposed to bright light, maximising the rate of photosynthesis.

★ **Spongy mesophyll cells** contain fewer chloroplasts and are more loosely packed.

   As a result, there are air spaces between the spongy mesophyll cells.

★ The spaces allow carbon dioxide and water vapour to circulate freely within the leaf, bringing the raw materials for photosynthesis to the leaf cells.

   STOMATA Page 62.

★ Each **stoma** is flanked by guard cells which control the size of the opening of the stoma.

   As a result, the rate of diffusion of gases into and out of the leaf through the stomata is controlled.

★ The cells of the lower leaf surface lack chloroplasts, except the guard cells.

4 ★ Chloroplasts pack the inside of each palisade cell.

   ★ Chloroplasts stream in the cytoplasm (**cyclosis**) to the region of the palisade cell where light is brightest.

   As a result, the rate of photosynthesis is maximised.

5 ★ Membranes inside the chloroplasts are covered with the green pigment **chlorophyll**.

   ★ Chlorophyll absorbs light, especially wavelengths in the red and blue parts of the spectrum.

   ★ The membranes are arranged like stacks of pancakes, maximising the surface area of chlorophyll exposed to light.

6 ★ During photosynthesis, light energy is converted into the energy of chemical bonds of glucose (sugar).

   ★ Chlorophyll makes light energy available for the synthesis (making) of sugar.

   ★ The region between membranes contains enzymes which convert water and carbon dioxide into sugar. The energy needed for the conversion comes from the light absorbed by chlorophyll.

Green plants as organisms

GETTING SUNLIGHT

The leaves of plants fit together in a mosaic pattern like a jigsaw.

CHECK LIST 1

GETTING THE RAW MATERIALS

Water and carbon dioxide are both abundant in the environment.

leaf stalk

pores (stomata) on the underside of the leaf through which carbon dioxide and water vapour are exchanged between the inside of the leaf and the atmosphere

Key
- water molecule
- carbon dioxide molecule
- → movement of water molecules
- → movement of carbon dioxide molecules

Track the route of water molecules and carbon dioxide molecules to the chloroplast.

Water is absorbed from the soil.

CHECK LIST 2

PHOTOSYNTHESIS IN ACTION

membrane of chloroplast

Water molecules and carbon dioxide molecules combine to form sugar. The chemical reactions produce oxygen.

carbon dioxide + water → sugar + oxygen

CHECK LIST 6

INSIDE THE CHLOROPLAST

CHLOROPLAST ×50 000

membranes covered with chlorophyll

lining of chloroplast cut away

Track the route of water molecules and carbon dioxide molecules into the chloroplast.

CHECK LIST 5

INSIDE THE CELL

PALISADE CELL ×400

cytoplasm, chloroplast, plasma membrane, nucleus, cell wall, vacuole

carbon dioxide in the air dissolves in the film of moisture on the cell's surface and diffuses into the cell

water diffuses into the cell

Track the route of water molecules and carbon dioxide molecules to the chloroplasts.

CHECK LIST 4

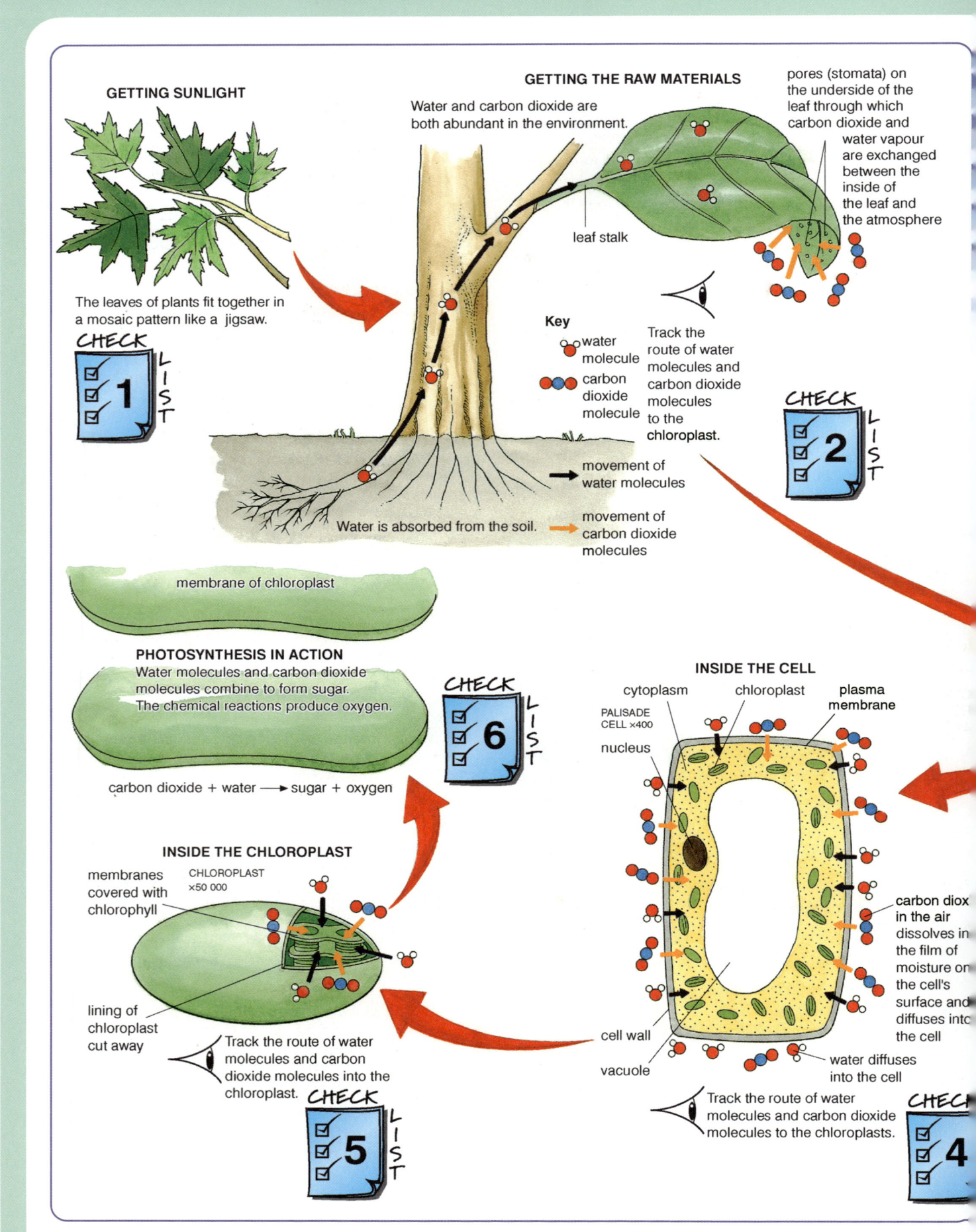

Photosynthesis (Checklist numbers refer to the checklist on page 59.)

Green plants as organisms

4.2 Transport in plants

PREVIEW

At the end of this section you will:
- know that xylem tissue transports water and that phloem tissue transports food
- understand the processes of transpiration and translocation
- know that xylem tissue and phloem tissue form vascular bundles which reach all parts of the plant.

Transport systems in plants

On pages 62–63 is the concept map for **transport in plants**, and its checklist. Study them carefully.

Remember that **stomata** are the tiny pores perforating the underside of leaves through which water vapour and carbon dioxide are exchanged between the inside of the leaf and the atmosphere. The loss of water vapour from the leaf is called **transpiration**. Most plants have a waxy layer (**cuticle**) which covers the outer surfaces of the leaf, preventing it from losing too much water. The leaves of plants growing in dry environments are often covered by a cuticle that is thicker than the cuticle covering the leaves of plants growing in wetter conditions.

Factors affecting transpiration

Think of the ways plants lose and gain water.

★ Loss of water is through transpiration.

★ Gain is through the uptake of water by the roots.

If the loss of water is greater than the gain, then the stomata close.

As a result, transpiration is reduced.

If the loss of water is still more than the gain, then the cells of the plant lose turgor and the plant **wilts**.

Remember that the turgor of the cells of a non-woody (**herbaceous**) plant helps to keep it upright.

The graphs show the effect of other factors on the rate of transpiration. Light stimulates the stomata to open wide. The rate of transpiration is therefore greater during the day than at night.

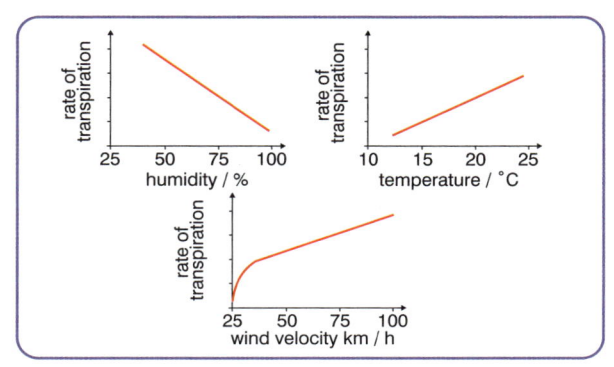

Factors affecting the rate of transpiration

INSIDE THE LEAF

SECTION THROUGH LEAF x80

- waxy cuticle
- cells of the upper leaf surface (upper epidermis)
- palisade cell
- air space
- spongy mesophyll cells
- xylem
- phloem
- stoma
- guard cell
- cells of the lower leaf surface (lower epidermis)

Track the route of water molecules and carbon dioxide molecules to the cells.

CHECKLIST 3

Green plants as organisms

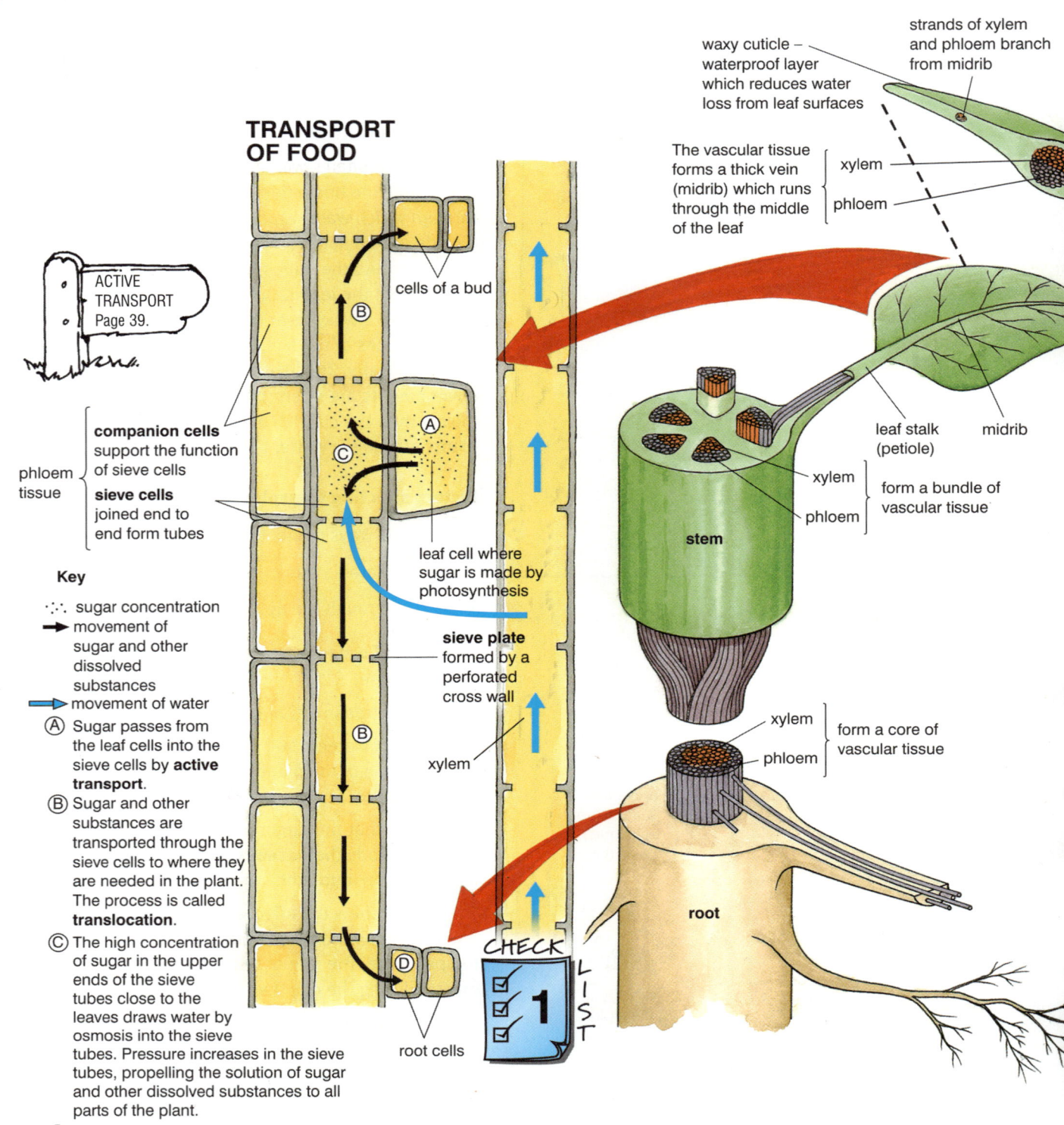

TRANSPORT OF FOOD

ACTIVE TRANSPORT Page 39.

phloem tissue {
companion cells support the function of sieve cells
sieve cells joined end to end form tubes
}

Key
- ∴ sugar concentration
- → movement of sugar and other dissolved substances
- ⇨ movement of water

(A) Sugar passes from the leaf cells into the sieve cells by **active transport**.

(B) Sugar and other substances are transported through the sieve cells to where they are needed in the plant. The process is called **translocation**.

(C) The high concentration of sugar in the upper ends of the sieve tubes close to the leaves draws water by osmosis into the sieve tubes. Pressure increases in the sieve tubes, propelling the solution of sugar and other dissolved substances to all parts of the plant.

(D) Root cells convert sugar to starch, which is stored. Sugar is also used in aerobic respiration. Therefore, the concentration of sugar in the lower ends of the sieve tubes is less than in their upper ends. Less water is drawn into them by osmosis, so the pressure within is less.

Translocation depends on the differences in the concentration of sugar in different parts of the plant and, therefore, the differences in pressure within the sieve tubes.

- cells of a bud
- leaf cell where sugar is made by photosynthesis
- **sieve plate** formed by a perforated cross wall
- xylem
- root cells

- waxy cuticle – waterproof layer which reduces water loss from leaf surfaces
- strands of xylem and phloem branch from midrib
- The vascular tissue forms a thick vein (midrib) which runs through the middle of the leaf
- xylem
- phloem
- leaf stalk (petiole)
- midrib
- xylem
- phloem
- form a bundle of vascular tissue
- stem
- xylem
- phloem
- form a core of vascular tissue
- root

Transport in plants

Green plants as organisms

TRANSPORT OF WATER

- stomata – gaps through which gases diffuse
- upper leaf surface
- xylem
- phloem
- air space
- lower leaf surface
- stoma
- guard cell

TRANSPIRATION

Xylem cells join end to end. Cross walls separating a cell from neighbouring cells are broken down. A continuous tube is formed, rather like a drinking straw.

Key
→ movement of water

Ⓐ Root hairs absorb water from the soil by **osmosis**. Mineral ions are **actively transported** into the root.
Ⓑ Water passes through the root tissue into the xylem by **osmosis**.
Ⓒ Water travels through the xylem of the root and stem in unbroken columns – the **transpiration stream**.
Ⓓ Water moves through the xylem of the leaf stalk and veins of the leaf.
Ⓔ Water evaporates into the large air spaces within the leaf. The air spaces are saturated with water vapour.
Ⓕ The concentration of water vapour in the atmosphere is lower than that in the air spaces. Water vapour therefore diffuses from the leaf through the stomata. The process is called **transpiration**.
Ⓖ Water lost by cells through evaporation is replaced with water drawn through the cells by osmosis. Cells next to the xylem draw water from the xylem by osmosis.

- root cells
- soil particles
- root hair cell

Checklist for transport in plants

1 ★ Phloem consists of *living cells*.
   ★ The concentration of sugar in the leaf is often lower than the concentration of sugar in the upper ends of the sieve tubes.
   As a result, sugar moves from the leaf into the sieve cells by **active transport**.
   ★ Osmosis draws water from the xylem and increases the pressure in the sieve tubes.
   As a result, sugar solution moves to all parts of the plant.
   ★ Pressure in the sieve tubes drops as cells use sugar or store it as starch.

2 ★ Xylem consists of *dead cells*.
   ★ The walls of xylem tubes are waterproofed with a substance called **lignin**.
   ★ As water transpires, more is drawn from the xylem in the leaf.
   As a result, water is 'sucked' upwards through the xylem of the stem.
   As a result, more water is supplied to the bottom of the xylem by the roots.
   As a result, there are unbroken moving columns of water from the roots to the leaves.

Green plants as organisms

Controlling the size of stomata

Two sausage-shaped **guard cells** surround the opening which forms the stoma. The guard cells contain chloroplasts. Think of the sequence:

★ During the day, there is an increase in the concentration of potassium ions in the guard cells. There is, therefore, a net flow of water by osmosis into the guard cells making them turgid. The guard cells bow out, opening the stoma.

★ At night, the concentration of potassium ions in the guard cells falls. There is a net outflow of water and the guard cells lose turgor. The guard cells bow in, closing the stoma.

Surviving arid conditions

Losing too much water is a constant threat to plants living in hot, dry (arid) deserts. Different features, which reduce water loss, help the plants to survive. For example, a cactus has:

- leaves that are little more than spines, reducing the area of the surfaces from which water is lost
- a thick, waxy, waterproof cuticle, which covers the plant's surfaces
- shiny surfaces that reflect heat and light
- a thick stem, which stores water
- stomata sunk in hair-fringed pits. Water vapour is trapped in the pits resulting in a humid micro-environment around the stomatal opening.

As a result, the concentration gradient of water between the tissues of the cactus and the micro-environment of the stomatal opening is reduced, reducing the rate of transpiration.

4.3 Plant responses

PREVIEW

At the end of this section you will know that:
- plants grow in response to stimuli
- there are two sorts of growth movement – nastic movements and tropic movements (tropisms)
- plant growth regulators affect the growth of plants
- auxin is an example of a plant growth regulator
- commercial applications of plant growth regulators include weed control and the production of 'seedless' fruits.

Plants move by growing in response to stimuli. One part of the plant grows faster than another. There are two types of growth movement.

★ **Nastic movements** are responses to stimuli that come from all directions. For example, flowers open and close in response to changes in temperature.

★ **Tropic movements** (tropisms) are responses to stimuli which come mainly from one direction. For example, shoots bend towards light.

How plants respond

The diagram at the bottom of page 65 and the checklist below are your revision guide to **plant responses**. Study them carefully.

Remember that plant responses are the result of growth. **Growth regulators** (sometimes called growth hormones) affect the growth of plants. **Auxin** is an example of a plant growth regulator.

Checklist for plant responses

1 ★ Tropisms are **positive** if the plant grows towards the stimulus and **negative** if it grows away.

> As a result of different positive and negative tropisms, the different parts of the plant grow in a way that increases the plant's chances of survival. For example, the roots 'find' water, leaves receive as much light as possible to enable photosynthesis to occur at a maximum rate.

64

Green plants as organisms

★ The growing tips (shoot/root) of a plant are receptors for different stimuli.

2 ★ Auxin makes the cellulose wall of plant cells more elastic.

As a result, the cells elongate rapidly.

As a result, the cells on the shady side of the shoot tip grow *more* rapidly than the cells on the brightly lit side.

As a result, the shoot tip bends towards the light.

3 ★ The effect of the growth regulator produced by the root cap is different from auxin produced by the shoot tip. It *slows down* growth in the underside of the root tip.

As a result, the root bends down and grows into the soil.

Fact file

Plant growth regulators used to be called plant hormones or plant growth substances. You may come across these terms in other books. In this book, the more up-to-date term is used.

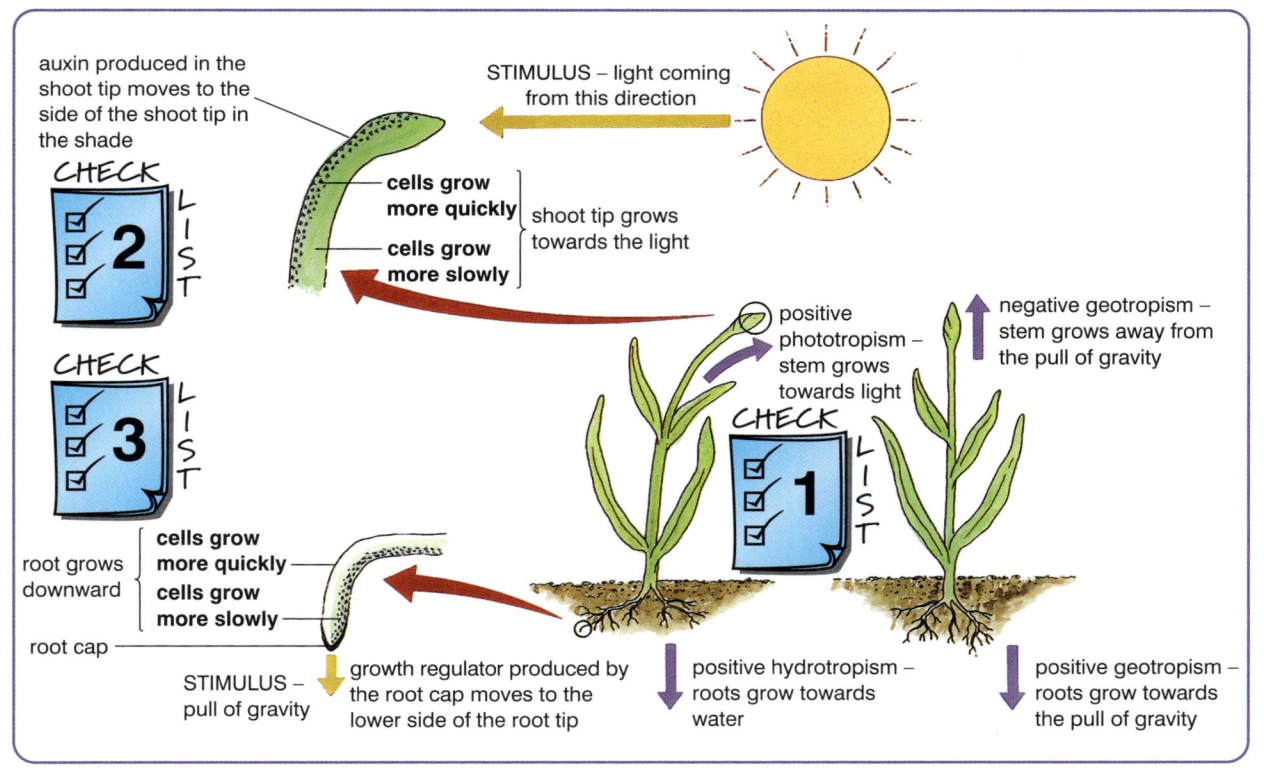

Fact file

★ The stems of some types of plant respond to the touch of an object by growing in a spiral around the object. The response is called **thigmotropism**. Sweet peas and runner beans show thigmotropism. They spiral round wooden canes stuck into the ground to support them.

★ Does it matter which way up a seed is planted? Positive phototropism means that the shoot will always grow upwards. Positive geotropism means that the roots will always grow downwards. So, no matter which way up a seed is, its shoot and roots will always grow in the right direction.

★ Auxin sometimes prevents growth. It diffuses down the stem and prevents the growth of side shoots. Lopping the top off a plant removes the source of auxin and side branches then develop. This is why a gardener trims a hedge to make it more bushy.

Tropisms – the response of the shoot tip to light and of the root cap to gravity and water (Checklist numbers refer to the checklist on pages 64–65.)

Green plants as organisms

The shoot tip

The table below shows the sorts of experiments carried out by scientists investigating the response of plants to light. These experiments suggest that there is a growth regulator (auxin) which:
- is produced in the shoot tip
- diffuses to the region behind the shoot tip
- stimulates growth so that the shoot bends towards light.

Using plant hormones

★ **Ripening** – fruit is quickly ripened in sheds in an atmosphere which contains one part of **ethene** per million parts of air.

★ **Weedkillers** – 2,4-D (2,4-dichlorophenoxyethanoic acid) is a synthetic auxin which kills plants by making them grow too fast. Broad-leaved weed plants like docks, daisies and dandelions are more sensitive to 2,4-D than narrow-leaved crop plants like wheat and barley.

★ **Seedless fruit** – an auxin paste smeared over the carpels (female sex organs) of some crop species produces fruit without fertilisation. Seedless cucumbers and seedless tomatoes are produced in this way.

★ **Rooting** – gardeners use 'rooting powder' which contains auxin that encourages roots to sprout from stem cuttings. The method allows large numbers of identical plants to be grown quickly.

symbol	treatment	response to light	conclusion
	Uncovered intact barley seedling	✔	control, which shows that the shoot tip is sensitive to light
	Uncovered barley seedling with its shoot tip removed	✘	shows that the shoot tip contains a substance which controls the response of the shoot to light
	Intact barley seedling covered with aluminium foil which excludes light	✘	shows that the shoot tip is sensitive to light
	Barley seedling with its tip cut off. The tip is placed on a slip of metal foil and replaced on the rest of the shoot. The metal slip prevents diffusion of chemicals from the shoot tip to the rest of the shoot.	✘	shows that a substance produced in the shoot tip diffuses to the region behind the shoot tip, where it controls the shoot's response to light
	Barley seedling with its tip removed. The tip is placed on an agar block and replaced on the rest of the shoot.	✔	The agar block allows diffusion of a substance produced in the shoot tip to the region behind the shoot tip. Result confirms conclusion from the experiment with a slip of metal foil above.
	Barley seedling with its tip removed. An agar block is placed on the rest of the shoot after it has been soaked in a mash made of the shoot tip.	✔	shows that a substance produced in the shoot tip controls the response of the shoot to the light
	Barley seedling with its tip removed. An agar block is placed on the rest of the shoot after it has been soaked in a solution of auxin.	✔	shows that the substance produced in the shoot tip which controls the response of the shoot to light is auxin
	Barley seedling with its tip removed. An agar block is placed on the remaining part of the shoot.	✘	control for the experiment which shows that auxin, not agar, controls the response of the shoot to light

Response of the shoot tip to light

Green plants as organisms

ROUND UP

How much have you improved? Work out your improvement index on pages 157–8.

1. Name the different cells in the leaf that contain chloroplasts. [3]

2. Briefly explain why most chloroplasts are found in palisade cells lying just beneath the upper surface of the leaf. [4]

3. List the major factors which limit the rate of photosynthesis. Briefly explain how a greenhouse overcomes the effect of limiting factors on the growth of plants. [8]

4. Complete the following paragraph using the words below. Each word may be used once, more than once or not at all.

   **xylem   transport   sugar   translocation
   transpiration   phloem   pressure
   active transport   water**

   Leaves produce _____ by photosynthesis. The concentration of _____ in leaf cells is often less than that in nearby _____ tissue. _____ therefore moves from the leaf cell into the _____ by _____. Osmosis draws _____ into the _____ tissue increasing _____ which helps transport sugar. The transport of sugar is called _____. Storage of _____ in the root cells reduces _____ in the _____. [13]

5. Describe the probable weather on a day when the transpiration rate of a plant is at a maximum. [4]

6. Briefly explain what happens if a plant loses more water through transpiration than it gains through absorption of water by its roots. [3]

7. Compare the characteristics of xylem tissue with those of phloem tissue. List the comparisons in two columns headed 'xylem' and 'phloem' respectively. [5]

8. Complete the following paragraph using the words below. Each word may be used once, more than once or not at all.

   **weedkiller   ripens   growth regulator
   unfertilised   tip   seedless   slowly**

   Auxin is a _____ produced in the _____ of the shoot. Synthetic auxin is used as a _____ to kill unwanted plants. Auxin paste applied to the _____ carpels of some crop species produces _____ fruits. Fruit stored in an atmosphere containing ethene _____ more quickly. [6]

9. The diagram shows an experiment on the shoots of growing seedlings. In experiment A a thin piece of metal was placed between the tip of the shoot and the rest of the stem. In experiment B a thin piece of metal was placed further down, separating the shoot into an upper part and a lower part.

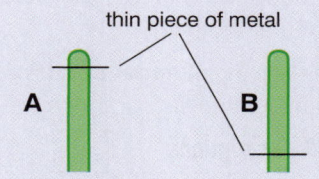

   The growing seedlings were placed in a box which was light-tight except for a slit on one side. The seedlings were illuminated for three days.

   a) What hypothesis was the scientist trying to test? [2]

   b) In each case, what do you think the response of the seedling will be to the light source? (Assume the seedlings survived the treatment for the time of the experiment.) [2]

   Explain your answer. [4]

Well done if you've improved. Don't worry if you haven't. Take a break and try again.

Chapter 5 Humans (and other animals) as organisms

How much do you already know? Work out your score on page 158.

Test yourself

1 The nutrients in food are listed below. Match the nutrients to the following questions.

carbohydrates   fats   proteins   vitamins   minerals

   a) Which nutrients give food its energy content? [3]
   b) Which nutrient is a source of energy, but is more important for the growth and repair of the body? [1]
   c) Which nutrient releases the most energy per gram? [1]
   d) Which nutrients are needed only in small amounts, but play an important role in the control of metabolism? [2]

2 Match each term in column **A** with its correct description in column **B**.

A terms	B descriptions
ingestion	the removal of undigested food through the anus
digestion	digested food passes into the body
absorption	food is taken into the mouth
egestion	food is broken down

[4]

3 Explain the differences between
   a) bronchi and bronchioles [2]
   b) lungs and alveoli [2]
   c) aerobic respiration and anaerobic respiration [4]
   d) breathing and gaseous exchange. [3]

4 Explain how the heart functions as a double pump. [4]

5 The different components of blood are listed in column **A**. Match each component with its correct description in column **B**.

A components	B descriptions
plasma	contain haemoglobin
red blood cells	promote the formation of blood clots
white blood cells	contains dissolved food substances
platelets	produce antibodies

[4]

6 The components of the reflex arc are listed as follows: sensory neurone, effector, relay neurone, receptor, motor neurone. Write the components in their correct order. [4]

7 What is the function of each of these parts of the ear?
   a) the eardrum   b) the bones of the middle ear
   c) the pinna   d) the hair cells [8]

8 What are hormones and how are they transported around the body? [2]

9 Distinguish between the roles of the hormones insulin and glucagon in keeping the blood glucose level steady. [2]

10 The structures of the kidney tubule and its blood supply are listed below. Rewrite them in the order in which a molecule of urea passes from the renal artery to the outside of the body.

tubule   urethra   bladder   glomerulus   Bowman's capsule   ureter   collecting duct [7]

11 How are the teeth of a dog adapted for grasping and cutting food? [4]

12 The mussel is a bivalve (two shells) mollusc. Briefly explain how a mussel filters food from the water in which it lives. [6]

13 Match the different types of skeleton in column **A** with their correct description in column **B**.

A skeletons	B descriptions
endoskeleton	the skeleton is a body space filled with fluid
exoskeleton	the skeleton lies inside the body
hydrostatic skeleton	the skeleton surrounds the body

[3]

Humans (and other animals) as organisms

5.1 Food and diet

PREVIEW

At the end of this section you will:
- understand that different foods contain different amounts of energy
- be able to identify the components of a diet
- know the role of different foods in the body.

Nutrients in food

The **nutrients** in food are **carbohydrates**, **fats** and **oils** (lipids), **proteins**, **vitamins** and **minerals**. **Water** and **fibre** are not thought of as nutrients but are also components of food. Different foods contain nutrients, water and fibre in different proportions. Our **diet** is the food and drink we take in. Remember the sequence:

nutrient + water + fibre $\xrightarrow{\text{components of}}$ food $\xrightarrow{\text{eaten}}$ diet

All living things (including us) need food and the nutrients it contains.

★ Carbohydrates and lipids are sources of **energy** which powers life's activities
★ Protein is a source of materials for the **growth** and **repair** of bodies
★ Vitamins and minerals are substances which control the **metabolism** of cells.

Checklist for food and diet

1 ★ The **energy value** of food is measured using an instrument called a **bomb calorimeter**, shown below.

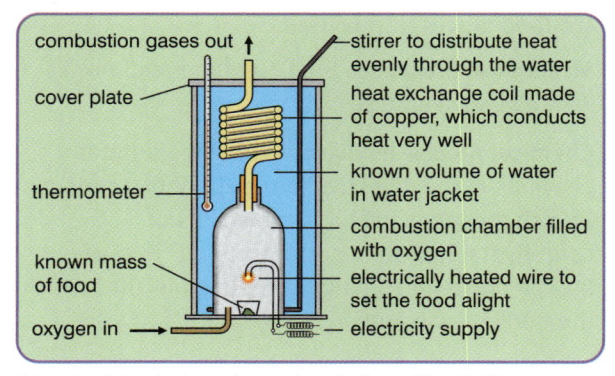

A bomb calorimeter is made to reduce the loss of heat to the surroundings and maximise the transfer of heat from the burning food to the water in the water jacket. In this way the accuracy of the data on the energy values of foods burnt in the calorimeter is improved.

The burning food heats the surrounding water. The change in temperature of the water is used to work out the energy value of the food:

$$\frac{\text{energy released}}{\text{per gram}} = \frac{\text{volume of water in water jacket} \times \text{temperature rise} \times 4.2}{\text{mass of food}}$$

★ The energy released from food depends on the nutrients it contains.
- 17.2 kJ/g for carbohydrate
- 22.2 kJ/g for protein
- 38.5 kJ/g for fat

Although protein can be a source of energy, its most important use in the body is for growth and repair.

★ People have different energy requirements depending on their:
- **age** – on average young people have greater energy requirements than older people
- **gender** – pregnancy and lactation (milk production) increase the energy requirements of women
- **activities** – any kind of activity increases a person's energy requirements.

★ The rate at which the body uses energy is called the **metabolic rate**. It is lowest (called the **basal metabolic rate**) when the body is at rest.

★ If a person eats more food than is necessary for his/her energy needs, the excess is turned into fat.
As a result, the person puts on weight.

★ To lose weight, a person can:
- take more exercise, which increases energy output
- eat less high-energy food, decreasing energy input.

2 ★ **Additives** are put into food to:
- make it tastier
- make it more attractive
- improve its texture
- prevent it from spoiling.

★ Some additives can make some people unwell.

3 ★ A **balanced diet** is a mixture of foods which together provide sufficient nutrients for healthy living.

★ The 'basic four' food groups help us choose a balanced diet. Careful selection of items provides a balanced diet for vegetarians.

Humans (and other animals) as organisms

4 ★ The amount of **alcohol** people consume is measured in units, as shown below.

unit of alcohol	one measure of whisky	one glass of sherry	one glass of table wine	half a pint of beer or lager
1	=	=	=	=

Units of alcohol

★ How much alcohol is too much? It depends on a person's age, size, gender (male or female) and metabolic rate.

5 ★ Vitamin A gives resistance to disease and helps you to see in the dark. Deficiency of vitamin A increases the risk of infections. Vision is poor in dim light.

★ Vitamin C helps cells to join together. It also controls the use of calcium by bones and teeth. Deficiency of vitamin C results in scurvy (bleeding gums and internal organs).

★ Vitamin D helps the body to absorb calcium. Deficiency of vitamin D results in rickets (soft bones in children and brittle bones in adults).

★ Iron is needed to make haemoglobin (the pigment in red blood cells that absorbs oxygen). Deficiency of iron is a common cause of anaemia.

★ Calcium is needed to make bones and teeth. It also helps blood to clot. Deficiency of calcium results in rickets (soft bones).

5.2 The digestive system

PREVIEW

At the end of this section you will:

- know that the digestive system is a muscular tube through which food moves and into which juices produced by the liver and pancreas flow
- understand that as food moves through the digestive system it is processed (digested) into substances which the cells of the body can absorb and use
- be able to identify enzymes responsible for digesting food
- know that digestive systems are adapted to type of diet.

Testing your understanding

The terms:

gut
intestine   all refer to the digestive system.
alimentary canal

Digesting food

Food is processed through the digestive system in the following sequence:

ingestion
food is taken into the mouth

↓

digestion
large insoluble molecules of food are broken down into smaller soluble molecules

↓

absorption → **assimilation** follows the absorption of digested food. It describes the processes in cells that convert digested food materials into living matter.
the small molecules of digested food pass into the body

↓

egestion
undigested food is removed from the body through the anus

The digestive system is a muscular tube through which food moves. It processes food.

★ **Mechanical processes** break up food and mix it with digestive juices.

★ **Chemical processes** digest food using different enzymes in the digestive juices. The body cannot absorb the large insoluble molecules of carbohydrate, protein and fat in food. They are broken down into smaller soluble molecules which the body can absorb.

Humans (and other animals) as organisms

On pages 72–73 is the concept map for **the digestive system**. The **liver** and **pancreas** are connected by ducts to the digestive system. They play an important role in the digestion of food. The numbers on the concept map refer to the checklist below.

Checklist for the digestive system

(M) = mechanical processes of digestion

(C) = chemical processes of digestion

1. ★ **(M) Teeth** chew food, breaking it into small pieces.

    As a result, the surface area of food exposed to the action of digestive enzymes is increased.

    As a result, food is digested more quickly.

2. ★ **(C) Saliva**, produced by the salivary glands, contains the enzyme **amylase**.

    As a result, the digestion of starch begins in the mouth.

    ★ **(M)** Saliva moistens the food.

    As a result, the food is made slippery for easy swallowing.

3. ★ **(M)** Muscles of the **stomach** wall and **small intestine** mix food thoroughly with different juices containing digestive enzymes.

    As a result, a liquid paste called **chyme** is formed.

    As a result, food and digestive enzymes are brought into intimate contact.

    ★ **(C)** Gastric juice, produced by **pits** in the stomach wall, contains **hydrochloric acid** and the enzymes **pepsin** and **renin**.

    Hydrochloric acid:
    - increases the acidity of the stomach contents.

    As a result, bacteria in the food are killed.

    As a result, the action of salivary amylase is stopped.

    Pepsin:
    - begins the digestion of protein.

    Renin:
    - clots milk, making it semi-solid.

    As a result, milk stays in the gut long enough to be digested.

4. ★ **(C) Bile**, produced by the **liver**, is a green alkaline liquid which is stored in the gall bladder before release into the small intestine through the bile duct. It:
    - neutralises acid from the stomach
    - breaks fats and oils into small droplets (**emulsification**).

    As a result, the surface area of fats and oils exposed to the action of the enzyme **lipase** is increased.

    As a result, fats and oils are digested more quickly.

5. ★ **(C) Pancreatic juice**, produced by the **pancreas**, is released into the small intestine through the pancreatic duct. It contains:
    - **sodium carbonate** which neutralises stomach acid
    - **carbohydrases**, **proteases** and **lipases** which digest carbohydrate, protein, fats and oils.

6. ★ **(C) Intestinal juice**, produced by glands in the wall of the **duodenum** and **ileum**, contains:
    - **carbohydrases** and **lipases** that complete the digestion of carbohydrates and fats and oils.

Chemistry of digestion

Digestive enzymes catalyse the breakdown of food by **hydrolysis**. Water splits large insoluble molecules of food into smaller soluble molecules which are suitable for absorption into the body. The table on page 74 summarises the process.

Humans (and other animals) as organisms

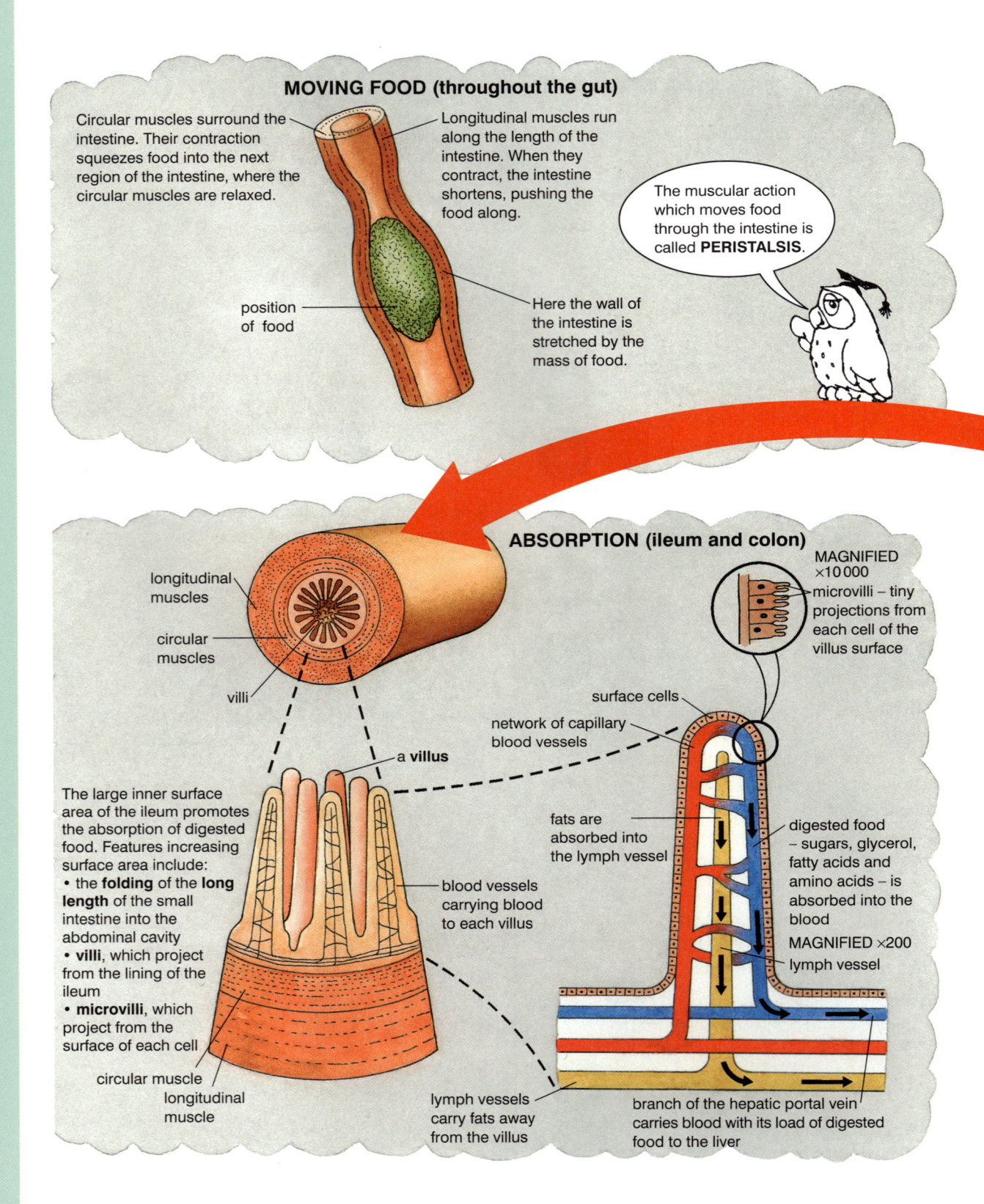

MOVING FOOD (throughout the gut)

Circular muscles surround the intestine. Their contraction squeezes food into the next region of the intestine, where the circular muscles are relaxed.

Longitudinal muscles run along the length of the intestine. When they contract, the intestine shortens, pushing the food along.

position of food

Here the wall of the intestine is stretched by the mass of food.

*The muscular action which moves food through the intestine is called **PERISTALSIS**.*

ABSORPTION (ileum and colon)

- longitudinal muscles
- circular muscles
- villi

MAGNIFIED ×10 000
microvilli – tiny projections from each cell of the villus surface

surface cells
network of capillary blood vessels

a **villus**

The large inner surface area of the ileum promotes the absorption of digested food. Features increasing surface area include:
- the **folding** of the **long length** of the small intestine into the abdominal cavity
- **villi**, which project from the lining of the ileum
- **microvilli**, which project from the surface of each cell

circular muscle
longitudinal muscle

blood vessels carrying blood to each villus

fats are absorbed into the lymph vessel

digested food – sugars, glycerol, fatty acids and amino acids – is absorbed into the blood
MAGNIFIED ×200
lymph vessel

lymph vessels carry fats away from the villus

branch of the hepatic portal vein carries blood with its load of digested food to the liver

The digestive system – its structure and functions (Checklist numbers refer to the checklist on page 71.)

72

Humans (and other animals) as organisms

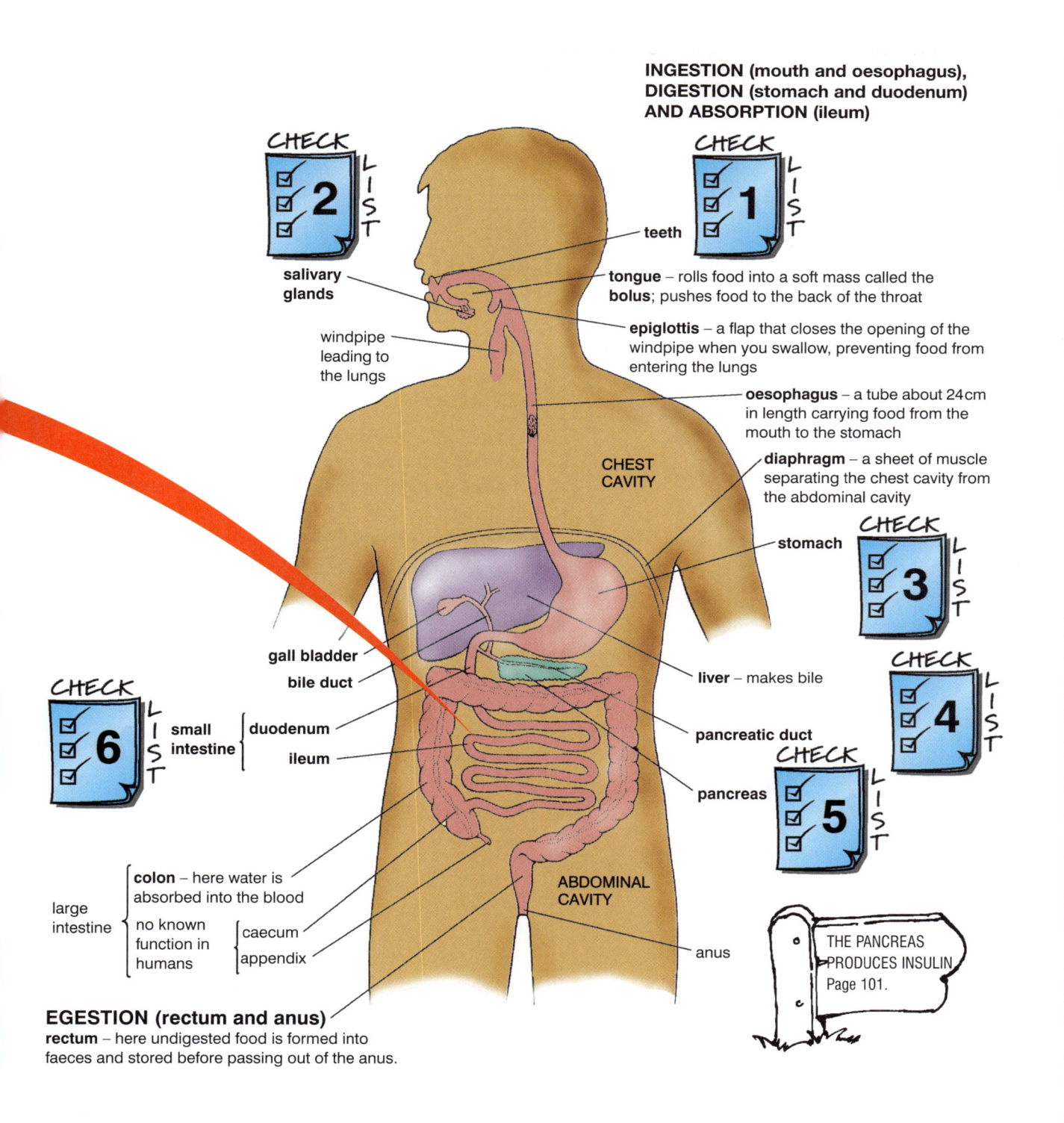

INGESTION (mouth and oesophagus), **DIGESTION** (stomach and duodenum) **AND ABSORPTION** (ileum)

CHECK LIST 1

CHECK LIST 2

- **teeth**
- **tongue** – rolls food into a soft mass called the **bolus**; pushes food to the back of the throat
- **epiglottis** – a flap that closes the opening of the windpipe when you swallow, preventing food from entering the lungs
- **salivary glands**
- **windpipe** leading to the lungs
- **oesophagus** – a tube about 24cm in length carrying food from the mouth to the stomach
- **diaphragm** – a sheet of muscle separating the chest cavity from the abdominal cavity

CHEST CAVITY

CHECK LIST 3

- **stomach**
- **liver** – makes bile
- **gall bladder**
- **bile duct**
- **pancreatic duct**
- **pancreas**

CHECK LIST 4

CHECK LIST 5

CHECK LIST 6

- small intestine { **duodenum**, **ileum** }
- large intestine {
  - **colon** – here water is absorbed into the blood
  - no known function in humans { **caecum**, **appendix** }
}

ABDOMINAL CAVITY

- **anus**

THE PANCREAS PRODUCES INSULIN Page 101.

EGESTION (rectum and anus)
rectum – here undigested food is formed into faeces and stored before passing out of the anus.

Humans (and other animals) as organisms

enzyme group	example	where found	food component	after digestion
carbohydrases (catalyse the digestion of carbohydrates)	amylase	mouth	starch	maltose
	maltase	small intestine	maltose	glucose
proteases (catalyse the digestion of proteins)	pepsin	stomach	protein	polypeptides
	chymotrypsin dipeptidase	small intestine	polypeptides dipeptides	dipeptides amino acids
lipases (catalyse the digestion of fats and oils)	lipase	small intestine	fats and oils	fatty acids + glycerol

Enzymes that digest carbohydrates, proteins and fats and oils

What happens to digested food?

VEINS Page 87.
LYMPH VESSELS Page 88.

Digested food is carried away from the ileum in the blood within the hepatic portal vein and in the fluid of the lymph vessels.

★ Blood transports water, sugars, fatty acids, glycerol and amino acids to the liver.

★ Lymph transports fats, oils and fat-soluble vitamins to a vein in the neck where the substances enter the bloodstream.

The **liver** plays a major role in the metabolism of food substances after they have been absorbed into the body.

★ Glucose may be converted to **glycogen** and stored in the liver. Glycogen may be hydrolysed to glucose and released back into the blood in response to the body's needs.

★ Iron, obtained from destroyed red blood cells, is stored in the liver.

★ Amino acids in excess of the body's needs are broken down (a process called **deamination**) in the liver. Urea is formed and excreted in urine.

★ Amino acids are converted from one type into another in the liver (a process called **transamination**) according to the body's needs.

Digestive system and diet

Remember that:
- omnivores eat both plants and meat
- herbivores eat plants
- carnivores eat meat.

Most humans are omnivores, and the human digestive system is adapted to deal with a mixture of plant and animal foods. Rabbits and cattle are herbivorous, with digestive systems adapted to deal with plant food; cats are carnivorous with a digestive system adapted to deal with meat.

FOOD CHAINS AND WEBS Pages 15–17.

Humans (and other animals) as organisms

Fact file

Most animals do not produce enzymes (called cellulases) to digest the cellulose in the walls of plant cells. Different species of bacteria and protists do produce cellulases.

Cattle have a large stomach in four parts. The **rumen** and **reticulum** receive the food first. The rumen contains microorganisms which produce cellulases that digest the cellulose in the plant material. Here the food forms into balls of **cud** which return to the mouth where they are thoroughly re-chewed before being re-swallowed. Animals that chew cud are called **ruminants**. The **omasum** and **abomasum** receive the cud and protein digestion then takes place.

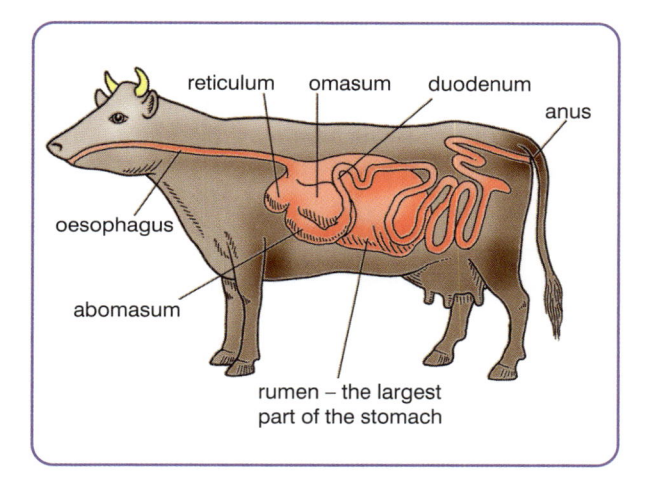

Rabbits do not chew cud. Instead they eat the pellets of faeces produced from the food's first journey through the gut.

★ Pellets are soft and contain a lot of undigested food.

As a result, microorganisms which live in the **appendix** have another chance of dealing with the food second time through. Faecal pellets produced after the food's second journey through are hard.

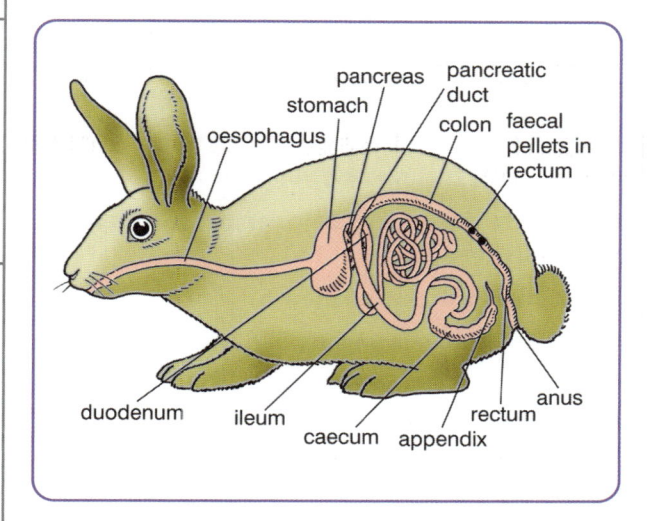

Cats do not chew their food. Having caught it, they swallow it whole or in large chunks. The stomach is large so that it can store the meal while it is digested bit by bit.

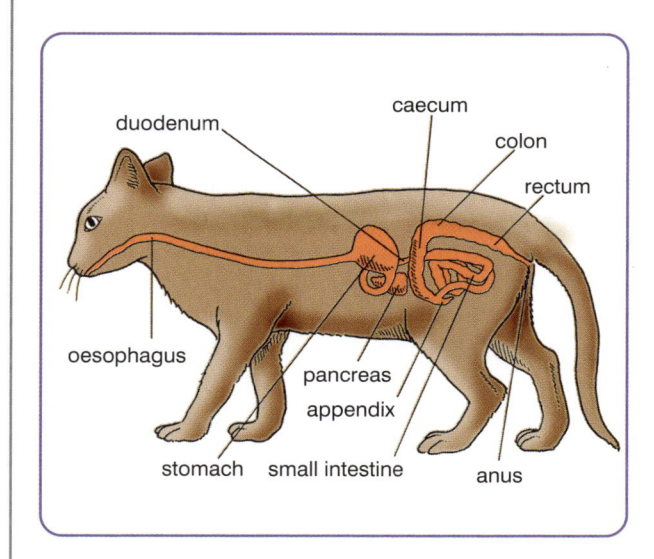

75

Humans (and other animals) as organisms

5.3 Obtaining food

> **PREVIEW**
>
> At the end of this section you will:
> - be able to distinguish between filter feeders and fluid feeders
> - know the structure of a tooth
> - understand the arrangement of teeth in the mouth
> - be able to identify adaptations of the skull and teeth to different diets.

When animals take in (**ingest**) food, we say that they are **feeding**. Different animals have different structures for feeding.

Filter feeders

Animals that feed by straining food from the water in which they live are called **filter feeders**. Bivalve (two-shelled) molluscs and whales are examples of filter feeders.

Mussels are bivalve molluscs. They live in shallow water near the sea-shore. The mussel attaches itself to rocks and stones by a muscular **foot**. Two shells close round the animal. The diagram at the top of the next column shows the shells prized open and the arrangement of body parts within. The **gills** are covered with beating cilia which draw a current of water containing microscopic organisms between the shells. The mussel filters the microscopic organisms from the water by trapping them in mucus that covers the mantle and gills. The mucus and entrapped food are then drawn into the mouth.

CILIA Page 40.

Krill (greatly magnified)

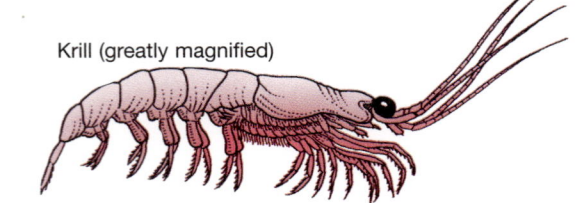

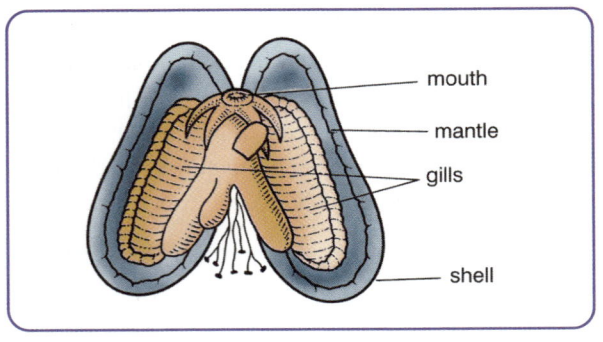

Inside a mussel

Baleen whales like the blue whale feed on the minute protists that form the dense plankton layer at the ocean's surface.

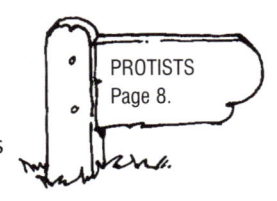

PROTISTS Page 8.

The blue whale also feeds on huge quantities of tiny shrimps called **krill**, filtered from the water. The diagram below shows how the water is strained through a series of horny plates (called **baleen**) that grow down from the sides of the upper jaw. The shrimps are caught in the bristles of the baleen plates and then swallowed.

The mouth opens, drawing food organisms into the mouth cavity in a large volume of water.

The mouth closes, the tongue is raised and water is sieved through the spaces between the baleen plates. Food organisms are caught on the bristles of the baleen plates and then swallowed

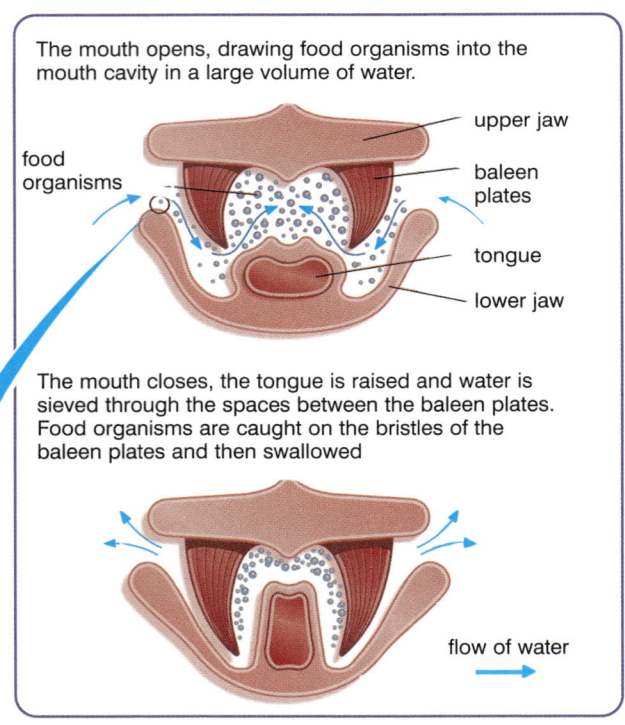

Cross-section through the head of a baleen whale

Humans (and other animals) as organisms

Fluid feeders

Insects feed on the fluids of animals or plants in different ways. They may:
- suck fluids directly
- pierce tissues and then suck the fluids in them
- suck food which is first liquefied by enzymes in the insect's saliva.

The diagram on page 78 shows examples of the categories of insect fluid feeders.

Teeth

Teeth are the feeding structures of most vertebrates except birds.

The diagram below shows the internal structure of a human tooth.

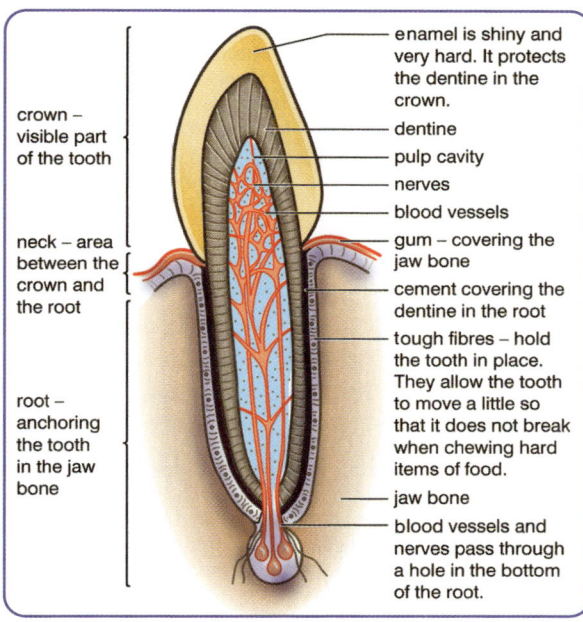

Structure of a human tooth

Labels:
- crown – visible part of the tooth
- neck – area between the crown and the root
- root – anchoring the tooth in the jaw bone
- enamel is shiny and very hard. It protects the dentine in the crown.
- dentine
- pulp cavity
- nerves
- blood vessels
- gum – covering the jaw bone
- cement covering the dentine in the root
- tough fibres – hold the tooth in place. They allow the tooth to move a little so that it does not break when chewing hard items of food.
- jaw bone
- blood vessels and nerves pass through a hole in the bottom of the root.

Types of teeth

Mammals deal with food in different ways, and their teeth are adapted accordingly.

★ **Incisors** are chisel shaped for biting and cutting food.

★ **Canines** are pointed for piercing, slashing and tearing food.

★ **Premolars** and **molars** are large, with broad surfaces made uneven by bumps called **cusps**, for crushing and grinding food.

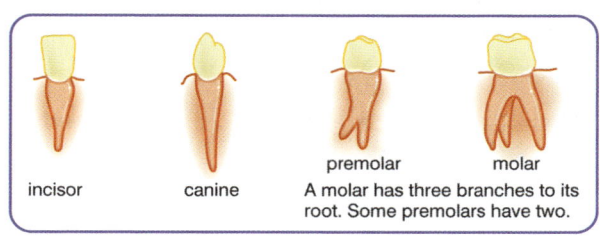

incisor   canine   premolar   molar

A molar has three branches to its root. Some premolars have two.

The four basic types of human teeth

The word **dentition** is used to describe the number and arrangement of teeth in an animal. Tooth enamel is the hardest substance in the body. It consists of calcium salts bound together by the protein **keratin**.

Humans (and other animals) as organisms

Aphids pierce plant tissues and suck the fluids in them. The aphid inserts its hollow needle-like mouthparts (stylets) through the surface of a plant stem into a sieve tube (see page 64). Sap, under pressure in the sieve tubes, is forced through the mouthparts and into the aphid gut.

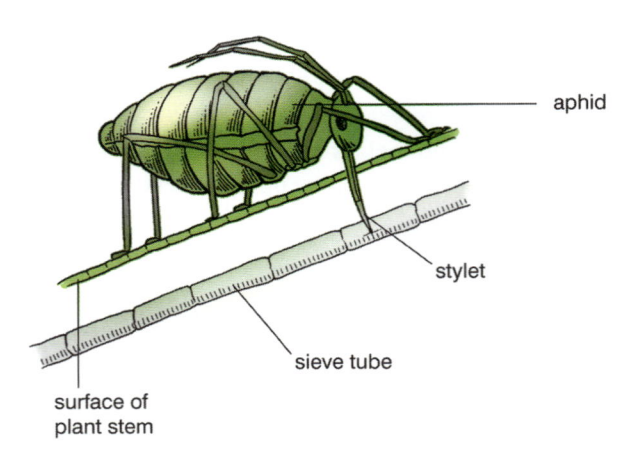

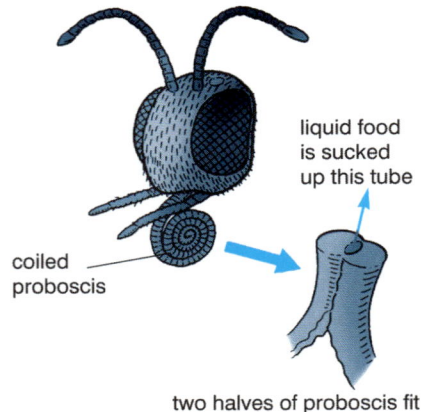

Butterflies suck nectar from flowers. The mouthparts are in the form of a long **proboscis**. Grooves along each half of the proboscis fit together to make a tube. The tip of the proboscis is placed in the nectar which is sucked up the tube like water up a drinking straw. When the proboscis is not in use, it is coiled up like a clock spring.

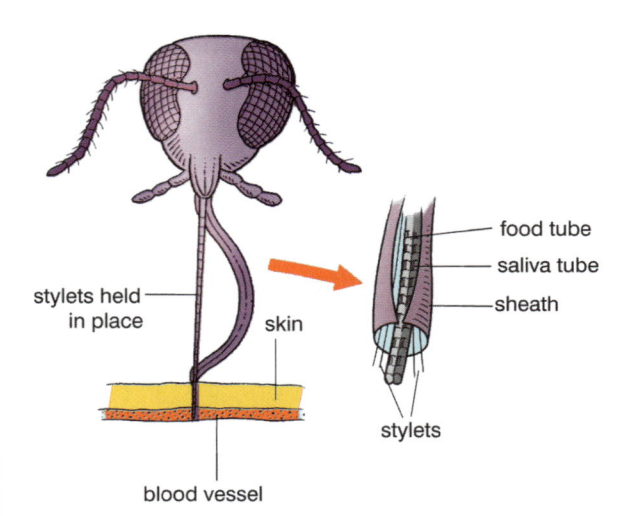

Houseflies first liquefy food externally and then suck it up. The mouthparts of the housefly form a proboscis which has a two-lobed pad at its tip. In the pad are many thin tubes. During feeding, saliva is pumped down these tubes onto the food. Enzymes in saliva liquefy the food. The liquid food is then sucked up the tubes and into the mouth.

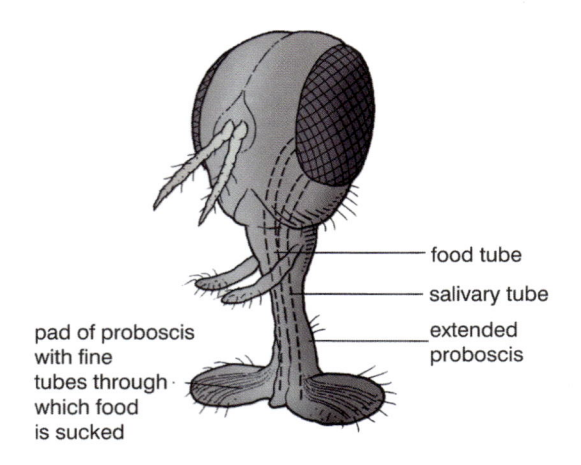

Mosquitoes pierce animal tissues and suck the fluids in them. Female mosquitoes feed on blood. Their mouthparts are long and sharply pointed, forming stylets surrounded by a sheath-like structure. Inside are a food tube and a tube through which saliva passes. The stylets pierce the victim's skin until a blood vessel is reached. The food tube is then pushed in and saliva pumped down through the salivary tube into the wound. Chemicals in the saliva stop the blood clotting as it is sucked up into the mouth.

Insect fluid feeders

Humans (and other animals) as organisms

Omnivore dentition

Humans and other omnivores have all four basic types of teeth. The dentition is described in a **dental formula** using the letters shown here.

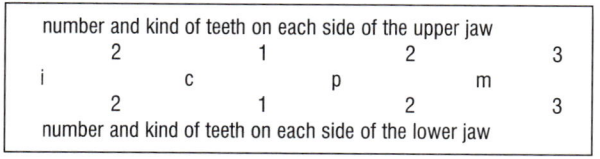

number and kind of teeth on each side of the upper jaw							
	2		1		2		3
i		c		p		m	
	2		1		2		3
number and kind of teeth on each side of the lower jaw							

Human dental formula

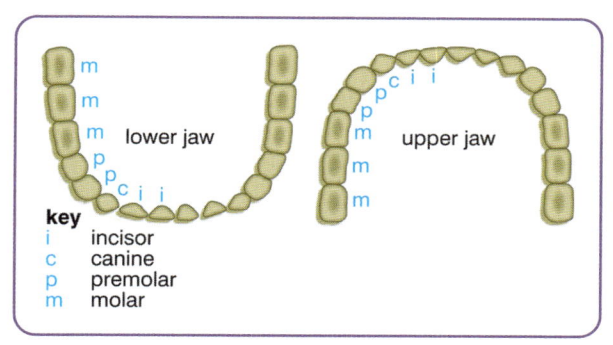

key
i   incisor
c   canine
p   premolar
m   molar

The arrangement of teeth in the adult human jaw

There are 32 teeth in total in the adult human jaw. In children there are 24 teeth, 20 of which have been gradually replaced by the permanent teeth by the age of about twelve. The teeth in children are called **milk teeth**. The third molars of the permanent teeth are called the **wisdom teeth** and do not appear until the age of about 20.

Herbivore dentition

The dentition of sheep and cattle is adapted to:
- sweep grass into the mouth with the tongue poking through the **diastema** (gap between the canines and premolars)
- cut off the grass by the lower incisors nipping against the pad in the upper jaw
- grind the grass between the ridged, broad surfaces of the premolars and molars. The joint of the jaw moves from side to side as well as up and down which makes grinding food easier.

number and kind of teeth on each side of the upper jaw							
	0		0		3		3
i		c		p		m	
	3		1		3		3
number and kind of teeth on each side of the lower jaw							

Sheep dental formula

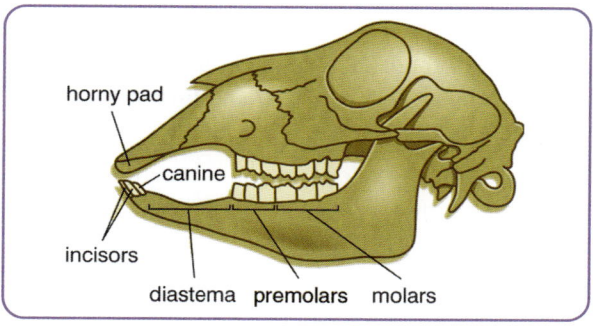

The arrangement of teeth in the jaws of a sheep. Notice that there are no canines in the upper jaw, and the canines in the lower jaw look like incisors.

Carnivore dentition

The dental formula of dogs suggests that their dentition is adapted to:
- catch, hold and tear struggling prey with long, well developed canines
- cut through flesh and bone with incisors, premolars and molars.

Powerful jaw muscles ensure a firm grip and bite. The jaw joint only allows up-and-down movements.

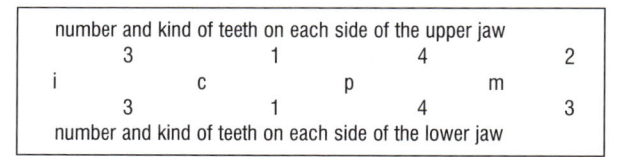

number and kind of teeth on each side of the upper jaw							
	3		1		4		2
i		c		p		m	
	3		1		4		3
number and kind of teeth on each side of the lower jaw							

Dog dental formula

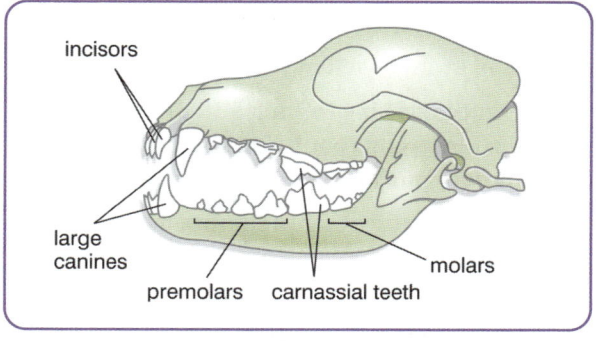

The arrangement of teeth in the jaws of a dog. Notice that the last premolar on each side of the upper jaw and the first molar on each side of the lower jaw are fused to form the large **carnassial teeth**. They work like scissors, cutting through flesh and bone.

Humans (and other animals) as organisms

Looking after your teeth

Sugary food is especially bad for your teeth. It encourages bacteria to multiply and form **plaque** on the surfaces of the teeth.

★ The bacteria break down sugar in the mouth and acids are formed.

★ The acids soften the enamel which begins the process of decay (called **caries**).

★ The decay penetrates the layer of dentine, eventually reaching the pulp cavity.

The result is the agony of toothache. The pain is caused by nerves in the pulp cavity responding when decay penetrates the tooth.

Owl's routine for helping to prevent tooth decay

★ *Reduce* the amount of sugary food in your diet.

★ *Clean* your teeth regularly with a toothbrush – at least after breakfast and last thing at night.

★ *Floss* between your teeth where the toothbrush cannot reach.

★ *Visit* the dentist for a check-up every six months.

5.4 Breathing, gaseous exchange and respiration

> **PREVIEW**
>
> At the end of this section you will:
>
> - know that breathing in (inhalation) draws air into the lungs and that breathing out (exhalation) pushes air out from the lungs
> - be able to describe how breathing movements take place
> - know that the exchange of gases (oxygen and carbon dioxide) happens in the lungs, between the gases in the air sacs (alveoli) and the blood of the vessels supplying blood to the alveoli
> - understand that the blood transports oxygen to cells which use it for aerobic respiration
> - be able to distinguish between aerobic respiration and anaerobic respiration.

Respiration

Remember the distinction between respiration and gaseous exchange. Oxygen is used by cells to oxidise digested food substances (glucose) to release energy. The process is called **aerobic respiration**. The energy released from the oxidation of glucose powers the activities which define the characteristics of life. The table shows that there is less oxygen in exhaled air than in inhaled air. This is because some of the oxygen is used by cells for aerobic respiration. There is more carbon dioxide in exhaled air than in inhaled air because carbon dioxide is produced by the chemical reactions of aerobic respiration.

gas	amount in inhaled air / %	amount in exhaled air / %
nitrogen	78	78
oxygen	21	16
noble gases	1	1
carbon dioxide	0.035	4
water vapour	0	1

Differences between inhaled and exhaled air

★ How does oxygen reach cells?

★ How does carbon dioxide leave cells?

The answer is by gaseous exchange.

The diagram opposite shows the links between breathing air, gaseous exchange and aerobic respiration.

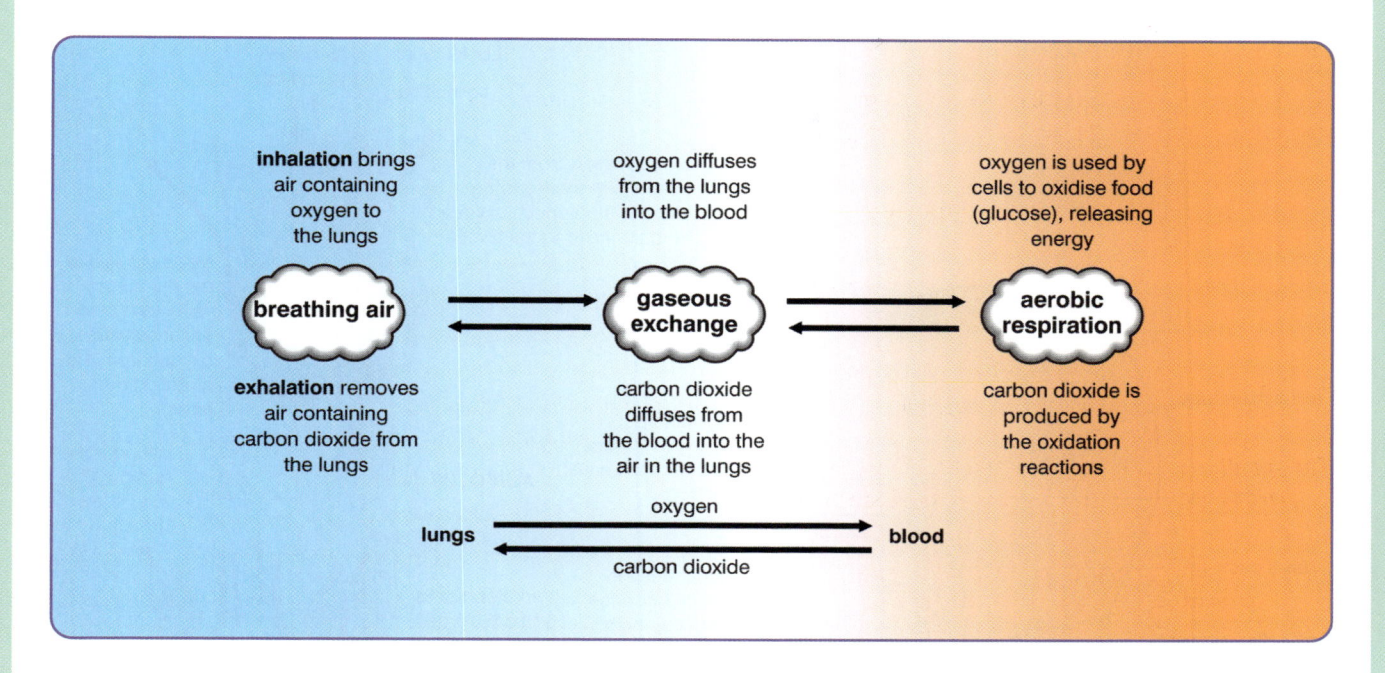

Humans (and other animals) as organisms

inhalation brings air containing oxygen to the lungs

breathing air → **gaseous exchange** ← **aerobic respiration**

oxygen diffuses from the lungs into the blood

oxygen is used by cells to oxidise food (glucose), releasing energy

exhalation removes air containing carbon dioxide from the lungs

carbon dioxide diffuses from the blood into the air in the lungs

carbon dioxide is produced by the oxidation reactions

lungs ⟶ oxygen ⟶ blood
lungs ⟵ carbon dioxide ⟵ blood

On page 82 is the concept map for **breathing, gaseous exchange and respiration**. The numbers on the concept map refer to the checklist below.

Checklist for breathing, gaseous exchange and respiration

1 ★ The **upper respiratory tract** consists of tubes from the nostrils and mouth to the lungs.
 • The tubes are well supplied with blood.

 As a result, inhaled air is warmed to body temperature.

 • Hairs in the nasal passage filter out large dust particles.
 • The lining of **mucus**, produced by **goblet cells**, traps bacteria, viruses and dust particles.
 • Hair-like **cilia** sweep the mucus into the **pharynx**, where it is either swallowed, sneezed out or coughed up.

 As a result, the air entering the lungs is cleaned and freed of disease-causing microorganisms.

2 ★ The network of **bronchioles** in the lungs form the **bronchial tree**.

 ★ The millions of **alveoli** in a pair of human lungs form a surface area of about 90 m².

 As a result, gaseous exchange is very efficient.

3 ★ Gases diffuse rapidly across the wall of each alveolus because each wall is:
 • *thin* and therefore not a barrier to the rapid diffusion of gases
 • *moist*; gases dissolve in the layer of moisture and diffuse in solution
 • *well supplied with blood vessels*; gases are quickly carried away from the alveoli in the bloodstream. The concentration gradient of gases between the blood and the air in the alveoli is steep.

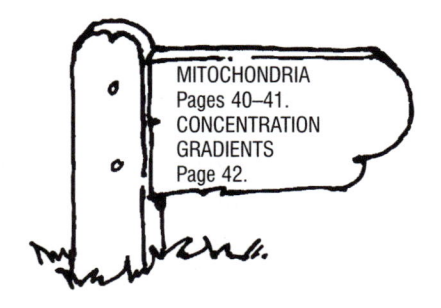

MITOCHONDRIA Pages 40–41.
CONCENTRATION GRADIENTS Page 42.

Humans (and other animals) as organisms

LUNG detail

Key: → blood flow

- bronchiole
- air moves in and out
- alveoli
- blood vessels from the pulmonary arteries bring blood without much oxygen from the heart to the alveoli
- blood vessels to the pulmonary veins take blood enriched with oxygen from the alveoli to the heart

ALVEOLUS detail

- blood with a low [O_2] and a high [CO_2]
- air moves in and out
- blood with a high [O_2] and a low [CO_2]
- red blood cells absorb oxygen
- CO_2 diffuses out of blood
- O_2 diffuses into blood
- wall of capillary – only one cell thick
- wall of alveolus – only one cell thick

CHECK LIST 3

- eustachian tube
- middle ear
- nasal passage
- pharynx
- epiglottis – prevents food from entering the larynx
- larynx (voice box)
- oesophagus
- nostril through which air passes to one of the nasal passages
- palate – separates the nasal passages from the mouth
- mouth through which air passes

CHECK LIST 1

UPPER RESPIRATORY TRACT detail

- mucus produced by a goblet cell
- cilia sweep mucus along
- sheet of mucus
- cell of the membrane lining the upper respitory tract

- larynx
- incomplete rings of cartilage support the trachea and bronchi
- right lung
- right bronchus
- bronchial tree { bronchiole, alveolus }
- trachea (windpipe)
- left lung
- left bronchus
- intercostal muscles (between ribs)
- heart
- cut end of rib
- pleural fluid stops the lungs from sticking to the chest wall
- pleural membranes line the rib cage and cover the lungs
- diaphragm – a sheet of muscle that separates the thoracic (chest) cavity from the abdominal cavity

CHECK LIST 2

Breathing, gaseous exchange and respiration (Checklist numbers refer to the checklist on page 81.)

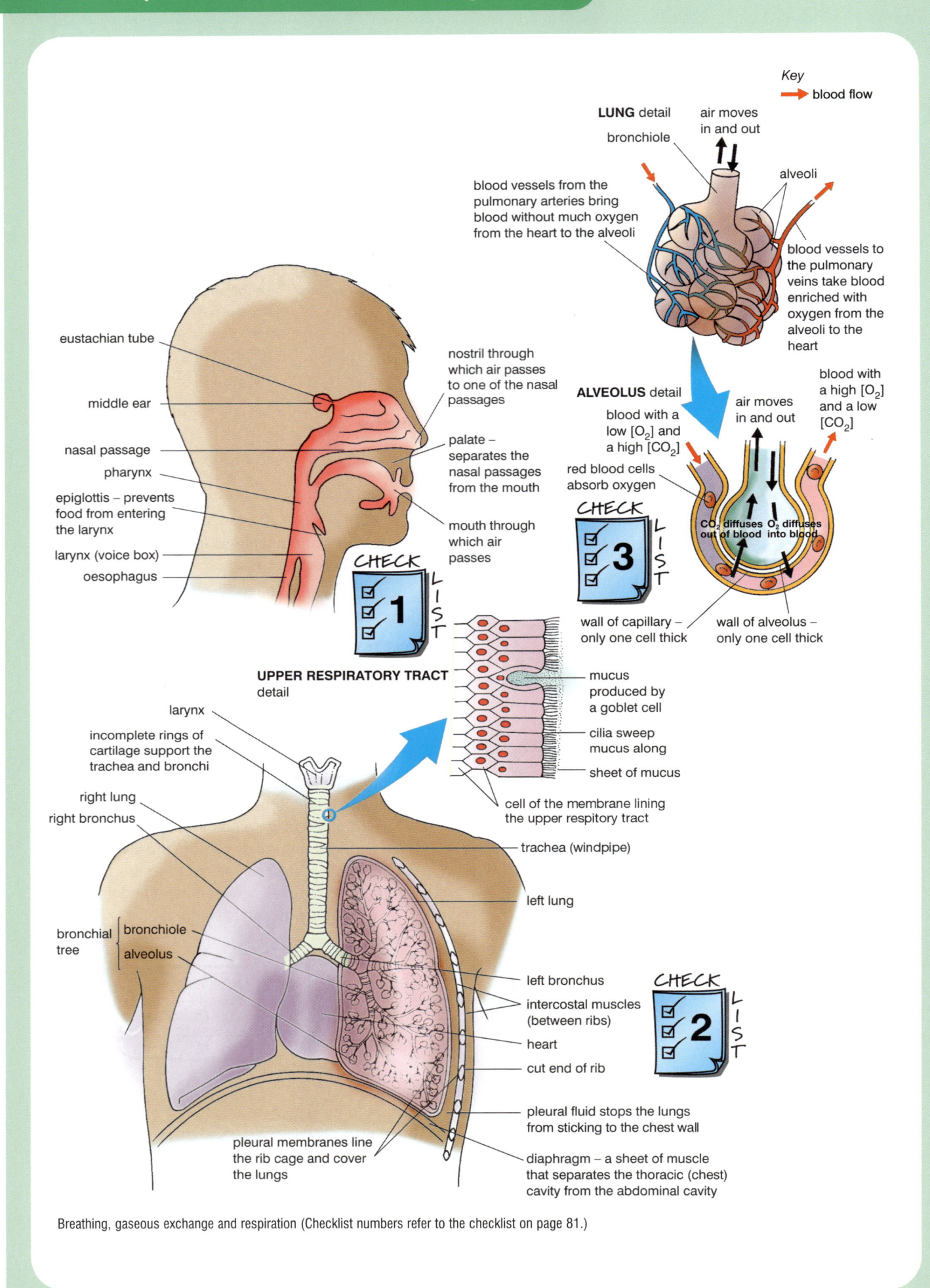

Humans (and other animals) as organisms

Breathing movements

The **ribs** and **diaphragm** form an elastic cage around the lungs. As they move, the pressure in the lungs changes. This change in pressure causes **inhaling** (breathing in) and **exhaling** (breathing out).

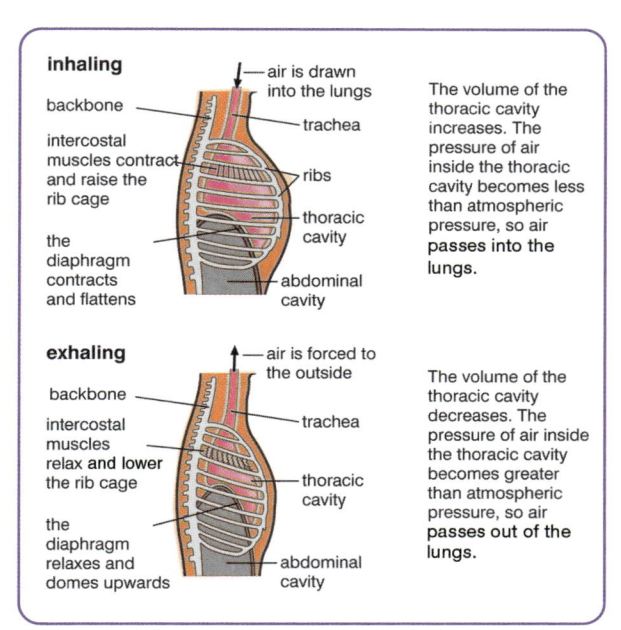

inhaling
- backbone
- intercostal muscles contract and raise the rib cage
- the diaphragm contracts and flattens
- air is drawn into the lungs
- trachea
- ribs
- thoracic cavity
- abdominal cavity

The volume of the thoracic cavity increases. The pressure of air inside the thoracic cavity becomes less than atmospheric pressure, so air passes into the lungs.

exhaling
- backbone
- intercostal muscles relax and lower the rib cage
- the diaphragm relaxes and domes upwards
- air is forced to the outside
- trachea
- thoracic cavity
- abdominal cavity

The volume of the thoracic cavity decreases. The pressure of air inside the thoracic cavity becomes greater than atmospheric pressure, so air passes out of the lungs.

Inhaling and exhaling

Remember

★ **All** cells respire – animal cells, plant cells and the cells of fungi and single-celled organisms.

★ **Most** cells respire aerobically.

★ **Some** cells, such as muscle cells, the cells of plant roots, yeast cells and some types of bacteria, are able to respire anaerobically when supplies of oxygen are low.

★ **Some** cells, such as the bacterium that causes tetanus, can *only* respire anaerobically.

Fact file

The gills of fish are adapted for efficient gaseous exchange in water. **Remember** that gaseous exchange depends on diffusion processes.

★ Each gill consists of rows of leaf-like tissue (called **lamellae**) projecting from each side of a thin bar of bone called the **gill arch**.

★ Each lamella is folded into **gill plates**.

As a result, the surface area available for the exchange of gases is greatly increased.

★ The lamellae are well supplied with blood, which transports gases to and from the gas exchange surfaces.

★ The flow of blood through the lamellae and the flow of water over the lamellae are in opposite directions resulting in a **counter current** effect.

As a result of the counter current effect, the concentration gradients of oxygen and carbon dioxide between blood and water are steep, enhancing exchange of gases.

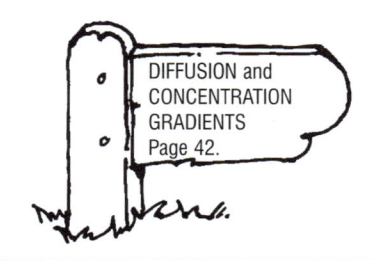

DIFFUSION and CONCENTRATION GRADIENTS Page 42.

Mutual friends!

The muscles of the man and dog are working hard. At first, aerobic respiration in their muscle cells gives them a flying start.

glucose + oxygen → carbon dioxide + water

$C_6H_{12}O_6(aq) + 6O_2(g) \rightarrow 6CO_2(g) + 6H_2O(l)$

energy released = 16.1 kJ/g glucose

The man and dog are both panting. However, in spite of rapid breathing and strenuous pumping by the heart, oxygen cannot reach the muscles fast enough to supply their needs.

The muscles then switch from **aerobic respiration** to **anaerobic respiration** which does *not* use oxygen. **Lactic acid** is produced, which collects in the muscles (the **oxygen debt**).

Humans (and other animals) as organisms

glucose → lactic acid
$C_6H_{12}O_6(aq)$ $2CH_3CHOHCO_2H(aq)$

energy released = 0.83 kJ/g glucose

Notice that the energy released per gram of glucose is less than in aerobic respiration. As lactic acid accumulates, the muscles stop working. The man and dog will be unable to run any further until the lactic acid has been removed from their muscles. This removal process uses oxygen. Lactic acid stimulates the body to pant vigorously, bringing a rush of oxygen to the muscles. During the recovery period, the lactic acid is oxidised and the **oxygen debt** is repaid. Aerobic respiration can then start again.

Fact file

Why is there a difference in energy output between aerobic respiration and anaerobic respiration?

★ During aerobic respiration glucose is completely oxidised to carbon dioxide and water, releasing all of the available energy from each glucose molecule.

★ During anaerobic respiration glucose is incompletely oxidised and ethanol or lactic acid is formed. Molecules of ethanol and lactic acid represent a considerable store of chemical bond energy, which is only released when the substances are oxidised aerobically. The chemical reactions of anaerobic respiration are the **fermentation** reactions that provide us with food, drink and a range of other products – see Chapter 8.

5.5 Blood and the circulatory system

PREVIEW

At the end of this section you will:
- be able to identify the different components of blood
- understand the functions of blood
- understand why the heart is a double pump
- know that capillary blood vessels link arteries and veins
- understand how different factors (diet, exercise and stress) affect the circulatory system.

Fact file

★ The **heart** is a pump.
★ **Blood** is a liquid containing different cells.
★ **Arteries**, **veins** and **capillaries** are tube-like vessels through which blood flows.

heart —pumps→ blood —through→ blood vessels

Moving blood around

The circulatory system consists of tubes (arteries, veins and capillaries) through which blood is pumped by the heart. Blood carries oxygen, digested food, hormones and other substances *to* the tissues and organs of the body that need them. Blood also carries carbon dioxide and other waste substances produced by the metabolism of cells *from* the tissues and organs of the body. On pages 86–87 is the concept map for **blood and the circulatory system**. The numbers on the concept map refer to the checklist on page 85.

Fact file

The English scientist William Harvey (1578–1657) discovered the circulation of blood in 1628. He identified arteries and veins but, in the absence of microscopes, could not see the capillary blood vessels connecting them. However, he predicted the existence of capillaries, a prediction confirmed by Marcello Malpighi in 1661 who observed them through a microscope, which by then had been invented.

Humans (and other animals) as organisms

Checklist for blood and the circulatory system

1. ★ **Red blood cells** are made in the **marrow** of the limb bones, ribs and vertebrae.
   - ★ Old red blood cells are destroyed in the liver.
   - ★ **White blood cells** originate in the **bone marrow** and **spleen**.
   - ★ **Antibodies** produced against a particular **antigen** will attack only that antigen. The antibody is said to be **specific** to that antigen. Antibodies are produced by white blood cells called B-lymphocytes.

LIVER Pages 71 and 74.

Fact file

Red blood cells look alike under the microscope. However, they may carry different antigens, called **antigen A** and **antigen B**, on the cell surface. A person's blood plasma contains antibodies, which attack foreign red cell antigens, but does not contain antibodies that would attack its own red cell antigens. The combinations of antibody and antigen are the basis of the ABO system of blood grouping. The possible combinations are shown in the table below.

Antigen on red cells	Antibody in plasma	Blood group
A	Anti-B	A
B	Anti-A	B
A and B	Neither	AB
Neither	Anti-A and Anti-B	O

2. ★ **Arteries** carry blood *from* the heart.
   Veins carry blood *to* the heart (except the hepatic portal vein).

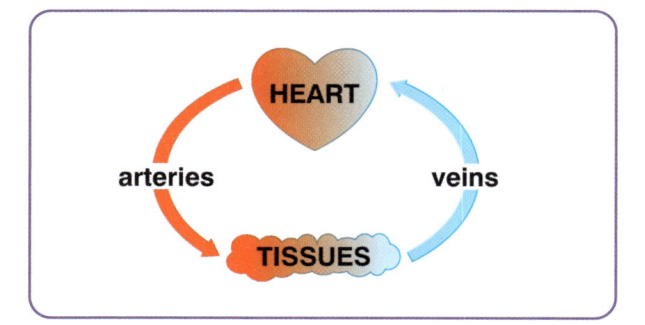

   HEART → arteries → TISSUES → veins → HEART

3. ★ Heart (**cardiac**) muscle contracts and relaxes rhythmically for a lifetime.
   - ★ The heartbeat is a two-tone sound:
     - **diastole** – the heart muscles are relaxed
     - **systole** – the heart muscles contract. During **auricular** (atrial) **systole**, contraction of the auricles (atria) forces blood into the ventricles. During **ventricular systole**, contraction of the ventricles forces blood into the pulmonary artery (from the right ventricle) and aorta (from the left ventricle).
   - ★ **Valves** direct the flow of blood through the heart.
     - During auricular (atrial) systole, the increase in the pressure of the blood in the right and left auricles forces open the tricuspid valve and bicuspid valve, respectively.
     - During ventricular systole, the increase in the pressure of the blood in the ventricles closes the tricuspid and bicuspid valves and forces open the semi-lunar valves guarding the opening of the pulmonary artery and aorta, respectively.
   - ★ A constant blood pressure is needed for the kidneys to work properly.
     - The heart is a **double pump**.
     - The beating of the heart is controlled by a **pacemaker**.

     As a result, the heart beats on average 72 times a minute.
   - ★ The pacemaker is supplied by two sets of nerves from the brain. One set speeds up the heart rate; the other slows it down.

     As a result, the heart can adjust to meet the body's changing demands for blood.

4. ★ The arteries and veins in the human body form two circuits:
   - the lung circuit
   - the head and body circuit.

Testing your understanding

Examinations test your understanding of ideas and important principles. Be sure you have grasped the arrangement of the **hepatic portal vein** and the role of the **pulmonary artery** and **pulmonary vein** (see page 88).

85

Humans (and other animals) as organisms

Fact file
★ Haemoglobin combines with oxygen to form **oxyhaemoglobin**. This breaks down to release oxygen in tissues where the concentration of oxygen is low.

$$\text{haemoglobin} + \text{oxygen} \rightleftharpoons \text{oxyhaemoglobin}$$

★ Blood that contains a lot of oxyhaemoglobin is bright red in colour. It is called **oxygenated** blood. Blood with little oxyhaemoglobin looks a deep red-purple. It is called **deoxygenated** blood.

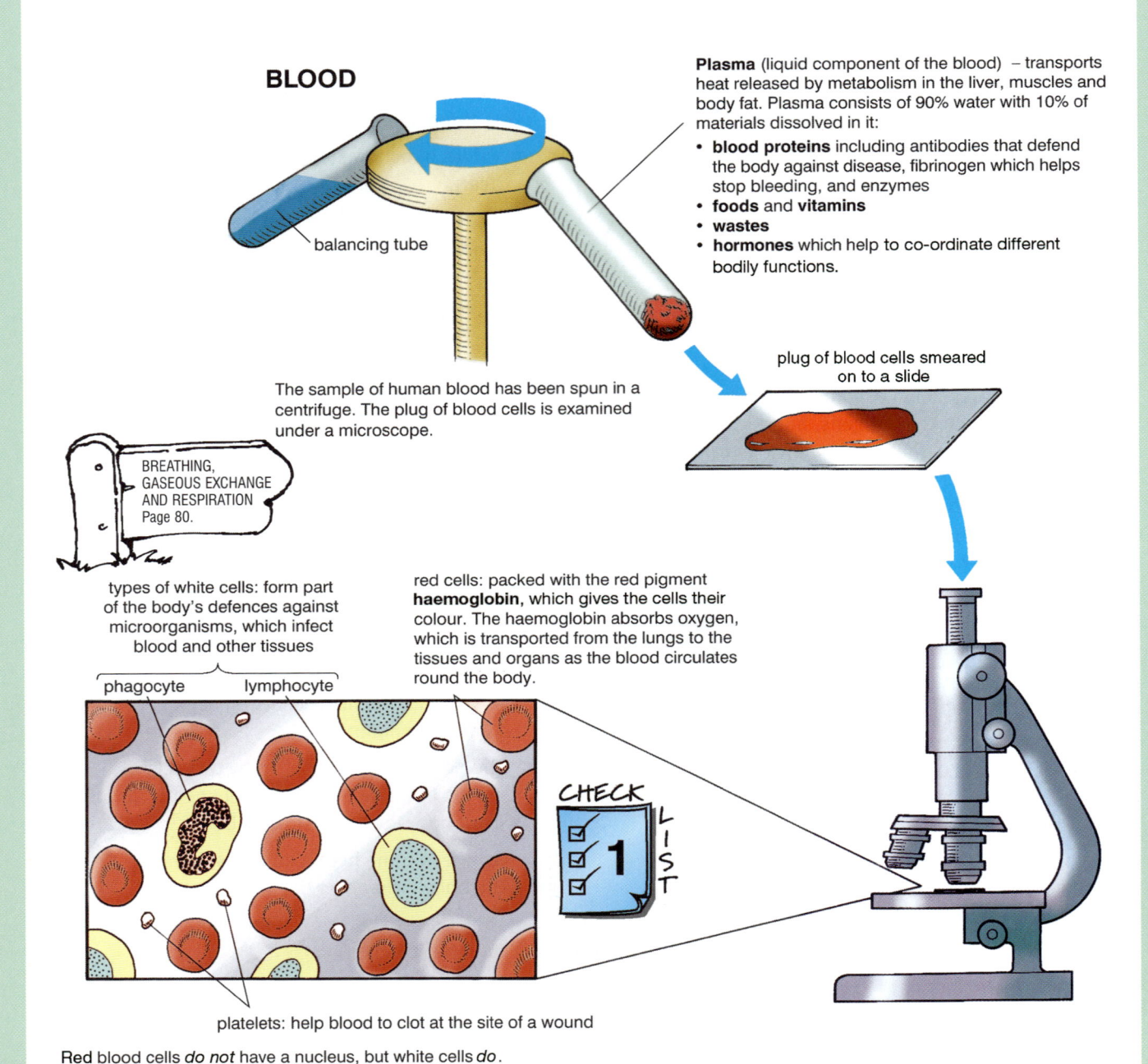

BLOOD

balancing tube

The sample of human blood has been spun in a centrifuge. The plug of blood cells is examined under a microscope.

Plasma (liquid component of the blood) – transports heat released by metabolism in the liver, muscles and body fat. Plasma consists of 90% water with 10% of materials dissolved in it:
- **blood proteins** including antibodies that defend the body against disease, fibrinogen which helps stop bleeding, and enzymes
- **foods** and **vitamins**
- **wastes**
- **hormones** which help to co-ordinate different bodily functions.

plug of blood cells smeared on to a slide

BREATHING, GASEOUS EXCHANGE AND RESPIRATION Page 80.

types of white cells: form part of the body's defences against microorganisms, which infect blood and other tissues

phagocyte   lymphocyte

red cells: packed with the red pigment **haemoglobin**, which gives the cells their colour. The haemoglobin absorbs oxygen, which is transported from the lungs to the tissues and organs as the blood circulates round the body.

CHECK LIST 1

platelets: help blood to clot at the site of a wound

Red blood cells *do not* have a nucleus, but white cells *do*. **Notice** the characteristic shapes of the nuclei of phagocytes and lymphocytes. Platelets look like fragments of red cells.

Blood and the circulatory system (Checklist numbers refer to the checklist on page 85.)

Humans (and other animals) as organisms

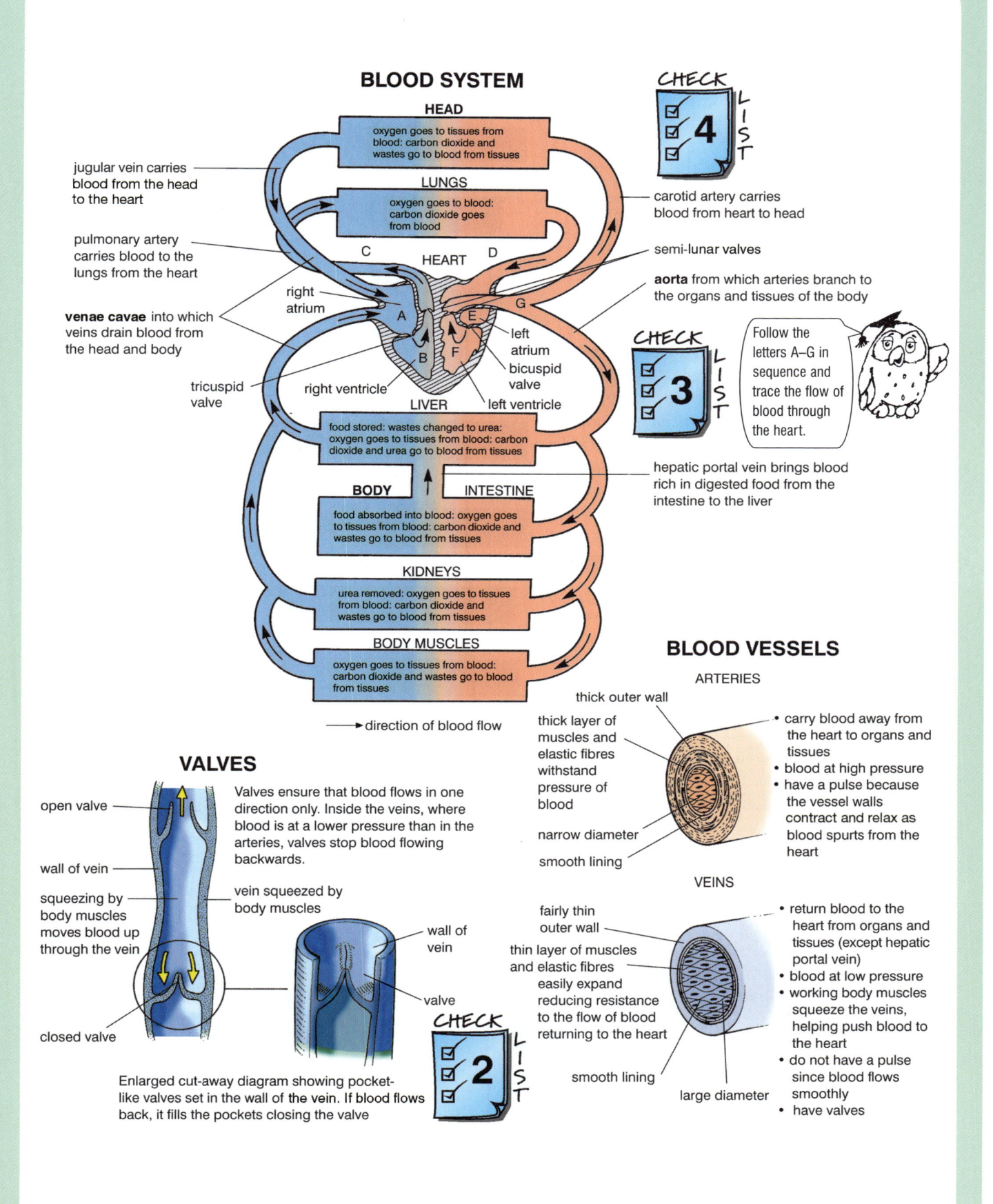

BLOOD SYSTEM

HEAD — oxygen goes to tissues from blood: carbon dioxide and wastes go to blood from tissues

LUNGS — oxygen goes to blood: carbon dioxide goes from blood

HEART (C, D, A, B, E, F, G — right atrium, right ventricle, left atrium, left ventricle, tricuspid valve, bicuspid valve)

LIVER — food stored: wastes changed to urea: oxygen goes to tissues from blood: carbon dioxide and urea go to blood from tissues

BODY INTESTINE — food absorbed into blood: oxygen goes to tissues from blood: carbon dioxide and wastes go to blood from tissues

KIDNEYS — urea removed: oxygen goes to tissues from blood: carbon dioxide and wastes go to blood from tissues

BODY MUSCLES — oxygen goes to tissues from blood: carbon dioxide and wastes go to blood from tissues

- jugular vein carries blood from the head to the heart
- pulmonary artery carries blood to the lungs from the heart
- **venae cavae** into which veins drain blood from the head and body
- tricuspid valve
- right atrium
- right ventricle
- carotid artery carries blood from heart to head
- semi-lunar valves
- **aorta** from which arteries branch to the organs and tissues of the body
- left atrium
- bicuspid valve
- left ventricle
- hepatic portal vein brings blood rich in digested food from the intestine to the liver

→ direction of blood flow

CHECK LIST 3: Follow the letters A–G in sequence and trace the flow of blood through the heart.

VALVES

Valves ensure that blood flows in one direction only. Inside the veins, where blood is at a lower pressure than in the arteries, valves stop blood flowing backwards.

- open valve
- wall of vein
- squeezing by body muscles moves blood up through the vein
- closed valve
- vein squeezed by body muscles
- wall of vein
- valve

Enlarged cut-away diagram showing pocket-like valves set in the wall of the vein. If blood flows back, it fills the pockets closing the valve

CHECK LIST 2

BLOOD VESSELS

ARTERIES

- thick outer wall
- thick layer of muscles and elastic fibres withstand pressure of blood
- narrow diameter
- smooth lining

- carry blood away from the heart to organs and tissues
- blood at high pressure
- have a pulse because the vessel walls contract and relax as blood spurts from the heart

VEINS

- fairly thin outer wall
- thin layer of muscles and elastic fibres easily expand reducing resistance to the flow of blood returning to the heart
- smooth lining
- large diameter

- return blood to the heart from organs and tissues (except hepatic portal vein)
- blood at low pressure
- working body muscles squeeze the veins, helping push blood to the heart
- do not have a pulse since blood flows smoothly
- have valves

CHECK LIST 4

87

Humans (and other animals) as organisms

Understanding the hepatic portal vein

Veins carry blood to the heart. The **hepatic portal vein** is the exception. Notice on page 87 that it carries blood with its load of digested food from the intestine to the liver.

ABSORPTION OF FOOD Page 72.

Understanding the pulmonary artery and the pulmonary vein

Arteries are sometimes described as carriers of oxygenated blood (often coloured red on diagrams), and veins as carriers of deoxygenated blood (often coloured blue on diagrams). However, the **pulmonary artery** carries deoxygenated blood from the heart to the lungs. The **pulmonary vein** carries oxygenated blood from the lungs to the heart.

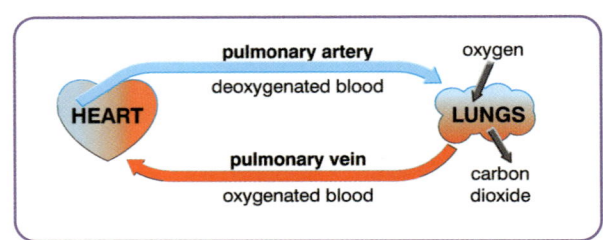

- ★ **Tissue fluid** carries oxygen, food and other substances to the cells. This fluid is blood plasma that has been forced out through the thin capillary walls by the pressure of the blood inside.

- ★ Red blood cells squeeze through the smallest capillaries in single file.

  As a result, the pressure drops as blood passes through the capillaries from the artery to the vein.

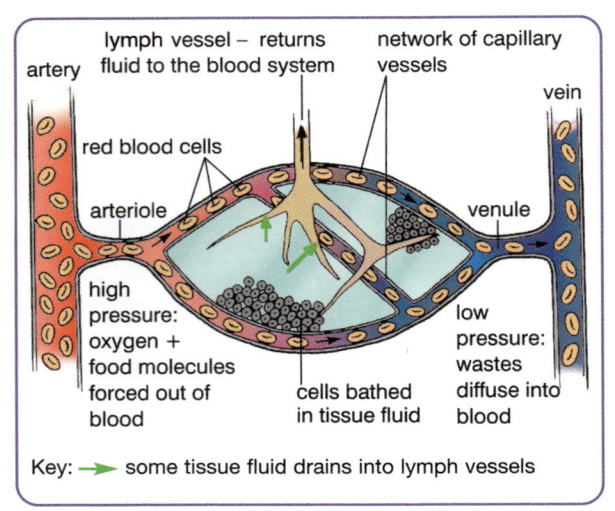

Capillaries at work

Fact file

Capillaries are tiny blood vessels, 0.001 mm in diameter. They join each artery with its corresponding vein.

- ★ The walls of capillary blood vessels are one cell thick.

  As a result, substances easily diffuse between blood in the capillaries and the surrounding tissues.

- ★ Capillaries form dense networks called **beds** in the tissues of the body.

  As a result, no cell is very far away from a capillary.

- ★ The blood in capillaries supplies nearby cells with oxygen, food molecules and other substances. It also carries away carbon dioxide and other wastes produced by the cells' metabolism.

Disorders of the blood

- ★ **Leukaemia** results from the production of abnormal white blood cells.

  As a result, there are too few red blood cells.

  Treatments of the disorder include using drugs that slow the production of white blood cells, and radiotherapy which kills the abnormal cells.

- ★ **Haemophilia** is a genetic disease which runs in families. The blood does not clot properly because factor VIII, one of the substances in the blood needed for blood clots to form, is missing.

  As a result, **haemophiliacs** (people suffering from haemophilia) lose a lot of blood if they injure themselves.

  Treatment is by injections of factor VIII.

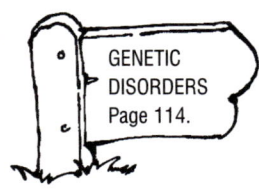

GENETIC DISORDERS Page 114.

Humans (and other animals) as organisms

AIDS

AIDS (**A**cquired **I**mmune **D**eficiency **S**yndrome) is caused by the **H**uman **I**mmunodeficiency **V**irus (**HIV**). The virus attacks a particular type of white blood cell.

As a result, a person infected with HIV has reduced protection from disease-causing microorganisms.

Once HIV has destroyed a sufficient number of lymphocytes, the symptoms of AIDS develop. Common diseases include:
- pneumonia – a disease of the lungs
- thrush – a fungal infection
- Kaposi's sarcoma – a skin cancer.

Transmission of HIV is usually by sexual intercourse, the communal use of syringes and needles contaminated with HIV infected blood by drug abusers and, early on in the history of the infection, by transfusion of infected blood or blood products. However, the introduction of a programme of screening and sterilisation of donated blood for HIV (the procedures have been in place in the UK since 1985) means that the risk of HIV transmission from the use of donated blood and blood products is now virtually non-existent.

Treatment and control

Drugs with different effects on HIV are used to treat people infected with the virus. At least three types of drug are given to the infected person each day (**combination treatment**). Since the introduction of combination treatment in the mid-1990s, there has been a significant reduction in the death rates of HIV infected people in the UK and in other countries.

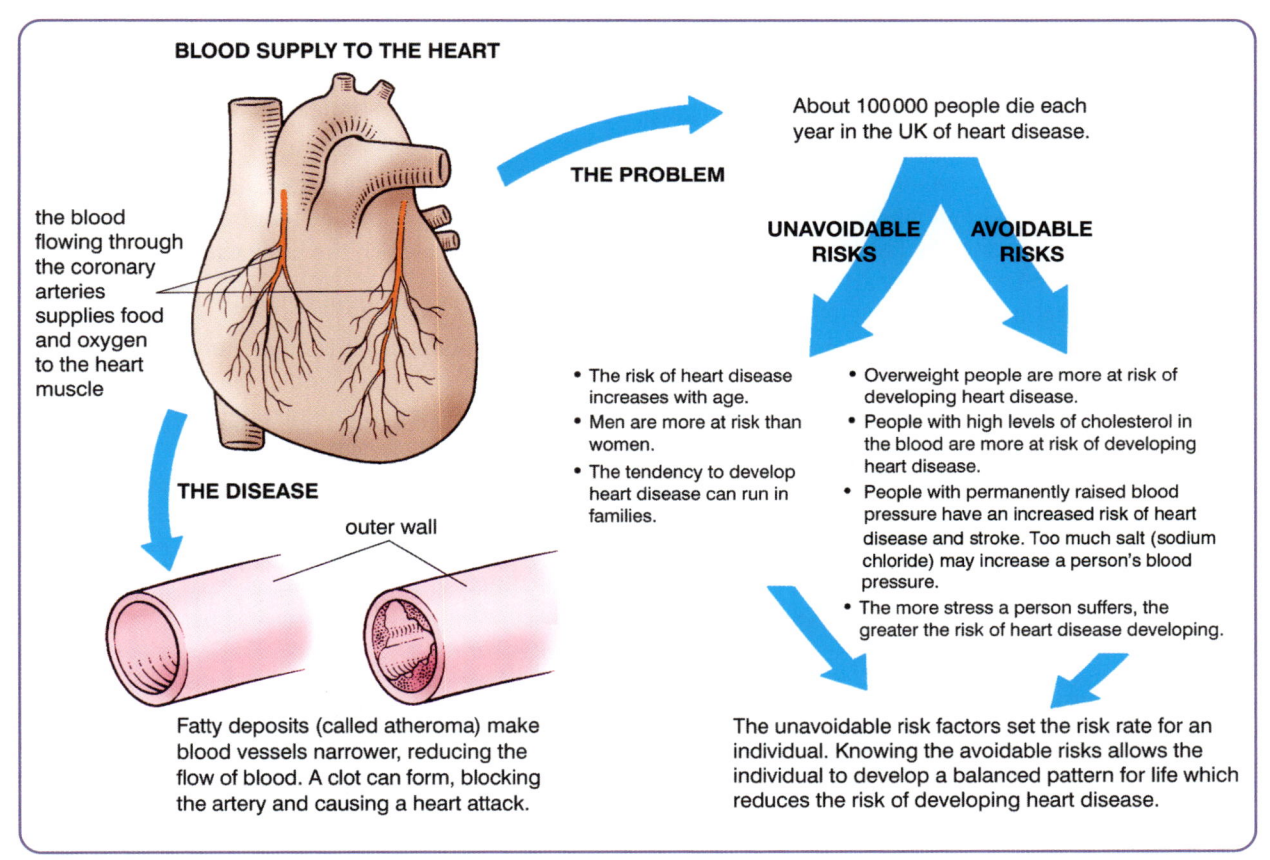

BLOOD SUPPLY TO THE HEART

the blood flowing through the coronary arteries supplies food and oxygen to the heart muscle

THE PROBLEM

About 100 000 people die each year in the UK of heart disease.

UNAVOIDABLE RISKS
- The risk of heart disease increases with age.
- Men are more at risk than women.
- The tendency to develop heart disease can run in families.

AVOIDABLE RISKS
- Overweight people are more at risk of developing heart disease.
- People with high levels of cholesterol in the blood are more at risk of developing heart disease.
- People with permanently raised blood pressure have an increased risk of heart disease and stroke. Too much salt (sodium chloride) may increase a person's blood pressure.
- The more stress a person suffers, the greater the risk of heart disease developing.

THE DISEASE

outer wall

Fatty deposits (called atheroma) make blood vessels narrower, reducing the flow of blood. A clot can form, blocking the artery and causing a heart attack.

The unavoidable risk factors set the risk rate for an individual. Knowing the avoidable risks allows the individual to develop a balanced pattern for life which reduces the risk of developing heart disease.

The risk of heart disease

Humans (and other animals) as organisms

While the search for new drugs (and the development of vaccines) continues, taking precautions to control the spread of HIV is important.

★ Using condoms during sexual intercourse provides a barrier to transmission of the virus.

★ Providing sterile syringes and needles reduces the risk of infection with HIV (and other pathogens in the blood) among drug abusers.

★ Screening donated blood for HIV, and rejecting infected blood, protects people who need the transfusion of blood and blood products.

Hepatitis B

Hepatitis B virus causes serious liver disease. Medical workers and patients in places where there may be human blood contaminated with the virus and families of hepatitis B carriers are at risk from the disease. They are high-priority groups for the hepatitis B vaccine.

Understanding heart disease

The **coronary arteries** supply blood to the heart muscle, as shown in the diagram on page 89. The lining of blood vessels can be damaged and roughened by a fatty deposit called **atheroma**. The build-up of atheroma in the coronary arteries is one cause of **heart disease**. It increases the risk of blood clots forming. A blood clot in the coronary arteries can interrupt the blood supply to the heart, and the person suffers a **heart attack**.

The symptoms are:
- severe pain in the chest, neck and arms
- sweating
- faintness and sickness.

The clot is called a **thrombus**, and the blockage a **thrombosis**.

The diagram on page 89 shows some of the factors affecting the risk of a person developing heart disease.

5.6 Senses and the nervous system

> **PREVIEW**
>
> At the end of this section you will know that:
> - stimuli are converted by receptors into signals called nerve impulses, to which the body can respond
> - neurones (nerve cells) conduct nerve impulses to muscles, which respond by contracting
> - muscles and glands are effectors
> - nerves are formed from bundles of neurones and are the link between stimulus and response.

Stimulus and response

A **stimulus** is a change in the environment which causes a living organism to take action. A **response** is the action that the living organism takes. The **nervous system** links stimuli and responses. The sequence of events is:

★ **Sensory receptor cells** detect stimuli and convert them into **nerve impulses** that transmit information, to which the body can respond.

★ Nerve impulses are minute electrical disturbances.

★ **Neurones** (nerve cells) conduct nerve impulses to **effectors** (muscles or glands). Muscles respond to nerve impulses by contracting; glands respond by secreting substances. For example, the adrenal glands respond to nerve impulses by producing the hormone adrenaline, which helps the body cope with sudden stress.

HORMONES Page 97.

The process runs:

stimulus → receptor → nerves → effector → response

The nervous system

On pages 92–93 is the concept map for **the nervous system**. The numbers on the concept map refer to the checklist on page 91.

Humans (and other animals) as organisms

Checklist for the nervous system

1. ★ Each **nerve** of the nervous system consists of a bundle of **neurones**.
   ★ Neurones transmit nerve impulses to an **effector** (muscle or gland).
   ★ Nerve impulses are minute electrical disturbances which carry information about stimuli.
   ★ Nerve impulses stimulate effectors to respond to stimuli in a useful way.
   ★ A nerve impulse takes just milliseconds to travel along a neurone.

2. ★ A **neurotransmitter** is a chemical substance released from the end of a neurone into the **synapse**.
   ★ A neurotransmitter is produced only from the end of the neurone before the synapse.

   As a result, nerve impulses always travel *from* the receptor *to* the effector.

   ★ Once neurotransmitter has stimulated the neurone after the synapse to fire off new nerve impulses, it is destroyed by an enzyme. If it were not destroyed, it would stimulate the neurone after the synapse to continue to fire off nerve impulses.

   As a result, muscles (the effectors) would be permanently contracted: a condition called **tetanus**. Death quickly follows.

3. ★ **Reflex responses** happen before the brain has had time to process the nerve impulses carrying the information about the stimulus (track the sequence 1–5 in the diagram on page 92).
   ★ When the brain catches up with events, it brings about the next set of reactions – such as a shout of pain.
   ★ **Ascending fibres** form synapses with sensory neurones. The ascending fibres carry nerve impulses to the brain.

   As a result, the brain receives information about the stimulus causing the reflex response.

   ★ Nerve impulses from the brain are carried by the **descending fibres**, which synapse with motor neurones.

   As a result, the reflex response is brought under conscious control.

4. ★ The human brain weighs approximately 1.3 kg and occupies a volume of about 1500 cm^3.
   ★ Around 6 million neurones make up 1 cm^3 of brain matter.
   ★ Memory and learning are under the brain's control.
   ★ Different drugs affect the brain. For example, ethanol (the alcohol in beers, wines and spirits) depresses the activity of the cerebral cortex, affecting judgement and the control of movement.

Fact file

A reflex response is said to be **conditioned** when the stimulus that caused the response in the first place is replaced by another, alternative stimulus. For example, to feed the cat you may head for the cupboard in the kitchen where the food is kept. At first the cat only notices when the food is seen and smelt in the feeding bowl. However, it is not long before the cat shows great interest when you just head for the kitchen cupboard, long before it has seen or smelt the food. Its feeding responses have been conditioned.

Responding to changes in the environment

The diagram below shows different types of European woodlice.

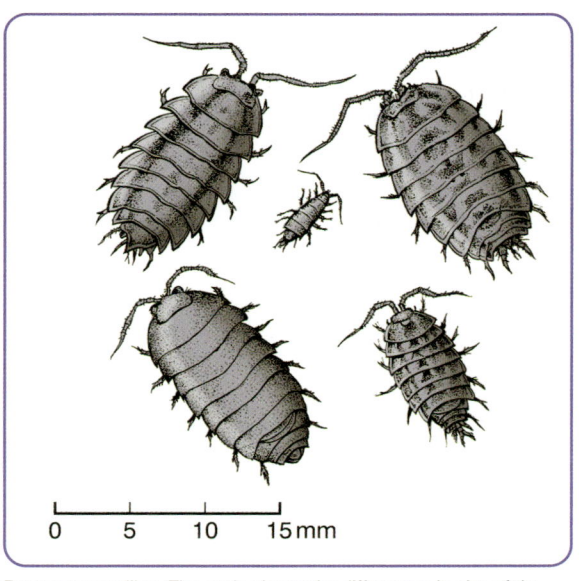

European woodlice. The scale shows the differences in size of the different types (after J L Cloudsley-Thompson)

Humans (and other animals) as organisms

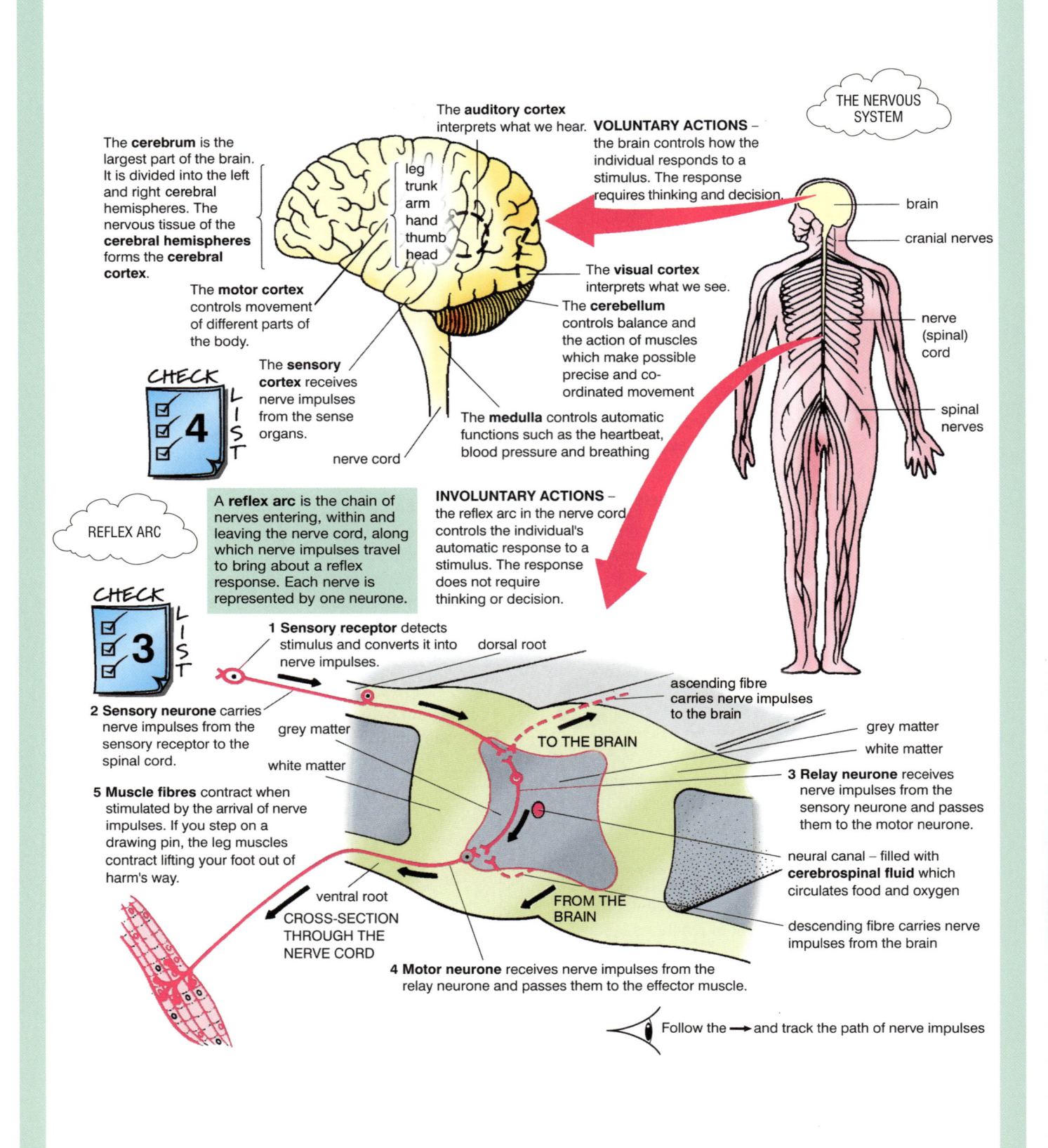

THE NERVOUS SYSTEM

The **cerebrum** is the largest part of the brain. It is divided into the left and right cerebral hemispheres. The nervous tissue of the **cerebral hemispheres** forms the **cerebral cortex**.

The **auditory cortex** interprets what we hear.

VOLUNTARY ACTIONS – the brain controls how the individual responds to a stimulus. The response requires thinking and decision.

leg, trunk, arm, hand, thumb, head

The **motor cortex** controls movement of different parts of the body.

The **sensory cortex** receives nerve impulses from the sense organs.

The **visual cortex** interprets what we see.

The **cerebellum** controls balance and the action of muscles which make possible precise and co-ordinated movement

The **medulla** controls automatic functions such as the heartbeat, blood pressure and breathing

nerve cord

CHECK LIST 4

- brain
- cranial nerves
- nerve (spinal) cord
- spinal nerves

REFLEX ARC

A **reflex arc** is the chain of nerves entering, within and leaving the nerve cord, along which nerve impulses travel to bring about a reflex response. Each nerve is represented by one neurone.

INVOLUNTARY ACTIONS – the reflex arc in the nerve cord controls the individual's automatic response to a stimulus. The response does not require thinking or decision.

CHECK LIST 3

1 Sensory receptor detects stimulus and converts it into nerve impulses.

2 Sensory neurone carries nerve impulses from the sensory receptor to the spinal cord.

5 Muscle fibres contract when stimulated by the arrival of nerve impulses. If you step on a drawing pin, the leg muscles contract lifting your foot out of harm's way.

dorsal root

grey matter

white matter

ascending fibre carries nerve impulses to the brain

TO THE BRAIN

grey matter

white matter

3 Relay neurone receives nerve impulses from the sensory neurone and passes them to the motor neurone.

neural canal – filled with **cerebrospinal fluid** which circulates food and oxygen

descending fibre carries nerve impulses from the brain

ventral root

CROSS-SECTION THROUGH THE NERVE CORD

FROM THE BRAIN

4 Motor neurone receives nerve impulses from the relay neurone and passes them to the effector muscle.

Follow the ➝ and track the path of nerve impulses

Neurones, nerves and the nervous system (Checklist numbers refer to the checklist on page 91.)

Humans (and other animals) as organisms

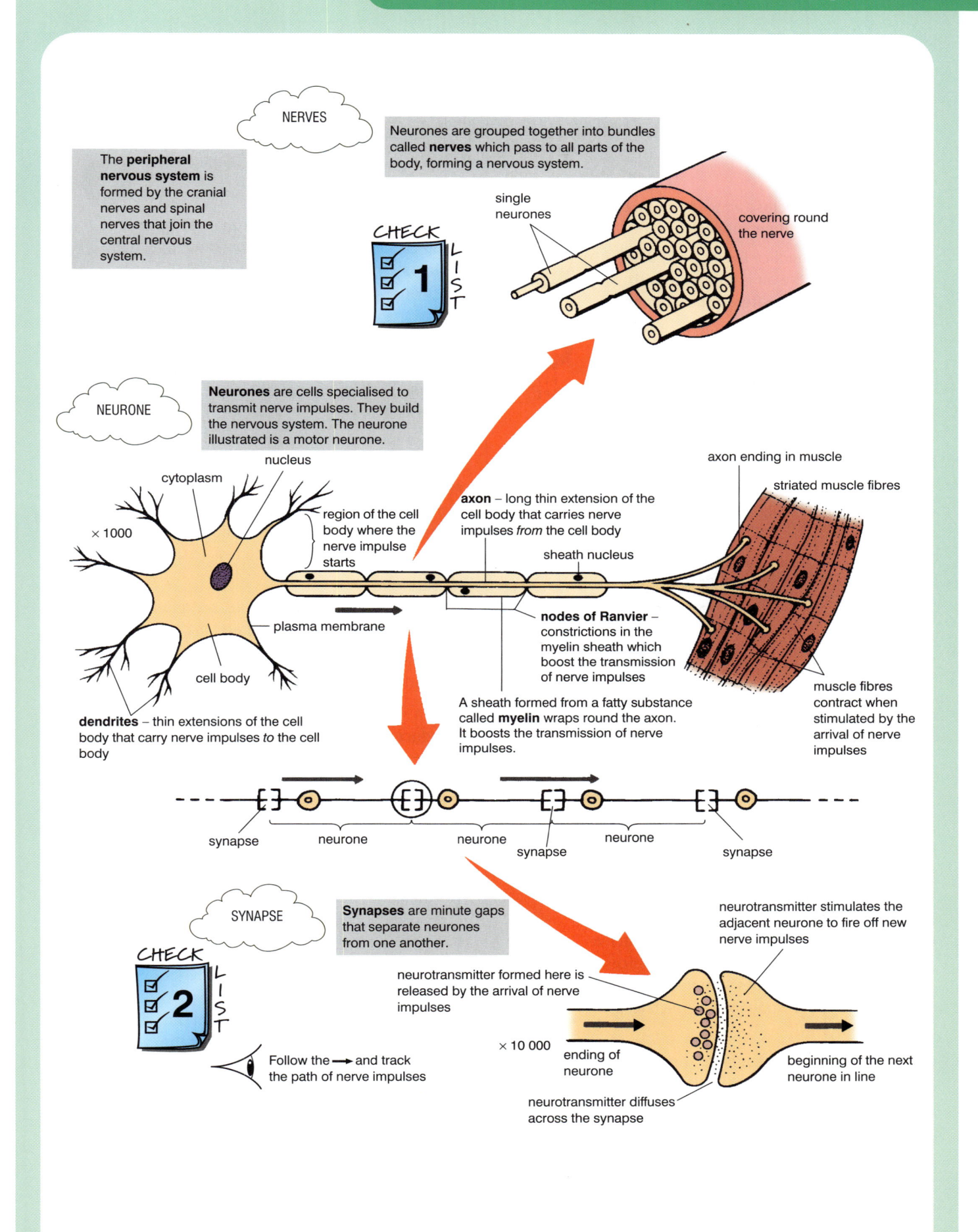

NERVES

The **peripheral nervous system** is formed by the cranial nerves and spinal nerves that join the central nervous system.

Neurones are grouped together into bundles called **nerves** which pass to all parts of the body, forming a nervous system.

CHECK LIST 1

- single neurones
- covering round the nerve

NEURONE

Neurones are cells specialised to transmit nerve impulses. They build the nervous system. The neurone illustrated is a motor neurone.

× 1000

- cytoplasm
- nucleus
- region of the cell body where the nerve impulse starts
- **axon** – long thin extension of the cell body that carries nerve impulses *from* the cell body
- sheath nucleus
- axon ending in muscle
- striated muscle fibres
- plasma membrane
- cell body
- **dendrites** – thin extensions of the cell body that carry nerve impulses *to* the cell body
- **nodes of Ranvier** – constrictions in the myelin sheath which boost the transmission of nerve impulses
- A sheath formed from a fatty substance called **myelin** wraps round the axon. It boosts the transmission of nerve impulses.
- muscle fibres contract when stimulated by the arrival of nerve impulses

- synapse
- neurone
- neurone
- synapse
- neurone
- synapse

SYNAPSE

Synapses are minute gaps that separate neurones from one another.

CHECK LIST 2

Follow the ➡ and track the path of nerve impulses

× 10 000

- neurotransmitter formed here is released by the arrival of nerve impulses
- neurotransmitter stimulates the adjacent neurone to fire off new nerve impulses
- ending of neurone
- beginning of the next neurone in line
- neurotransmitter diffuses across the synapse

93

Humans (and other animals) as organisms

Why do they live under stones, in layers of detritus and other dark, damp places?

DETRITUS LAYER Page 13.

Woodlice quickly lose water from the body in dry air, threatening their survival.

As a result, woodlice live in dark, damp places where the air is saturated with water vapour (**humid**).

As a result, loss of water from the body is reduced.

Look at *Moving molecules* on page 39. **Remember** that substances diffuse from where the substance is in high concentration to where it is in low concentration. For woodlice the process runs:

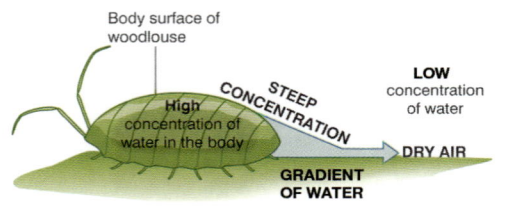

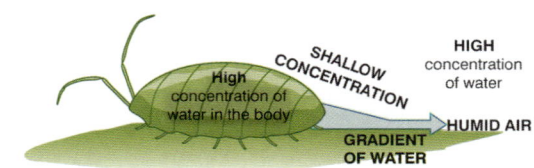

[Diagram: Body surface of woodlouse — High concentration of water in the body, STEEP CONCENTRATION, LOW concentration of water, DRY AIR, GRADIENT OF WATER]

[Diagram: High concentration of water in the body, SHALLOW CONCENTRATION, HIGH concentration of water, HUMID AIR, GRADIENT OF WATER]

How do woodlice find dark, damp places to live? Their **behaviour** makes sure they avoid environments where there would be a danger of them drying out.

★ The activity (walking) of woodlice depends on how **dry** the environment is (intensity of stimulus). The dryer it is the more active woodlice are, increasing their chances of finding damp environments. When they find a damp environment woodlice are much less active (stop moving).

★ Woodlice also respond to the intensity of **light**. The lighter it is, the more active woodlice are.

★ Light means lack of shelter.

Why?

As a result, the environment is more likely to be dry.

As a result, woodlice are more likely to lose body water and die.

You can use a **choice chamber** to investigate the responses of woodlice to dry/wet and light/dark environments. The diagram on page 95 gives you the idea.

Rhythms of animal behaviour

Woodlice also have regular patterns of activity (**rhythms**) during the day and night (24 hours) and between seasons.

Daily rhythms

★ At night, woodlice do not respond to humidity as much as during daylight hours. When it is dark the environment is more humid and woodlice can leave their shelter with less risk of drying out.

As a result, woodlice are able to explore new environments for food and mates.

★ As the intensity of light increases (early morning) woodlice return to their dark, damp shelters.

As a result, the risk of drying out is reduced.

Seasonal rhythms

★ In spring, rain brings woodlice out of **hibernation**.

As a result, the **distribution** (where living things are found in the environment) of woodlice is affected, increasing their chances of finding new (damp!) environments in which to live.

Advantages of rhythmical activity

The intensity of light and humidity of the environment are stimuli which trigger the rhythmical activity of woodlice.

Why are the responses important to the living things described?

Humans (and other animals) as organisms

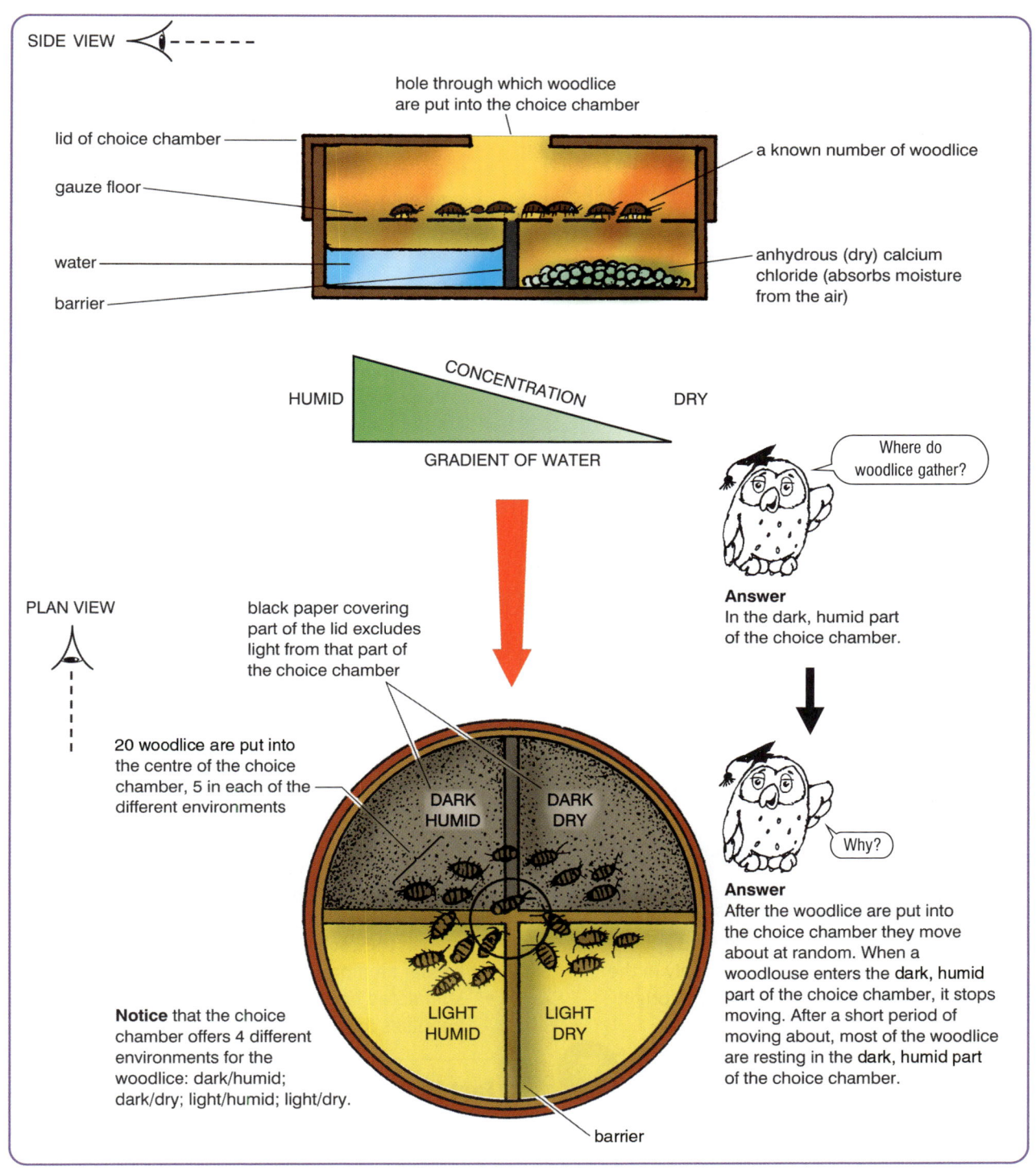

SIDE VIEW

- lid of choice chamber
- gauze floor
- water
- barrier
- hole through which woodlice are put into the choice chamber
- a known number of woodlice
- anhydrous (dry) calcium chloride (absorbs moisture from the air)

HUMID ← CONCENTRATION → DRY
GRADIENT OF WATER

PLAN VIEW

- black paper covering part of the lid excludes light from that part of the choice chamber
- 20 woodlice are put into the centre of the choice chamber, 5 in each of the different environments
- DARK HUMID / DARK DRY / LIGHT HUMID / LIGHT DRY
- barrier

Notice that the choice chamber offers 4 different environments for the woodlice: dark/humid; dark/dry; light/humid; light/dry.

Where do woodlice gather?

Answer
In the dark, humid part of the choice chamber.

Why?

Answer
After the woodlice are put into the choice chamber they move about at random. When a woodlouse enters the **dark, humid** part of the choice chamber, it stops moving. After a short period of moving about, most of the woodlice are resting in the **dark, humid** part of the choice chamber.

The choice chamber allows woodlice to choose different environments

★ *Tropical toads and frogs* are active when it rains, finding mates and reproducing. Their fertilised eggs and the **tadpoles** (young stages) which hatch from them need water in which to develop into adults.

★ *Birds* reproduce in spring because the increase in day length coincides with an increase in the supply of food on which their young depend. The chances of the young surviving to become adults are improved.

Humans (and other animals) as organisms

5.7 Sense organs

> **PREVIEW**
>
> At the end of this section you will know that:
> - the sense organs consist of sensory cells which are adapted to detect a particular type of stimulus.

Handy hint

The sensory cells of the:

- **S**kin detect heat and cold, touch and pain
- **N**ose detect chemicals
- **E**ye detect light
- **E**ar detect sound
- **T**ongue detect chemicals.

Thinking of the memory aid **SNEET** will help you remember the major sense organs of the body.

Sensing the surroundings

On pages 98–99 is the concept map for **sense organs**. The numbers refer to the checklist below.

Checklist for sense organs

1. ★ **Tears** lubricate the surface of the eye. They contain the enzyme **lysozyme** which kills bacteria.
   - ★ The **iris** of the eye is usually coloured brown, blue or green.
   - ★ A pair of human eyes contains around 130 million **rods** and 7 million **cones**.
   - ★ **Cone** cells are packed most densely in the region of the **fovea** and respond to bright light.
     As a result, brightly lit objects are seen most clearly if looked at straight on.
   - ★ **Rod** cells occur mostly near the edges of the retina and respond to dim light.
     As a result, dimly lit objects are seen more clearly out of the corner of the eye.

2. ★ Loudness is measured in **decibels**. The faintest sound that the ear can hear is defined as zero decibels.
   - ★ The response of the ear to different levels of loudness varies with frequency. The ear is most sensitive to frequencies around 3000 Hz, and can detect the softest sounds. It is completely insensitive to sounds over 18 000 Hz and cannot detect them.
   - ★ The walls of the ear tube produce wax, which keeps the eardrum soft and supple.

3. ★ The nerve impulses from **temperature receptors** are interpreted by the brain, enabling us to feel whether our surroundings are hot or cold.
   - ★ Sensitivity to **touch** depends on which part of the body is stimulated. The tip of the tongue and the fingertips can distinguish between two pin pricks 1.0 mm apart. Two pinpricks on the thigh may have to be more than 60 mm apart before they are detected as separate stimuli.

4. ★ **Taste buds** help us to decide whether food is safe. A bitter taste is usually a warning signal not to swallow.
   - ★ **Smell** is defined as the detection of substances carried in the air.
   - ★ To be detected, substances which are tasted or smelt must first be dissolved in the watery environment covering the receptor cells.

Check the vibrations

In the concept map (pages 98–99), notice the different structures in the ear vibrating in response to sound waves striking the eardrum. The sequence reads:

- eardrum
- bones of the middle ear
- oval window
- fluid in the cochlea
- basilar membrane
- stimulated hair cells (receptors) fire off nerve impulses to the brain along the auditory nerve.

Fact file

★ The ear becomes less and less sensitive if it is regularly exposed to very loud sounds. At noisy discos, you can protect your ears by plugging them with cotton wool.

★ In most humans the ear lobe (pinna) is fixed. Cats and dogs, however, can adjust the pinna and turn it towards sources of sound.

★ A cat's tongue contains very few taste receptors which respond to sugar. Cats, therefore, are among the few animals that do not prefer substances with a sweet taste.

Humans (and other animals) as organisms

The eye at work

Look up from this page and gaze out of the window at some distant object. Your eye lens becomes thinner to keep your vision in focus. This change in lens shape to keep a nearby object and then a distant object in focus is called **accommodation**.

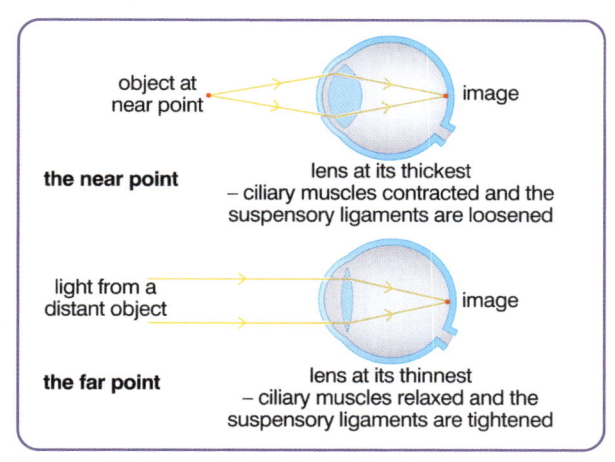

- object at near point → image
- the near point: lens at its thickest – ciliary muscles contracted and the suspensory ligaments are loosened
- light from a distant object → image
- the far point: lens at its thinnest – ciliary muscles relaxed and the suspensory ligaments are tightened

Accommodation keeps objects in focus

Fact file

★ Human eyes are damaged by ultraviolet light. However, insects' eyes can see in ultraviolet light.

★ A normal eye can see clearly any object from far away (at the **far point**) to 25 cm from the eye (the **near point**).

★ The image of an object on the retina is inverted, but the brain interprets it so you see it the right way up.

Light control

The **iris** controls the amount of light entering the eye. The intensity of light causes a **reflex response**. In bright light:
- the muscle of the iris contracts.

  As a result, the pupil narrows.

  As a result, the amount of light entering the eye is reduced.

In dim light:
- the muscle of the iris relaxes.

  As a result, the pupil widens.

  As a result, the amount of light entering the eye is increased.

5.8 Hormones

PREVIEW

At the end of this section you will know that:
- chemicals called hormones regulate the activities of the body
- hormones are produced in the tissues of endocrine glands
- endocrine glands are ductless glands – they release their hormones directly into the bloodstream
- hormones circulate in the blood and cause specific effects on the body
- the tissue on which a particular hormone or group of hormones acts is called a target tissue.

The hormonal system

The blood system is the link between a hormone and its **target tissue**. The sequence reads:

endocrine gland $\xrightarrow{produces}$ hormone $\xrightarrow{circulates}$ blood $\xrightarrow{hormone\ affects}$ target tissue

Hormones affect many of the body's activities. For example, the hormones **insulin** and **glucagon** help regulate the level of glucose in the blood and cope with the surge of glucose at mealtimes and when you eat a snack, such as a bar of chocolate.

Fact file

Most hormones produce their effects rather slowly. They bring about long-term changes in the body such as growth and sexual development.

Hormones called anabolic steroids are used illegally by some athletes to improve their performance. The hormones help to develop muscle tissue, giving an unfair advantage over other athletes who do not use them.

How hormones work

On pages 100–101 is the concept map which revises **hormones**. The numbers on the concept map refer to the checklist on page 102.

Humans (and other animals) as organisms

TASTE BUDS
receptor cells sensitive to chemicals in food × 400

× 100
section through tongue
nerve to brain

TONGUE
detects chemicals – taste

bitter
sour / sweet / sour
sweet and salt

CHECK LIST 4

THE NOSE detects chemicals – smell

patch of tissue sensitive to chemicals – contains **olfactory receptor cells**

CHEMICALS

THEY'RE SENSATIONAL!

SENSE ORGANS
The receptor cells of sense organs are **transducers** – they convert the energy of stimuli (e.g. light energy, sound energy) into electrical energy (nerve impulses)

HOT AND COLD
TOUCH AND PAIN

RECEPTOR CELLS IN THE SKIN

detect hot and cold, touch and pain

receptor cells sensitive to changes in pressure

hair
surface of the skin
touch
pain
cold
heat
receptor cells sensitive to changes in temperature

nerve fibres along which impulses pass to the brain

CHECK LIST 3

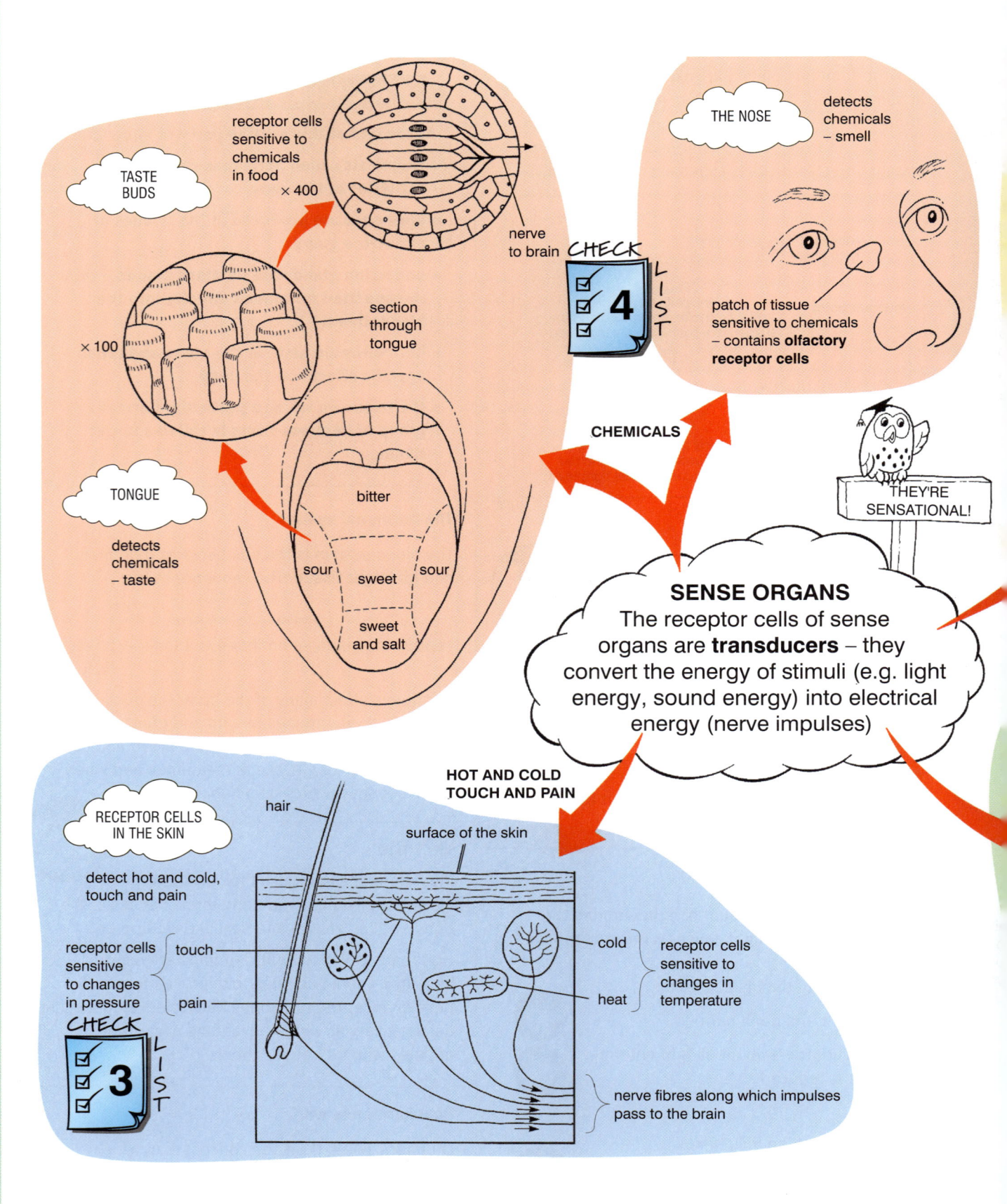

Sense organs (Checklist numbers refer to the checklist on page 96.)

98

Humans (and other animals) as organisms

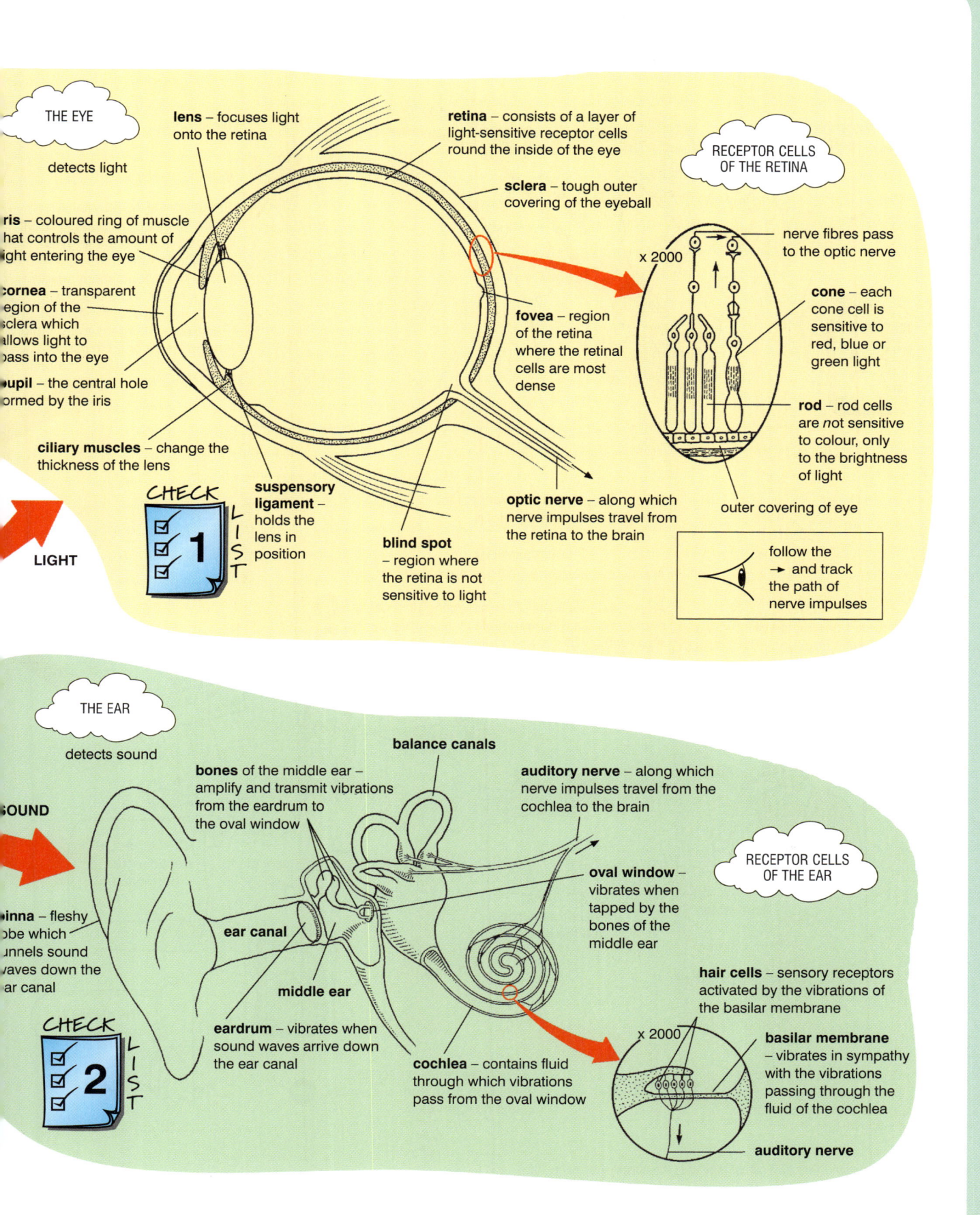

THE EYE
detects light

- **lens** – focuses light onto the retina
- **retina** – consists of a layer of light-sensitive receptor cells round the inside of the eye
- **sclera** – tough outer covering of the eyeball
- **iris** – coloured ring of muscle that controls the amount of light entering the eye
- **cornea** – transparent region of the sclera which allows light to pass into the eye
- **pupil** – the central hole formed by the iris
- **ciliary muscles** – change the thickness of the lens
- **suspensory ligament** – holds the lens in position
- **fovea** – region of the retina where the retinal cells are most dense
- **optic nerve** – along which nerve impulses travel from the retina to the brain
- **blind spot** – region where the retina is not sensitive to light

LIGHT

CHECK LIST 1

RECEPTOR CELLS OF THE RETINA
x 2000

- nerve fibres pass to the optic nerve
- **cone** – each cone cell is sensitive to red, blue or green light
- **rod** – rod cells are *not* sensitive to colour, only to the brightness of light
- outer covering of eye

follow the → and track the path of nerve impulses

THE EAR
detects sound

SOUND

- **pinna** – fleshy lobe which funnels sound waves down the ear canal
- **bones** of the middle ear – amplify and transmit vibrations from the eardrum to the oval window
- **balance canals**
- **auditory nerve** – along which nerve impulses travel from the cochlea to the brain
- **ear canal**
- **middle ear**
- **eardrum** – vibrates when sound waves arrive down the ear canal
- **oval window** – vibrates when tapped by the bones of the middle ear
- **cochlea** – contains fluid through which vibrations pass from the oval window

CHECK LIST 2

RECEPTOR CELLS OF THE EAR
x 2000

- **hair cells** – sensory receptors activated by the vibrations of the basilar membrane
- **basilar membrane** – vibrates in sympathy with the vibrations passing through the fluid of the cochlea
- **auditory nerve**

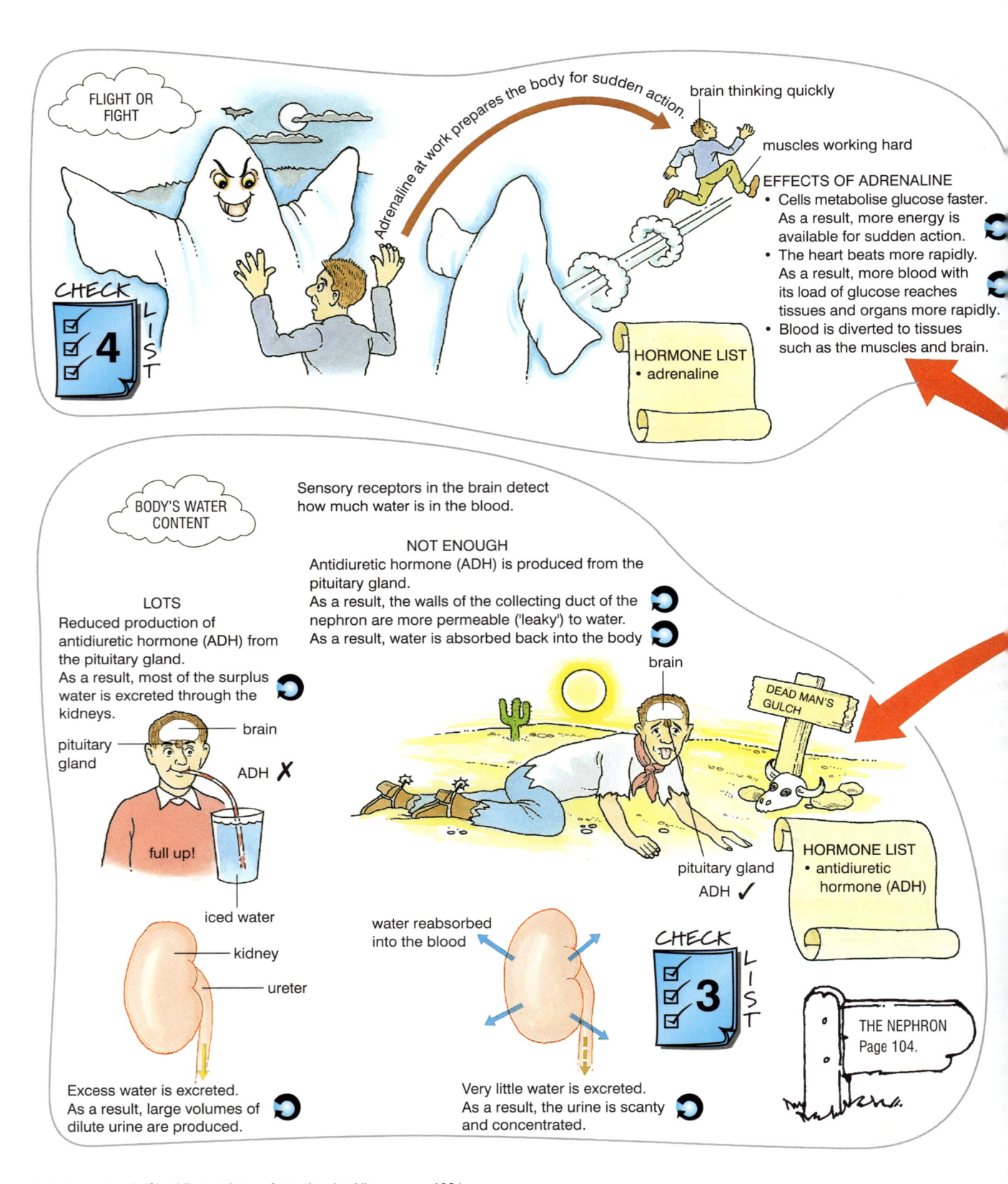

Humans (and other animals) as organisms

FLIGHT OR FIGHT

Adrenaline at work prepares the body for sudden action.

brain thinking quickly

muscles working hard

EFFECTS OF ADRENALINE
- Cells metabolise glucose faster. As a result, more energy is available for sudden action.
- The heart beats more rapidly. As a result, more blood with its load of glucose reaches tissues and organs more rapidly.
- Blood is diverted to tissues such as the muscles and brain.

HORMONE LIST
- adrenaline

CHECK LIST 4

BODY'S WATER CONTENT

Sensory receptors in the brain detect how much water is in the blood.

NOT ENOUGH
Antidiuretic hormone (ADH) is produced from the pituitary gland.
As a result, the walls of the collecting duct of the nephron are more permeable ('leaky') to water.
As a result, water is absorbed back into the body

brain

DEAD MAN'S GULCH

pituitary gland
ADH ✓

water reabsorbed into the blood

Very little water is excreted. As a result, the urine is scanty and concentrated.

LOTS
Reduced production of antidiuretic hormone (ADH) from the pituitary gland.
As a result, most of the surplus water is excreted through the kidneys.

brain
pituitary gland
ADH ✗
full up!
iced water
kidney
ureter

Excess water is excreted. As a result, large volumes of dilute urine are produced.

CHECK LIST 3

HORMONE LIST
- antidiuretic hormone (ADH)

THE NEPHRON Page 104.

Hormones at work (Checklist numbers refer to the checklist on page 102.)

Humans (and other animals) as organisms

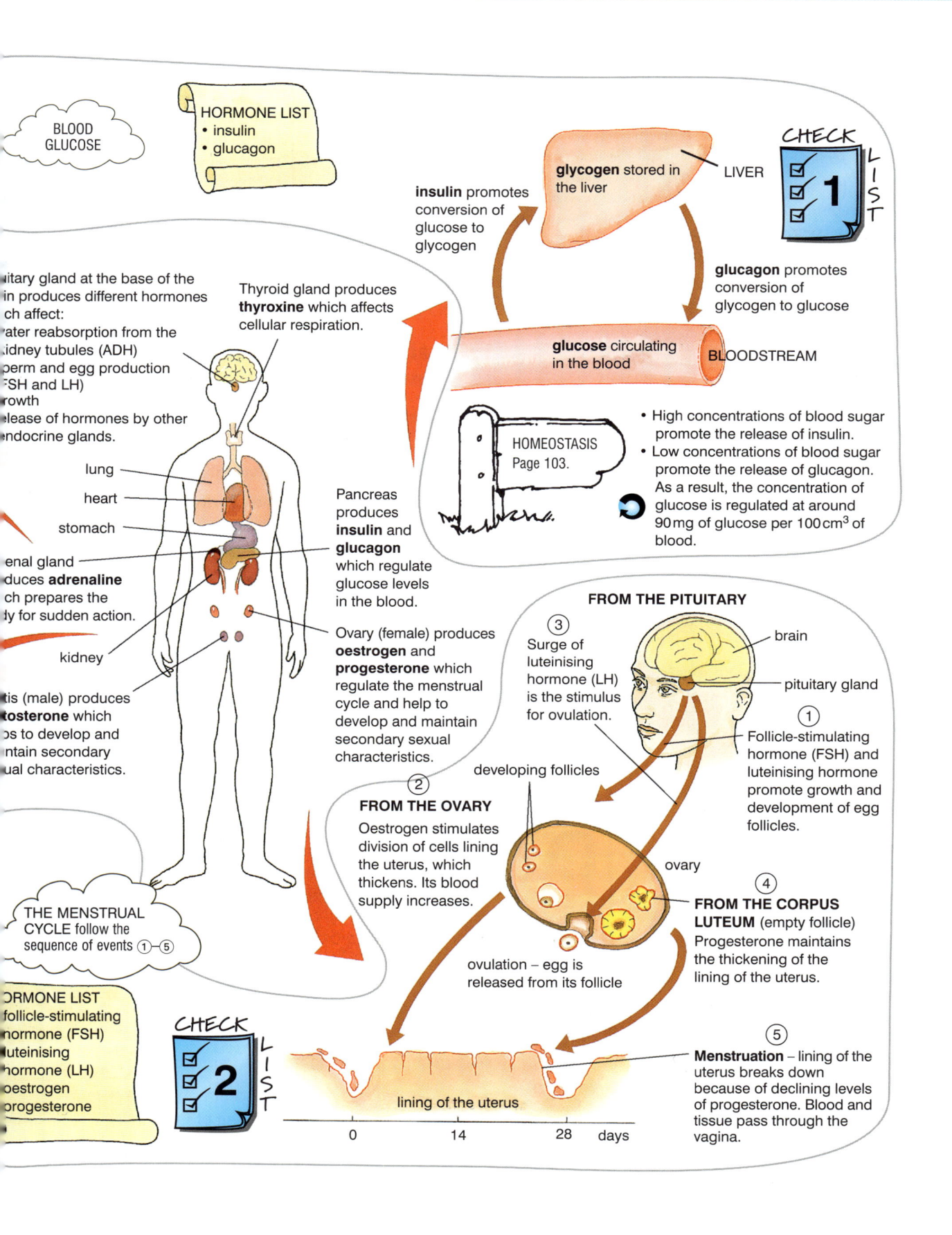

BLOOD GLUCOSE

HORMONE LIST
- insulin
- glucagon

insulin promotes conversion of glucose to glycogen

glycogen stored in the liver — LIVER

glucagon promotes conversion of glycogen to glucose

glucose circulating in the blood — BLOODSTREAM

CHECK LIST 1

HOMEOSTASIS Page 103.
- High concentrations of blood sugar promote the release of insulin.
- Low concentrations of blood sugar promote the release of glucagon. As a result, the concentration of glucose is regulated at around 90 mg of glucose per 100 cm^3 of blood.

...itary gland at the base of the ...in produces different hormones ...ch affect:
- ...ater reabsorption from the ...idney tubules (ADH)
- ...perm and egg production (FSH and LH)
- ...rowth
- ...lease of hormones by other ...ndocrine glands.

- lung
- heart
- stomach

...enal gland ...duces **adrenaline** ...ch prepares the ...dy for sudden action.

- kidney

...tis (male) produces **...tosterone** which ...s to develop and ...ntain secondary ...ual characteristics.

Thyroid gland produces **thyroxine** which affects cellular respiration.

Pancreas produces **insulin** and **glucagon** which regulate glucose levels in the blood.

Ovary (female) produces **oestrogen** and **progesterone** which regulate the menstrual cycle and help to develop and maintain secondary sexual characteristics.

THE MENSTRUAL CYCLE follow the sequence of events ①–⑤

...ORMONE LIST
- follicle-stimulating hormone (FSH)
- luteinising hormone (LH)
- oestrogen
- progesterone

CHECK LIST 2

FROM THE PITUITARY

③ Surge of luteinising hormone (LH) is the stimulus for ovulation.

- brain
- pituitary gland

① Follicle-stimulating hormone (FSH) and luteinising hormone promote growth and development of egg follicles.

developing follicles

② **FROM THE OVARY**
Oestrogen stimulates division of cells lining the uterus, which thickens. Its blood supply increases.

ovary

④ **FROM THE CORPUS LUTEUM** (empty follicle)
Progesterone maintains the thickening of the lining of the uterus.

ovulation – egg is released from its follicle

⑤ **Menstruation** – lining of the uterus breaks down because of declining levels of progesterone. Blood and tissue pass through the vagina.

lining of the uterus

0 — 14 — 28 days

Humans (and other animals) as organisms

Checklist for hormones at work

1. ★ If the pancreas does not produce enough insulin, a condition called **diabetes mellitus** occurs.

   ↻ As a result, the glucose level in the blood becomes dangerously high and can cause kidney failure and blindness.

   ★ People suffering from diabetes (**diabetics**) are taught to inject themselves regularly with insulin to lower their blood glucose level.

   ★ Glycogen is a polysaccharide whose molecules consist of hundreds of glucose units.

2. ★ The human female usually produces one mature egg each month from the onset of **puberty** (age 11–14 years) to the approach of the menopause (age about 45 years). Egg production becomes more irregular and then stops at the **menopause** (average age around 51 years).

   ★ The contraceptive pill contains one or both of the hormones oestrogen and progesterone. The hormones stop the ovaries from producing eggs.

   ★ Treatment with **fertility drugs** aims to stimulate egg development by raising the level of follicle-stimulating hormone (FSH) in the body.

3. ★ **Diuresis** refers to the production of urine. Antidiuretic hormone (ADH) counteracts diuresis.

   ↻ As a result, the flow of urine from the body is reduced.

   ★ Ethanol (the alcohol in beer, wine and spirits) increases diuresis.

4. ★ Unlike most hormones, adrenaline produces its effect very quickly.

   ↻ As a result, the body is able to respond to sudden shock or danger.

Fact file

Secondary sexual characteristics are the physical features which distinguish boys from girls. Testosterone helps develop and maintain the secondary sexual characteristics of boys. Oestrogen and progesterone help develop and maintain the secondary sexual characteristics of girls.

boys	girls
pubic hair develops	pubic hair develops
penis gets larger	breasts develop and fat is laid down around the thighs
voice breaks	menstruation starts
hair grows on armpits, chest, face and legs	hair grows on armpits

Secondary sexual characteristics

5.9 Maintaining the internal environment

PREVIEW

At the end of this section you will:

- understand that for cells to work efficiently, the composition of the tissue fluid which surrounds them should be kept fairly constant
- know about the important systems which maintain a constant environment in the body: the pancreas and liver (blood glucose), the kidneys (water content) and the skin (temperature).

Conditions in the body

The cells of the body work efficiently when they are:
- at an appropriate temperature
- supplied with an appropriate mixture and concentration of substances
- supplied with sufficient water
- at an appropriate acidity/alkalinity (pH).

These conditions are part of the body's **internal environment**. Different mechanisms help regulate the body, keeping its internal environment fairly constant. Keeping conditions constant is called **homeostasis**.

★ The **skin** regulates the body's temperature.

★ The **kidneys** regulate the concentration of salts in the blood, and the water content of the body.

★ The **liver** and **pancreas** regulate the concentration of sugar in the blood.

Humans (and other animals) as organisms

Homeostasis

Homeostasis depends on **negative feedback** mechanisms, which enable different processes to correct themselves when they change. In other words, the processes of life are **self-adjusting**. A level of a chemical or a temperature that deviates from a **set point** (a normal value) is returned to that set point. The menstrual cycle pictured on page 101 illustrates the principles. Rising levels of follicle-stimulating hormone and luteinising hormone stimulate the ovaries to produce the hormone oestrogen. Increasing levels of oestrogen feed back negatively, inhibiting further release of follicle-stimulating hormone. The level of the hormone returns to normal, its role of promoting the growth of egg follicles complete.

On pages 104–105 is the concept map for **homeostasis**. The numbers on the concept map refer to the checklist of points below. Study the concept map and its checklist carefully.

Checklist for homeostasis

1. ★ Each kidney consists of about one million tiny tubules called **nephrons**.
   - ★ The nephron is the working unit of the kidney. It is the structure that brings about homeostatic control of the:
     - concentration of salts in the blood
     - water content of the body.

   The kidney tubules are also responsible for the excretion of urea and other wastes from the body.

   - ★ **Diuresis** is the flow of urine from the body.
   - ★ Antidiuretic hormone counteracts diuresis.

     As a result, the flow of urine from the body is reduced.

     As a result, the loss of water from the body is reduced.

   - ★ Ethanol (the alcohol in beer, wine and spirits) increases diuresis.
   - ★ Antidiuretic hormone is one of the hormones produced by the pituitary gland at the base of the brain.

   ANTIDIURETIC HORMONE Page 100.

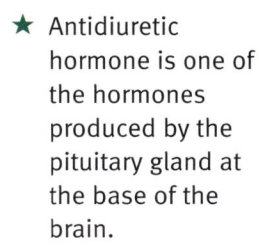

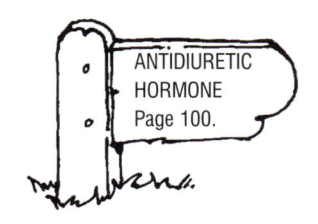

2. ★ Hair is made of the protein keratin.
   - ★ **Goose pimples** are bumps on the skin formed when empty hair follicles contract in response to cold.

Fact file

Liver metabolism releases a lot of heat energy, which is distributed all over the body by the blood. Humans (and other mammals and birds) have a high metabolic rate, which releases a large amount of heat. This is why mammals and birds are able to keep body temperature constant, even if the temperature of the environment changes. We say that they are **warm blooded**. Warm bloodedness means that the activity of enzymes (and therefore the activity of cells and the body as a whole) is at the optimum (most efficient) irrespective of the temperature of the surroundings.

Kidney disease

If a person's kidneys are not working (**kidney failure**) then:
- poisonous urea accumulates in the blood
- water accumulates in the tissues of the body.

As a result, the person dies unless treated quickly.

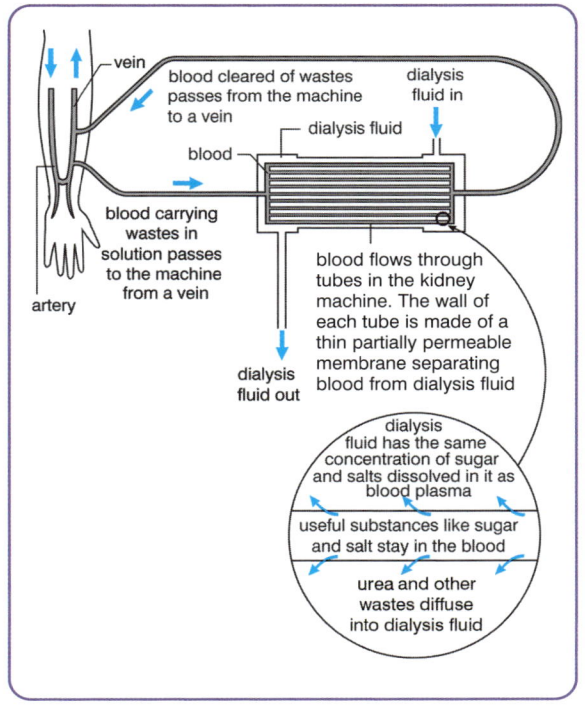

How a kidney machine works

- vein — blood cleared of wastes passes from the machine to a vein
- dialysis fluid in
- dialysis fluid
- blood
- artery — blood carrying wastes in solution passes to the machine from a vein
- blood flows through tubes in the kidney machine. The wall of each tube is made of a thin partially permeable membrane separating blood from dialysis fluid
- dialysis fluid out
- dialysis fluid has the same concentration of sugar and salts dissolved in it as blood plasma
- useful substances like sugar and salt stay in the blood
- urea and other wastes diffuse into dialysis fluid

Humans (and other animals) as organisms

CONTROLLING WATER CONTENT

- cortex
- medulla
- nephron
- ureter

- vena cava
- aorta
- diaphragm
- left kidney
- renal artery ⎫ the blood
- renal vein ⎭ supply to the kidneys
- ureter – urine passes through the ureter from each kidney to the bladder
- bladder – stores urine
- sphincter muscle – keeps the bladder closed. When it contracts, the bladder opens and urine passes to the outside.
- urethra – tube through which urine passes to the outside

Section lengthways through a kidney. Two zones of tissue, the cortex and the medulla, can be seen. The horseshoe-shaped Bowman's capsule is in the cortex. The rest of the nephron dips down into the medulla. (The nephron is drawn much larger than life.)

CHECK LIST 1

THE NEPHRON AT WORK

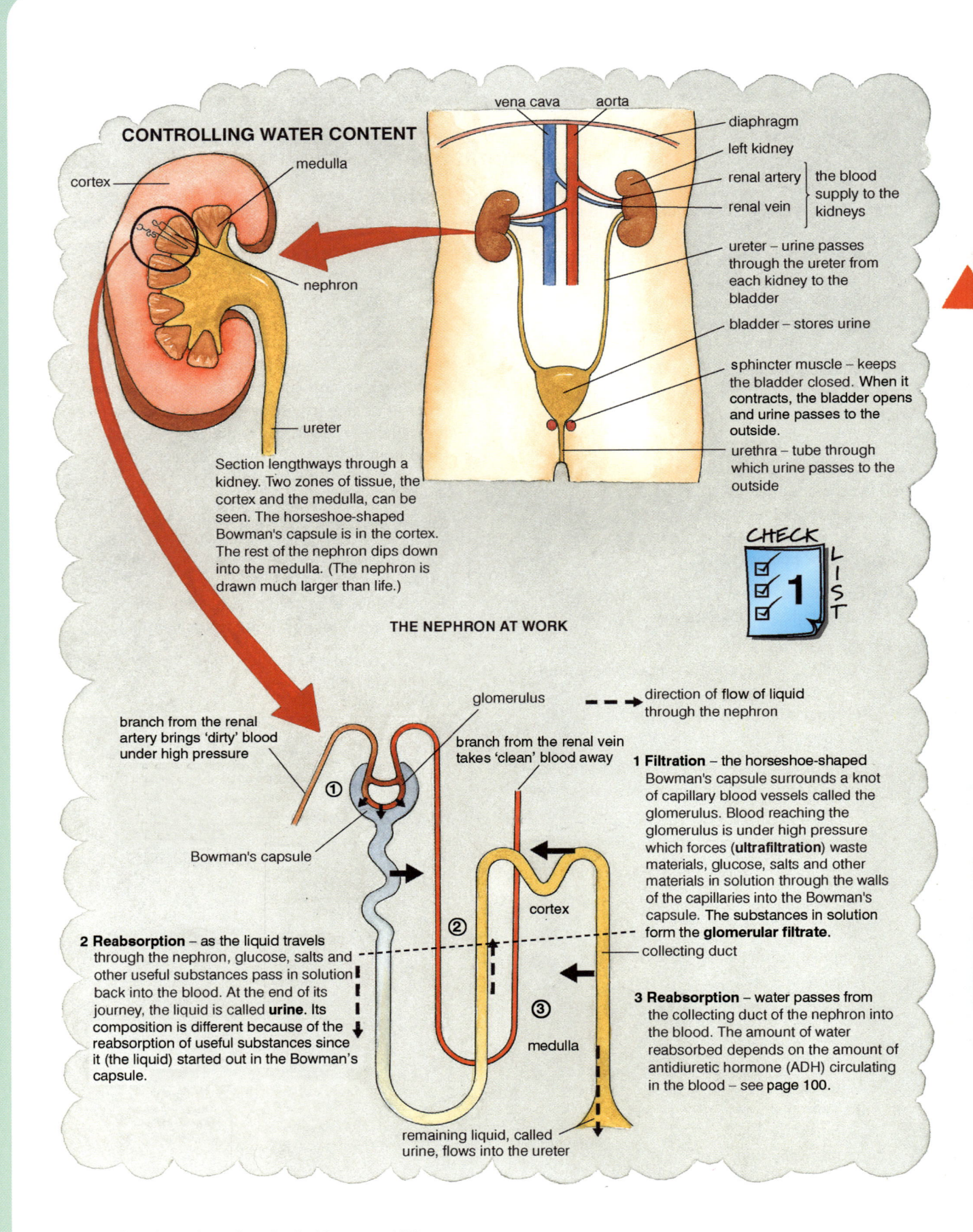

- branch from the renal artery brings 'dirty' blood under high pressure
- glomerulus
- branch from the renal vein takes 'clean' blood away
- Bowman's capsule
- cortex
- medulla
- collecting duct
- remaining liquid, called urine, flows into the ureter

- - - → direction of flow of liquid through the nephron

1 Filtration – the horseshoe-shaped Bowman's capsule surrounds a knot of capillary blood vessels called the glomerulus. Blood reaching the glomerulus is under high pressure which forces (**ultrafiltration**) waste materials, glucose, salts and other materials in solution through the walls of the capillaries into the Bowman's capsule. The substances in solution form the **glomerular filtrate**.

2 Reabsorption – as the liquid travels through the nephron, glucose, salts and other useful substances pass in solution back into the blood. At the end of its journey, the liquid is called **urine**. Its composition is different because of the reabsorption of useful substances since it (the liquid) started out in the Bowman's capsule.

3 Reabsorption – water passes from the collecting duct of the nephron into the blood. The amount of water reabsorbed depends on the amount of antidiuretic hormone (ADH) circulating in the blood – see page 100.

Homeostasis (Checklist numbers refer to the checklist on page 103.)

Humans (and other animals) as organisms

MAINTAINING A CONSTANT INTERNAL ENVIRONMENT

CONTROLLING TEMPERATURE

CHECK LIST 2

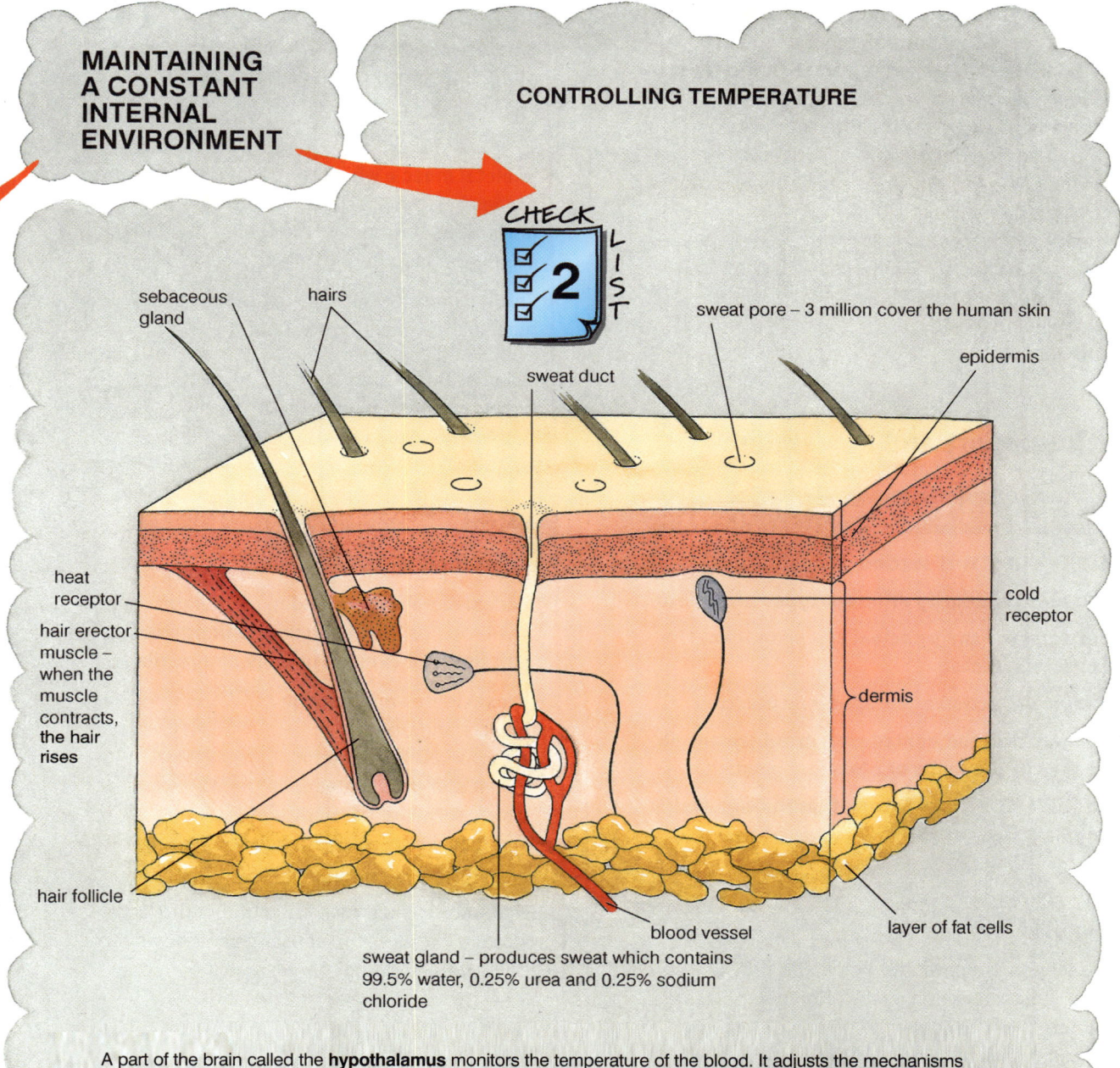

Labels on diagram:
- sebaceous gland
- hairs
- sweat duct
- sweat pore – 3 million cover the human skin
- epidermis
- heat receptor
- hair erector muscle – when the muscle contracts, the hair rises
- cold receptor
- dermis
- hair follicle
- blood vessel
- sweat gland – produces sweat which contains 99.5% water, 0.25% urea and 0.25% sodium chloride
- layer of fat cells

A part of the brain called the **hypothalamus** monitors the temperature of the blood. It adjusts the mechanisms of the body, so that the body's temperature remains constant. Different mechanisms help to control the body's temperature.
- Hairs raised by erector muscles trap a layer of air which insulates the body in cold weather (air is a poor conductor of heat). In warm weather, hair lays flat to the skin. Air is not trapped.
- Fat insulates the body and reduces heat loss. It is a poor conductor of heat.
- Sweat cools the body because it carries heat energy away from the body as it evaporates.
- Millions of temperature-sensitive sense receptors cover the skin. Nerves connect them to the brain which controls the body's response to changes in temperature in the environment.
- When it is warm, blood vessels in the skin dilate (**vasodilation**). More blood flows through the vessels in the skin and loses heat to the environment. In cold weather, the blood vessels in the skin constrict (**vasoconstriction**). Less blood flows through the skin and less heat, therefore, is lost to the environment.
- Shivering helps warm the body when it is cold. Small muscles under the skin contract and relax repeatedly. The contractions and relaxations release heat.

Humans (and other animals) as organisms

Kidney failure is usually treated by:
- **dialysis**. A **kidney machine** removes urea and other waste substances from the patient's blood. The diagram on page 103 shows you how the kidney machine works.
- **transplant surgery**. A healthy kidney taken from a person (the donor) who has just died or from a living person (often a close relative) who wants to help the patient, is put inside the patient's body. The transplanted kidney is connected to the blood supply and to the bladder.

BLOOD SYSTEM Page 84.

5.10 Support and movement

PREVIEW

At the end of this section you will:
- be able to identify different types of skeleton
- understand the principal components of the human skeleton
- know the action of antagonistic muscles
- understand the pentadactyl arrangement of bones in the limbs of birds and mammals
- be able to analyse locomotion through water and air.

Making the link

The skeleton supports the body, and provides surfaces for the attachment of muscles. Nerve impulses stimulate muscles to contract. They pull on the skeleton, moving it. The sequence reads:

nerve impulses $\xrightarrow{\text{stimulate}}$ muscles contract $\xrightarrow{\text{pull}}$ skeleton → ANIMAL MOVES

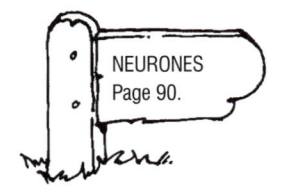

NEURONES Page 90.

Remember the different types of muscle in the human body.

★ **Smooth muscle** which is found in the walls of the intestines, blood vessels and air passages. It contracts slowly and steadily, and does not fatigue.

★ **Skeletal muscle** which is attached to the bones of the skeleton. Its quick, strong contractions move different parts of the skeleton. It fatigues after prolonged periods of contraction.

★ **Cardiac muscle** which is similar to skeletal muscle. However, it does not fatigue.

Muscle tissue contains fibres that contract when supplied with energy released by respiration.

RESPIRATION Page 80.

Skeletons

There are three types of skeleton.

1. **Endoskeletons** are found in vertebrates. The skeleton lies inside the body, surrounded by the soft tissue. It is made of **bone** and **cartilage**.

2. **Exoskeletons** are found in insects and other arthropods. The skeleton is made of hard plates which surround the body. The plates consist of the polysaccharide **chitin**, protein and other substances.

POLYSACCHARIDES Page 50.

3. **Hydrostatic skeletons** are found in the larger worms. The skeleton consists of a body space filled with fluid under pressure.

The human skeleton is shown opposite.

Humans (and other animals) as organisms

Appendicular skeleton | **Axial skeleton**

- pectoral girdle: clavicle (collar bone), scapula (shoulder blade)
- limb bones of the arm: humerus, elbow joint, radius, ulna
- pelvic girdle
- five fingers
- limb bones of the leg: femur, knee joint, tibia, fibula
- five toes

Axial: skull, sternum, ribs, one vertebra of the vertebral column

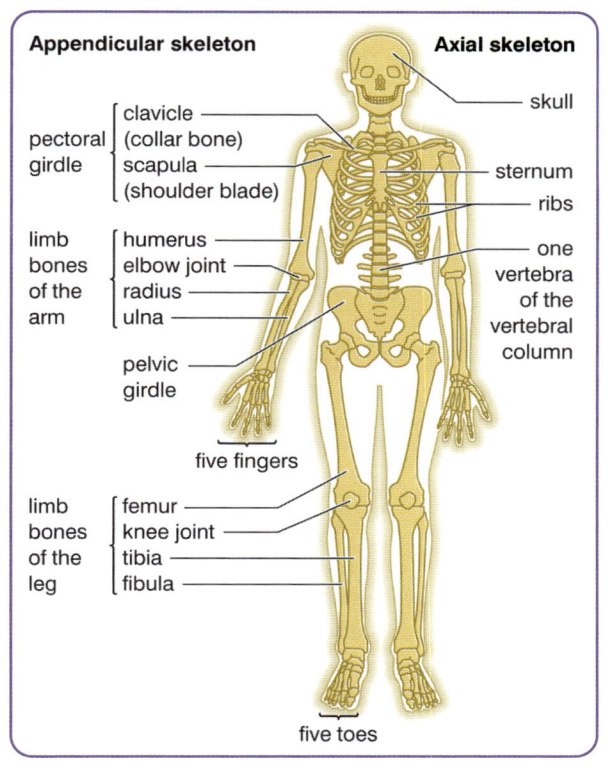

The human skeleton

★ **Joints** are formed where the bones of the skeleton connect to one another.

★ **Ligaments** hold joints together.

★ **Tendons** attach muscles to the skeleton.

As muscles contract and relax, they move the bones at the joints.

There are two parts to the human skeleton.

1. The **axial skeleton** consists of the:
   - **skull**, which encloses and protects the brain
   - **vertebral column** (backbone), made up of a series of bones called **vertebrae**. At the centre of each vertebra is a channel called the **neural canal**, which forms a continuous space in the vertebral column through which runs the **nerve cord**. The vertebral column supports the skull and the **pectoral** and **pelvic** girdles.
   - **ribs**, which form a bony cage protecting the heart and lungs.

BRAIN AND NERVE CORD Pages 92–93.

The axial skeleton protects the delicate tissues and organs of the body.

2. The **appendicular skeleton** consists of the:
   - **pelvic girdle**, which links the legs with the vertebral column. Its rigid framework allows forces on the legs to be transmitted to the rest of the body.
   - **pectoral girdle**, which links the arms with the vertebral column. Its flexibility gives the shoulders and arms freedom of movement.
   - **limb bones**, which in humans are long bones jointed at the elbows in the arms and at the knees in the legs. The limb bones also form joints with the girdles at the hips and shoulders, and with the hands at the wrists and the feet at the ankles. The joints at the elbows, knees, wrists and ankles enable the limbs to move freely.

Notice that the bones in each hand and foot are arranged as five **digits** (fingers and toes). The arrangement of digits and the long bones to which they are attached form the **pentadactyl limb** ('penta' means five). The limbs of vertebrates (except most types of fish) are based on the pentadactyl arrangement – EVEN MY WINGS!

wing

Types of joint

The diagram on page 108 shows a section through the joint of the elbow. Notice how friction in the joint is reduced to a minimum. There are different types of joint.

1. **Sutures** are fixed joints, for example the bones of the skull.

2. **Ball-and-socket joints** are formed where the upper long bones meet their respective girdles. The flexibility of these joints allows movement in all planes.

3. **Hinge joints** are formed at the elbow and knee. They allow movement in one plane only.

Humans (and other animals) as organisms

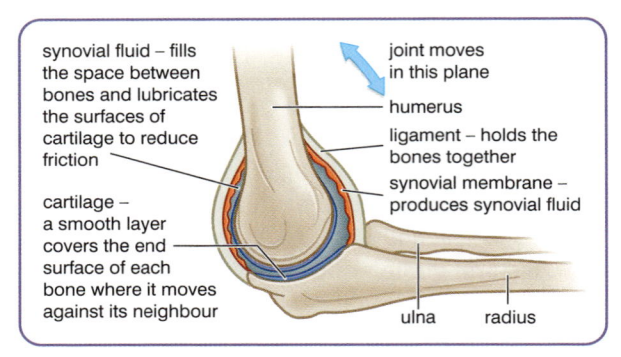

The structure of the elbow joint

Bone and cartilage

Bone is a mixture of materials. **Collagen** is a flexible fibrous material made of protein, in which are deposited **calcium salts** that strengthen the bone.

Blood vessels run through canals in the bone called **Haversian canals**, supplying the bone tissue with oxygen and food substances.

Cartilage is softer than bone. It contains fewer calcium salts. In humans, cartilage covers the ends of limb bones and helps reduce friction in the joints as bones move over one another.

Muscles in action

Contracting muscles pull on bones. A muscle will pull a bone in one direction; another muscle will pull the same bone in the opposite direction. In other words, muscles work in pairs, where one muscle of the pair has the opposite effect to its partner. We call these pairs **antagonistic pairs**.

The diagram at the top of the next column shows you how the **biceps** and **triceps** raise (flex) and lower (extend) the arm.

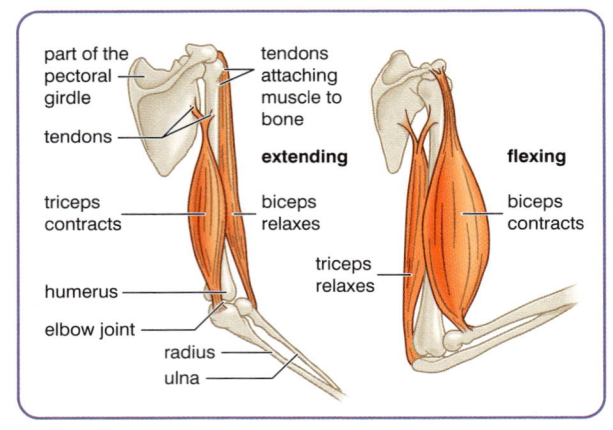

Antagonistic pairs of muscles flap my wings!

Moving the lower arm. The biceps and triceps work as an antagonistic pair of muscles.

How fish swim

The diagram opposite shows how fish swim. Blocks of muscle attached to each side of the fish's vertebral column work as antagonistic pairs, flexing the body from side to side. The side of the body pushes against the water, driving the fish forward. The fins control the direction of movement, and stability.

★ **Rolling** (rotation about the long axis of the body) and **yawing** (side-to-side movement of the head) are prevented by the dorsal and ventral fins.

★ **Pitching** (the tendency to nose-dive) is prevented by the pectoral and pelvic fins.

How birds fly

Birds are adapted to fly in the following ways.

★ Hollow bones reduce weight.

★ Flight muscles move the wings up and down.

★ Feathers smoothly shape the body.

The diagram on pages 110–111 shows how birds fly.

This is my spot folks – fame at last!

108

Humans (and other animals) as organisms

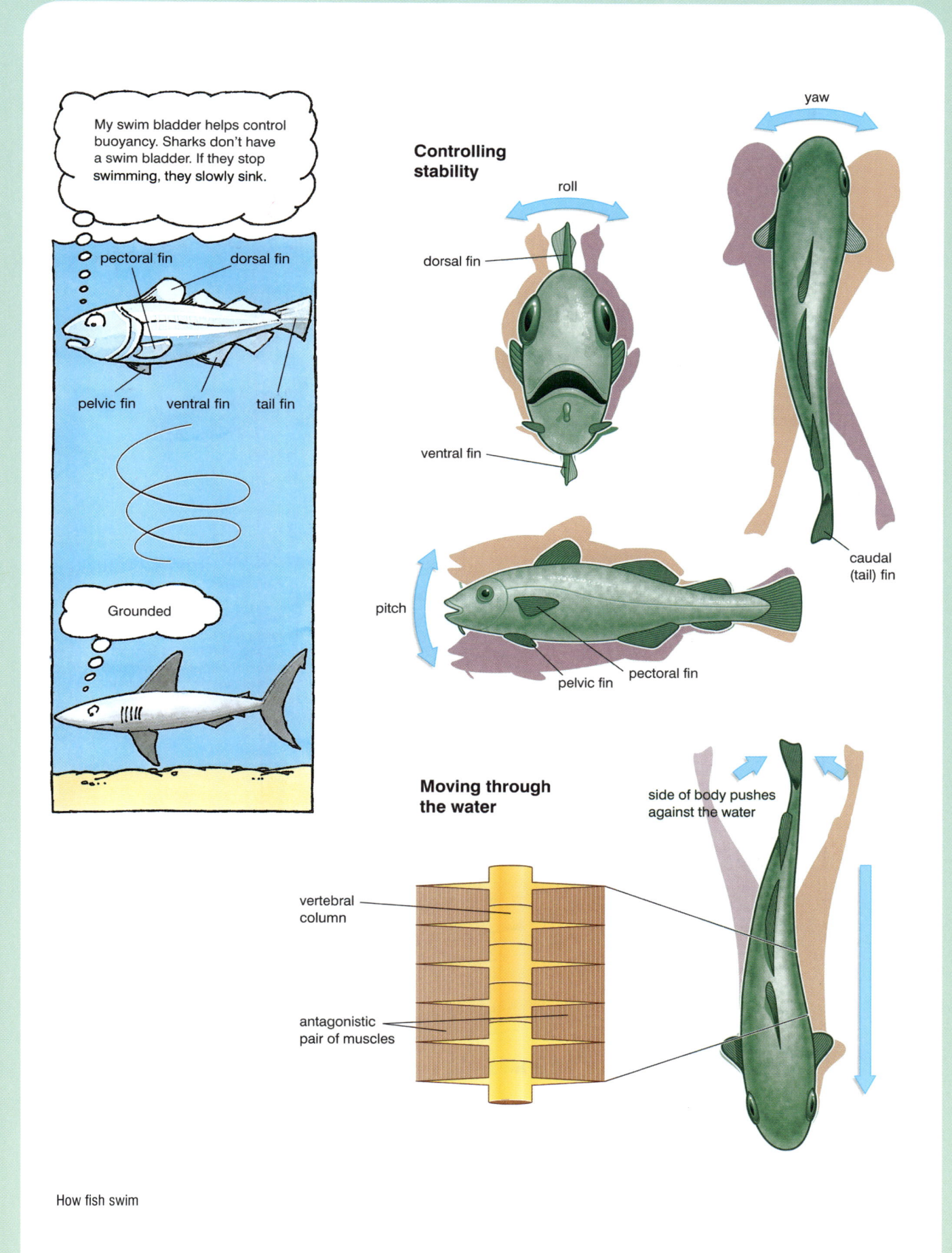

My swim bladder helps control buoyancy. Sharks don't have a swim bladder. If they stop swimming, they slowly sink.

- pectoral fin
- dorsal fin
- pelvic fin
- ventral fin
- tail fin

Grounded

Controlling stability

- roll
- dorsal fin
- ventral fin
- yaw
- caudal (tail) fin
- pitch
- pelvic fin
- pectoral fin

Moving through the water

- vertebral column
- antagonistic pair of muscles
- side of body pushes against the water

How fish swim

Humans (and other animals) as organisms

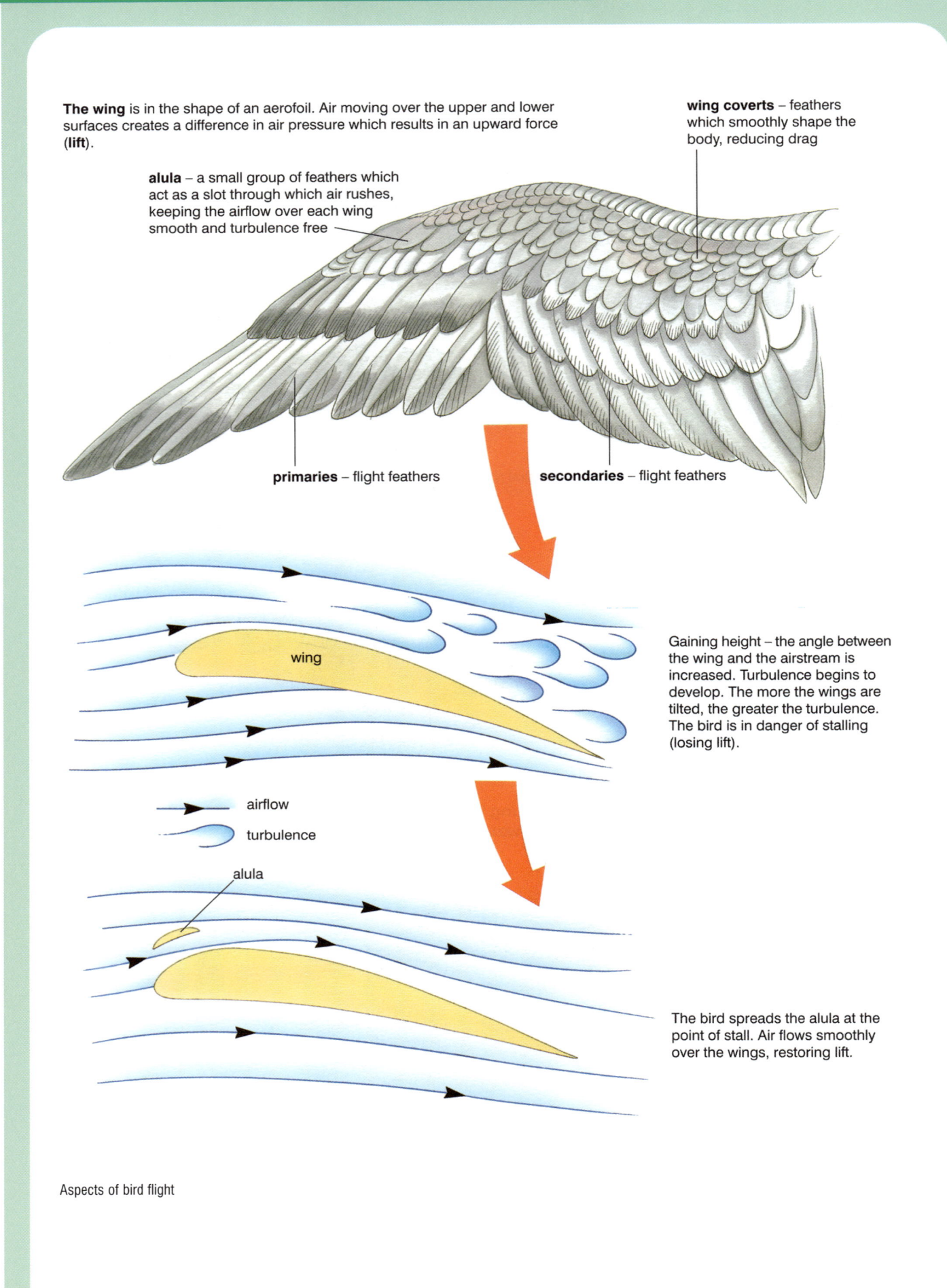

The wing is in the shape of an aerofoil. Air moving over the upper and lower surfaces creates a difference in air pressure which results in an upward force (**lift**).

alula – a small group of feathers which act as a slot through which air rushes, keeping the airflow over each wing smooth and turbulence free

wing coverts – feathers which smoothly shape the body, reducing drag

primaries – flight feathers

secondaries – flight feathers

Gaining height – the angle between the wing and the airstream is increased. Turbulence begins to develop. The more the wings are tilted, the greater the turbulence. The bird is in danger of stalling (losing lift).

→ airflow

↝ turbulence

alula

The bird spreads the alula at the point of stall. Air flows smoothly over the wings, restoring lift.

Aspects of bird flight

110

Humans (and other animals) as organisms

Upstroke – the recovery stroke which produces little air movement. The flight feathers separate and air passes through the gaps between them. Minimum air resistance means that the upstroke needs less effort.

humerus — 'rope and pulley' — upstroke
scapula
sternum
levator muscle (contracted) pulls on a tendon which forms a 'rope and pulley' system attached to the humerus, raising the wing on the upstroke
depressor muscle (relaxed)

section of the body through the line AB

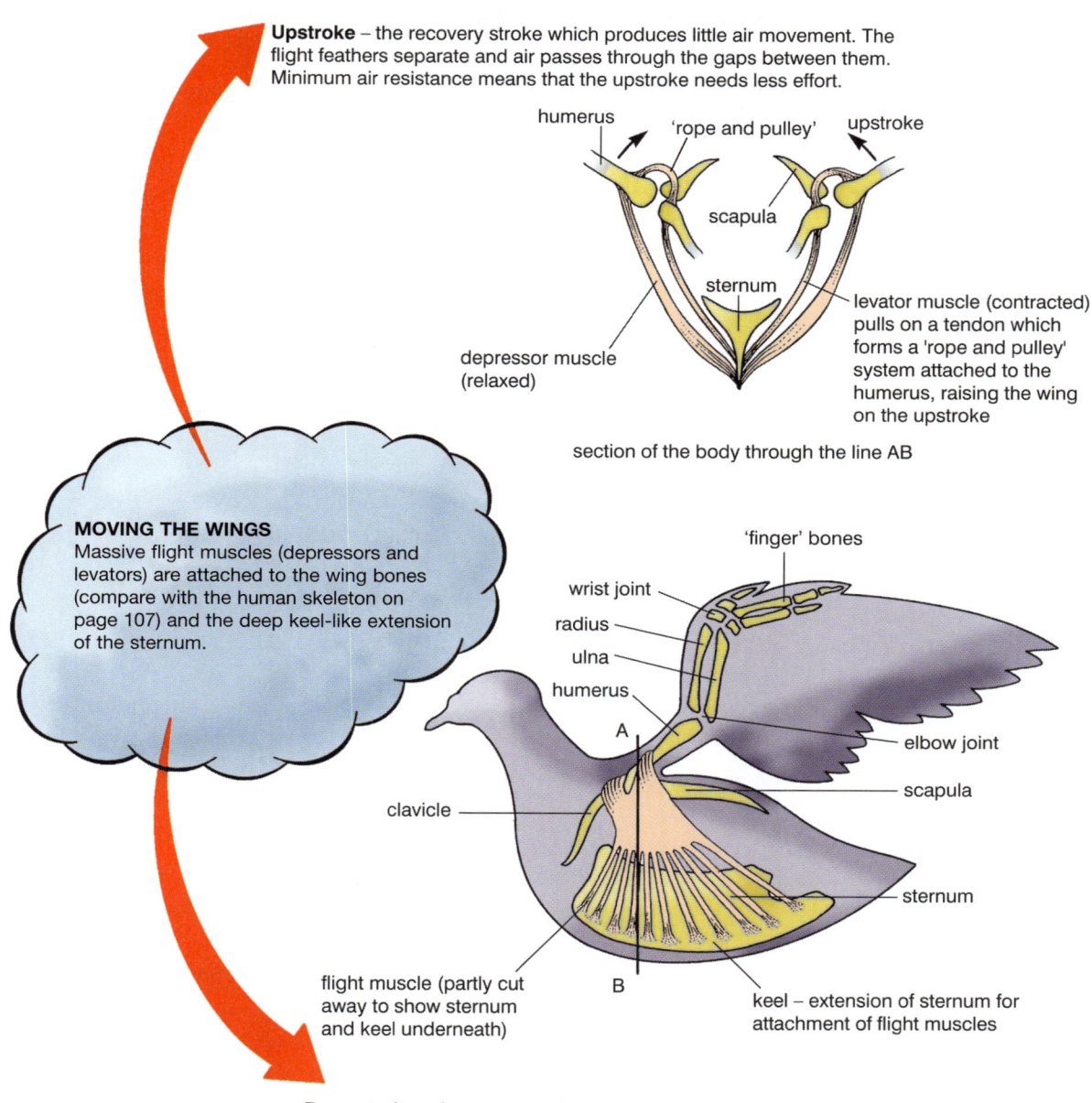

MOVING THE WINGS
Massive flight muscles (depressors and levators) are attached to the wing bones (compare with the human skeleton on page 107) and the deep keel-like extension of the sternum.

'finger' bones
wrist joint
radius
ulna
humerus
elbow joint
scapula
clavicle
sternum
flight muscle (partly cut away to show sternum and keel underneath)
keel – extension of sternum for attachment of flight muscles

Downstroke – the power stroke pushes air downwards, supporting the weight of the bird. The flight feathers form an unbroken surface which provides maximum resistance to the air underneath, generating lift.

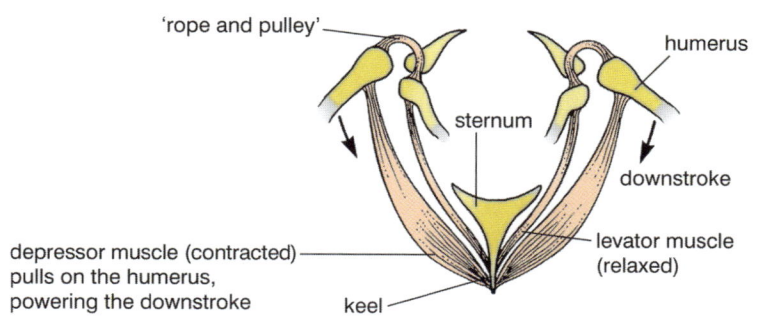

'rope and pulley'
humerus
sternum
downstroke
levator muscle (relaxed)
depressor muscle (contracted) pulls on the humerus, powering the downstroke
keel

section of the body through the line AB

111

Humans (and other animals) as organisms

ROUND UP

How much have you improved? Work out your improvement index on page 159.

1. Simple tests identify the nutrients in different foods. Match the nutrient in column **A** with the test result that identifies the nutrient in column **B**.

A nutrients	B test results
starch	forms a milky emulsion when mixed with warm dilute ethanol
glucose	produces a violet/purple colour when mixed with dilute sodium hydroxide and a few drops of copper sulphate solution
fat	produces a blue/black colour when mixed with a few drops of iodine solution
protein	produces an orange colour when heated with Benedict's solution [4]

2. Match each enzyme in column **A** with its role in digestion in column **B**.

A enzymes	B roles
amylase	digests maltose to glucose
pepsin	digests fat to fatty acids and glycerol
lipase	digests starch to maltose
maltase	digests protein to polypeptides [4]

3. Complete the following paragraph using the words below. Each word may be used once, more than once or not at all.

   **thin   exhalation   fat   oxygen   inhalation
   moist   carbon dioxide   exchange
   alveoli   surface area**

   The uptake of _____ and removal of _____ occur in the _____ of the lungs. These provide a large _____ for efficient gas _____. They are _____-walled, have an excellent blood supply, are _____ and kept well supplied with air by breathing. _____ takes air into the lungs; _____ removes air from the lungs. [9]

4. Distinguish between the following pairs of terms.
   a) oxygenated and deoxygenated blood [4]
   b) antibody and antigen [5]
   c) HIV and AIDS [3]
   d) haemoglobin and haemophilia [5]
   e) thrombus and thrombosis [3]

5. The different parts of a motor nerve cell are listed in column **A**. Match each part with its description in column **B**.

A parts of a cell	B descriptions
axon	minute electrical disturbance
dendrite	boosts the transmission of nerve impulses
sheath	transmits nerve impulses from the cell body
nerve impulse	carries nerve impulses to the cell body [4]

6. Explain the differences between the following pairs of terms.
   a) blind spot and fovea
   b) pupil and iris
   c) cornea and retina [6]

7. How do endocrine glands differ from other glands in the body? [2]

8. Briefly explain how antidiuretic hormone (ADH) keeps the water content of the body steady. [2]

9. Briefly explain
   a) why raised body hair helps us keep warm [3]
   b) why sweating helps us keep cool. [2]

10. Relative to the size of the rest of the body, frog tadpoles have a long coiled digestive system and frog adults a short one. Briefly explain why this suggests that frog tadpoles are herbivores and frog adults are carnivores. [4]

11. Complete the following paragraph using the words below. Each word may be used once, more than once or not at all.

    **dentist   hardest   softest   softens
    keratin   acid   alkali   calcium   sugar**

    Tooth enamel consists of _____ salts bound by the protein _____. This enamel is the _____ substance in the body. Bacteria in the mouth break down _____ to produce _____ which _____ the enamel, beginning the process of decay. Regular cleaning of the teeth and visits to the _____ help prevent tooth decay. [7]

Health and disease — Chapter 6

How much do you already know? Work out your score on pages 159–60.

Test yourself

1. Distinguish between non-infectious diseases and infectious diseases. Give *two* examples of each category. [7]
2. Match each body structure in column **A** with its role in the defence of the body against disease in column **B**.

A body structures	B roles
tear gland	produces sebum which kills bacteria and fungi
glands in the stomach wall	white cells produce antibodies which destroy antigens
skin	produce hydrochloric acid which kills bacteria
cilia lining the upper respiratory tract	produces the enzyme lysozyme which destroys bacteria
blood	sweep away mucus containing trapped microorganisms and particles

   [5]
3. Mumps and chickenpox are infectious diseases. Explain why we do not usually catch these diseases more than once in a lifetime. [5]
4. Distinguish between the following terms, which refer to aspects of tissue transplantation.
   a) donor and recipient [2]
   b) human lymphocyte antigens and red blood cell antigens [4]
   c) immunosuppressive drugs and antibiotic drugs [4]
5. List five different methods used to preserve food. [5]
6. Describe how domestic rubbish may be disposed of. [3]
7. Distinguish between antiseptics, disinfectants and asepsis. [5]
8. Briefly explain how mosquitoes transmit the parasite that causes malaria from person to person. [7]

6.1 Introducing health and disease

PREVIEW

At the end of this section you will:
- be able to distinguish between different categories of disease
- know about the defence mechanisms of the body
- understand the harmful effects of smoking
- understand the effects of drug abuse and solvent abuse on the body.

What is disease?

There are several categories of disease.

Infectious diseases are caused by a range of organisms. Disease-causing organisms are called **pathogens**:
- **bacteria**, for example, cause cholera, typhoid fever, tuberculosis, syphilis, gonorrhoea, whooping cough, tetanus
- **viruses**, for example, cause AIDS, 'flu, poliomyelitis, German measles, the common cold
- **fungi**, for example, cause thrush, athlete's foot, ringworm
- **protists**, for example, cause malaria, sleeping sickness.

Notice that microorganisms are the cause of numerous diseases. In favourable conditions (warmth, moisture, for example) microorganisms have the potential for reproducing very rapidly. If the microorganism is a pathogen, then the symptoms of disease soon appear as numbers build up. This is one reason why it is not a good idea to wear other people's shoes. Warm, sweaty feet are an ideal environment for the multiplication of the fungus causing athlete's foot. The fungus quickly spreads on contact with an infected person's footwear.

113

Health and disease

Fact file

Microorganisms are so called because they are only visible under a microscope.

Non-infectious diseases develop because the body is not working properly.

★ **cancer** – the uncontrolled division of cells leads to the development of a cancerous growth (**tumour**)

★ **degenerative illnesses** – organs and tissues work less well with wear and tear, for example, joints become arthritic and sight and hearing deteriorate with age

★ **allergies** – reactions to substances which are normally harmless, for example sensitivity to pollen and dust causes **hay fever**

★ **deficiency** – a poor diet may deprive the body of vitamins and other essential substances, for example scurvy (deficiency of vitamin C), rickets (deficiency of vitamin D), kwashiorkor (deficiency of protein).

Genetic disorders result from genetic defects and may be inherited. About 4000 genetic disorders affect humans. Genetic make-up also influences our vulnerability to diseases such as diabetes and heart disease.

★ **Down's syndrome** is caused by an extra copy of chromosome 21.

★ **Sickle-cell anaemia** is caused by a mutation of the gene (**allele**) controlling the synthesis of the blood pigment haemoglobin.

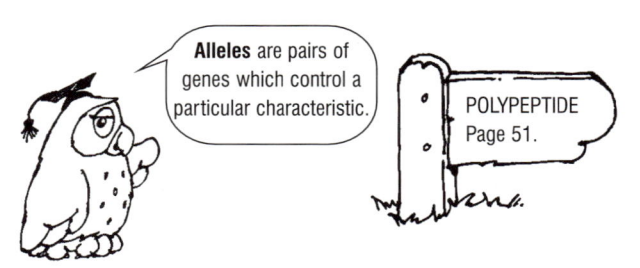

MUTATION Page 53.

POLYPEPTIDE Page 51.

Alleles are pairs of genes which control a particular characteristic.

★ **Cystic fibrosis** is caused by the mutation of an allele on chromosome 7. The allele controls the production of a polypeptide important for the transport of chloride ions (Cl⁻) across the cell membrane.

★ **Haemophilia** is caused by the mutation of an allele on the X chromosome, as described below.

The allele on the X chromosome normally controls production of **factor VIII**, a substance required for the blood to clot. The defective allele is recessive. The Y chromosome does not carry a dominant allele to mask the effect of the defective recessive allele on the X chromosome. Therefore a man with the defective allele produces no factor VIII, and suffers from haemophilia. For a woman to suffer from haemophilia, she would have to receive the recessive allele from both her father and her mother – a rare occurrence. A woman who has the defective allele on *one* of the X chromosomes is called a **carrier**. She does not suffer from haemophilia because the normal allele on the other X chromosome is dominant and therefore masks the effect of the recessive allele.

Muscular dystrophy is another genetic disease linked to the X chromosome.

Fact file

A disease is said to be **endemic** if it affects a small proportion of a country's population for most of the time. A disease is **epidemic** when it affects a significant proportion of a country's population for a limited period.

Fighting disease

The body's natural defences against disease are shown opposite. **Physical** barriers and **chemical** barriers keep us healthy for most of our lives.

White blood cells

Bacteria, viruses and other microorganisms may infect the blood and tissues of the body and cause disease. Two types of white blood cell, **lymphocytes** and **phagocytes**, protect the body. They work quickly to destroy bacteria, viruses or other cells or substances which the body does not recognise as its own. Such materials 'foreign' to the body are called **antigens**.

Health and disease

mucus – lines the upper respiratory tract. It **traps** bacteria and **particles** and is swept away by cilia.

stomach – glands produce hydrochloric acid which kills bacteria on food.

platelets – release a substance that promotes formation of clots which seals cuts.

cervix (part of the female reproductive system) – is plugged with mucus which is a barrier to microorganisms.

tears – contain the enzyme lysozyme which destroys bacteria.

skin – glands produce an oily substance called sebum which kills bacteria and fungi.

white blood cells – are produced in the bone marrow and lymph glands. They destroy bacteria, viruses and other organisms which cause disease.

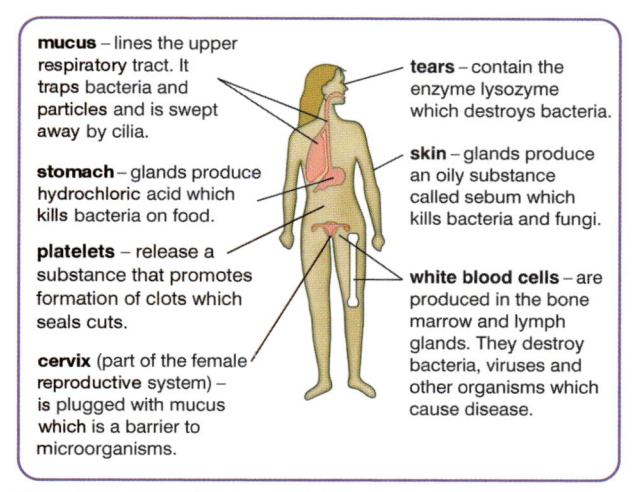

The body's natural defences against disease

There are two types of lymphocyte.

★ **B-lymphocytes** produce **antibodies** which are proteins that attack antigens.

★ **T-lymphocytes** do not produce antibodies. Instead they bind with an antigen and destroy it.

Phagocytes in the blood engulf and destroy antigens. Some phagocytes pass through the walls of blood vessels and migrate through tissues to attack antigens that have entered the body through cuts or scratches. Their action causes an **inflammatory response** – swelling, redness and heat as the phagocytes destroy the invading antigens at the site of the infection. The diagram above, right shows B-lymphocytes and phagocytes at work in the blood.

Diseases of the upper respiratory tract and lungs

Despite its filtering and cleaning mechanisms, the upper respiratory tract may become infected by disease-causing microorganisms. Infection of the:
- throat (pharynx) is called **pharyngitis**
- voicebox (larynx) is called **laryngitis**
- windpipe (trachea) is called **tracheitis**
- bronchi and bronchioles is called **bronchitis**.

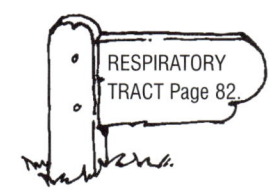

RESPIRATORY TRACT Page 82.

Pneumonia is an infection of the lungs caused by a particular type of bacterium. In pneumonia:
- fluid collects in the lungs.

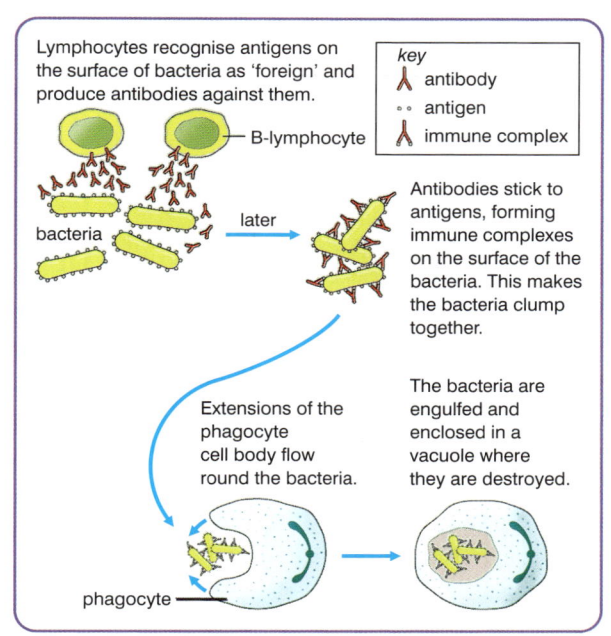

Lymphocytes recognise antigens on the surface of bacteria as 'foreign' and produce antibodies against them.

key
- antibody
- antigen
- immune complex

B-lymphocyte

bacteria → later

Antibodies stick to antigens, forming immune complexes on the surface of the bacteria. This makes the bacteria clump together.

Extensions of the phagocyte cell body flow round the bacteria.

The bacteria are engulfed and enclosed in a vacuole where they are destroyed.

phagocyte

B-lymphocytes produce antibodies which damage bacteria 'foreign' to the body (antigens). Phagocytes engulf the bacteria. (The cells are not drawn to scale.)

As a result, the surface area available for the absorption of oxygen is reduced.

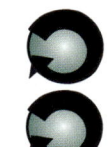

As a result, the patient becomes breathless.

Pleurisy is an infection of the pleural membranes caused by a particular type of bacterium. In pleurisy:
- infection makes the membranes rough.

As a result, there is pain when the membranes rub together.

Antibiotic drugs are used to treat pneumonia and pleurisy.

However, they are not an effective treatment for diseases caused by viruses because viruses can only reproduce inside cells. It is difficult to develop drugs that destroy viruses without also damaging the body's tissues. For example, influenza ('flu) is caused by a virus. Normally, treating a victim of 'flu amounts to little more than bed rest and good care, although the drugs **amantadine** and **zanamivir** are given to patients who are at high risk of serious illness. Amantadine seems to prevent the 'flu virus from multiplying; zanamivir relieves the symptoms of the disease.

Health and disease

Vaccination also helps to prevent the spread of 'flu. However, the surface proteins of 'flu virus, which act as antigens against which a vaccinated person produces antibodies, often change as a result of mutations. To be effective, new vaccines must be developed quickly in response to the changes.

'Flu virus is spread from person to person in air. An infected individual sneezes and the virus particles are carried in the jet of moisture droplets that shoot out of the nose and mouth. In this way 'flu virus (and other air-borne pathogens) infect people nearby, spreading rapidly in crowded places like schools and hospitals.

ANTIGENS Page 85.
ANTIBODIES Page 85.
MUTATIONS Page 53.

Fact file

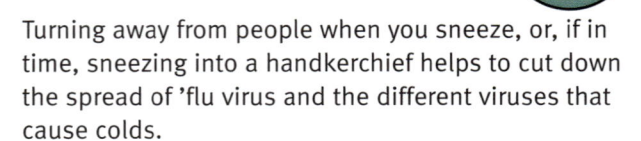

Turning away from people when you sneeze, or, if in time, sneezing into a handkerchief helps to cut down the spread of 'flu virus and the different viruses that cause colds.

Smoking

Smoking cigarettes is a major cause of lung cancer and heart disease. Cigarette smoke is acidic and contains various substances harmful to health.

★ **Nicotine** is a powerful drug which increases the heart rate and blood pressure.

★ **Carbon monoxide** is a poisonous gas which combines 300 times more readily with haemoglobin than oxygen does.

As a result, the level of oxygen in the blood is reduced.

★ **Tar** is a mixture of many compounds, some of which cause cancer (are **carcinogens**).

Some substances in cigarette smoke irritate the membrane lining the upper respiratory tract.

As a result, extra mucus (phlegm) forms in the trachea and bronchi.

As a result, the person may develop 'smoker's cough'. Coughing helps remove the excess phlegm.

Other substances in cigarette smoke stop the cilia from beating.

As a result, particles and microorganisms enter the lungs.

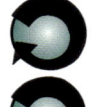

As a result, the risk of infection is increased.

Emphysema is caused by repeated coughing, which destroys the walls of the alveoli.

As a result, the surface area available for the absorption of oxygen is reduced.

As a result, the person becomes breathless.

Lung cancer is caused by the carcinogens in tar. Abnormal cell division in lung tissue leads to the development of tumours (growths) which may be difficult to cure. Cancer cells may break away from the tumours and circulate in the blood to start **secondary** growths elsewhere in the body.

The smoking habit

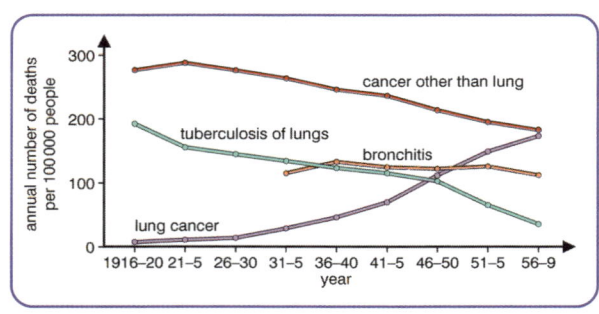

Deaths from lung cancer increased sharply in England and Wales from 1916 to 1960, which was the period when more and more people were smoking cigarettes. Other types of lung disease were declining.

Health and disease

Smoking cigarettes was fashionable in the early 1900s, and many people became smokers. Scientists soon suspected a link between smoking cigarettes and lung cancer.

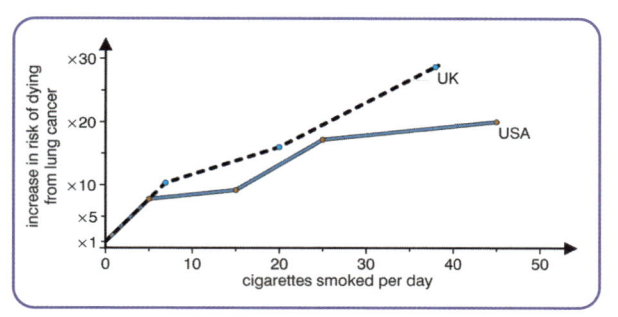

Studies have shown that the more cigarettes smoked, the greater is the risk of dying from lung cancer.

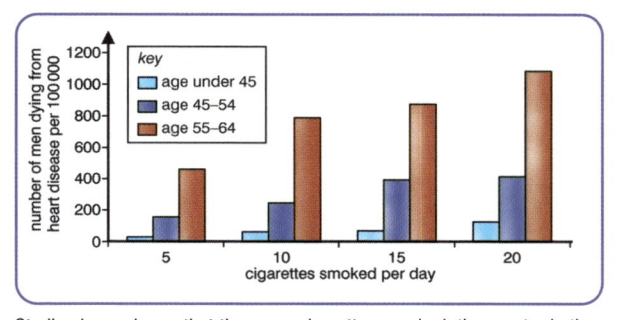

Studies have shown that the more cigarettes smoked, the greater is the risk of dying from heart disease.

Today there are fewer smokers than non-smokers in the United Kingdom. However, of the people who do smoke, there are many young people. SMOKING IS A MUG'S GAME – DO NOT START!

REMEMBER – IF YOU DO SMOKE YOU CAN GIVE IT UP. Advice and help are available.

Drugs

Drugs are used to help in the fight against disease. For example:
- **antibiotics** are used to attack the different types of bacteria that cause disease
- **analgesics** are drugs that reduce pain (painkillers).

Some drugs are highly **addictive** and may be **abused**. This means they are used for non-medical purposes.

Alcohol

Ethanol (the alcohol in beers, wine and spirits) depresses the activity of the nervous system. Small amounts affect the **cortex** of the brain which controls judgement. Large quantities affect the **motor cortex** which controls movement. Even more impairs memory. Drinking increasing amounts of alcohol affects other areas of the brain until it reaches brain centres that keep us alive. Death may follow.

Solvents

Glues, paints, nail varnish and cleaning fluids (dry cleaners) contain volatile solvents such as esters and ethanol. These are liquids in which other substances dissolve, and which readily produce a vapour at room temperature. Breathing them in gives a warm sense of well-being, but also produces dangerous disorientation. Long-term solvent abuse can damage the brain, kidneys and liver.

BRAIN Page 92.

6.2 More about immunology

PREVIEW

At the end of this section you will:
- understand the mechanism of the immune response
- be able to distinguish between B-cell lymphocytes and T-cell lymphocytes
- understand the basis of immunological memory
- be able to explain why tissue transplants are vulnerable to rejection.

Some definitions

★ **Immunology** is the study of processes that establish specific immunity in the body.

★ **Immunity** is the ability of an individual's immune system to destroy antigens, especially microorganisms and parasites that cause disease (pathogens).

Health and disease

★ The **immune system** consists of different categories of white blood cell – B-cell lymphocytes, T-cell lymphocytes and phagocytes – which destroy antigens.

> Read (or re-read) Sections 5.5 and 6.1 to check up on antibodies, antigens, lymphocytes, phagocytes and pathogens.

The immune response and immunological memory

The body's immune response to a particular antigen occurs in two phases.

1. a **primary response** when an antigen first invades the body. The body takes a few days to produce antibodies (part of the **immune reaction**) against a first-time infection. The delay may allow symptoms of disease to develop if the antigen is a pathogen.

2. a **secondary response** should the same antigen invade the body again. The secondary response to the antigen is much quicker than the primary response because:
   - **memory cells** left over from the division of lymphocytes during the primary response recognise the antigen and quickly divide.

     As a result of the rapidity of the secondary response, the immune reaction is almost immediate, destroying the antigen.

     As a result, symptoms of the disease do not develop.

Memory cells specific for particular antigens prevent us from catching diseases like mumps and chickenpox more than once. The rapid secondary response destroys the pathogens before they make us ill.

Lymphocytes

Lymphocytes are the white blood cells that recognise and react to antigens. They originate in the **bone marrow,** a yellow fatty material that fills the hollow centre of the shafts of the long bones.

Remember that there are two categories of lymphocytes.

★ **B-cell lymphocytes** produce antibodies specific to the antigen that triggers their response.

★ **T-cell lymphocytes** do not produce antibodies but:
  - bind with an antigen and
  - divide to form a variety of cell types that have different functions, for example **T-helper** cells control the production of antibodies by B-cell lymphocytes and **T-cytotoxic** cells destroy virus-infected cells.

Transplants and rejection

Tissue transplants help people recover from serious illnesses. The most frequent types of transplant are:
- skin – treatment for burns
- kidney – treatment for kidney failure as an alternative to dialysis
- heart – treatment for heart failure.

The **donor** is the person from whom the tissue is taken.
The **recipient** is the person who recieves the transplant.

> Why are transplanted tissues vulnerable to rejection?

Answer

The antigens on the cell membranes of the donor are different from the antigens on the cell membranes of the recipient. The antigens are called **human lymphocyte antigens** (**HLA**).

As a result, the recipient's immune system mounts an immune response to the 'foreign' donor tissue.

As a result, T-cell lymphocytes and phagocytes invade the donor tissue.

As a result, the donor tissue is rejected and the transplant fails.

Different methods are used to reduce the chance of rejection.

- ★ **Identical twins** have identical genotypes. Their HLA antigens are therefore the same, preventing rejection if one twin donates tissue to the other.
- ★ **Tissue typing** identifies the different HLA antigens in the donor and recipient. Matching the HLA antigens between donor and recipient as closely as possible reduces the risk of rejection.
- ★ **Immunosuppressive drugs** prevent the recipient's T-cell lymphocytes from acting against the antigens in the transplanted tissue. **Cyclosporine** is one of the most effective immunosuppressive drugs.

Sterile conditions are provided for the recipient's recovery, reducing the risk of infection while s/he is immunosuppressed.

Radiation treatment of the recipient's bone marrow stops production of T-cell lymphocytes which would otherwise act against the antigens in the transplanted tissue. The recipient's immune system is even more suppressed, so the provision of sterile conditions for the recipient's recovery is very important.

6.3 Controlling the spread of disease

PREVIEW

At the end of this section you will understand public health issues:

- disposal of sewage
- treatment of water
- storage of food
- disposal of waste
- immunisation programmes.

Making the link

Good health depends not only on the treatment of disease, but also on preventing disease. Hygienic disposal of sewage and waste, the safe storage of food, a healthy diet, the absence of military conflict and immunisation programmes are particularly important measures which control the spread of disease. Education that informs people of the importance of these measures to good health helps to improve the well-being of the public at large.

Disposal of sewage

On average a person produces 1.5 dm^3 of urine and faeces each day. Urine and faeces are components of sewage; so too are industrial and household wastes and the water and grit that drain from roads and paths.

Untreated sewage is a health hazard. It contains microorganisms causing diseases such as cholera, typhoid, poliomyelitis and diphtheria. It also attracts insects which help to spread disease.

Other microorganisms help us treat sewage by breaking it down into harmless and even useful substances. This treatment occurs in sewage works. The sequence of processes is shown in the diagram overleaf.

Treatment of water

Four-fifths of the diseases in developing countries are caused by people drinking dirty water. Providing water which is safe to drink is the single most effective measure for controlling the spread of disease. The process runs:

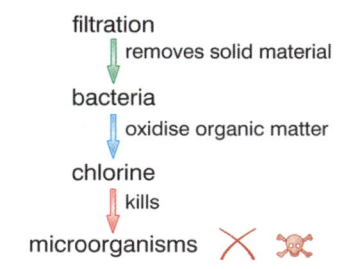

filtration
↓ removes solid material
bacteria
↓ oxidise organic matter
chlorine
↓ kills
microorganisms

✓ Result: the control of water-borne pathogens which cause diseases such as cholera and typhoid fever

Health and disease

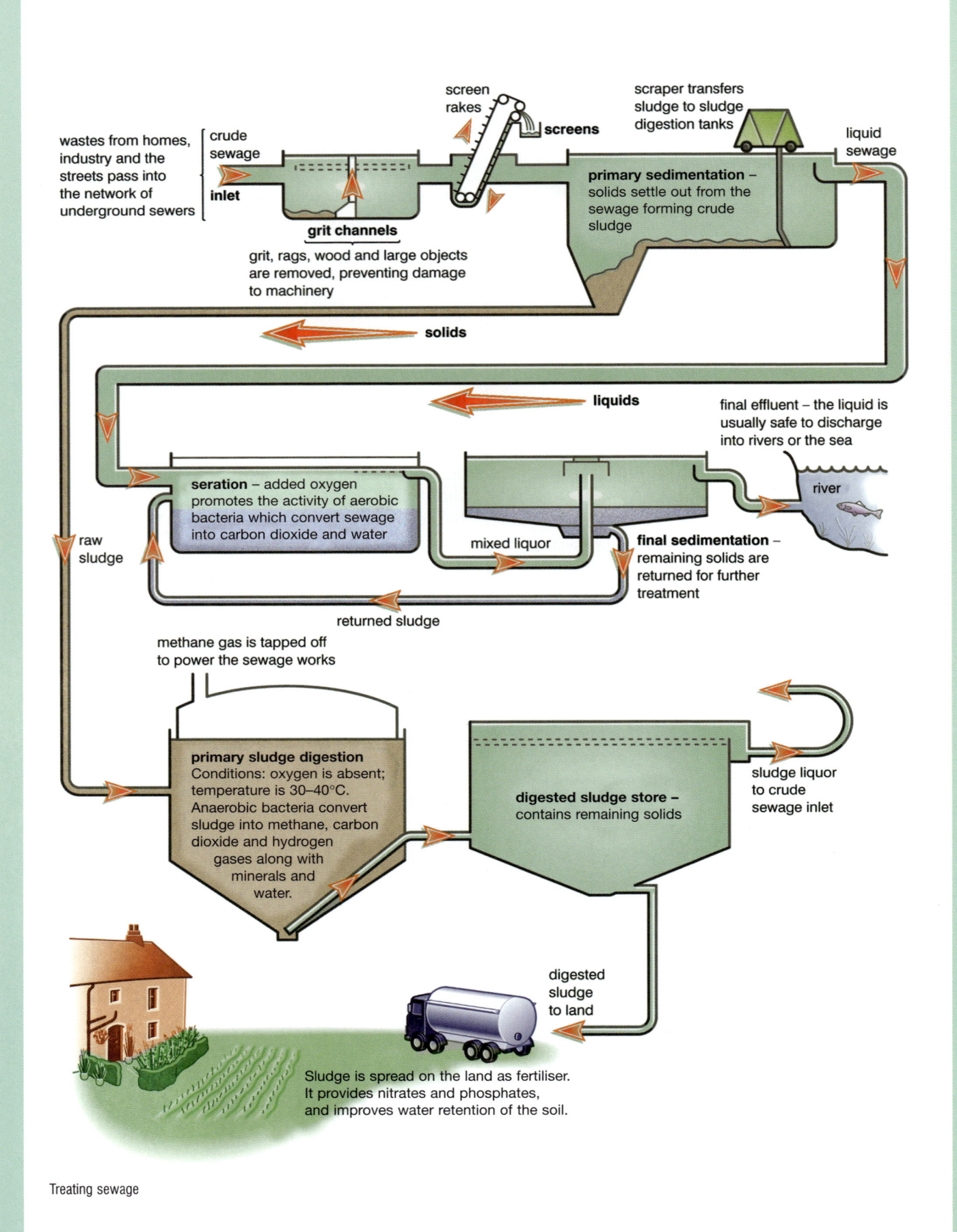

wastes from homes, industry and the streets pass into the network of underground sewers

crude sewage → inlet

grit channels — grit, rags, wood and large objects are removed, preventing damage to machinery

screen rakes → **screens**

scraper transfers sludge to sludge digestion tanks

primary sedimentation – solids settle out from the sewage forming crude sludge

liquid sewage

← solids

← liquids

seration – added oxygen promotes the activity of aerobic bacteria which convert sewage into carbon dioxide and water

mixed liquor

final sedimentation – remaining solids are returned for further treatment

final effluent – the liquid is usually safe to discharge into rivers or the sea

river

raw sludge

returned sludge

methane gas is tapped off to power the sewage works

primary sludge digestion
Conditions: oxygen is absent; temperature is 30–40°C. Anaerobic bacteria convert sludge into methane, carbon dioxide and hydrogen gases along with minerals and water.

digested sludge store – contains remaining solids

sludge liquor to crude sewage inlet

digested sludge to land

Sludge is spread on the land as fertiliser. It provides nitrates and phosphates, and improves water retention of the soil.

Treating sewage

Health and disease

Storage of food

Fungi and bacteria can easily come into contact with food, and some of them cause diseases. Methods of preserving food and preventing food-borne diseases include the following.

★ **Sterilisation** kills bacteria. Food is heated to a high temperature and then sealed in air-tight containers, such as tins.

★ **Pasteurisation** of milk and cheese means flash-heating the milk to 72 °C for 15 seconds, which kills most bacteria.

★ **Refrigeration** at a temperature between 0 °C and 4 °C stops bacteria from reproducing and slows their other activities.

★ **Freezing** at between −18 °C and −24 °C stops all bacterial activity.

★ **Drying** prevents bacteria reproducing.

★ **Ohmic heating** cooks and sterilises food by passing an electric current through it.

★ **Chemical preservatives** either stop the growth of bacteria, or kill them. Some chemical preservatives may cause irritation to the lining of the intestine.

★ **Pickling** stops the growth of bacteria.

★ **Jam-making** preserves food in concentrated sugar solution. Bacteria lose water by osmosis and are killed.

★ **Smoking** food over burning wood or peat deposits substances that kill bacteria and moulds on the food.

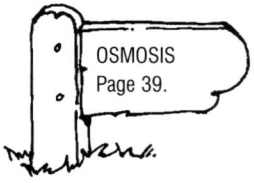

OSMOSIS Page 39.

★ **Irradiation** exposes food to gamma-radiation, killing bacteria and moulds. However, if the bacteria and moulds release toxins (poisons) into the food before it is irradiated, the toxins are not affected by the treatment and may cause illness if the irradiated food is eaten. The irradiation of food reduces spoilage and increases shelf-life. However, some people are concerned that there may be risks to human health.

Fact file

Cooking and boiling water are the means by which bacteria in food are destroyed. However, some types of bacteria produce **spores** that resist heat. Even if food is thoroughly heated, the spores can survive to produce new colonies of bacteria that may cause disease. Spores can also survive low temperatures, loss of water (desiccation) and the effect of different chemicals. They may develop into new bacterial cells when conditions favourable to growth return.

Food hygiene

Frozen food should be thawed before cooking unless the instructions say that the food can be cooked from frozen. It is especially important to thaw chicken and then cook it to a temperature of at least 68 °C, which kills bacteria, otherwise the centre of the carcass may not reach the 'safe' temperature. Chicken carcasses are often infected with *Salmonella* bacteria after slaughter, because the crowding in poultry houses provides an ideal environment for spreading the bacterium from bird to bird. Someone who eats food contaminated with *Salmonella* soon develops the symptoms of food poisoning, because of the production of bacterial toxin (poison) in the intestine. Symptoms include:
- fever
- pain
- vomiting
- diarrhoea.

The victim loses water and the body quickly dehydrates. Young children and elderly people are particularly vulnerable to the effects of food poisoning. As well as thoroughly cooking the carcass, improvements in the rearing of chickens (the birds are less crowded) and the suitable storage of meat help to avoid food poisoning by *Salmonella* bacteria. The bacterium *Escherichia coli* (*E. coli*) can also cause the symptoms of food poisoning.

Health and disease

Fact file

Flies release pathogens in the digestive juices they secrete through their mouthparts onto the organic material on which they are feeding. If the organic material is human food, then people are in danger of being infected with the pathogens the flies leave behind. We say that flies are **vectors** of disease because they spread pathogens from person to person. Keeping food covered helps to prevent the spread of fly-borne diseases, such as cholera and typhoid fever.

Disposal of waste

Insects are attracted by decomposing waste and may spread disease. Most household waste in the UK is therefore dumped into large holes in the ground. The operation is called **landfill**. Bacteria naturally present in the soil decompose the waste. When the hole has been filled, it is covered with soil and returned to agricultural use.

There are problems with landfill.

★ Decomposition of waste produces methane gas, which is inflammable. If the gas accumulates, it may explode. Modern landfill sites pipe off the methane for industrial and domestic use as fuel.

★ Water percolating through the waste dissolves salts of lead, cadmium and copper. These heavy metals are very poisonous and may leak from landfill sites into domestic water supplies.

Other ways of disposing of waste include **incineration** and **recycling**.

Immunisation programmes

The action of lymphocytes and phagocytes against invading microorganisms in the body is called an **immune reaction** (see page 118). The responses are the components of an **active immunity** against disease. **Immunisation** promotes active immunity to a particular infection. A doctor or nurse gives a person an injection, or a substance to swallow. The substance injected or swallowed is a **vaccine** and the process of being immunised is called **immunisation** (or **vaccination**).

Vaccines are made from one of the following:
- killed microorganisms which cause disease when alive
- a weakened (**attenuated**) form of the microorganism, which causes disease when fully active
- a substance produced by the microorganism which does not cause disease
- genetically engineered microorganisms.

GENETIC ENGINEERING Page 145.

A vaccine contains antigens from the pathogen which has been used to make it (the vaccine). The antigens stimulate the person's B-cell lymphocytes to produce antibodies. When the harmful form of the pathogen invades the body, the memory cells left over from the immune response to the vaccine quickly produce antibodies which destroy the pathogen. The active immunity produced by vaccines can protect a person from disease for a long time. **Booster** vaccinations keep up the level of antibodies and so maintain a person's immunity.

Children in the UK are immunised against different diseases that used to cause many deaths: diphtheria, tetanus, whooping cough, poliomyelitis, tuberculosis and German measles (*Rubella*).

Not all vaccines contain antigens that stimulate the body to produce antibodies. Instead, antibodies can come ready-made from other animals. For example, anti-tetanus vaccine contains anti-tetanus antibodies produced by horses. Immunity that comes from antibodies made in another animal is called **passive immunity**.

Remember that the work of the British doctor Edward Jenner (1749–1823) on the viral disease smallpox established immunisation as a powerful weapon in the fight against disease. The French scientist Louis Pasteur (1822–1895) established the field of **microbiology** (the study of microorganisms). He developed a vaccine against the viral disease rabies.

Controlling the spread of parasites

Remember that parasites live on or in their hosts to which they cause harm. Parasites can transmit pathogens to humans or release toxins (poisons) which damage tissues and organs.

★ The **head louse** lives in hair to which it firmly cements its eggs. The eggs hatch into nymphs, which develop into adults. An itchy head may indicate the presence of head lice. The adults feed on dead skin and heavy infestation may lead to skin complaints in the affected person. People huddling together makes it easier for head lice to pass from person to person. Washing hair with a special shampoo helps to control infestations.

★ The **tapeworm** lives in the human intestine. In the case of the pork tapeworm, the young stages (larvae) of the tapeworm become embedded in the muscles (the pork meat we eat) of the pig. If the muscle is eaten as undercooked pork, then the larvae develop into adult tapeworms inside the intestine. The tapeworms release toxins that make the person ill. Inspecting meat for tapeworm larvae before it is sold for human consumption, and cooking meat thoroughly are important precautions that help to control the spread of tapeworms.

Fact file

Each year, air travel moves millions of people at great speed around the world. Speed means that travellers may reach their destination infected with pathogens before the symptoms of disease are apparent. Vaccination of travellers helps to prevent the spread of infectious diseases.

Health and disease

6.4 Fighting infectious diseases

PREVIEW

At the end of this section you will:
- be able to distinguish between antisepsis and asepsis
- know that drugs are used to attack different pathogens
- understand how pathogens develop resistance to drugs
- be able to explain why mosquitoes are vectors of different diseases, especially malaria.

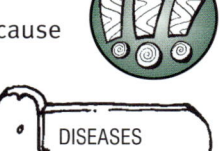

★ **Remember** that organisms that cause disease are called **pathogens**.

★ Diseases are said to be **infectious** if the organisms can be passed from one person to another.

DISEASES Pages 113–4.

Antiseptics, disinfectants and aseptic surgery

Antiseptics and disinfectants are chemicals that we use outside the body to attack microorganisms which might otherwise cause disease.

★ **Antiseptics** stop microorganisms from multiplying. They can be used to swab a wound or before an injection to clean the area of skin where the hypodermic needle is to be inserted.

★ **Disinfectants** are usually stronger than antiseptics. They kill microorganisms and are used to keep surfaces such as lavatory bowls and kitchen tables free from microorganisms.

★ **Washing** regularly with soap (or soap solutions) kills and/or removes microorganisms from the surfaces of the body. It helps, therefore, to prevent the build up of possible pathogens on the individual and to prevent their spread to food and other people.

123

Health and disease

Aseptic surgery aims to prevent microorganisms from infecting a wound. The following procedures keep the operating theatre, where surgery takes place, as sterile as possible.

- Sterilised gowns and gloves are worn by surgeons and their assistants.
- Air entering the operating theatre is filtered.
- Equipment, furniture and surfaces are designed to be easy to clean.

Chemotherapy

The word **chemotherapy** means using drugs to combat pathogens. **Antibiotic** drugs attack bacteria which cause disease.

- **Bactericides** such as penicillin kill bacteria.
- **Bacteristats** such as tetracycline prevent bacteria from multiplying.

The diagram below shows how different antibiotics affect bacteria. A range of microorganisms produces a variety of antibiotics.

- **Penicillins** are produced by a number of genetically different strains of the fungus *Penicillium*.
- **Cephalosporins** are produced by the fungus *Cephalosporium*.
- **Tetracyclines** are produced by the bacterium *Streptomyces*.

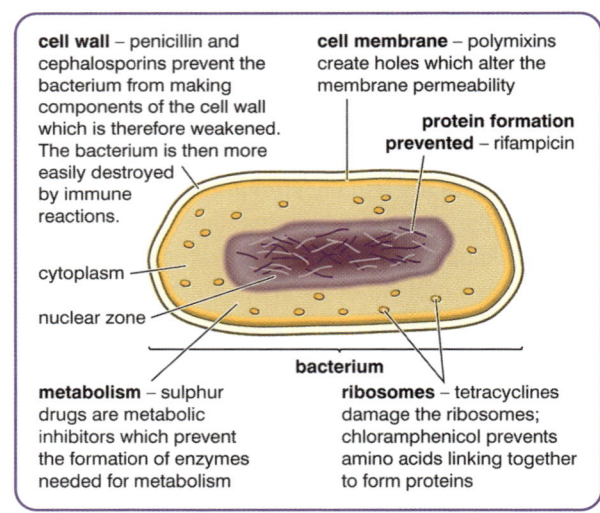

cell wall – penicillin and cephalosporins prevent the bacterium from making components of the cell wall which is therefore weakened. The bacterium is then more easily destroyed by immune reactions.

cell membrane – polymixins create holes which alter the membrane permeability

protein formation prevented – rifampicin

cytoplasm

nuclear zone

bacterium

metabolism – sulphur drugs are metabolic inhibitors which prevent the formation of enzymes needed for metabolism

ribosomes – tetracyclines damage the ribosomes; chloramphenicol prevents amino acids linking together to form proteins

Antibiotic drugs at work. Ribosomes are the places within the cell where proteins are made.

Fact file

Three scientists were involved in the discovery and development of penicillin.

★ In 1928 **Alexander Fleming** noticed that the mould *Penicillium notatum* killed bacteria. He isolated the active substance and called it **penicillin**.

★ In 1938 **Howard Florey** and **Ernst Chain** began to develop methods to produce enough penicillin for clinical trials. *P. notatum* was replaced by *P. chrysogenum*, which produces more penicillin.

★ By 1944 penicillin was in large-scale production, following the move of production from Britain to the USA at the onset of the Second World War.

Penicillium is grown in large fermenters. In the 1950s, 1 dm^3 batch of *Penicillium* and nutrient solution produced 60 mg of penicillin. Today, 20 g of penicillin can be extracted from the same volume of material owing to advances in biotechnology and control of fermentation processes.

Resistance

Bacteria can become **resistant** to a particular antibiotic. The antibiotic becomes less effective for the treatment of disease.

★ The dosage of a drug to which bacteria are becoming resistant has to be gradually increased as symptoms continue.

As a result, the drug becomes increasingly inefficient as resistance develops.

As a result, the drug may become poisonous to the patient.

How can we slow the spread of resistance?

Answer

★ Avoid using antibiotics by practising good hygiene to prevent the spread of infection.

★ Use antibiotics sparingly when drugs are needed to treat infection.

★ Finish a prescribed course of antibiotics.

★ Reduce the antibiotics given to farm animals.

How do doctors deal with resistant infections?

Answer

★ Different types of antibiotic are prescribed to treat different diseases, and drugs are switched if resistance develops.

★ Research scientists work continually to develop new antibiotics.

However, the race to develop new drugs as bacteria develop resistance to existing ones is a close one. It is an example of the 'Red Queen Effect'. Find out what the Red Queen says to Alice in *Through the Looking Glass* by Lewis Carroll.

Mosquitoes and malaria

The transmission of malaria involves the steps given below.

★ *Plasmodium* species are protists that cause human malaria. The parasites infect liver cells and red blood cells.

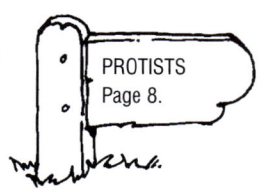

PROTISTS Page 8.

★ Female *Anopheles* mosquitoes feed on human blood.

★ The mosquitoes suck up the parasites in the red blood cells when they feed on infected people.

★ A mosquito that has fed on infected people transmits the parasite to new human hosts when it feeds on them.

The diagram overleaf shows the relationship beween parasite, mosquito and people.

★ The **host** is a person who is infected with a parasite.

★ The **vector** transmits the disease. The female *Anopheles* mosquito is the vector for malaria because it transmits the *Plasmodium* parasite from host to new host.

Treatment and prevention of malaria

Fighting malaria depends on the factors listed below.

★ **Treatment:**
  - drugs like malorone, chloroquine and quinacrine destroy the parasite in the host
  - vaccines (under development) inhibit different stages in the parasite's life cycle.

★ **Destroying the mosquito vector:**
  - draining marshes, ponds and ditches prevents the female mosquito from laying eggs, and the eggs from developing into larvae
  - spraying insecticides onto the water's surface kills mosquito larvae and pupae
  - introducing fish which eat mosquito larvae (an example of **biological control**).

★ **Preventing contact between mosquitoes and people:**
  - bed nets soaked with insecticide protect people from mosquitoes while they are asleep
  - chemical repellant sprayed on the skin and clothes deters mosquitoes from landing on the body.

Health and disease

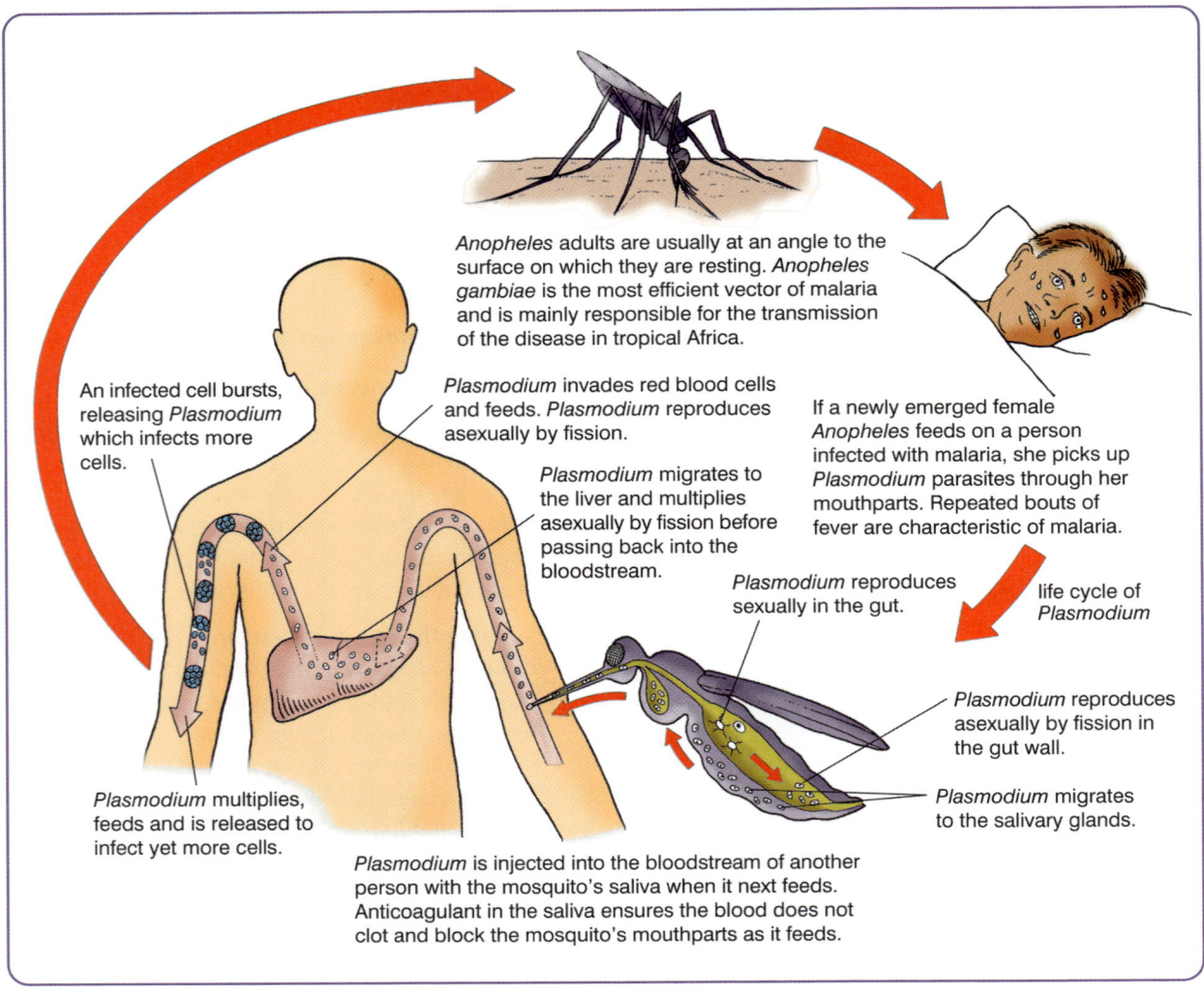

Anopheles adults are usually at an angle to the surface on which they are resting. *Anopheles gambiae* is the most efficient vector of malaria and is mainly responsible for the transmission of the disease in tropical Africa.

An infected cell bursts, releasing *Plasmodium* which infects more cells.

Plasmodium invades red blood cells and feeds. *Plasmodium* reproduces asexually by fission.

Plasmodium migrates to the liver and multiplies asexually by fission before passing back into the bloodstream.

If a newly emerged female *Anopheles* feeds on a person infected with malaria, she picks up *Plasmodium* parasites through her mouthparts. Repeated bouts of fever are characteristic of malaria.

Plasmodium reproduces sexually in the gut.

life cycle of *Plasmodium*

Plasmodium reproduces asexually by fission in the gut wall.

Plasmodium migrates to the salivary glands.

Plasmodium multiplies, feeds and is released to infect yet more cells.

Plasmodium is injected into the bloodstream of another person with the mosquito's saliva when it next feeds. Anticoagulant in the saliva ensures the blood does not clot and block the mosquito's mouthparts as it feeds.

Transmission of the malaria parasite

ROUND UP

How much have you improved? Work out your improvement index on pages 160–161.

1. Identify the cause of each disease in the list by writing either **B** (for bacterium) or **V** (for virus) next to each one.
   cholera AIDS syphilis 'flu pneumonia [5]

2. List the different types of white blood cell. Explain the role of each type of cell in the defence of the body against disease. [6]

3. Match each of the body's natural defences against disease in column A with its correct description in column B. [5]

A defences	B descriptions
mucus	a substance which kills bacteria and fungi on the skin
lysozyme	destroy antigens
hydrochloric acid	traps particles and bacteria which are removed from the body by cilia
antibodies	destroys bacteria, preventing infection of the eye
sebum	kills bacteria on food

4. How many glasses of table wine contain the same amount of alcohol (ethanol) as $2\frac{1}{2}$ pints of beer? [1]

5. Distinguish between the following terms.
   a) antibiotics and analgesics [2]
   b) B-lymphocytes and T-lymphocytes [4]
   c) lung cancer and emphysema [2]

6. Identify the substances in cigarette smoke which are harmful to health. Briefly explain why they are harmful. [6]

7. Distinguish between the following terms.
   a) primary immune response and secondary immune response [5]
   b) lymphocytes and phagocytes [9]
   c) T-helper cells and T-cytotoxic cells [3]

8. Briefly explain why
   a) tissue typing and immunosuppressive drugs help prevent rejection by the recipient of transplanted tissue [4]
   b) the transplantation of tissue between identical twins carries the least risk of rejection. [2]

9. Distinguish between the following pairs of terms.
   a) vaccine and vaccination [3]
   b) refrigeration and freezing [2]
   c) activated sludge process and trickling filter process [4]

10. How do booster vaccinations help to maintain a person's immunity to disease? [1]

11. Why are the symptoms of vomiting and diarrhoea associated with food poisoning a serious risk to health? [2]

12. Distinguish between the following terms.
    a) host and vector [4]
    b) bactericides and bacteristats [4]
    c) chemotherapy and resistance [4]

13. Briefly explain the precautions which can be taken to slow the development of bacterial resistance to different drugs. [6]

14. List the methods available for the treatment and prevention of malaria. [9]

Well done if you've improved. Don't worry if you haven't. Take a break and try again.

Chapter 7   Inheritance and evolution

How much do you already know? Work out your score on page 161.

Test yourself

1. The diagram shows the reproductive system of a man. Name parts A–E. [5]

2. Match each structure in column **A** with its correct description in column **B**.

A structures	B descriptions
corm	a horizontal stem running above ground
runner	a short, swollen underground stem
tuber	a large underground bud
bulb	a swelling at the end of a rhizome

   [4]

3. In humans, the gene for brown eyes (**B**) is dominant to the gene for blue eyes (**b**).

   a) Using the symbols **B** and **b**, state the genotypes of the children that could be born from a marriage between a heterozygous father and a blue-eyed mother. [2]

   b) State whether the children are brown eyed or blue eyed. [2]

4. Why are acquired characteristics not inherited? [3]

5. List the different sources of variation in living things. [6]

6. Why does sexual reproduction produce much more genetic variation than asexual reproduction? [5]

7. Distinguish between the following terms.

   a) ancestors and descendants [1]
   b) adaptation and extinction [2]
   c) evolution and natural selection [3]

8. How are fossils formed? [4]

7.1 Reproduction

PREVIEW

At the end of this section you will:
- know that reproduction gives rise to offspring
- understand that sexual reproduction gives rise to variation in offspring and that asexual reproduction gives rise to identical offspring
- be able to identify the components of the human reproductive system
- know how sexual reproduction occurs in humans and in flowering plants.

Sexual or asexual?

Reproduction passes genetic material from parents to their offspring. There are two types of reproduction.

GENES AND GENETICS Pages 53–54 and 134.

★ In **sexual reproduction**, *two* parents (male and female) produce sex cells called **gametes**. Gametes are formed by **meiosis**. The male gametes are **sperm**. The female gametes are **eggs**. The sperm and egg fuse – this is called **fertilisation**. The fertilised egg cell is called a **zygote**. The zygote divides repeatedly, producing a ball of cells called an **embryo** which develops into the new individual. The offspring formed by sexual reproduction inherit one of each pair of alleles (genes) from each parent, and are genetically *different* from one another and from their parents. In other words, they show **variation**.

IMPORTANT ANNOUNCEMENT
Section 3.3 about meiosis and mitosis is **REALLY REALLY** important to your understanding of sexual and asexual reproduction.

Inheritance and evolution

★ In **asexual reproduction**, *one* parent divides by **mitosis**. The daughter cells produced divide by mitosis and develop into new individuals. These offspring are genetically *identical* to one another and to their parent because DNA replicates exact copies of itself during mitosis.

Fact file

Most types of bacteria reproduce by **fission**: the bacterial cell splits into two. In this way solid material, such as food contaminated with bacteria, becomes covered with **colonies** as the bacterial cells multiply. In water, fission results in cloudiness (**turbidity**) as the number of bacterial cells increases. Counting colonies and measuring turbidity are methods for estimating the size of populations of bacteria.

Sexual reproduction in humans and flowering plants

How much do you recall about the structure of the reproductive organs in flowering plants and humans?

Remember that **flowers** are shoots which are specialised for reproduction. The **genitalia** are the visible parts of the human reproductive system.

Checklist for reproduction

1 ★ The testes hang down between the legs.

As a result, the testes are protected from injury.

★ The position of the testes keeps them about 3 °C lower than body temperature.

As a result, sperm develop properly in the slightly cooler conditions.

★ A woman's genitalia cover and protect the opening to the rest of the reproductive system inside her body.

2 ★ A fertilised egg is called a **zygote**. It develops into a new individual. The sequence reads as follows:

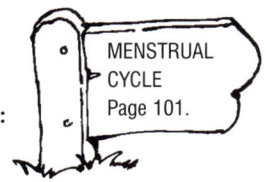

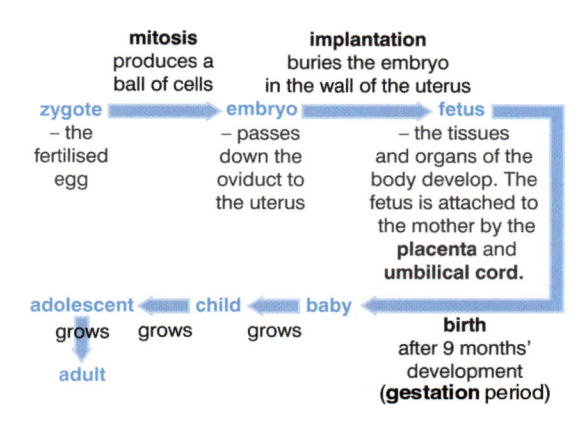

MENSTRUAL CYCLE Page 101.

mitosis produces a ball of cells — **implantation** buries the embryo in the wall of the uterus

zygote – the fertilised egg → **embryo** – passes down the oviduct to the uterus → **fetus** – the tissues and organs of the body develop. The fetus is attached to the mother by the **placenta** and **umbilical cord**.

adolescent ← grows ← **child** ← grows ← **baby** ← grows ← **birth** after 9 months' development (**gestation** period)

adult grows

★ Cells from a developing animal embryo may be split apart before they become specialised. The process, called **embryo cloning**, produces many genetically identical copies (**clones**) of the animal. The identical embryos may then be transplanted into host mothers. The embryos develop normally, resulting in genetically identical offspring. In this way, beneficial characteristics, such as milk producing abilities, are conserved from generation to generation.

★ Clones of animals can also be produced by inserting the nuclei of the body cells of an animal into its egg cells after the nucleus of each egg cell has been removed. Each egg cell, with the new body nucleus in place, is 'tricked' into developing as if it had been fertilised. Since the nuclei of the animal's body cells are genetically identical, the offspring that result from the treated egg cells are also genetically identical, forming a clone.

★ In humans, pregnancy usually results in the birth of only one baby. However, sometimes **twins** are born.

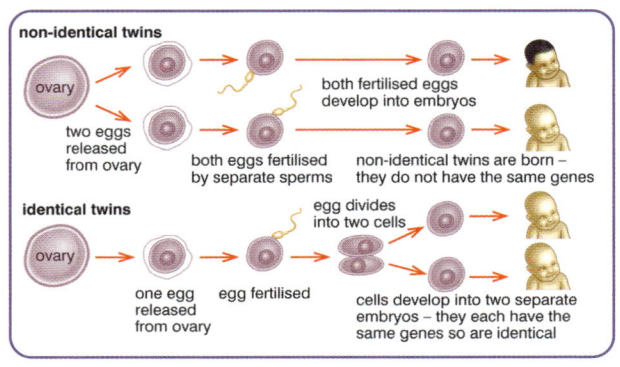

Producing twins

129

Inheritance and evolution

3. ★ **Contraception** aims to prevent pregnancy by:
   - preventing sperm from reaching the egg,
     or
   - preventing eggs from being produced,
     or
   - preventing the fertilised egg from developing in the uterus.

4. ★ In flowering plants, sexual reproduction involves **pollination**, **fertilisation** and the formation of **fruits** and **seeds**. The diagram below shows the sequence.

Pollination is the transfer of pollen from the anther to the stigma.
* **Cross-pollination** is the transfer of pollen between anthers and stigma(s) of different plants.
* **Self-pollination** is the transfer of pollen between the anthers and stigma(s) on the same plant.

Fertilisation is the fusion of a male sex nucleus with the female egg nucleus. The male sex nucleus passes down the **pollen tube** which grows from a pollen grain.

Seed is formed from the fertilised egg. It contains the embryo plant with its food store. The **fruit** (usually formed from the wall of the ovary) surrounds and protects the seed.

Flowers have features which make pollination more certain.

- **Insect-pollinated** flowers are often brightly coloured and produce nectar and scent. Insect visitors are attracted to them.
- **Wind-pollinated** flowers are often dull in colour. Clouds of light, smooth pollen grains are easily carried in the wind, scattering them far and wide.

Fact file

The shape of flowers helps to bring about pollination. The white dead nettle is an example.

★ In the young flower, the stigma is unripe and closed. The weight of an insect landing on the flower's lower petal brings down the ripe anthers, brushing pollen onto the insect's back.

★ In the older flower, the anthers are shrivelled and the stigma is ripe and open. The weight of a landing insect visiting an older flower brings down the stigma, which picks up pollen from the insect's back.

Remember that the anthers produce pollen grains each containing a male sex cell; the stigma is the part of the carpel (female sex organ) to which pollen is transferred.

★ Fruits and seeds may be distributed by animals or wind.

- **Spines** and **hooks** attach the fruit to passing animals.
- Animals are attracted to feed on **brightly coloured** fruits. The seeds are protected from the digestive juices in the animal's intestine, and eventually pass out in the animal's faeces.
- **Parachutes** and **wings** increase the surface area of fruits, helping them to travel long distances in the wind.

7.2 Asexual reproduction in plants

PREVIEW

At the end of this section you will:
- be able to identify the organs of asexual reproduction in flowering plants
- know that cuttings, graftings and micropropagation are used by farmers and gardeners to produce many identical plants
- understand that asexual reproduction preserves desirable characteristics and so guarantees plant quality.

Remember that asexual reproduction gives rise to **genetically identical** individuals, because DNA replicates during mitosis. This process passes on exact copies of the parent's genetic material to the daughter cells.

parent cells → (replication of DNA) mitosis → (exact copy of parent's genetic material is inherited) daughter cells → (develop) offspring

130

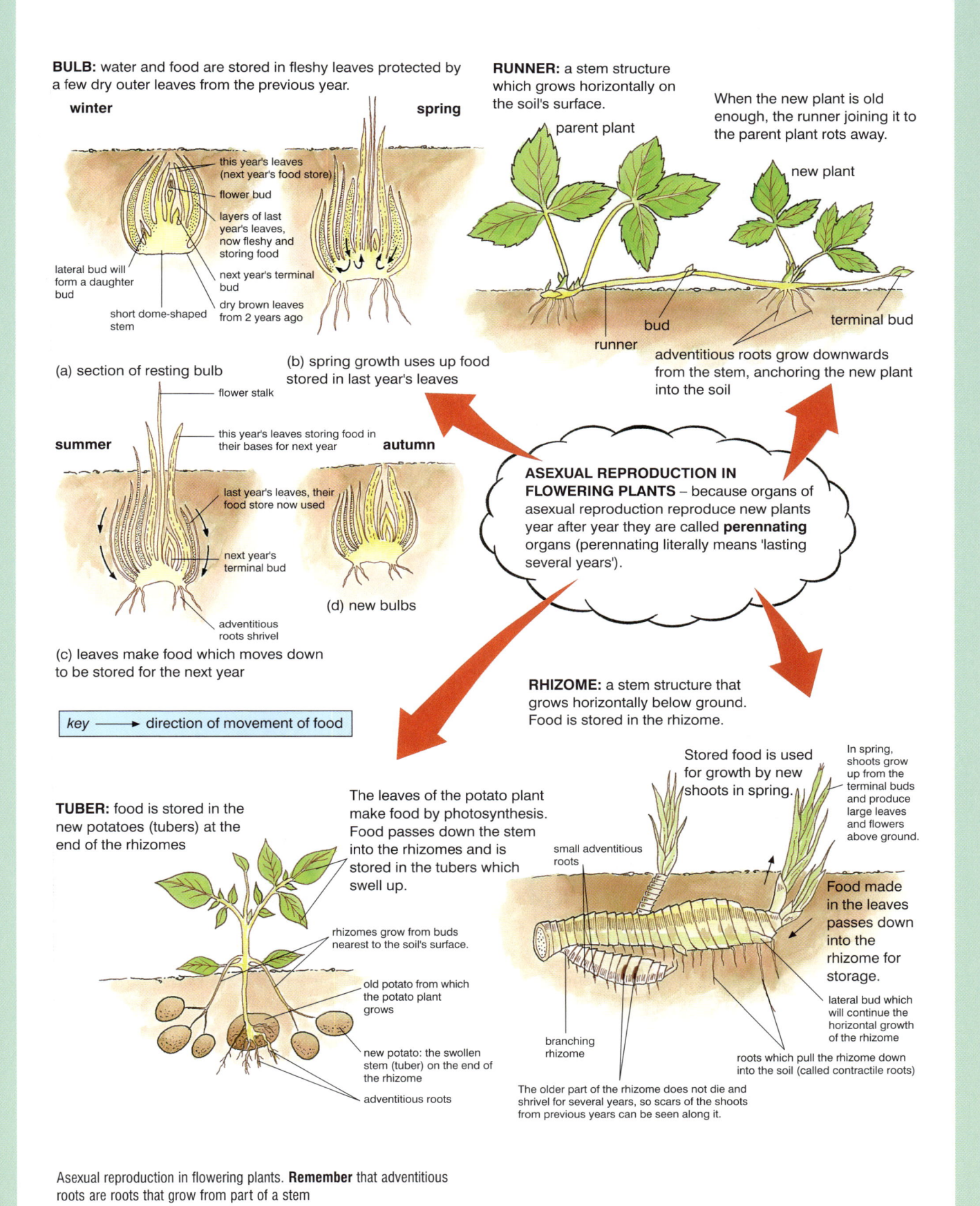

Inheritance and evolution

BULB: water and food are stored in fleshy leaves protected by a few dry outer leaves from the previous year.

winter — (a) section of resting bulb
- this year's leaves (next year's food store)
- flower bud
- layers of last year's leaves, now fleshy and storing food
- next year's terminal bud
- dry brown leaves from 2 years ago
- lateral bud will form a daughter bud
- short dome-shaped stem

spring — (b) spring growth uses up food stored in last year's leaves

summer — (c) leaves make food which moves down to be stored for the next year
- flower stalk
- this year's leaves storing food in their bases for next year
- last year's leaves, their food store now used
- next year's terminal bud
- adventitious roots shrivel

autumn — (d) new bulbs

key → direction of movement of food

RUNNER: a stem structure which grows horizontally on the soil's surface.
- parent plant
- When the new plant is old enough, the runner joining it to the parent plant rots away.
- new plant
- bud
- runner
- terminal bud
- adventitious roots grow downwards from the stem, anchoring the new plant into the soil

ASEXUAL REPRODUCTION IN FLOWERING PLANTS – because organs of asexual reproduction reproduce new plants year after year they are called **perennating** organs (perennating literally means 'lasting several years').

TUBER: food is stored in the new potatoes (tubers) at the end of the rhizomes

The leaves of the potato plant make food by photosynthesis. Food passes down the stem into the rhizomes and is stored in the tubers which swell up.
- rhizomes grow from buds nearest to the soil's surface.
- old potato from which the potato plant grows
- new potato: the swollen stem (tuber) on the end of the rhizome
- adventitious roots

RHIZOME: a stem structure that grows horizontally below ground. Food is stored in the rhizome.

Stored food is used for growth by new shoots in spring.

In spring, shoots grow up from the terminal buds and produce large leaves and flowers above ground.

Food made in the leaves passes down into the rhizome for storage.
- small adventitious roots
- branching rhizome
- lateral bud which will continue the horizontal growth of the rhizome
- roots which pull the rhizome down into the soil (called contractile roots)

The older part of the rhizome does not die and shrivel for several years, so scars of the shoots from previous years can be seen along it.

Asexual reproduction in flowering plants. **Remember** that adventitious roots are roots that grow from part of a stem

Inheritance and evolution

Remember that genetically identical individuals are called **clones** (see page 129).

Vegetative reproduction

Different parts of flowering plants can reproduce asexually. They are called the **vegetative parts** and are formed from the **root, leaf** or **stem**. Asexual reproduction in flowering plants is sometimes called **vegetative reproduction**. Since the new plants come from a single parent, and develop as a result of mitosis, they are genetically the same and are therefore **clones**.

The vegetative parts of plants store food. The stored food is used for the development of the new plant(s). We sometimes eat the organs which store the food, for example, potatoes, carrots.

The concept map for **asexual reproduction in plants** is shown on page 131. It is your revision guide, so study it carefully.

Artificial vegetative reproduction

Gardeners and farmers need to produce fresh stocks of plants that have desirable characteristics such as disease resistance, colour of fruit or shape of flower. The diagram opposite shows how plants are propagated vegetatively.

Micropropagation is used to grow plants from small pieces, using a technique called **tissue culture**.

★ Small fragments of plant tissue are grown in a liquid or gel that contains all the ingredients the pieces need to grow.

★ Conditions are sterile.

   As a result, the new plants are free of disease.

★ The temperature is carefully controlled.

All the plants grown from pieces of one parent plant will be genetically identical. They are clones. The advantages are that the plants:
- are healthy
- are the same
- retain the desirable characteristics of the parent plant.

The widespread use of clones by gardeners and farmers reduces variation. Fewer alleles are available for the selective breeding of new varieties of crops and animals for food.

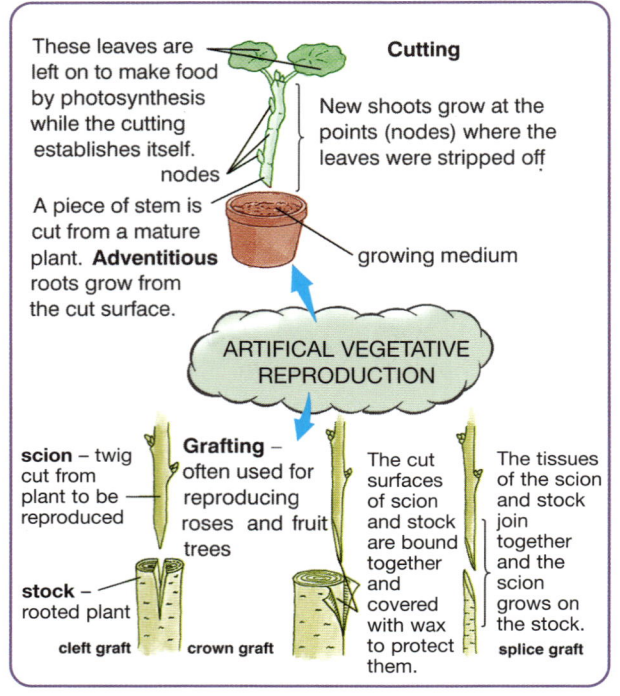

Cutting
- These leaves are left on to make food by photosynthesis while the cutting establishes itself.
- nodes
- A piece of stem is cut from a mature plant. **Adventitious** roots grow from the cut surface.
- New shoots grow at the points (nodes) where the leaves were stripped off
- growing medium

ARTIFICAL VEGETATIVE REPRODUCTION

Grafting – often used for reproducing roses and fruit trees
- scion – twig cut from plant to be reproduced
- stock – rooted plant
- cleft graft
- crown graft
- The cut surfaces of scion and stock are bound together and covered with wax to protect them.
- The tissues of the scion and stock join together and the scion grows on the stock.
- splice graft

Exploiting vegetative reproduction. Adventitious roots are roots that grow from a part of a stem. A node is the point where a leaf stalk joins the stem.

7.3 Monohybrid inheritance

PREVIEW

At the end of this section you will:
- understand genetic terms
- be able to work out the expected outcome of a monohybrid cross
- understand the inheritance of gender
- understand sex-linked inheritance.

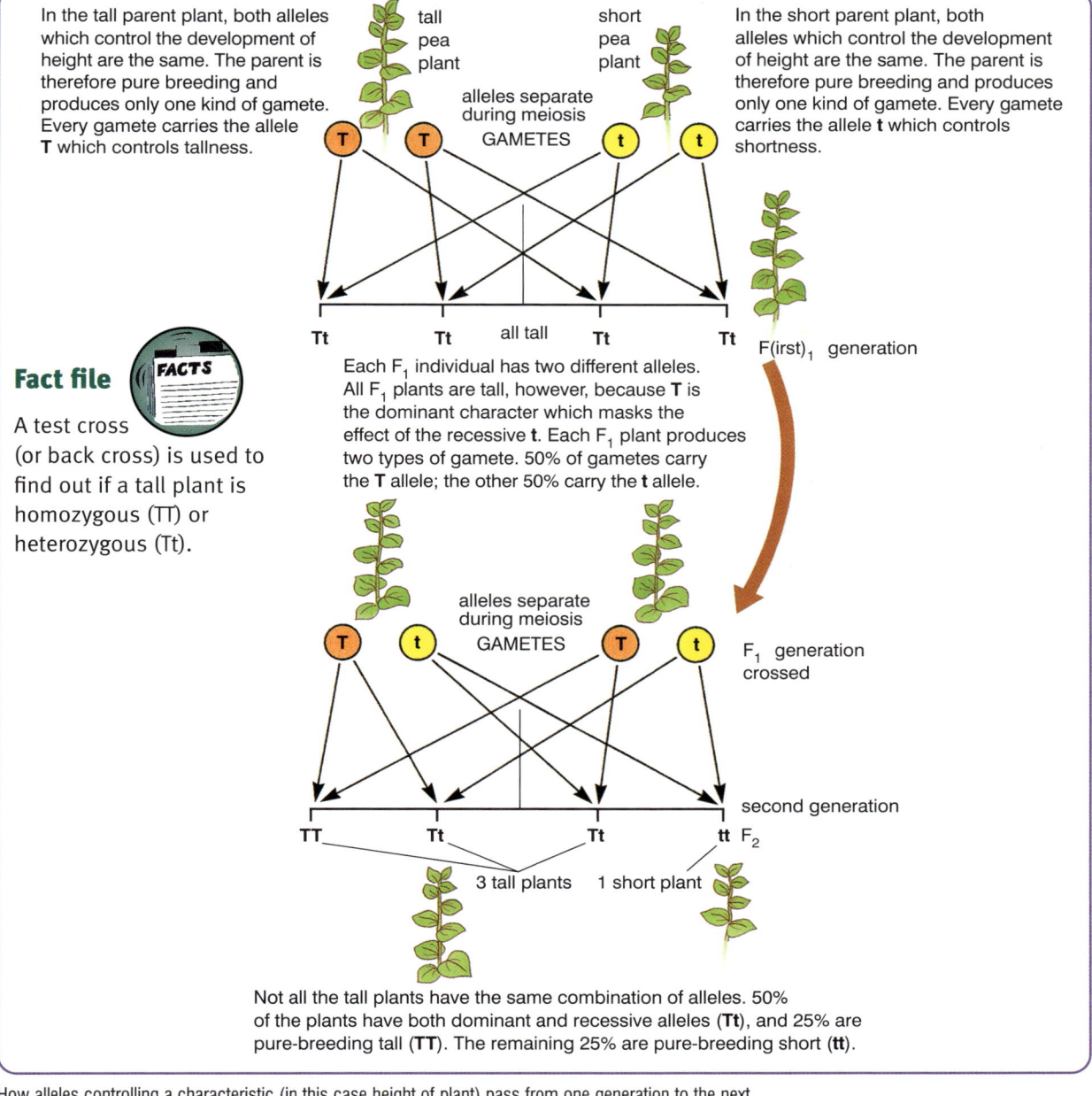

Inheritance and evolution

In the tall parent plant, both alleles which control the development of height are the same. The parent is therefore pure breeding and produces only one kind of gamete. Every gamete carries the allele **T** which controls tallness.

In the short parent plant, both alleles which control the development of height are the same. The parent is therefore pure breeding and produces only one kind of gamete. Every gamete carries the allele **t** which controls shortness.

alleles separate during meiosis
GAMETES

Tt   Tt   all tall   Tt   Tt   F(irst)$_1$ generation

Each F$_1$ individual has two different alleles. All F$_1$ plants are tall, however, because **T** is the dominant character which masks the effect of the recessive **t**. Each F$_1$ plant produces two types of gamete. 50% of gametes carry the **T** allele; the other 50% carry the **t** allele.

Fact file

A test cross (or back cross) is used to find out if a tall plant is homozygous (TT) or heterozygous (Tt).

alleles separate during meiosis
GAMETES

F$_1$ generation crossed

second generation
TT   Tt   Tt   tt F$_2$
3 tall plants   1 short plant

Not all the tall plants have the same combination of alleles. 50% of the plants have both dominant and recessive alleles (**Tt**), and 25% are pure-breeding tall (**TT**). The remaining 25% are pure-breeding short (**tt**).

How alleles controlling a characteristic (in this case height of plant) pass from one generation to the next

Fact file

Gregor Mendel was a monk who lived in the Augustinian monastery at the town of Brünn (now Brno in the Czech Republic). He observed the inheritance of different characteristics in the garden pea, and reported the results of his experiments in 1865. The work established the basis of modern genetics. However, at the time, nobody realised what Mendel was talking about. The reason probably lay with Mendel's training: he was a mathematician as well as a biologist, which was an unusual combination of skills in the mid-nineteenth century. His report was ignored because then, most scientists were unfamiliar with the mathematical analysis of biological problems.

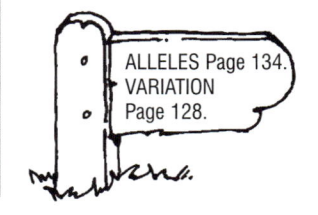

ALLELES Page 134.
VARIATION Page 128.

Inheritance and evolution

The vocabulary of genetics

★ **monohybrid inheritance** – the processes by which a single characteristic is passed from parents to offspring, for example flower colour or eye colour

★ **pure breeding** – characteristics that breed true, appearing unchanged generation after generation

★ **parental generation** (symbol **P**) – individuals that are pure breeding for a characteristic

★ **first filial generation** (symbol F_1) – the offspring produced by a parental generation

★ **second filial generation** (symbol F_2) – the offspring produced by crossing members of the first filial generation

★ **gene** – a length of DNA which codes for the whole of one protein

GENES Page 52.

★ **allele** – one of a pair of genes that control a particular characteristic

★ **homozygote** – an individual with identical alleles controlling a particular characteristic. Individuals that are pure breeding for a particular characteristic are **homozygous** for that characteristic

★ **heterozygote** – an individual with different alleles controlling a particular characteristic

★ **expressed** – a gene is expressed when a protein is produced from the activity of the gene

★ **dominant** – any characteristic that appears in the F_1 offspring of a cross between pure-breeding parents with contrasting characteristics, such as tallness and shortness in pea plants, *or* any characteristic expressed by an allele in preference to the form of the characteristic controlled by the allele's partner

★ **recessive** – any characteristic present in the parental generation that misses the F_1 generation but reappears in the F_2 generation, *or* any characteristic of an allele that is not expressed because the form of the characteristic of the allele's partner is expressed in preference, *or* any characteristic of an allele that is only expressed in the absence of the allele's dominant partner

★ **genotype** – the genetic make-up (all of the genes) of an individual

★ **phenotype** – the outward appearance and internal structure and function of an individual which results from the activity of those genes of the genotype actively expressing characteristics.

Some rules of genetics

★ Paired genes controlling a particular characteristic are called alleles.

★ Letters are used to symbolise alleles.

★ A capital letter is used to symbolise the dominant member of a pair of alleles.

★ A small letter is used to symbolise the recessive member of a pair of alleles.

★ The letter used to symbolise the recessive allele is the same letter as that for the dominant allele.

A monohybrid cross

The diagram on the previous page sets out the results of crosses between tall and short pea plants. Notice that **T** is used to symbolise the allele that produces tallness in pea plants, and **t** is used to symbolise the allele that produces shortness. Other contrasting characteristics of the pea plant such as seed shape (round or wrinkled), flower colour (purple or white) and pod shape (smooth or wrinkled) are inherited in a similar way.

From his results on the inheritance of different characteristics of pea plants, Mendel realised that parents passed 'something' on to their offspring that made them look like their parents. When these offspring became parents, they passed on the 'something' to their offspring, and so on, from generation to generation. Mendel called the 'something' particles; today we know them as **genes**.

Fact file

Some scientists thought that Mendel's ratio of 3:1 in the F_2 generation was statistically too perfect. The doubts do not mean that Mendel's conclusions were wrong; just that 'experimental error' was not properly taken into account.

Inheritance and evolution

Inheritance of sex

The photograph shows the chromosomes that determine the sex of a person. The larger chromosome is the **X** chromosome; the smaller chromosome is the **Y** chromosome. The body cells of a woman each carry two **X** chromosomes; those of a man each carry an **X** chromosome and a **Y** chromosome.

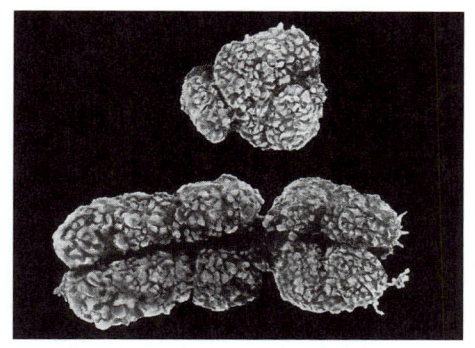

Human sex chromosomes

The diagram below shows how a person's sex is inherited. **Notice** that:
- a baby's sex depends on whether the egg is fertilised by a sperm carrying an X chromosome or one carrying a Y chromosome
- the birth of (almost) equal numbers of girls and boys is governed by the production of equal numbers of X and Y sperms at meiosis.

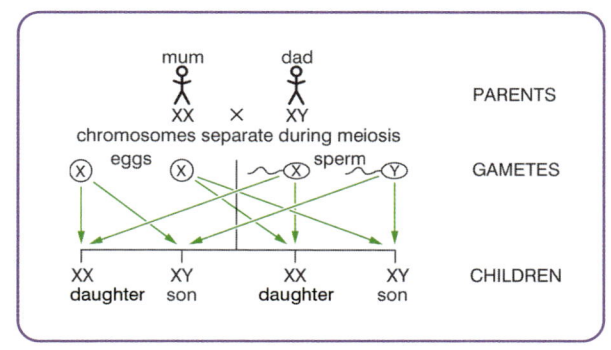

Inheritance of sex in humans

Haemophilia: a sex-linked genetic disease

Characteristics controlled by alleles situated on the sex chromosomes are said to be **sex-linked** characteristics. The genetic disease **haemophilia** is an example. The diagrams show what happens.

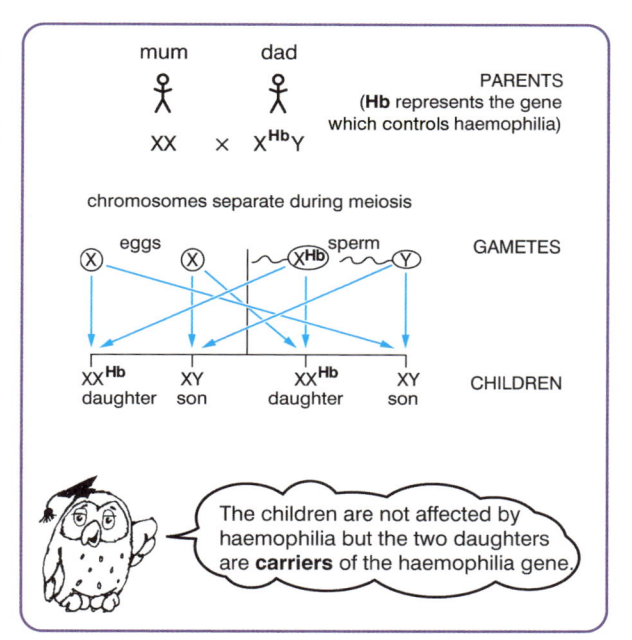

The outcome when a man affected by haemophilia becomes a father

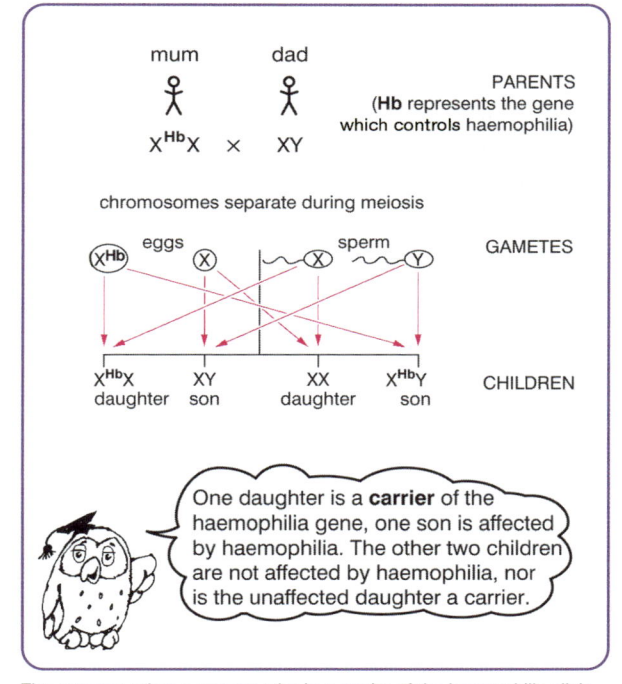

The children are not affected by haemophilia but the two daughters are **carriers** of the haemophilia gene.

The outcome when a woman who is a carrier of the haemophilia allele becomes a mother

One daughter is a **carrier** of the haemophilia gene, one son is affected by haemophilia. The other two children are not affected by haemophilia, nor is the unaffected daughter a carrier.

Inheritance and evolution

A haemophiliac (a person suffering from haemophilia) has a mutant version of the allele responsible for the expression of the blood clotting agent factor VIII. The affected person does not produce **factor VIII**, which means that if s/he is cut, it takes a long time for a clot to form and a lot of blood may be lost. The mutant allele is recessive and located on the X chromosome. The diagrams on page 135 show how it passes from one generation to the next in two different circumstances: when the father is haemophiliac and the mother is a carrier.

Fact file

Haemophiliacs are usually male. Although the mutant allele is recessive, the male Y chromosome (remember that men have an X chromosome and a Y chromosome) carries few alleles and does not have a normal dominant partner allele to mask the effects of the mutant allele on the X chromosome. For a female to have haemophilia, she would have to inherit the recessive mutant allele from both of her parents. This happens only very occasionally as the mutant allele is very rare.

Cystic fibrosis: a recessive genetic disease

Cystic fibrosis is a genetic disease that is not sex-linked. It affects the lungs and the pancreas. The bronchioles and the pancreatic duct become blocked with excess mucus and have to be cleared regularly. The mutant allele responsible is recessive. A person suffers from the disease only if s/he has two mutant alleles. A person with a single mutant allele is a carrier. The diagram below shows how it passes from one generation to the next when two parents who are carriers have children.

Huntington's chorea: a dominant genetic disease

Like cystic fibrosis, **Huntington's chorea** is a genetic disease which is not sex-linked. However, unlike cystic fibrosis, the mutant allele responsible is dominant. Involuntary muscular movement and mental deterioration are characteristics of the disease. A person suffers from the disease even if s/he has only one mutant allele. Unfortunately, the age of onset of symptoms of the disease is about 35 years. Affected people, therefore, can have a family before being aware of their own condition. The diagram on page 137 shows how the mutant allele passes from one generation to the next when one of the parents is affected.

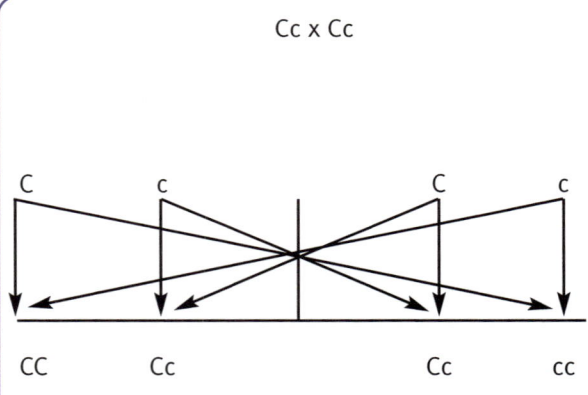

Cc x Cc

C   c   C   c

CC   Cc   Cc   cc

PARENTS
chromosomes separate during meiosis
(C represents the allele which controls the development of normal lungs and pancreas; c represents the allele which controls the development of cystic fibrosis)

GAMETES

CHILDREN

One child is affected by cystic fibrosis; another is not affected, nor is it a carrier of the cystic fibrosis allele. The other two children are carriers but are not affected by cystic fibrosis.

Inheritance and evolution

HChc x hchc   PARENTS
chromosomes separate during meiosis   (HC represents the allele which controls the
                                                   development of Huntington's chorea;
                                                   hc represents the normal allele)
HC   hc   hc   hc   GAMETES

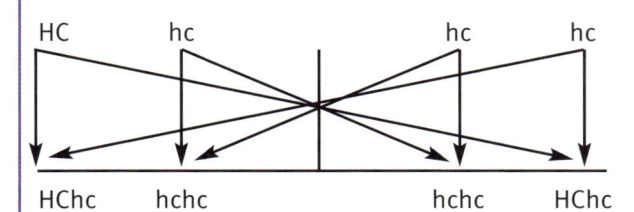

HChc   hchc   hchc   HChc   CHILDREN

Two children are affected by Huntington's chorea; the other two are not. The unaffected children cannot be carriers because the mutant allele is dominant.

7.4 Variation

PREVIEW

At the end of this section you will:

- understand the difference between continuous variation and discontinuous variation
- be able to identify the sources of variation
- know that variation is either inherited or acquired.

Genetic and environmental variation

Look closely at your family, friends and classmates. Notice the differently coloured hair and eyes, and the differently shaped faces. We all show **variations** in the different characteristics that make up our physical appearance (**phenotype**).

GENOTYPE and PHENOTYPE Page 134.

Variation arises from **genetic** causes.

Sexual reproduction (see pages 128–129) involves the fusion of the nucleus of a **sperm** with the nucleus of the **egg**. The process of fusion is called **fertilisation** and recombines the genetic material from each parent in new ways within the **zygote**.

Mutations are either the result of abnormalities in the number of chromosomes (**chromosome mutations**) or of a change (or changes) in the genes themselves (**gene mutations**). Down's syndrome is an example of a chromosome mutation. The affected person has an extra copy of chromosome 21. Gene mutations arise as a result of mistakes in the **replication** of DNA (see page 53). Occasionally the wrong base adds to the growing strand of DNA, making the new DNA slightly different from the original. **Ionising radiation** and some **chemicals** increase the probability of gene mutation.

★ Ionising radiation strips electrons from matter exposed to it (ionises the atoms). Emissions from radioactive substances are ionising radiations. They may cause mutations by damaging DNA directly, or by generating highly active components of molecules called **free radicals** which cause the damage indirectly.

★ Chemicals such as the **carcinogens** (substances that cause cancer) in tobacco may lead to mutations of the genes that normally inhibit cell division.

As a result, cell division runs out of control and a cancer develops.

★ **Crossing over** during **meiosis** exchanges a segment of one chromosome (and the genes it carries) with the corresponding segment of its homologous chromosome (see page 45).

As a result, the sex cells produced by meiosis have a different combination of genes from the parent cell.

Inheritance and evolution

Fact file

In rare cases, a mutation may increase an organism's chances of survival. The mutant gene will be favoured by natural selection and, therefore, so inherited by future generations. Some mutations do not affect an organism's chances of survival one way or another. Such mutations are neutral in their effects.

Variations that arise from genetic causes are inherited from parents by their offspring, who pass them on to their offspring, and so on from generation to generation. Inherited variation is the raw material on which **natural selection** acts, resulting in **evolution**.

NATURAL SELECTION and EVOLUTION Pages 139–141

Variation also arises from **environmental** causes. Here, 'environmental' means all the external influences affecting an organism, for example:

★ **nutrients** in the food we eat and minerals that plants absorb in solution through the roots. In many countries, children are now taller and heavier, age for age, than they were 50 years ago because of improved diet and standards of living.

★ **drugs**, which may have a serious effect on appearance. **Thalidomide** was given to pregnant women in the 1960s to prevent them feeling sick and to help them sleep. The drug can affect the development of the fetus and some women who were prescribed thalidomide gave birth to seriously deformed children.

★ **temperature** affects the rate of enzyme-controlled chemical reactions. Warmth increases the rate of photosynthesis, for instance, and therefore improves the rate of growth of plants kept under glass.

★ **physical training** uses muscles more than normal, increasing their size and power. Weightlifters, therefore, develop bulging muscles as they train for their sport.

Variations that arise from environmental causes are *not* inherited, because the sex cells are not affected. Instead the characteristics are said to be **acquired**. The fact that the weightlifter has developed bulging muscles does not mean that his or her children will have bulging muscles – unless they take up weightlifting as well! Because variations as a result of acquired characteristics are not inherited, they do not affect evolution.

Continuous and discontinuous variation

The variations shown by some characteristics are spread over a range of measurements. All intermediate forms of a characteristic are possible between one extreme and the other.
We say that the characteristic shows **continuous variation**. The height of a population is an example of continuous variation.

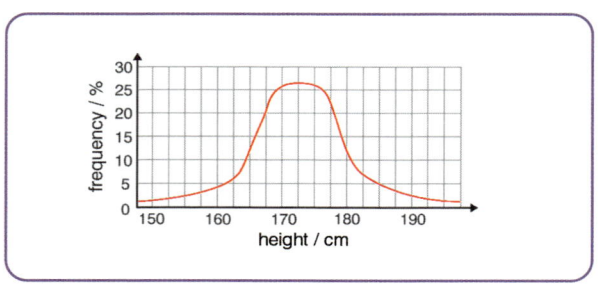

Variation in the height of the adult human population – an example of continuous variation

Other characteristics do not show a continuous trend in variation from one extreme to another. They show categories of the characteristic without any intermediate forms. The ability to roll the tongue is an example – you can either do it or you can't. There are no half-rollers! We say that the characteristic shows **discontinuous variation**.

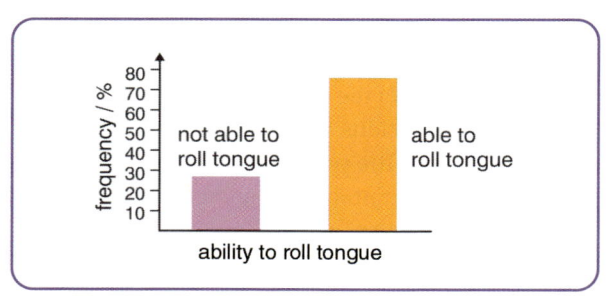

Ability to roll the tongue – an example of discontinuous variation

Inheritance and evolution

7.5 Evolution

> **PREVIEW**
>
> At the end of this section you will:
> - know that the British naturalist Charles Darwin was the first person to explain *how* species can evolve
> - understand Darwin's evidence showing that evolution occurs, and that natural selection is the mechanism of evolution
> - be able to interpret examples of evolution in action
> - know that fossils are a record of organisms that have become extinct.

Charles Darwin

Charles Darwin (1809–82) was a keen British naturalist who abandoned medicine at Edinburgh and studied theology at Cambridge. His world voyage on HMS *Beagle* (1831–6) provided much of the evidence that:
- organisms **evolve** and that
- **natural selection** is the mechanism of evolution.

It was another 20 years before he published these proposals in his book *Origin of species*.

The process of evolution

Present-day living things are descended from ancestors that have changed through thousands of generations. The process of change is called **evolution**. The concept map for evolution is shown overleaf. It shows that other people's ideas influenced Darwin's thinking on how species can evolve. The numbers on the concept map refer to the checklist of points on this page and on page 141. The concept map and its checklist are your revision guide to evolution.

Fact file

Charles Darwin was not the first person to propose a mechanism by which species evolve. In 1809, the French biologist Jean-Baptiste de Lamarck proposed that organisms evolve because changes in the environment cause changes in the characteristics of organisms. The characteristics are said to be acquired (see page 138) and Lamarck believed them to be inherited by offspring.

Checklist for evolution

1. A survey of the South American coast was among the tasks undertaken by the crew of HMS *Beagle* during its world voyage. At that time Darwin took over as the ship's naturalist. He:
   - collected **fossils** and specimens of plants and animals on expeditions inland
   - noticed that one type of organism gave way to another as the *Beagle* sailed around the coast of South America
   - observed that the animals along the Pacific coast of South America were different from those along the Atlantic coast
   - compared the wildlife of the Galapagos Islands with the wildlife of the South American mainland, noting the differences between similar species.

   The variety of species that Darwin discovered on his expeditions in South America and the Galapagos Islands convinced him that species change through time; that is, they **evolve**.

2. The famous geologist Charles Lyell (1797–1875) believed that:
   - Earth's rocks are very old, and
   - natural forces produce continuous geological change during the course of Earth's history
   - fossils can be used to date rocks
   - the fossil record was laid down over hundreds of millions of years.

   Darwin read Lyell's books.

   As a result, Darwin reasoned that if rocks have changed slowly over long periods of time, living things might have a similar history.

3. In 1798 the Reverend Thomas Malthus wrote *An Essay on the Principle of Population*. He stated that the size of a population would increase indefinitely unless kept in check by shortages of resources such as food and living space. Darwin read the essay in 1838 and reasoned that in nature a 'struggle for existence' must occur. In modern language we say that organisms **compete** for resources in limited supply.

Inheritance and evolution

Evidence
- The fossils that Darwin collected on expeditions inland showed him that organisms today are not the same as organisms that lived a long time ago. In other words, organisms change through time – they evolve.
- There is an enormous variety of living things.

Darwin travelled around the coast of South America on HMS *Beagle*.

CHECKLIST 1

Evidence
- Lyell's work showed that the geology of the Earth changed through long periods of time.
- Darwin reasoned that if the geology of Earth had changed then so too could organisms.

Charles Lyell
Darwin and Lyell became friends on Darwin's return to England from the voyage in the *Beagle*. Lyell believed that the Earth was very old.

CHECKLIST 2

Charles Darwin (1809–82)

THE COMPONENTS OF EVOLUTION

variation + natural selection —time→ evolution

Evidence
- Artificial selection helped confirm natural selection in Darwin's mind as the mechanism of evolution.

The variety of pigeons bred by 'fanciers' over hundreds of years originated from a 'wild type' common ancestor.

CHECKLIST 4

Evidence
- Darwin reasoned that since the number of individuals in a population does not increase indefinitely, then limiting factors must check the increase in numbers.

Reverend Thomas Malthus
Malthus suggested that the growth in numbers of a population outstrips resources in limited supply, leading to competition between individuals for the resources, e.g. food, habitats (see page 13), mates.

CHECKLIST 3

How Darwin arrived at a theory of evolution through natural selection (Checklist numbers refer to the checklist on pages 139 and 141.)

Inheritance and evolution

COMPETITION
Pages 20–22.

4 For centuries we have selected animals and plants for their desirable characteristics, and bred from them. This is called **artificial selection**. For example, dogs have been bred for shape, size and coat colour, resulting in a wide variety of breeds; different varieties of cereal crops (wheat, barley, rice) have been selectively bred from wild grasses. Darwin investigated the work of breeders of animals and plants, and added to his experience by breeding pigeons. He reasoned that if artificial selection produced change in domestic animals and plants, then natural selection should have the same effect on wildlife.

Fact file

Francis Galton was a rich Victorian scientist and cousin to Charles Darwin. He believed that the human race could be improved by only allowing couples with 'desirable' characteristics to have children. In other words, he supported the idea of the artificial selection of human beings. This idea is called **eugenics** and is a controversial subject.

The checklist on page 139 and above sets out the different components which were the key to Darwin's understanding of how species evolve.
Variation: Darwin's work during the voyage of HMS *Beagle* and his experience of selectively breeding pigeons provided evidence for the large amount of variation in the characteristics of different species (checklist **1** and **4**).

Natural selection: Malthus' work contributed to Darwin's idea of a 'struggle for existence' (competition for resources). The result is the natural selection of those organisms best suited (**adapted**) to survive (checklist **3**).

Time: The work of Lyell showed Darwin that the Earth is very old, giving time for the evolution of species to occur (checklist **2**).

Fact file

Evidence suggests that Earth was formed about 4600 million years ago and that very simple forms of life first appeared around 4000 million years ago.

How species evolve – the modern argument summarised

1 Because individuals vary genetically, individuals are slightly different from one another.

2 This variation in a population of individuals is the raw material on which natural selection works, resulting in evolution.

3 All organisms potentially over-reproduce. Individuals, therefore, compete for resources in short supply. Resources include food and space – both required for individuals to survive.

4 Individuals with genes that express characteristics which adapt the individuals to obtain scarce resources are more likely to survive than other less well adapted individuals.

5 The best adapted individuals are more likely to survive and reproduce, and so their offspring will inherit the genes which control those favourable characteristics.

6 In this way organisms accumulate genes which control favourable characteristics and change through time; that is, they evolve over many generations.

7 If the environment in which individuals are living changes, then genes which control different characteristics might favour survival. Individuals with these characteristics will survive to reproduce and so evolution continues from generation to generation.

It took Darwin nearly 30 years to develop a theory of evolution through natural selection. The ideas were a revolution in scientific thinking.

Evolution in action

Evolution is still happening. Maintaining the balance between the pale (peppered) and the dark (melanic) forms of the peppered moth *Biston betularia* is an example. The diagram on page 142 shows what happens.

The development of resistance of bacteria to antibiotic drugs is another example of evolution in action. Populations of bacteria always contain a few individuals with genes which enable them to resist the effects of an antibiotic. These individuals survive exposure to the antibiotic and reproduce. The new generation of bacteria inherits the genes which control resistance. Resistance quickly develops in bacteria because they reproduce rapidly.

Inheritance and evolution

The fossil record

Fossils are the remains of dead organisms, which do not decay easily, or impressions made by them, such as footprints. Fossilisation also occurs when parts of organisms have not decayed because one or more of the conditions (e.g. warmth, oxygen) necessary for decomposition to occur are absent, or when parts of organisms are replaced by other materials (e.g. mineral particles) as they decompose. Fossils are usually preserved in sedimentary rocks which are formed layer on layer by the deposition of mud, sand and silt over millions of years. Provided the layers are undisturbed, then the more recent the layer, the nearer it is to the Earth's surface.

As a result, the fossils in each rock layer are a record of life on Earth at the time when the layer was formed.

As a result, a sequence of undisturbed layers each with its fossils traces the history of life on Earth.

Extinction

Species may die out (become **extinct**) because of the harmful effects of human activities on the environment. Natural extinction also happens over longer periods of time. It makes room for new species to evolve and replace the previous ones. Naturally occurring extinctions are caused by:
- competition between species
- changes in the environment.

The mass extinction of whole groups of organisms has occurred at intervals throughout the history of life on Earth. Extinction of the dinosaurs and many other species of reptile about 70 million years ago is a well known example. Their extinction made way for mammals and birds to fill the vacant spaces in the environment.

That's why you and I are here!

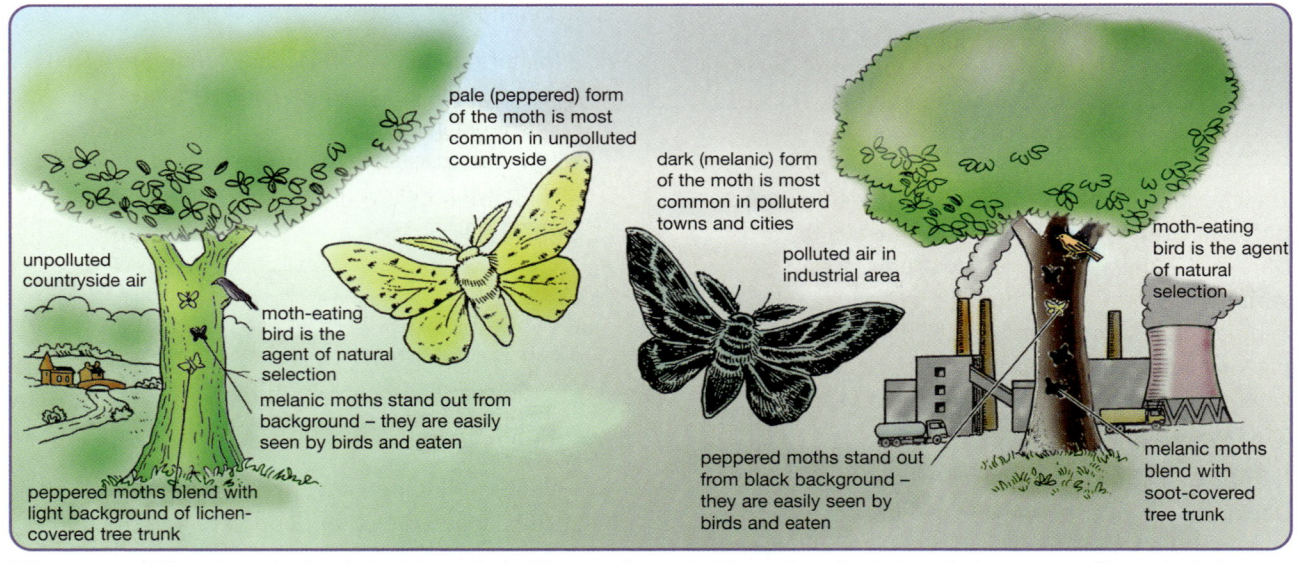

- pale (peppered) form of the moth is most common in unpolluted countryside
- unpolluted countryside air
- moth-eating bird is the agent of natural selection
- melanic moths stand out from background – they are easily seen by birds and eaten
- peppered moths blend with light background of lichen-covered tree trunk
- dark (melanic) form of the moth is most common in polluterd towns and cities
- polluted air in industrial area
- peppered moths stand out from black background – they are easily seen by birds and eaten
- moth-eating bird is the agent of natural selection
- melanic moths blend with soot-covered tree trunk

Different forms of *Biston betularia* adapt the moth to survive in different environments. The numbers of melanic moths in towns and cities are in decline as pollution control makes the urban environment cleaner. At the same time, the numbers of peppered moths are increasing.

Inheritance and evolution

ROUND UP

How much have you improved? Work out your improvement index on page 162.

1. Match each structure in column **A** with its correct description in column **B**.

A structures	B descriptions
seed	structure to which pollen grains attach
ovule	produces a sugar solution
fruit	contains the egg nucleus
stigma	a fertilised ovule
nectary	develops from the ovary after fertilisation

   [5]

2. What are the advantages to growers of reproducing crops asexually? [3]

3. Name the food stored in the organs of asexual reproduction of plants. [1]

4. Briefly explain why the production of clones depends on the process of mitosis. [5]

5. Match each term in column **A** with its correct description in column **B**.

A terms	B descriptions
allele	the processes by which a single characteristic passes from parents to offspring
pure breeding	offspring of the offspring of the parental generation
second filial generation	characteristics that appear unchanged from generation to generation
monohybrid inheritance	one of a pair of genes that control a particular characteristic

   [4]

6. In a population of 300 goldfish, variations in two characteristics were measured and the results displayed as charts. Chart A shows variation in the length of the fish; chart B shows variation in their colour.

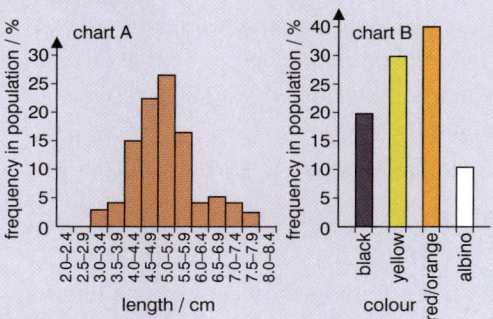

   a) Which chart shows
   - (i) continuous variation
   - (ii) discontinuous variation?
   - (iii) Briefly give reasons for your answers. [6]

   b) Using chart B, calculate the number of yellow goldfish in the population. [1]

   c) Albino goldfish are relatively rare. Give a possible genetic explanation for the occurrence of albino goldfish. [1]

7. a) Look at the diagram on page 142. Briefly explain why the population densities of pale peppered moths and dark peppered moths are different in the countryside from those in industrial areas. [8]

   b) Why is the moth-eating bird called an agent of natural selection? [2]

8. Briefly explain why genes which control characteristics that favour the survival of individuals tend to accumulate from generation to generation. [4]

9. Outline the contributions of the ideas of Charles Lyell and Thomas Malthus to Darwin's development of a theory of evolution through natural selection. [5]

Well done if you've improved. Don't worry if you haven't. Take a break and try again.

Chapter 8　Biotechnology

How much do you already know? Work out your score on pages 162–3.

Test yourself

1. Briefly explain why the production of wine depends on the incomplete breakdown of glucose molecules during anaerobic respiration. [3]

2. Distinguish between the following.
   a) restriction enzyme and ligase (splicing enzyme) [7]
   b) biotechnology and genetic engineering [5]
   c) batch culture and continuous culture [7]

3. Plants are a store of energy. Briefly explain how biotechnology converts the stored energy in plants into fuel. [8]

4. Many types of washing powder contain enzymes. Which types of enzyme are best for washing food-stained clothing? [6]

5. Nitrogen-fixing bacteria, which convert nitrogen in the atmosphere into nitrates, live in swellings on the roots of leguminous plants. Cereal plants do not contain nitrogen-fixing bacteria. How do you think food production and the environment would benefit from biotechnology which manipulates nitrogen-fixing bacteria to live in the roots of cereal plants? [9]

6. a) What is single cell protein? [2]
   b) Single cell protein is produced from bacteria grown on methanol in a fermenter at 40°C.
      (i) Explain the importance of keeping the fermenter at a constant temperature of 40°C. [4]
      (ii) State two forms in which single cell protein is sold. [2]
      (iii) State three advantages of using bacteria to produce protein food. [4]
      (iv) Briefly explain the importance of methanol in the process. [3]

7. Why do you think people might be reluctant to eat food made from microorganisms? [1]

8.1 Introducing biotechnology

PREVIEW

At the end of this section you will:
- know that the processes of biotechnology have a long history in the production of bread and alcoholic drinks
- understand that the techniques of genetic engineering manipulate genes to human advantage
- realise that genetic engineering has transformed biotechnology into a rapidly expanding industry which provides food, medicines and a range of industrial chemicals.

Fact file

The word **biotechnology** describes the way we use plant cells, animal cells and microorganisms to produce substances that are useful to us.

Using biotechnology

The long history of biotechnology demonstrates the importance of this area of biology to human welfare.

The traditional: for thousands of years humans have exploited microorganisms to produce food, using:
- **yeast** to make wine, beer and bread
- **moulds** to make cheese
- **bacteria** to make yogurt and vinegar.

The diagram on page 146 sets out the production processes.

Anaerobic respiration (see pages 83–4) by yeast cells converts glucose into **ethanol** ('alcohol' in wines and beers) and **carbon dioxide** (the gas that makes bread rise). The reactions of anaerobic respiration are **fermentations**. Biotechnology exploits a range of fermentation reactions to produce different substances.

144

Biotechnology

Fact file

Yeasts are fungi. Most fungi are made up of a mass of thread-like cells called **hyphae**. Yeasts, however, do not grow hyphae, but are single-celled. They reproduce by **budding**, which is a form of asexual reproduction.

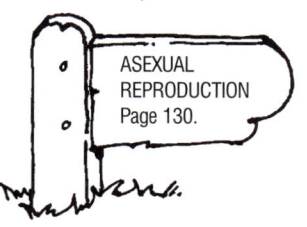

ASEXUAL REPRODUCTION Page 130.

The new: in the 1970s scientists developed the techniques of **genetic engineering,** which introduced the modern era of biotechnology. New methods of manipulating genes became possible because of the discovery of different enzymes in bacteria.

★ **Restriction enzymes** cut DNA into pieces, making it possible to isolate desirable genes (those which are useful to us).

★ **Ligase** (splicing enzyme) allows desirable genes to be inserted into the genetic material of host cells.

Genetic engineering uses the methods to identify and insert genes of one type of organism into the DNA of the cells of another different organism (the recipient). A **vector** may be used to transfer genes from donor to recipient. Different viruses and loops of bacterial DNA are commonly used as gene vectors.

Using genetic engineering we can create **genetically modified** (GM) organisms with specific genetic characteristics, such that they produce substances that we need and want. For example, microorganisms are cultured in a solution containing all the substances (nutrients) they require for rapid growth and multiplication inside huge containers called **fermenters**. In this way, medicines, foods and industrial chemicals can be made on an industrial scale. The diagram below shows how genetically engineered insulin is made.

INSULIN Page 101.

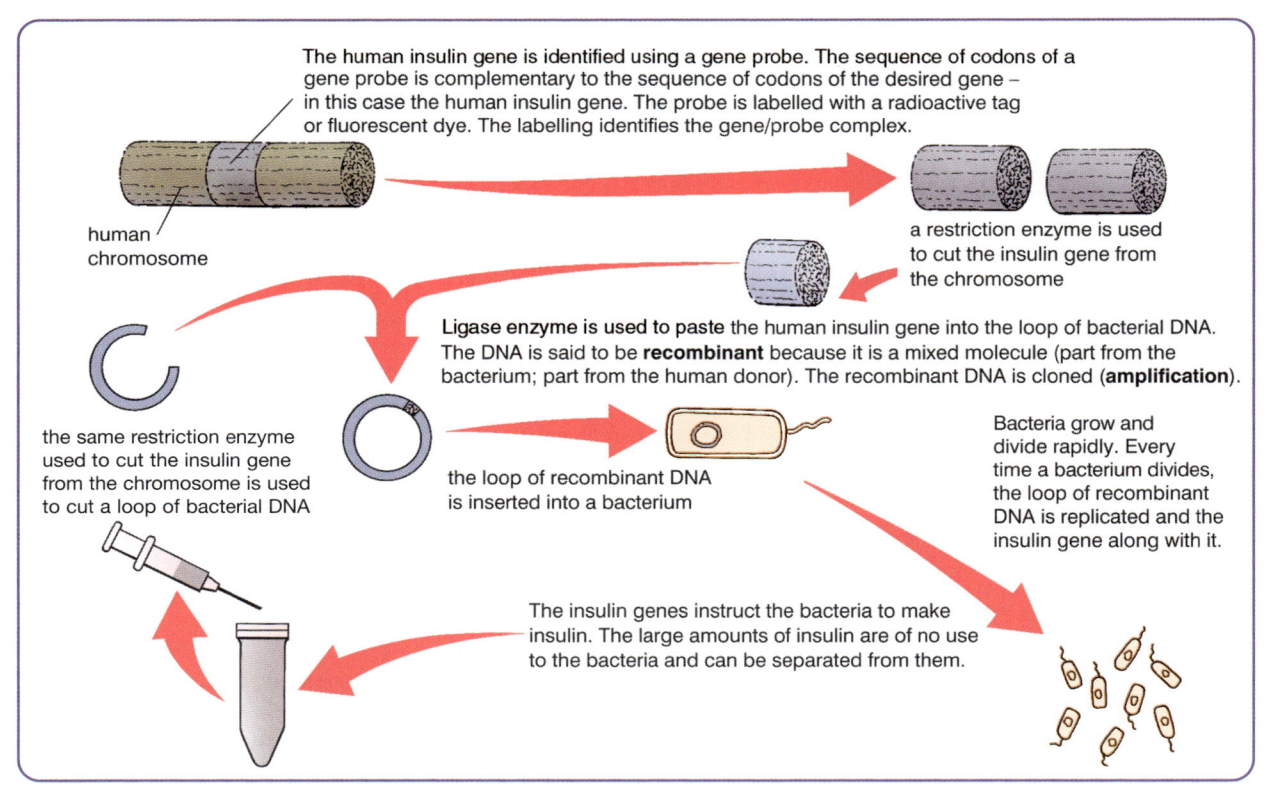

The human insulin gene is identified using a gene probe. The sequence of codons of a gene probe is complementary to the sequence of codons of the desired gene – in this case the human insulin gene. The probe is labelled with a radioactive tag or fluorescent dye. The labelling identifies the gene/probe complex.

human chromosome

a restriction enzyme is used to cut the insulin gene from the chromosome

the same restriction enzyme used to cut the insulin gene from the chromosome is used to cut a loop of bacterial DNA

Ligase enzyme is used to paste the human insulin gene into the loop of bacterial DNA. The DNA is said to be **recombinant** because it is a mixed molecule (part from the bacterium; part from the human donor). The recombinant DNA is cloned (**amplification**).

the loop of recombinant DNA is inserted into a bacterium

Bacteria grow and divide rapidly. Every time a bacterium divides, the loop of recombinant DNA is replicated and the insulin gene along with it.

The insulin genes instruct the bacteria to make insulin. The large amounts of insulin are of no use to the bacteria and can be separated from them.

Making genetically engineered insulin. Gene probes are used to detect and identify faulty genes

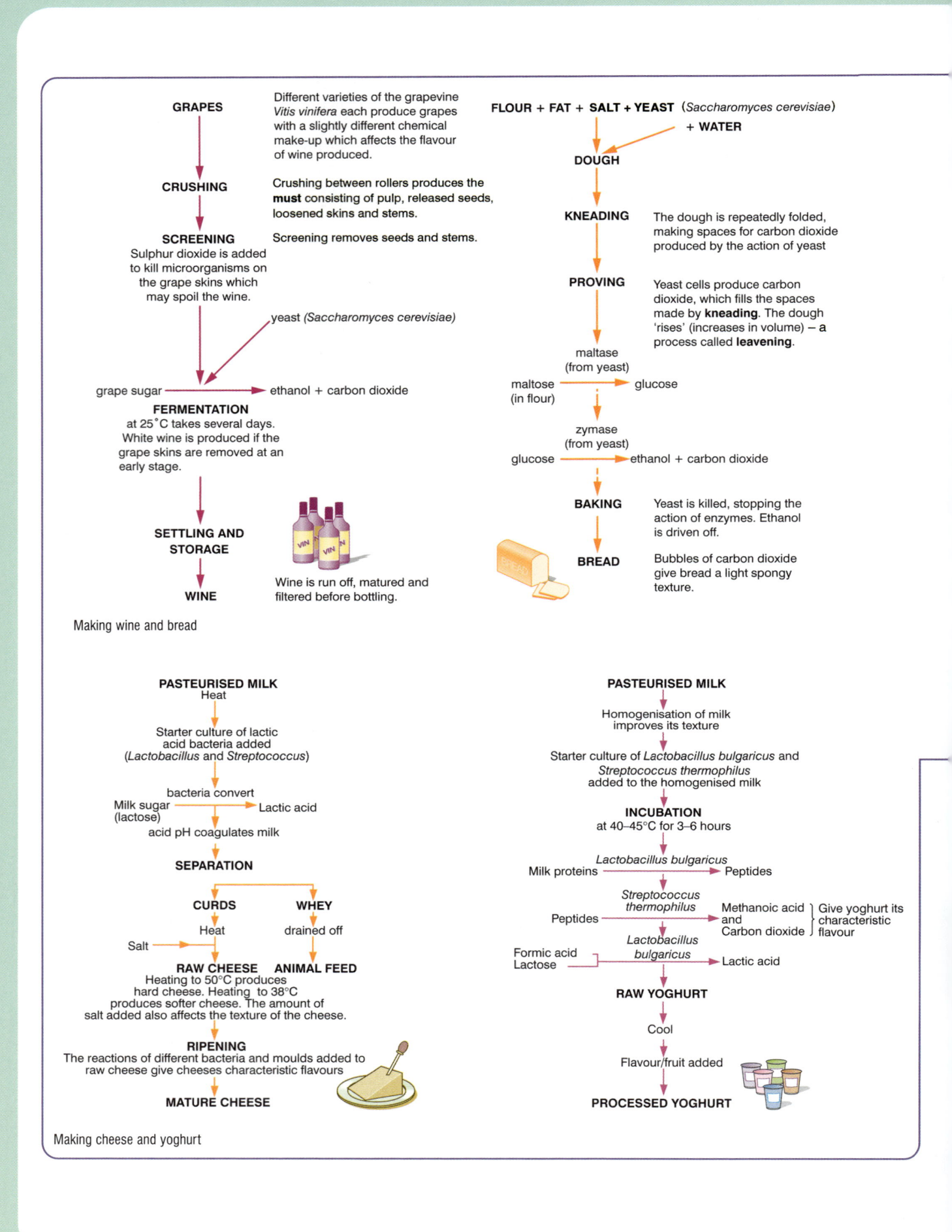

Biotechnology

Making wine and bread

GRAPES — Different varieties of the grapevine *Vitis vinifera* each produce grapes with a slightly different chemical make-up which affects the flavour of wine produced.

↓

CRUSHING — Crushing between rollers produces the **must** consisting of pulp, released seeds, loosened skins and stems.

↓

SCREENING — Screening removes seeds and stems. Sulphur dioxide is added to kill microorganisms on the grape skins which may spoil the wine.

↓ yeast (*Saccharomyces cerevisiae*)

grape sugar ⟶ ethanol + carbon dioxide

FERMENTATION at 25°C takes several days. White wine is produced if the grape skins are removed at an early stage.

↓

SETTLING AND STORAGE

↓

WINE — Wine is run off, matured and filtered before bottling.

FLOUR + FAT + SALT + YEAST (*Saccharomyces cerevisiae*) + WATER

↓

DOUGH

↓

KNEADING — The dough is repeatedly folded, making spaces for carbon dioxide produced by the action of yeast.

↓

PROVING — Yeast cells produce carbon dioxide, which fills the spaces made by **kneading**. The dough 'rises' (increases in volume) — a process called **leavening**.

maltase (from yeast)
maltose (in flour) ⟶ glucose

zymase (from yeast)
glucose ⟶ ethanol + carbon dioxide

↓

BAKING — Yeast is killed, stopping the action of enzymes. Ethanol is driven off.

↓

BREAD — Bubbles of carbon dioxide give bread a light spongy texture.

Making cheese and yoghurt

PASTEURISED MILK
↓ Heat

Starter culture of lactic acid bacteria added (*Lactobacillus* and *Streptococcus*)

bacteria convert
Milk sugar (lactose) ⟶ Lactic acid
acid pH coagulates milk

↓

SEPARATION
↙ ↘
CURDS   **WHEY**
Heat   drained off
Salt ⟶
RAW CHEESE   **ANIMAL FEED**

Heating to 50°C produces hard cheese. Heating to 38°C produces softer cheese. The amount of salt added also affects the texture of the cheese.

↓

RIPENING — The reactions of different bacteria and moulds added to raw cheese give cheeses characteristic flavours.

↓

MATURE CHEESE

PASTEURISED MILK

↓ Homogenisation of milk improves its texture

Starter culture of *Lactobacillus bulgaricus* and *Streptococcus thermophilus* added to the homogenised milk

↓

INCUBATION at 40–45°C for 3–6 hours

Lactobacillus bulgaricus
Milk proteins ⟶ Peptides

Streptococcus thermophilus
Peptides ⟶ Methanoic acid and Carbon dioxide } Give yoghurt its characteristic flavour

Lactobacillus bulgaricus
Formic acid / Lactose ⟶ Lactic acid

↓

RAW YOGHURT

↓ Cool

Flavour/fruit added

↓

PROCESSED YOGHURT

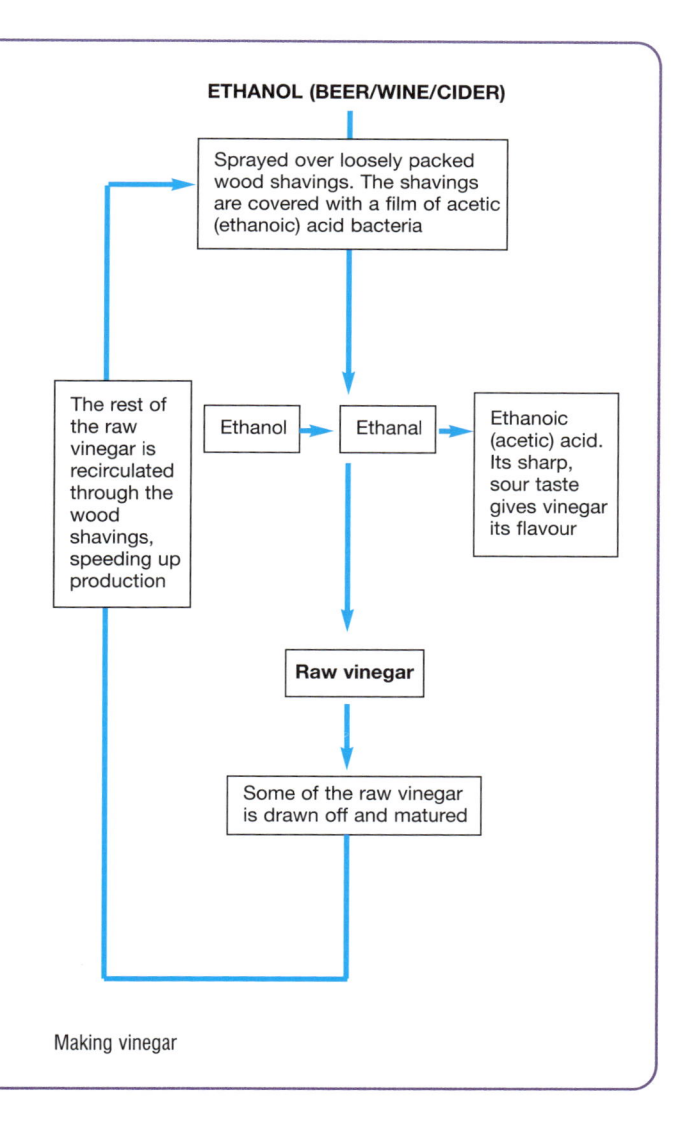

Biotechnology

ETHANOL (BEER/WINE/CIDER)

Sprayed over loosely packed wood shavings. The shavings are covered with a film of acetic (ethanoic) acid bacteria

Ethanol → Ethanal → Ethanoic (acetic) acid. Its sharp, sour taste gives vinegar its flavour

The rest of the raw vinegar is recirculated through the wood shavings, speeding up production

Raw vinegar

Some of the raw vinegar is drawn off and matured

Making vinegar

Remember that the products of biotechnology come from the action of **genes** producing useful substances.

Fact file

★ **Batch culture** produces batches of product in a fermenter. The fermenter is then emptied of the product and the nutrient solution. The fermenter is sterilised with super-heated steam ready for the next batch.

★ **Continuous culture** produces substances as an ongoing process. The product is drawn off the fermenter and nutrients are replaced as they are used.

8.2 Making use of biotechnology

PREVIEW

At the end of this section you will:
- know that enzymes are useful industrial catalysts
- understand that plant material is a store of energy which can be converted into fuel
- be able to list the different applications of biotechnology on the farm
- understand the significance of monoclonal antibodies
- realise the potential of gene therapy for curing inherited diseases.

Making the link

Modern biotechnology is branching out in new and exciting ways. Central to its success is our understanding that the products of biotechnology are the result of the action of **genes**.

GENES Page 54.

Enzymes

Enzymes are useful **industrial catalysts** for the following reasons.

★ Only a particular reaction is catalysed by an enzyme, making it easier to collect and purify the products.

★ Enzyme activity is high at moderate temperature and pH.

★ Only small amounts of enzyme are required.

★ The enzyme is not used up in the reaction.

Most industrial enzymes come from microorganisms grown in nutrient solution inside

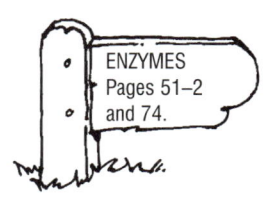

ENZYMES Pages 51–2 and 74.

147

Biotechnology

large fermenters. The enzymes secreted into the nutrient solution are filtered off, concentrated and packaged for sale as liquids or powders.

Enzymes have a range of uses.

★ **Industrial** – food production, leather-making, brewing and washing powder manufacture.

★ **Medical** – diagnosis and treatment.

★ **Analysis** – environmental pollution and crime detection.

Fact file

Washing liquids and powders may contain proteases and lipases. The enzymes help to wash food-stained clothing clean. They catalyse reactions that digest the protein and lipid components of food stains, producing products that are soluble in water.

Immobilised enzymes

Enzymes may be bonded to different insoluble materials which support them. They are then called **immobilised enzymes**, and their advantages are that they are:
- easily recovered and can be re-used
- active at temperatures that would destroy unprotected enzymes
- not diluted and therefore do not contaminate the product.

Immobilised enzymes are vital components of different types of **biosensor**.

DNA fingerprinting

A person's DNA is unique as their fingerprints. DNA 'fingerprinting' can help to identify criminals in cases where the criminal's body cells are found at the scene of the crime. Except in the case of identical twins, the chances of two people having the same DNA 'fingerprint' are millions to one against.

The principles of obtaining a genetic 'fingerprint' of someone suspected of a crime are given below.

★ DNA is obtained from the biological evidence (blood or semen, for example) left at the scene of the crime.

★ Restriction enzymes are used to break up the DNA into pieces of different length.

★ The pieces are separated and identified by a radioactively labelled tag.

★ The end result looks like a 'bar code'.

DNA is obtained from samples of cells of suspects and in each case a 'bar code' is prepared. The 'bar codes' of the suspects are compared with the 'bar code' of the DNA obtained from the biological evidence left at the scene of the crime. If the 'bar code' of one of the suspects matches the 'bar code' of the biological evidence, then it is almost certain that the person is the culprit. Look at the DNA 'bar codes' in the figure below. Who do you think is the most likely suspect to have committed the crime?

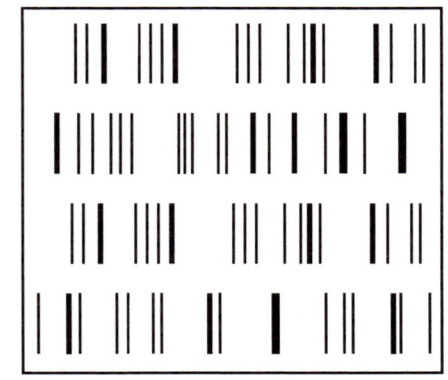

Biotechnology

Biofuel

Plants trap light energy to produce sugars by photosynthesis. Plant material therefore represents a store of energy which the processes of biotechnology convert into **fuels** such as ethanol. Countries that lack oil resources, such as Brazil, have developed gasohol programmes. Sugar cane grows rapidly in the warm sunny environment, and is used as a substrate which yeast ferments to produce ethanol. Most yeasts die when the concentration of ethanol is more than 15%. Sugar cane waste that has not been fermented (called **bagasse**) is burnt to provide the heat to distil off ethanol from the solution, and the gasohol fuel produced is 96% ethanol. After adjustments to carburettors and fuel pumps, car engines can run on pure ethanol or an ethanol–petrol mixture. The sequence runs:

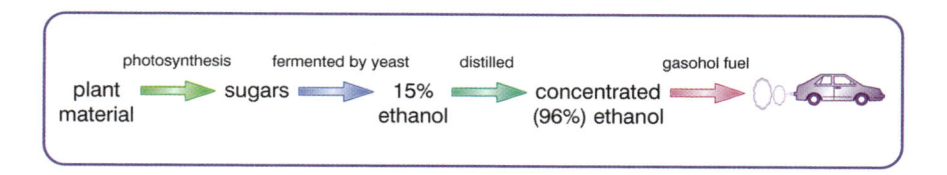

PHOTOSYNTHESIS Pages 57–60.

plant material →(photosynthesis)→ sugars →(fermented by yeast)→ 15% ethanol →(distilled)→ concentrated (96%) ethanol →(gasohol fuel)→ car

On the farm

Around 6.2 billion people populate the world. Feeding everybody is difficult, but biotechnology is helping to solve some of the problems. **Genetically modified** (GM) plants are being developed to improve the production of food. Developments include:

- genetically modifying crops to grow in places where at present there is little chance of success
- genetically modifying crops for resistance to pests and herbicides
- altering nitrogen-fixing bacteria so that they can live in the roots of cereal crops. If nitrogen-fixing bacteria can be made to live in the roots of cereal crops, the large amounts of nitrogen fertiliser used to boost cereal production would not be needed. Pollution of the environment would also be reduced.
- engineering bacteria to produce insecticides, and spraying the bacteria onto crops where they are taken up by the plants
- producing plants resistant to disease
- developing livestock to produce more and better quality meat and milk.

Soon crops will be able to tolerate cold, flourish in drought conditions and resist insects and disease – thanks to biotechnology.

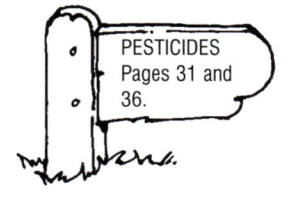

PESTICIDES Pages 31 and 36.

Why are GM crops an issue?

From the developments listed, GM crops would seem to have a number of advantages. For example controlling the weeds and insects that reduce food production is easier and safer for the farmer. Also, the volume of chemicals used to control them is cut back, resulting in less damage to wildlife and the environment. Why, then, are people concerned about the introduction of GM crops? Here are a number of points for you to think about:

★ People are worried that eating GM food may harm their health.

★ There are concerns that GM crops will harm wildlife.

★ Pollen from crops genetically modified for resistance to herbicides may transfer to wild plants. If these plants are weeds, there is a danger of the development of weeds resistant to herbicides.

★ Some people think that transferring genes between organisms in the laboratory is somehow 'not natural'.

Remember that whatever your views, there are different ways of thinking about the issues raised.

Biotechnology

Fact file

Tomatoes soften as a particular enzyme breaks down a substance called **pectin** in the walls of their cells. Softening limits the 'shelf-life' of tomatoes. The gene coding for the 'softening' enzyme has been identified and a reverse form of it has been made. When the reverse form is engineered into the tomato plant it silences the normal softening gene. 'Gene silencing' has been used to control the softening of tomatoes as they ripen, helping to prolong their 'shelf-life'.

Using transgenic animals

The term **transgenic** is used, as well as 'GM', to refer to organisms whose genetic material has been modified to produce useful substances. For example, genetic engineering has inserted the human gene for **factor VIII** (a blood-clotting protein) into the DNA of sheep. The sheep make factor VIII which is drawn off in the milk, purified and used to treat haemophilia. Modifying the milk of other livestock species (cattle, goats, rabbits) has made available other medically useful substances. The technique is particularly attractive because female mammals produce milk for long periods and engineering the desired gene into genetic material, which is only expressed in the tissue of the mammary glands, reduces the risk of side effects in other organs.

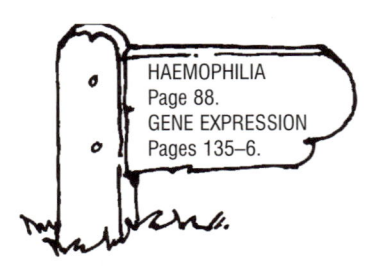

HAEMOPHILIA Page 88.
GENE EXPRESSION Pages 135–6.

Cloning

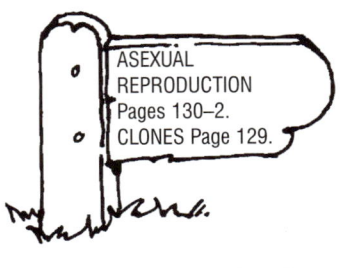

Cloning plants preserves the characteristics of previous generations of plants in the offspring. Desirable qualities, such as disease resistance, colour of fruit or shape of flower, are preserved and reliably reproduced in new stocks of plants.

ASEXUAL REPRODUCTION Pages 130–2.
CLONES Page 129.

Cloning animals is more difficult than cloning plants. However, clones of sheep, cattle, pigs, mice and other mammals are available. Their possible use for improvements in medicine and agriculture often makes the news headlines.

In 1996 Dolly the sheep was born. Dolly was the first mammal to be cloned from an adult cell. The process of producing Dolly runs:

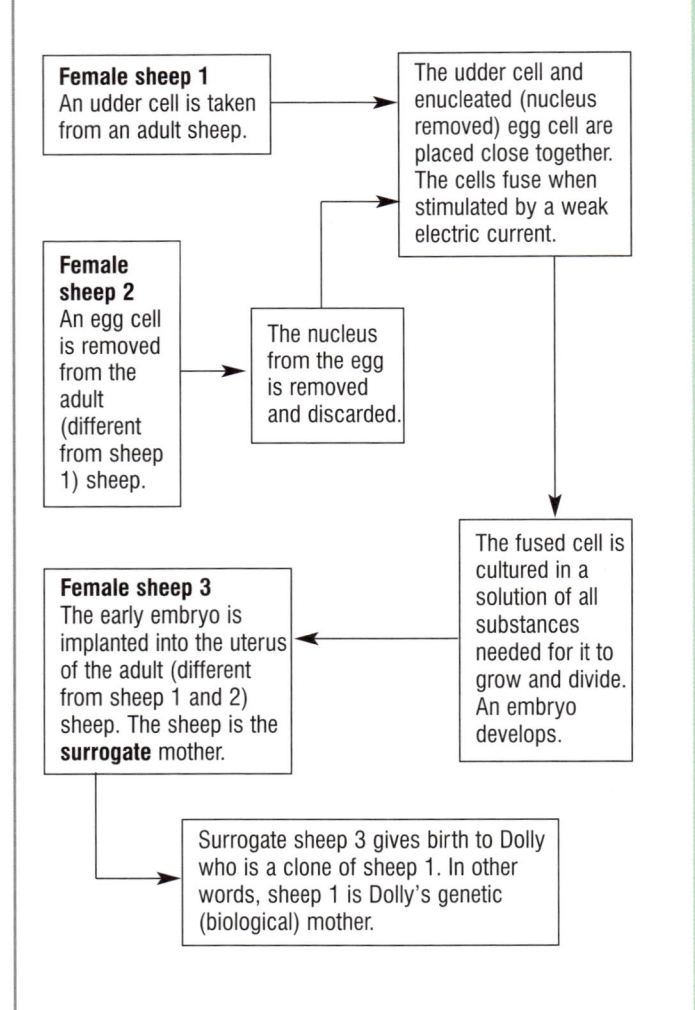

Female sheep 1
An udder cell is taken from an adult sheep.

→ The udder cell and enucleated (nucleus removed) egg cell are placed close together. The cells fuse when stimulated by a weak electric current.

Female sheep 2
An egg cell is removed from the adult (different from sheep 1) sheep.

→ The nucleus from the egg is removed and discarded.

→ The fused cell is cultured in a solution of all substances needed for it to grow and divide. An embryo develops.

Female sheep 3
The early embryo is implanted into the uterus of the adult (different from sheep 1 and 2) sheep. The sheep is the **surrogate** mother.

Surrogate sheep 3 gives birth to Dolly who is a clone of sheep 1. In other words, sheep 1 is Dolly's genetic (biological) mother.

Biotechnology

Some people think the benefits of animal cloning could be enormous; others point out serious moral and ethical concerns. Here are a number of points for you to think about:

★ Healthy cells taken from a sick person could be cloned and used to repair that person's damaged tissues.

★ A person needing a transplant could make use of a brain-dead clone of himself/herself as a source of tissues and organs for transplantation.

★ For some the thought of a brain-dead clone as a source of tissues and organs for transplantation is morally wrong. Respect for human life should outweigh the possible benefits to the patient.

★ If cloning animals that are not genetically modified like Dolly is possible, then cloning ones that are (including humans) should be relatively simple.

In 2003, Dolly was found to have arthritis in her joints. She also developed lung disease and was 'put down' to prevent her suffering distress. By sheep standards, Dolly was not old, and her death has added new life to the long-running argument over the ethics of cloning animals. Was her death linked to premature ageing because she was a clone? This and other questions raise important issues about the safety of cloning and the possible extension of the work to humans.

Remember that whatever your views, there are different ways of thinking about the issued raised.

Monoclonal antibodies

Antibodies defend the body from attack by pathogens. However, it is not possible to separate out different antibodies into pure samples to fight specific diseases. White blood cells which produce antibodies are very difficult to grow outside the body. However, cancer cells are not. Fusing white blood cells that produce the desired antibody with a certain type of cancer cell results in cells called **hybridomas** which do grow outside the body. The hybridomas produce pure samples of antibodies which are called **monoclonal antibodies**.

Remember that antibodies are **specific**. Each type will only bind with the antigen which stimulates its (the antibody) production in the first place. Some types of cancer cell make proteins (antigens) that are different from the proteins made by healthy cells. Monoclonal antibodies that bind only to the abnormal proteins are available. When combined with drugs that kill cells, the monoclonal antibody/drug combination targets the cancer cells without affecting healthy cells.

Monoclonal antibodies have a wide range of uses, such as:

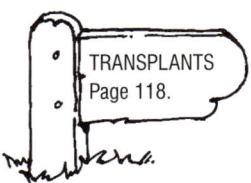

- diagnosis of diseases
- detection of pregnancy
- inactivation of poisons
- tissue matching to reduce the risk of rejection of transplanted tissues
- treatment of cancer.

TRANSPLANTS Page 118.

Gene therapy

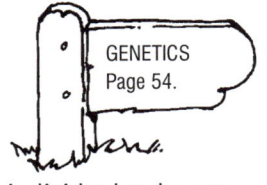

We all carry a few faulty alleles. Most of them are recessive, so their harmful effects are masked by their dominant partners. However, individuals who are homozygous for recessive faulty alleles or who are heterozygous for dominant faulty alleles show symptoms of disease.

GENETICS Page 54.

Gene therapy aims to replace the faulty alleles with normal ones. It is difficult to produce long-term cures for genetic diseases, although research is making progress. For example, **cystic fibrosis** is a genetic disease caused by a faulty recessive allele (see page 136). Healthy copies of the allele are engineered into tiny fat droplets called **liposomes**. These are carried as an aerosol spray deep into the lungs in an attempt to replace the faulty alleles in the cells of lung tissue with healthy ones. The cells seem to take up the liposomes with the healthy alleles, bringing some relief (albeit temporary) to sufferers of cystic fibrosis. Research continues to try to make the benefits long term.

Biotechnology

8.3 Eating microorganisms

PREVIEW

At the end of this section you will:
- know about the advantages of eating micro-organisms
- be able to summarise the stages in the production of single cell protein.

Making the link

How can we produce enough food to feed the world's growing population? Intensive farming and applying biotechnology to farming are options (see Sections 2.6 and 8.2). Eating microorganisms produced by biotechnology is another alternative.

Advantages of eating microorganisms

The problem of feeding the world's population requires imaginative solutions. Eating microorganisms produced by biotechnology is an option.

★ Populations of microorganisms grow quickly and are easy to manipulate. They may double their mass within hours. Plants and animals take weeks.

★ Microbial mass is at least 40% protein.

★ Microorganisms have a high vitamin and mineral content.

★ Growing microorganisms does not depend on the weather; growing crops like wheat and potatoes does.

High protein food produced from microorganisms is called **single cell protein** (**SCP**).

Producing SCP

Different nutrients, such as glucose syrup, waste from papermaking and fruit pulp, are used to grow SCP microorganisms in huge fermenters which are run continuously for months at a time (**continuous culture**). Nutrients are replaced as they are used up, and temperature and pH are carefully controlled.

CONTINUOUS CULTURE Page 147.

Microorganisms are harvested at regular intervals and processed into SCP. 'Quorn', made from the mould *Fusarium graminearum*, is an example. The food is called **mycoprotein** and, unlike meat, it is high in fibre and free of cholesterol. Quorn is made into soups, biscuits and drinks as well as substituting for different meats.

Inside fermenters making SCP, **warmth**, **food**, **moisture** and **oxygen** are controlled to make conditions ideal for the rapid **asexual reproduction** of the microorganisms harvested as food. Think of the sequence of numbers:

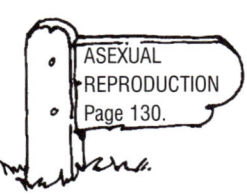

ASEXUAL REPRODUCTION Page 130.

2 4 8 16 32 64 128 256 512 1024 ... and so on

Notice that the next number in the sequence is double the previous number. If a population of microorganisms growing in a fermenter increases in this way, it means that each generation is double the size of the previous generation.

POPULATIONS Pages 22–24.

Remember that under ideal conditions some microorganisms can reproduce asexually every 20–30 minutes:

       divides   divide   divide
1 cell → 2 cells → 4 cells ... and so on

No wonder, with such rapid growth using cheap nutrients, microorganisms are commercially attractive for the production of protein-rich foods – for *animals* as well as humans.

Biotechnology

Microorganisms used for industrial processes and laboratory work need careful handling.

★ Unwanted microorganisms can *contaminate*:
  - industrial processes spoiling the product
  - laboratory experiments spoiling the results of scientific analysis and research.

★ Microorganisms which cause disease (**pathogens**) may represent a *health hazard* to people working on industrial processes and in laboratories.

Precautions for industry

★ *Superheated steam* at 120 °C is pumped through the fermenter and its pipelines.

As a result spores produced by bacteria and fungi, which may spoil the product and/or be a hazard to health, are destroyed.

Precautions for laboratories

★ *Protective* laboratory coats/face masks prevent bacteria from contaminating clothes and the face.

★ *Washing* hands *before* work and *after* work removes microorganisms from the skin.

★ *Swabbing* working surfaces prevents the build up of microorganisms in the laboratory.

★ *Flaming* wire loops and necks of culture bottles makes sure that the microorganisms under investigation are not contaminated with unwanted microorganisms.

★ *Autoclaving* heats laboratory equipment before use so that unwanted microorganisms are killed. It also kills all microorganisms on equipment after the equipment has been used. The precaution makes sure that any unwanted microorganisms that may have contaminated experiments are killed.

Remember to use only cultures of microorganisms that are described as *safe*. **Do not** culture microorganisms from other sources such as air, soil or water. The sources may contain microorganisms that are a hazard to health.

Biotechnology

ROUND UP

How much have you improved? Work out your improvement index on page 163.

1 Distinguish between the processes of kneading, proving and baking in the making of bread. [6]

2 Below is a list of the processes which start with identifying the human insulin gene and result in the production of genetically engineered human insulin. Write the letters in the correct order.

 A The human insulin gene is identified.

 B Bacteria genetically engineered with the human insulin gene grow and divide rapidly.

 C Restriction enzyme cuts open a ring of bacterial DNA.

 D Large amounts of insulin are separated from the nutrient solution in which the genetically engineered bacteria are growing.

 E The ring of genetically engineered bacterial DNA is inserted into a bacterium.

 F Restriction enzyme cuts the human insulin gene from the chromosome.

 G Ligase is used to insert the human insulin gene into a ring of bacterial DNA.

 H Human insulin is purified and packed. [6]

3 What are the advantages to diabetics of using insulin produced by bacteria into which the human insulin gene has been inserted? [4]

4 Describe how monoclonal antibodies could be used to treat cancer. [4]

5 Briefly explain the principles behind treating genetic diseases by gene therapy. [2]

6 How is biotechnology helping to feed the world's growing human population? [5]

7 What is an immobilised enzyme? [3]

8 People might be reluctant to eat SCP made from microorganisms. How do you think SCP might be made more acceptable as food? [4]

9 What contribution do you think that SCP production could make to helping feed the world's growing population? [7]

Well done if you've improved. Don't worry if you haven't. Take a break and try again.

Answers

1 Test yourself (page 4)
Introducing biology

1. a) It would increase (✓). b) It would decrease (✓).

2. a) | b) | c)
   movement | ✓ |
   respiration | ✓ | ✗
   sensitivity | ✓ | ✗
   growth | ✓ | ✗
   reproduction | ✓ | ✗
   excretion | ✓ | ✗
   nutrition | ✓ | ✗ [✓ × 10]

   d) No – plants do not move from place to place (✓).

3. Annual: a plant that grows from seed to maturity and produces new seeds all within one growing season (✓). It then dies (✓). Perennial: a plant that continues to grow and produce seeds for many years (✓).

4. a) To identify different living things by name (✓).
   b) These characteristics vary too much (✓) even between members of the same group of organisms (✓) to be reliable indicators for identification (✓).

5. Soil: is damp (✓); shields organisms from ultraviolet light (✓); maintains a relatively stable temperature compared with air (✓); contains food (✓).

Your score: ☐ out of 24

1 Round up (page 10)
Introducing biology

1. a) It would boil away (✓).
   b) It would freeze and form ice (✓).

2. a) oxygen (✓)
   b) carbon dioxide (✓)

3. a) Respiration releases energy from food (✓). Gaseous exchange takes in oxygen needed for respiration (✓) and removes carbon dioxide produced by respiration (✓).
   b) Excretion removes the waste substances produced by metabolism (✓). Defecation removes the undigested remains of food (✓).

4. The answer should include the idea that although cars move (✓), need fuel (= nutrition) (✓), burn fuel (= respiration) (✓) and produce waste gases (= excretion) (✓) they do not grow (✓) or reproduce (✓) and are not sensitive (✓). Cars therefore do not show all the characteristics associated with living things (✓).

5. | A characteristics | | B descriptions |
   |---|---|---|
   | movement | (✓) | changing position |
   | respiration | (✓) | releasing energy from food |
   | sensitivity | (✓) | responding to stimuli |
   | growth | (✓) | increasing in size |
   | reproduction | (✓) | producing new individuals |
   | excretion | (✓) | removing waste substances produced by cells |
   | nutrition | (✓) | making or obtaining food |

6. | A animals | | B descriptions |
   |---|---|---|
   | insect | (✓) | six legs |
   | worm | (✓) | no legs |
   | spider | (✓) | eight legs |
   | bird | (✓) | two legs |

7. The unfamiliar specimen is compared with the descriptions in the key (✓).
   The descriptions are followed through (✓) until the description that matches the specimen is found (✓).
   The matching description identifies the specimen (✓).

8. The system gives each living organism a name in two parts (✓). The first is the name of the genus (✓); the second is the species name (✓). The genus and species names identify the organism (✓).

9. paired statements (✓)

Your score: ☐ out of 37

Your improvement index: $\dfrac{\boxed{}/37}{\boxed{}/24} \times 100\% = \boxed{}\%$

2 Test yourself (page 11)
Organisms in the environment

1. | A terms | | B descriptions |
   |---|---|---|
   | biosphere | (✓) | all the ecosystems of the world |
   | community | (✓) | all the organisms that live in a particular ecosystem |
   | habitat | (✓) | the place where a group of organisms lives |
   | population | (✓) | a group of individuals of the same species |

2. a) Most animals eat more than one type of plant or other animal (✓). A food web shows the range of different foods eaten (✓).
   b) Plants produce food by photosynthesis (✓). Animals consume this food directly when they eat plants (✓) or indirectly when they eat other animals (✓) which depend on plant food (✓).

155

Answers

3 a) The pyramid of biomass takes into account differences in size (✓) of producers and consumers (✓).
 b) The energy pyramid shows the amount of food being produced (✓) and consumed (✓) in a given time (✓).

4 Improvements in food production (✓); more jobs (✓); new drugs (accept improvement in medicines/medical care) (✓); improvement in public health (✓).

5 Benefits: more food (✓), reliably produced (✓).
Costs: loss of wildlife (✓), loss of habitats (✓), pollution from agrochemicals (✓). (Accept other sensible alternatives.)

Your score: ☐ out of 24

2 Round up (page 37)
Organisms in the environment

1 physical *or* abiotic factors (✓), environment (✓), living *or* biotic factors (✓), community (✓), habitats (✓), niches (✓)

2 a) the non-living part of an ecosystem (✓)
 b) The amount of light affects the rate of photosynthesis (✓) and therefore the amount of plant growth under the canopy layer (✓). This in turn affects the animals that depend on plants for food and shelter (✓) and so on along the food chain (✓).

3 a) 3 (✓)
 b) water weed (✓)
 c) water weed makes food by photosynthesis (✓)
 d) tadpoles (✓)
 e) tadpoles eat water weed (accept plants) (✓)
 f) minnows (✓) and perch (✓)
 g) Minnow and perch eat tadpoles (accept meat) (✓).

4 Light is reflected from the leaf surface (✓). Light passes through the leaf (✓). Only some of the light is absorbed by chlorophyll (✓).

5 When the different organisms in the community show an approximation (are roughly the same) in size (✓).

6 a) saw wrack (✓)
 b) dog whelks (✓)
 c) The biomass of dog whelks would decrease (✓). The biomass of saw wrack would increase (✓).

7 a) Intraspecific competition – competition between individuals of the same species (✓). Interspecific competition – competition between individuals of different species (✓).
 b) Adaptation – an organism is adapted (suited) to survive (✓). Survival – an organism survives (lives) because of its adaptations (✓).
 c) Camouflage – coloration that conceals organisms (✓). Warning coloration – colours that deter predators from attacking prey (✓).

8 a) When prey is scarce predator numbers fall (✓). When prey numbers build up predator numbers follow because there is more prey food (✓). Predator breeds and reproduces more slowly than prey (✓).
 b) The population numbers of each species are stable (✓). (Allow: population numbers of each species fluctuated around a mean (average) number for that species.)
 c) Numbers would increase (✓).
 d) Numbers would decline (✓) to the former level (✓).
 e) Numbers would decline (✓) because of lack of food (✓). (Allow sensible alternative suggestions, e.g. increased mortality due to disease or parasites.)

9

A terms	B descriptions
fertiliser (✓)	supplies plants with nutrients
herbicide (✓)	kills plants
irrigation (✓)	supplies plants with water
monoculture (✓)	a crop grown over a large area
weed (✓)	an unwanted plant

Your score: ☐ out of 47

Your improvement index: $\dfrac{\Box/47}{\Box/24} \times 100\% = \Box\%$

3 Test yourself (page 38)
Cell activity

1

A structures	B functions
mitochondrion (✓)	where energy is released from the oxidation of glucose
plasma membrane (✓)	partially permeable to substances in solution
chloroplast (✓)	where light energy is captured
cell wall (✓)	fully permeable to substances in solution
nucleus (✓)	contains the chromosomes

2 Because molecules of the substance are moving against their concentration gradient (✓).

3 a) A plasmolysed cell is one from which water has passed out of the vacuole, out of the cytoplasm, and out of the cell through the plasma membrane and cell wall into the solution outside the cell (accept water has passed out of the cell) (✓). As a result the cytoplasm pulls away from the cell wall (accept cell content disrupted) (✓) and the cell becomes limp (✓). A turgid cell is one which contains as much water as it can hold (✓).
 b) A fully permeable membrane allows most substances to pass through it (✓). A partially permeable membrane allows some substances to pass through it (✓) and stops other substances (✓).

4 A group of genetically identical cells (or organisms) (✓).

5 During replication each chromosome (and its DNA) (✓) makes an exact copy of itself (✓).

6 a) Cells die (✓). New cells (✓) which are replicas of the old cells are produced by mitosis (✓).
   b) The daughter cells have the same number of chromosomes as the parent cell (✓). The chromosomes in the daughter cells are identical to those in the parent cells (✓).

7 Haploid cells receive half the diploid number of chromosomes (✓) from their parent cell (✓).
   Diploid cells receive the full number of chromosomes (✓) from their parent cell (✓).

8 cells (✓), cells (✓), tissues (✓), an organ (✓), organs (✓), an organ (✓)

9 cellulose in plant cell walls (✓); chitin in insect exoskeletons (✓)

10 Molecules of unsaturated fats have double bonds between some carbon atoms (✓). Molecules of saturated fats have only single bonds between carbon atoms (✓).

11 A nucleotide consists of the sugar ribose (✓) or deoxyribose (✓), one of five different bases (✓) and a phosphate group (✓).

Your score: ☐ out of 39

3 Round up (page 56)
Cell activity

1 a) nucleus (✓), plasma membrane (✓), mitochondria (✓), cytoplasm (✓)
   b) cell wall (✓), large vacuole (✓), chloroplasts (✓)

2 Water is taken into the cells (✓) by osmosis (✓). The cells become turgid (✓). The wilted plant (✓) will become upright again (✓) as its cells become turgid following watering.

3 down (✓), faster (✓), against (✓), energy (✓), partially (✓), osmosis (✓)

4 Damaged tissues can be replaced by new cells that are identical to the parent cells (✓).

5 Similarities: replication of each chromosome into chromatids (✓); lining up of the chromosomes on the equator of the cell (✓); separation of the chromatids (✓); chromatids form the new chromosomes in daughter cells (✓); break down and reformation of the nuclear membrane during the process of cell division (✓).
   Differences: chromosomes form homologous pairs in meiosis but not in mitosis (✓); there are two divisions during meiosis but only one division during mitosis (✓); meiosis results in four haploid daughter cells, mitosis in two diploid daughter cells (✓).

6 cells (✓), tissues (✓), organs (✓), organ systems (✓), organisms (✓)

7 A substances   B functions
   fat   (✓)   insulates the body
   cellulose   (✓)   a component of the plant cell wall
   DNA   (✓)   carries the genetic code
   polypeptide   (✓)   made of about 40 amino acids
   glycogen   (✓)   a food substance stored in the liver
   protein   (✓)   enzymes are made of this substance

8 a) 4 (✓)   b) 4 (✓)

Your score: ☐ out of 40

Your improvement index: $\dfrac{\Box/40}{\Box/39} \times 100\% = \Box\%$

4 Test yourself (page 57)
Green plants as organisms

1 a) carbon dioxide (✓) and water (✓)
   b) oxygen (✓)

2 A substances   B functions
   nitrogen   (✓)   used to make protein
   phosphorus   (✓)   used to make cell membranes
   magnesium   (✓)   used to make chlorophyll

3 increase (✓), xylem (✓), osmosis (✓), active transport (✓), xylem (✓), evaporates (✓), stomata (✓)

4 A tropisms   B descriptions
   phototropism   (✓)   growth movement in response to light
   geotropism   (✓)   growth movement in response to gravity
   hydrotropism   (✓)   growth movement in response to water
   thigmotropism (✓)   growth movement in response to touch

Your score: ☐ out of 18

4 Round up (page 67)
Green plants as organisms

1 palisade cells (✓), spongy mesophyll cells (✓), guard cells (✓)

2 The cells of the upper surface of the leaf do not contain chloroplasts (✓). Most light therefore reaches the palisade cells (✓) which are packed with chloroplasts (✓). Photosynthesis occurs at a maximum rate (✓)

3 temperature (✓), light intensity (✓), supplies of carbon dioxide (✓) and water (✓). A modern greenhouse provides warmth (✓), lighting (✓), a source of carbon dioxide (✓) and water from sprinkler systems (✓)

4 sugar (✓), sugar (✓), phloem (✓), sugar (✓), phloem (✓), active transport (✓), water (✓), phloem (✓), pressure (✓), translocation (✓), sugar (✓), pressure (✓), phloem (✓)

5 warm (✓), windy (✓), low humidity (✓) and bright sunlight (✓)

6 The stomata close (✓). If the plant continues to lose more water than it gains then its cells lose turgor (✓) and it wilts (✓)

Answers

7.
Xylem	Phloem
dead tissue (cells) (✓)	living tissue (cells) (✓)
tissue (cells) waterproofed with lignin (✓)	tissue (cells) not waterproofed with lignin (✓)
transports water and minerals (✓)	transports sugar and other substances (✓)
transport of materials is one way (✓)	transport of materials is two ways (✓)
xylem tissue does not have companion cells (✓)	phloem tissue has companion cells (✓)

8. growth regulator (✓), tip (✓), weedkiller (✓), unfertilised (✓), seedless (✓), ripens (✓)

9.
   a) Hypothesis: a substance produced in the shoot tip of a growing seedling (✓) controls the response of the shoot to light (✓).
   b) A: the shoot will remain upright and not bend towards the source of light (✓).
   Explanation: the piece of metal prevents the substance that controls the response of the shoot to light and which is produced in the shoot tip (✓) from diffusing to the region behind the shoot tip where it has its effect (✓).
   B: the shoot will bend towards the source of light (✓).
   Explanation: the substance that controls the response of the shoot to light and which is produced in the shoot tip (✓) is able to diffuse to the region behind the shoot tip where it has its effect (✓).

Your score: ☐ out of 54

Your improvement index: $\dfrac{\boxed{}/54}{\boxed{}/18} \times 100\% = \boxed{}\%$

5 Test yourself (page 68)

Humans (and other animals) as organisms

1.
   a) carbohydrates (✓), fats (✓), proteins (✓)
   b) protein (✓)
   c) fat (✓)
   d) minerals (✓) and vitamins (✓)

2.
A terms	B descriptions
ingestion (✓)	food is taken into the mouth
digestion (✓)	food is broken down
absorption (✓)	digested food passes into the body
egestion (✓)	the removal of undigested food through the anus

3.
   a) There are two bronchi, one branching to each lung (✓). Each bronchus branches many times into small tubes called bronchioles (✓).
   b) A person has two lungs (✓). Within each lung, bronchioles subdivide into even smaller tubes which end in clusters of small sacs called alveoli (✓).
   c) During aerobic respiration, cells use oxygen to oxidise digested food substances (accept glucose) (✓), releasing energy (✓). During anaerobic respiration, cells break down digested food substances (accept glucose) without oxygen (✓). Less energy is released during anaerobic respiration than during aerobic respiration (✓).
   d) Breathing takes in (inhales) (✓) and expels (exhales) (✓) air. Gaseous exchange occurs across the surfaces of the alveoli (✓).

4. The right ventricle pumps blood into the pulmonary artery (✓) on its way to the lungs (✓); the left ventricle pumps blood into the aorta (✓) which takes it around the rest of the body (✓).

5.
A components	B descriptions
plasma (✓)	contains dissolved food substances
red blood cells (✓)	contain haemoglobin
white blood cells (✓)	produce antibodies
platelets (✓)	promote the formation of blood clots

6. receptor (✓), sensory neurone (✓), relay neurone (✓), motor neurone (✓), effector

7.
   a) The eardrum vibrates (✓) in response to sound waves (✓).
   b) The bones pass vibrations through the middle ear (✓) and also amplify them (✓).
   c) The pinna funnels sound waves down the ear canal (✓) to the eardrum (✓).
   d) The hair cells are stimulated by the vibrations of the basilar membrane (✓). They fire off nerve impulses to the brain along the auditory nerve (✓).

8. Hormones are chemical substances (✓) which circulate in the blood (✓).

9. Insulin decreases the level of glucose in the blood (✓). Glucagon increases the level of glucose in the blood (✓).

10. glomerulus (✓), Bowman's capsule (✓), tubule (✓), collecting duct (✓), ureter (✓), bladder (✓), urethra (✓)

11. The large pointed canines (✓) allow the dog to grip the food firmly (✓). The carnassial teeth (✓) in the upper and lower jaws cut the food (✓).

12. Beating cilia covering the gills (✓) draw a current of water containing microscopic organisms (✓) between the shells (✓). The microscopic organisms are trapped (✓) in the mucus covering the gills (✓). The mucus and food are then drawn into the mouth (✓).

13.
A skeletons	B descriptions
endoskeleton (✓)	the skeleton lies inside the body
exoskeleton (✓)	the skeleton surrounds the body
hydrostatic skeleton (✓)	the skeleton is a body space filled with fluid

Your score: ☐ out of 66

Answers

5 Round up (page 112)
Humans (and other animals) as organisms

1.
A nutrients		B test results
starch	(✓)	produces a blue/black colour when mixed with a few drops of iodine solution
glucose	(✓)	produces an orange/red colour when heated with Benedict's solution
fat	(✓)	forms a milky emulsion when mixed with warm dilute ethanol
protein	(✓)	produces a violet/purple colour when mixed with dilute sodium hydroxide and a few drops of copper sulphate solution

2.
A enzymes		B roles
amylase	(✓)	digests starch to maltose
pepsin	(✓)	digests protein to polypeptides
lipase	(✓)	digests fat to fatty acids and glycerol
maltase	(✓)	digests maltose to glucose

3. oxygen (✓), carbon dioxide (✓), alveoli (✓), surface area (✓), exchange (✓), thin (✓), moist (✓), inhalation (✓), exhalation (✓)

4. a) Oxygenated blood contains a lot of oxyhaemoglobin (✓). It is bright red (✓). Deoxygenated blood contains little oxyhaemoglobin (✓). It is deep red-purple (✓).
   b) Antibodies are proteins (✓) produced by lymphocytes (accept white blood cells) (✓) in response to antigens (✓) which are materials 'foreign' to (accept not recognised by) the body (✓). Antibodies destroy antigens (✓).
   c) HIV is the abbreviation for human immunodeficiency virus (✓) which causes the diseases (✓) that characterise AIDS (✓).
   d) Haemoglobin is the protein (✓) in red blood cells (✓) that absorbs oxygen (✓). Haemophilia is a genetic disease (✓) characterised by the slow clotting time of blood (✓).
   e) A thrombus is a clot (✓) that causes a thrombosis (blockage) (✓) in a blood vessel (✓).

5.
A parts of cell		B descriptions
axon	(✓)	transmits nerve impulses from the cell body
dendrite	(✓)	carries nerve impulses from the cell body
myelin sheath	(✓)	boosts the transmission of nerve impulses
nerve impulse	(✓)	minute electrical disturbances

6. a) The blind spot is the region of the retina insensitive to light (✓). The fovea is the most sensitive region of the retina, where cone cells are most dense (✓).
   b) The pupil is the central hole formed by the iris (✓). The iris is the coloured ring of muscle that controls the amount of light entering the eye (✓).
   c) The cornea bends (refracts) light (✓) and helps to focus light onto the retina (✓).

7. Endocrine glands are ductless glands (✓) which release hormones directly into the blood (✓).

8. Antidiuretic hormone promotes reabsorption of water into the body (✓) by making the collecting duct of the nephron more permeable to water (✓).

9. a) Raised hairs trap a layer of air (✓) which insulates the body in cold weather (✓). Air is a poor conductor of heat (✓).
   b) Sweat cools the body because it carries heat energy away from the body (✓) as it evaporates (✓).

10. The extra length of the tadpole's digestive system means that cellulose-digesting microorganisms (✓) have more time (✓) to digest plant material (✓). The shorter adult digestive system suggests that microorganisms are not an important component of the adult's digestive processes (✓).

11. calcium (✓), keratin (✓), hardest (✓), sugar (✓), acid (✓), softens (✓), dentist (✓)

Your score: ☐ out of 67

Your improvement index: $\dfrac{\Box/67}{\Box/66} \times 100\% = \Box\%$

6 Test yourself (page 113)
Health and disease

1. Non-infectious diseases develop because the body is not working properly (✓); two from, for example, cancer, arthritis, scurvy, schizophrenia, haemophilia (allow sensible alternatives) (✓✓).
   Infectious diseases are caused by organisms (allow pathogens) (✓) which can be passed from one person to another (✓); two from, for example, 'flu, chickenpox, mumps, AIDS, tuberculosis (allow sensible alternatives) (✓✓).

2.
A body structures		B roles
tear gland	(✓)	produces the enzyme lysozyme which destroys bacteria
glands in the stomach wall	(✓)	produce hydrochloric acid which kills bacteria
skin	(✓)	produces sebum which kills bacteria and fungi
cilia lining the upper respiratory tract	(✓)	sweep away mucus containing trapped microorganisms and particles
blood	(✓)	white cells produce antibodies which destroy antigens

3. The body takes a few days to produce antibodies against a first-time infection (✓). The individual therefore develops symptoms of disease (✓). If the same pathogen infects again, the body reacts more quickly (✓) producing antibodies which destroy the pathogen before symptoms develop (✓). The rapid response on reinfection is due to immunological memory (✓).

4. a) Donor – the person from whom organs or tissues are taken for transplantation (✓).
   Recipient – the person who receives organs or tissues from the donor (✓).
   b) Human lymphocyte antigens are carried on cell membranes (✓) except the membranes of red blood cells (✓). Red blood cell antigens are called antigen A and antigen B (✓). They determine which blood group a person belongs to (✓).

159

Answers

c) Immunosuppressive drugs prevent an immune response (✓) between the recipient and the donor organs or tissues (✓). Antibiotic drugs destroy bacteria (✓), preventing infection (✓).

5 Any five from: sterilisation; pasteurisation; refrigeration; freezing; drying; irradiation; ohmic heating; chemical preservatives; pickling; jam-making; smoking (✓✓✓✓✓).

6 Household rubbish may be incinerated (✓), dumped into holes in the ground (landfill sites) (✓) or recycled (✓).

7 Antiseptics are chemicals that stop microorganisms from multiplying (✓) and can be used to clean skin (✓).
Disinfectants kill microorganisms (✓) and are used to keep surfaces free of microorganisms (✓).
Aseptic procedures aim to prevent microorganisms from infecting wounds (✓).

8 The mosquito feeds on the blood (✓) of a person infected with the malaria parasite. The mosquito sucks up the parasite with the blood (✓) through its hollow mouthparts (✓). The parasite develops within the gut of the mosquito (✓) before migrating to the mosquito's salivary glands (✓). When the mosquito next feeds on another person, the malaria parasite passes down the mouthparts (✓) and enters the new person's bloodstream (✓).

Your score: ☐ out of 47

6 Round up (page 127)
Health and disease

1 cholera (B) (✓), AIDS (V) (✓), syphilis (B) (✓), 'flu (V) (✓), pneumonia (B) (✓)

2 B-lymphocytes produce antibodies (✓) in recognition of particular antigens (✓).
T-lymphocytes do not produce antibodies (✓). They bind with an antigen (✓).
Phagocytes engulf and destroy bacteria (✓) which have been attacked by antibodies (✓).

3 | A defences | | B descriptions |
|---|---|---|
| mucus | (✓) | traps particles and bacteria which are removed from the body by cilia |
| lysozyme | (✓) | destroys bacteria, preventing infection of the eye |
| hydrochloric acid | (✓) | kills bacteria on food |
| antibodies | (✓) | destroy antigens |
| sebum | (✓) | a substance which kills bacteria and fungi on the skin |

4 5 (✓)

5 a) Antibiotics are drugs which kill bacteria (✓).
Analgesics are drugs which relieve pain (✓).
b) B-lymphocytes produce antibodies (✓) which destroy antigens (✓).
T-lymphocytes do not produce antibodies (✓) but bind directly with an antigen, destroying it (✓).
c) Lung cancer is a result of the uncontrolled division of cells in lung tissue (✓).
Emphysema is caused by the destruction of the walls of the alveoli (✓).

6 Nicotine is a poison which increases the heart rate (✓) and blood pressure (✓).
Carbon monoxide combines with haemoglobin (✓) more readily than oxygen does (✓).
Tar is a mixture of substances (✓), some of which cause cancer (accept are carcinogens) (✓).

7 a) The primary immune response occurs when an antigen first invades the body (✓). The body takes a few days to produce antibodies against the antigen (accept to mount an immune response) (✓).
The secondary immune response occurs when the same antigen invades the body again (✓). Antibody production is much more rapid than during the primary immune response (accept the body mounts a rapid immune response) (✓).
The rapid response is due to memory cells (✓).
b) Lymphocytes are categories of white blood cell (✓). B-cell lymphocytes (✓) produce antibodies when challenged by antigens (✓). T-cell lymphocytes (✓) have a variety of functions (✓).
Phagocytes are a type of white blood cell (✓) which engulf bacteria (and other antigens) (✓) which have been attacked by antibodies (✓), destroying them (✓).
c) T-helper cells control the production of antibodies (✓) by B-cell lymphocytes (✓).
T-cytotoxic cells destroy virus-infected cells (✓).

8 a) Tissue typing compares the HLA antigens of donor and recipient (✓), matching them as closely as possible (✓).
Immunosuppressive drugs prevent the T-cell lymphocytes (✓) of the recipient from acting against the antigens in the transplanted tissue (✓).
b) Because the HLA antigens of the donor and recipient (✓) are identical (✓).

9 a) Vaccine – contains a substance that stimulates the production of antibodies (✓) which protect the person from disease-causing microorganisms (✓).
Vaccination – the introduction of a vaccine into an individual (✓).
b) Refrigeration – food is stored at a temperature between 0°C and 5°C (✓).
Freezing – food is stored at a temperature between −18°C and −24°C (✓).
c) Activated sludge process – diffusers bubble air (✓) through primary sewage effluent (✓).
Trickling filter process – primary sewage effluent is sprayed (✓) onto a filter bed (✓).

10 Boosters maintain a person's immunity by keeping up the level of antibodies in circulation (✓).

11 The victim loses water (✓) and the body quickly dehydrates (✓).

12 a) Host – an organism infected (✓) by a parasite (✓).
Vector – an organism which transfers a parasite (✓) from host to new host (✓).

b) Bactericides are antibiotic drugs (✓) which kill bacteria (✓).
Bacteristats are antibiotic drugs (✓) which prevent bacteria from multiplying (✓).

c) Chemotherapy – treatments which use drugs (✓) to attack pathogens (✓).
Resistance – the ability of a pathogen to deactivate a drug (accept withstand the effects of a drug) (✓) which had previously been an effective treatment for the pathogen (✓).

13 Precautions to slow the development of resistance include: avoiding the use of antibiotics by practising good hygiene (✓); using antibiotics only when necessary (✓); finishing a prescribed course of antibiotics (✓); switching antibiotics (✓) to slow the development of resistance to a particular antibiotic (✓); reducing the antibiotics given to farm animals (✓).

14 Treatment with drugs (✓) which destroy the malaria parasite (*Plasmodium*) (✓); destroying the mosquito vector (✓) by draining marshes/ponds/ditches (accept sensible alternatives) (✓), spraying insecticides which destroy mosquito larvae/pupae (✓) and introducing fish which eat mosquito larvae (✓); preventing contact between mosquitoes and people (✓) using bed nets (✓) and chemical repellants (✓).

Your score: ☐ out of 93

Your improvement index: $\dfrac{\boxed{}/93}{\boxed{}/47} \times 100\% = \boxed{}\%$

7 Test yourself (page 128)

Inheritance and evolution

1 A sperm duct (✓), B urethra (✓), C scrotal sac (accept scrotum) (✓), D = testis (✓), E = penis (✓)

2
A structures	B descriptions
corm (✓)	a short, swollen underground stem
runner (✓)	a horizontal stem running above ground
tuber (✓)	a swelling at the end of a rhizome
bulb (✓)	a large underground bud

3 a) Bb (✓) or bb (✓)
b) 50% of the children would be brown eyed (✓); 50% blue eyed (✓).

4 Acquired characteristics are those produced in the individual as a result of the influence (effects) of the environment (✓). These characteristics are not the result of genetic influence (✓) and are therefore not inherited (✓).

5 Genetic recombination (✓) as a result of sexual reproduction (✓), mutation (✓), crossing over (✓) during meiosis (✓) and the effects of the environment (✓).

Well done if you mentioned crossing over!

6 During sexual reproduction, genetic material inherited from both parents (✓) recombines in the fertilised egg (✓) producing combinations of genetic material in the offspring different from the combination in each of the parents (✓). During asexual reproduction, offspring inherit identical genetic material from one parent (✓). Mutation is the only source of variation (✓).

7 a) Ancestors are organisms that give rise to offspring, who are their descendants (✓).
b) Adaptation – an organism with a structure and way of life that best suits it to survive is said to be adapted (✓). Extinction occurs when a species dies out (✓).
c) Evolution – the change that occurs through many generations of descendants from different ancestors (✓). Natural selection – the process whereby favourable variations survive (✓) so that descendants evolve from ancestors (✓). (Allow: the mechanism of evolution (✓) through the survival of favourable variations (✓).)

8 Fossil formation occurs under the following conditions:
- the replacement of decayed organic material with a permanent alternative (✓)
- the burying of an organism in hardening mud or cooling volcanic ash (✓) followed by the formation of a cast (allow: material that takes on the shape of the original organism) (✓)
- rapid freezing of the organism following its death (✓).

Your score: ☐ out of 37

Answers

7 Round up (page 143)

Inheritance and evolution

1.
A structures		B descriptions
seed	(✓)	a fertilised ovule
ovule	(✓)	contains the egg nucleus
fruit	(✓)	develops from the ovary after fertilisation
stigma	(✓)	structure to which pollen grains attach
nectary	(✓)	produces a sugar solution

2. Plants are healthy (✓), the same (accept uniform) (✓), and retain desirable characteristics (✓).

3. starch (✓)

4. During mitosis, the DNA of the parent cell replicates (✓) so that daughter cells receive exact copies of the parent cell's genetic material (✓). Daughter cells divide and develop into new individuals which inherit the exact characteristics of the parent (✓). Offspring of the parent are also genetically identical to one another (✓) and are clones (✓).

5.
A terms		B descriptions
allele	(✓)	one of a pair of genes that controls a particular characteristic
pure breeding	(✓)	characteristics that appear unchanged from generation to generation
second filial generation	(✓)	offspring of the offspring of the parental generation
monohybrid inheritance	(✓)	the processes by which a single characteristic passes from parents to offspring

6. a) (i) A (✓)
   (ii) B (✓)
   (iii) Chart A shows intermediate lengths of fish (✓) over a range of measurements (✓). Chart B shows categories of colour (✓) without any intermediate shades (✓).
   b) 90% (✓)
   c) Albino fish occur as a result of a mutation of the alleles controlling colour (✓).

7. a) In unpolluted countryside, pale peppered moths blend with the light background of (are camouflaged on) the lichen-covered tree trunk (✓). Fewer are eaten by moth-eating birds (suffer less predation) (✓) than dark peppered moths (✓) which are more conspicuous (✓). In polluted industrial areas, dark peppered moths are less conspicuous against the soot-covered tree trunks (✓). Fewer are eaten by moth-eating birds (suffer less predation) (✓) than pale peppered moths (✓) which are more conspicuous (✓).
   b) The bird eats the moths which are conspicuous (✓) and therefore not adapted to blend with their surroundings (✓).

8. Individuals with genes for characteristics that favour survival are more likely to reproduce (✓). Their offspring inherit the favourable genes (✓) and in turn are more likely to survive and reproduce (✓) so handing on the favourable genes to the next generation, and so on (✓).

9. Charles Lyell stated that the Earth was very old (✓). This suggested to Darwin that there was sufficient time for the process of evolution to occur (✓). Malthus suggested that limited resources regulated population numbers (✓) which would otherwise increase indefinitely (✓). Darwin concluded that there must be a struggle for existence (competition for limited resources) (✓).

Your score: ☐ out of 45

Your improvement index: $\dfrac{\Box/45}{\Box/37} \times 100\% = \Box\%$

8 Test yourself (page 144)

Biotechnology

1. In the absence of oxygen (✓), yeast breaks down glucose anaerobically (✓) to form ethanol and carbon dioxide (✓).

2. a) Restriction enzyme cleaves (cuts up) lengths of DNA into different fragments (✓) depending on the restriction enzyme used (✓). A particular DNA fragment corresponds to a desired gene (✓). (Accept sensible alternative explanations.) Ligase splices the desired gene from among the fragments of DNA produced by a restriction enzyme (✓) into a plasmid vector (✓) which is a loop of bacterial DNA (✓) into which the desired gene is inserted (✓).
   b) Biotechnology uses microorganisms (✓) on a large scale for the production of useful substances (✓). Genetic engineering manipulates genes (✓) to create organisms (✓) with specific genetic characteristics for producing a range of useful substances (✓).
   c) Batch culture produces substances in a fermenter (✓). The fermenter is then emptied of product and nutrient solution (✓) and sterilised (✓) in preparation for the next batch (✓). Continuous culture produces substances over an extended period (✓). Product is drawn off and nutrients replaced as they are used (✓) during an ongoing process (✓).

3. Photosynthesis produces sugar which is a store of energy (✓). Yeasts are used to ferment the sugar (✓), producing ethanol (✓). When the concentration of ethanol exceeds 15% the yeasts die (✓). To concentrate the ethanol so that it is a useful fuel (✓), excess water is driven off (accept distilled off) (✓) by burning sugar cane waste (accept bagasse) (✓) as a source of heat for the distillation process (✓).

4. carbohydrases (✓) which digest carbohydrates (✓); proteases (✓) which digest protein (✓); lipases (✓) which digest fats (✓)

Answers

5 Nitrogen-fixing bacteria living in the roots of cereals would provide the plants with nitrates (✓), increasing production (✓). The need for synthetic nitrate fertilisers would diminish, saving fuel in their production (✓), reducing the amount applied to crops (✓) and therefore reducing the amount of surplus fertiliser which runs off the land into rivers and lakes (✓). Eutrophication (accept excessive growth of algae) would be avoided (✓) and wildlife would therefore benefit (✓). Also nitrates would not pollute drinking water supplies (✓), reducing the associated hazards to health (✓).

6 a) high protein food (✓) produced from microorganisms (✓).
   b) (i) 40°C is the best temperature for fermentation reactions to take place (✓). Fermentation reactions quickly raise the temperature inside the fermenter (✓). Temperatures of more than 60°C (accept high temperatures) would kill the cell culture (✓). A cooling system is necessary to maintain a temperature of around 40°C (✓).
       (ii) Marmite (✓) and Quorn (✓) are two examples. (Accept sensible alternative suggestions.)
       (iii) Microorganisms double their mass within hours (accept very quickly) (✓) compared with weeks for plants and animals (✓).
            Microbial mass is at least 40% protein (✓).
            Microbial mass has a high vitamin and mineral content (✓).
       (iv) Methanol is a substrate (✓) which bacteria ferment (accept use as food) (✓) to produce single cell protein (✓).

7 People associate microorganisms with dirt and disease (✓).

   Your score: ☐ out of 61

8 Round up (page 154)
Biotechnology

1 Kneading – repeated folding of the dough (✓) makes spaces for carbon dioxide produced by the action of yeast enzymes on the sugar in the dough (✓).
   Proving – carbon dioxide fills the spaces produced by kneading (✓).
   Baking – kills yeast, stopping the action of enzymes (✓).
   Ethanol produced by yeast fermenting sugars (✓) is driven off (✓).

2 A, F, C, G, E, B, D, H (✓✓✓✓✓). A and H begin and end the process.

3 Genetically engineered insulin is cheaper (✓), available in large quantities (✓) and chemically the same as human insulin (✓), preventing a possible immune response to injection of the hormone (✓).

4 If monoclonal antibodies can be made that attach themselves only to cancer cell antigens (✓), and these antibodies are attached to drugs that kill cancer cells (✓), then it should be possible to target cancer cells (✓) without affecting healthy cells (✓).

5 The faulty genes are first identified (✓) using gene probes. Treatment then aims to add normal genes to the patient's genetic make-up (accept genotype) (✓).

6 Developments include:
   - genetically engineering crops to grow in places where at present there is little chance of success (✓)
   - altering nitrogen-fixing bacteria so that they can live in the roots of cereal crops (✓)
   - designing insecticides produced by bacteria and which are selective for particular insect pests (✓)
   - producing plants resistant to disease (✓)
   - developing livestock to produce more and better quality meat and milk (✓).

7 An immobilised enzyme is made by attaching the enzyme to an insoluble support (✓). This means that enzyme is not lost (✓) when the products are collected (✓).

8 addition of colours (✓) and flavours (✓); blending with meat (✓) produces acceptable food (✓)

9 High protein food (✓) which is also high in vitamins and minerals (✓) but low in cholesterol (accept cholesterol-free) (✓) is produced by industrial processes (✓) which occupy a small area of land compared with a farm (✓). Production processes can be closely controlled (✓) compared with crops and livestock which are exposed to a variety of uncontrollable environmental factors (✓).

Your score: ☐ out of 41

Your improvement index: $\dfrac{\boxed{}/41}{\boxed{}/61} \times 100\% = \boxed{}\%$

Index

aerobic respiration 5, 80, 86
AIDS (Acquired Immune Deficiency Syndrome) 89
alcohol 70, 117
alleles 134, 135
allergies 114
amino acids 48, 49, 83–4
anaerobic respiration 5, 145
animal kingdom 6
antibiotics 115
antibodies 85
antiseptics 123
artificial vegetative reproduction 133
aseptic surgery 124
asexual reproduction 131–3, 153
auxin 60, 61

bacteria 9, 113, 145
binomial system 8
biofuel 150
biomass 17
biotechnology 144–154
birds 108, 110–11
blood 84–90
  white blood cells 114
bone 108
brain 91, 94, 100–1
breathing 80–83

cancer 114, 116
capillaries 67
carbohydrates 49–50, 69
carbon 49
carnivores 15
cartilage 108
cats 77
cattle 77
cells
  division 43–45
  functions 40, 41
  movement of molecules in 39, 42
  and organ systems 46–7
  structures 41

surface area to volume ratio 48
  types 40
cellulose 50
characteristics of life 5
chemicals in living things 49–50
chemotherapy 123
chitin 50
chromosomes 52
circulatory system 84–90
classification of living things 5–9
competition between organisms 20–22
cystic fibrosis 114, 136, 151

deoxyribonucleic acid (DNA) 43, 52, 53, 54, 148
dichotomous keys 9
diet 69–72
diffusion 39
digestive system 72–76
disaccharides 49
diseases 113–116
  blood disorders 90–92
  controlling the spread of 121–122
  genetic 114
  heart 91, 92
  infectious 113
  natural defences 114–5
  non-infectious 114
  respiratory tract 115–6
disinfectants 123
distribution of organisms 20–22
DNA (deoxyribonucleic acid) 43, 52, 53, 54, 148
Down's syndrome 114
drugs 117, 138

ears 99
Earth 4–5
ecological pyramids 18–20
ecosystems 11–12
energy
  and farming 33

food energy 67, 70
  pyramids 20
environment 5, 11
  human impact on 24–32
enzymes 51–2, 74, 145, 147
evolution 139–142
extinction 142
eyes 99, 101

farming 30–33, 35–6
fats 50, 69
filter feeders 76
fish 108–9
fluid feeders 77–8
food
  and biotechnology 146–7
  and diet 67–70
  eating microorganisms 153–4
  energy from 67, 70
  hygiene 121
  production 32–4
  storage 121
food chains 15–16, 18
food webs 16–18
fossils 142
fruit 163
fungi 8, 12, 113, 145

gaseous exchange 80–3
gene therapy 151
genes 52, 54
genetic diseases 114
genetic engineering 145
genetics 134, 137
glycogen 50, 74
growth 5, 43

habitats 12
haemophilia 88, 114, 150
heart 84
hepatic portal vein 88
herbivores 15
HIV (Human Immunodeficiency Virus) 89

Index

homeostasis 51, 62, 64, 97, 100–1, 102
hormones 102–6
human population 23–4

immunisation programmes 121–2
immunology 119–121
inheritance 132–136
  of sex 135
insulin 97
intensive farming 32, 35–6
interspecific competition 20

joints 109–110

keys 9
kidneys 105–6, 108
kingdoms 5–9

leaves 57
leukaemia 88
ligaments 107
light 22, 58, 63
lipids 50, 67
liver 71, 74
lymphocytes 114–5, 118

malaria 124–5
meiosis 43, 45
mitosis 43
monohybrid inheritance 132–6
monosaccharides 49
mosquitoes 124–5
muscles 106, 108
muscular dystrophy 114
mutations 53, 137

names of living things 5–7
natural selection 139–141
nervous system 90–1, 94–5
neurones 90–1, 94–5
nitrogen cycle 13
nose 100

nucleic acids 52–4
nutrients 5, 67

oils 50
omnivores 15
organ systems 46–8
osmosis 39, 63
ozone 4

pancreas 71
penicillin 123
phloem 64
photosynthesis 14, 57–60
plants
  kingdom 7
  leaves 57
  mineral nutrients 58
  reproduction 130–32
  response to light 62–3
  transpiration 61
  transport systems 61–2, 64–5
  see also photosynthesis
pollution 24–5
polysaccharides 50
population size 22–4
predators 15, 22–3
prey 15, 22–3
proteins 50–1, 67
protista 8, 113
pulmonary artery 88
pulmonary vein 88
pyramids
  of biomass 19
  of energy 20
  of numbers 18–9

rabbits 75
replication 53
reproduction 127–132
respiration 5, 80–3
ribonucleic acid (RNA) 50
RNA (ribonucleic acid) 50

scavengers 15
senses 90, 96–7, 98–9
sensitivity 5
sewage disposal 119, 120
sexual characteristics 101
sexual reproduction 127–130
sickle-cell anaemia 114
single cell protein (SCP) 152
skeleton 106–8
skin 98, 105
smoking 116–7
soil 5
solvents 117
starch 50
stimuli 90
stomata 59
synapses 91, 95

teeth 71, 77, 79–80
tendons 107
tissues 46
tongue 98
transpiration 59
transplants 106, 120–1
trophic levels 18

vaccines 121
variation 127, 137–8
vegetative reproduction 132
viruses 9, 113
vitamins 67

waste disposal 121
water 5, 25, 67, 119
weedkillers 64
white blood cells 114

xylem 63

165